C++ Network Programming
Volume 2

The C++ In-Depth Series

Bjarne Stroustrup, Editor

"I have made this letter longer than usual, because I lack the time to make it short."
 —BLAISE PASCAL

T he advent of the ISO/ANSI C++ standard marked the beginning of a new era for C++ programmers. The standard offers many new facilities and opportunities, but how can a real-world programmer find the time to discover the key nuggets of wisdom within this mass of information? **The C++ In-Depth Series** minimizes learning time and confusion by giving programmers concise, focused guides to specific topics.

Each book in this series presents a single topic, at a technical level appropriate to that topic. The Series' practical approach is designed to lift professionals to their next level of programming skills. Written by experts in the field, these short, in-depth monographs can be read and referenced without the distraction of unrelated material. The books are cross-referenced within the Series, and also reference *The C++ Programming Language* by Bjarne Stroustrup.

As you develop your skills in C++, it becomes increasingly important to separate essential information from hype and glitz, and to find the in-depth content you need in order to grow. The C++ In-Depth Series provides the tools, concepts, techniques, and new approaches to C++ that will give you a critical edge.

Titles in the Series

Accelerated C++: Practical Programming by Example, Andrew Koenig and Barbara E. Moo

Applied C++: Practical Techniques for Building Better Software, Philip Romanik and Amy Muntz

The Boost Graph Library: User Guide and Reference Manual, Jeremy G. Siek, Lie-Quan Lee, and Andrew Lumsdaine

C++ Coding Standards: 101 Rules, Guidelines, and Best Practices, Herb Sutter and Andrei Alexandrescu

C++ In-Depth Box Set, Bjarne Stroustrup, Andrei Alexandrescu, Andrew Koenig, Barbara E. Moo, Stanley B. Lippman, and Herb Sutter

C++ Network Programming, Volume 1: Mastering Complexity with ACE and Patterns, Douglas C. Schmidt and Stephen D. Huston

C++ Network Programming, Volume 2: Systematic Reuse with ACE and Frameworks, Douglas C. Schmidt and Stephen D. Huston

C++ Template Metaprogramming: Concepts, Tools, and Techniques from Boost and Beyond, David Abrahams and Aleksey Gurtovoy

Essential C++, Stanley B. Lippman

Exceptional C++: 47 Engineering Puzzles, Programming Problems, and Solutions, Herb Sutter

Exceptional C++ Style: 40 New Engineering Puzzles, Programming Problems, and Solutions, Herb Sutter

Modern C++ Design: Generic Programming and Design Patterns Applied, Andrei Alexandrescu

More Exceptional C++: 40 New Engineering Puzzles, Programming Problems, and Solutions, Herb Sutter

For more information, check out the series web site at www.awprofessional.com/series/indepth/

C++ Network Programming
Volume 2

Systematic Reuse with ACE and Frameworks

Douglas C. Schmidt
Stephen D. Huston

✦Addison-Wesley

Boston • San Francisco • New York • Toronto • Montreal
London • Munich • Paris • Madrid
Capetown • Sydney • Tokyo • Singapore • Mexico City

Many of the designations used by manufacturers and sellers to distinguish their products are claimed as trademarks. Where those designations appear in this book, and Addison-Wesley was aware of a trademark claim, the designations have been printed with initial capital letters or in all capitals.

The authors and publisher have taken care in the preparation of this book, but make no expressed or implied warranty of any kind and assume no responsibility for errors or omissions. No liability is assumed for incidental or consequential damages in connection with or arising out of the use of the information or programs contained herein.

The publisher offers discounts on this book when ordered in quantity for bulk purchases and special sales. For more information, please contact:

U.S. Corporate and Government Sales
(800) 382-3419
corpsales@pearsontechgroup.com

For sales outside of the U.S., please contact:

International Sales
international@pearsoned.com

Visit Addison-Wesley on the Web: www.awprofessional.com

Library of Congress Cataloging-in-Publication Data

Schmidt, Douglas C.
    C++ network programming / Douglas C. Schmidt, Stephen D. Huston.
        p. cm.
    Includes bibliographical references and index.
    Contents: Vol. 2. Systematic reuse with ACE and frameworks.
    ISBN 0-201-79525-6 (v. 2 : pbk.)
    1. C++ (Computer program language) 2. Object-oriented programming (Computer science) 3. Computer networks. I. Huston, Stephen D. II. Title.

    QA 76.73.C153 S368 2002
    005.2'762—dc21

                                        2001053345

ISBN   0201795256

Text printed on recycled paper

6 7 8 9 1011 OPM   09 08 07

6th Printing, October 2007

Contents

Foreword

The ADAPTIVE Communication Environment (ACE) toolkit has achieved enormous success in the area of middleware for networked computing. Due to its flexibility, performance, platform coverage, and other key properties, ACE enjoys broad acceptance by the networked application software community, as evidenced by its use in thousands of applications, in scores of countries, and in dozens of domains. ACE has also received considerable attention beyond the middleware community since it's an open-source role model for high-quality and well-designed pattern-oriented software architectures.

But why is ACE so successful? Addressing this question properly takes some thought. To start off, let's reconsider the Foreword from *C++ Network Programming: Mastering Complexity with ACE and Patterns* (C++NPv1) and resume the mass transit analogy presented there by my colleague Steve Vinoski. Steve's right that a high-quality mass transit system consists of more than just aircraft, airports, trains, train stations, and rails. It also needs less obvious infrastructure, such as scheduling, routing, ticketing, maintenance, and monitoring. But even a complete collection of ingredients is still not sufficient to develop an effective mass transit system. Arranging these ingredients so they seamlessly fulfill their primary objective—fast and reliable transportation of people—is equally important. Would you use a mass transit system whose ticketing was located in a train maintenance location or an airport hangar, or whose planned and actual scheduling and routing weren't available to the public? I doubt it!

The success of mass transit systems depends on more than the knowledge of the infrastructure parts that are provided—it depends on how these different parts must be connected and integrated with their environment. This knowledge enables architects of mass transit systems to integrate individual parts into higher-level building blocks and to connect these building blocks effectively. For example, ticketing, information points, baggage offices, and boarding are integrated in train stations located at city centers or major suburban centers. Likewise, airports are often located near large cities and connected by frequent express trains.

Even mass transit centers themselves are arranged so that activities can be performed effectively. For example, when you enter a train station or airport via the main entrance, you find ticket agents, information centers, and timetables. You also find shops to satisfy your travel needs. As you enter the main train hall or airport concourse, you find other information centers, up-to-date scheduling information, and the platforms and gates for boarding the trains and planes. Mass transit centers thus not only provide all necessary services to begin and end a journey, they also organize their internal "control flows" effectively. While the core structures and control flows in most train stations and airports are similar, their concrete realization can differ widely. Yet we all recognize these mass transit center patterns immediately since they follow key invariants that we've learned through years of experience.

So what's the connection between successful mass transit system design and the success of ACE? The answer is simple: In addition to the basic network computing ingredients (the wrapper facades that Doug and Steve introduced in C++NPv1), ACE also includes useful object-oriented frameworks that build upon these wrapper facades and provide useful higher-level communication services, such as event demultiplexing and dispatching, connection management, service configuration, concurrency, and hierarchically layered stream processing. The ACE framework services satisfy many networked software needs by organizing the structures and internal control flows of your applications effectively via key patterns learned through years of experience.

The ACE frameworks offer you a number of important benefits:

- You needn't develop the capabilities provided by ACE, which will save considerable time and effort. You can therefore focus on your key responsibility: *implementing the application functionality required by your customers and end users.*

- The ACE frameworks reify the extensive network programming expertise that Doug, Steve, and their colleagues have gained over several decades. In particular, the ACE frameworks efficiently implement the canonical classes, class relationships, and control flows common to networked applications. The ACE frameworks are tested regularly by thousands of users from around the world, which has yielded many useful corrections and improvements. As an ACE user, you can directly leverage the correctness, effectiveness, and efficiency of the ACE frameworks in your applications.

- A framework isn't a framework if it can't be adapted to specific user needs. This means you can adapt the ACE frameworks at key points of variation in networked applications. For example, the ACE Reactor framework can be adapted to use different event demultiplexer functions, such as `WaitForMultipleObjects()` or `select()`. Likewise, the ACE Acceptor-Connector framework can be configured with different IPC mechanisms. While this adaptability is beneficial by itself, ACE goes a step further: for many adaptations you can configure the desired strategies from available and interchangeable implementations. In addition to the different Reactor implementations mentioned above, for instance, ACE provides wrapper facades for various IPC mechanisms, such as the Sockets, SSL, TLI, and shared memory, that help to configure the ACE Acceptor-Connector framework for specific platforms and applications.

- Last but not least, the ACE frameworks don't exist in isolation. You can therefore combine them in novel ways to create networked applications and entirely new types of middleware. For example, you can integrate the Reactor framework with the Acceptor-Connector framework to separate connection establishment from service processing functionality in event-driven applications. You can likewise introduce various forms of concurrency into your applications using the ACE Task framework.

As a result of advising and leading many software projects over the years, I've found that ACE greatly simplifies the task of employing reusable middleware that can be customized readily to meet the needs of networked applications. Not all networked applications need heavyweight middleware, such as application servers, web services, and complex component models. Yet most networked applications can benefit from portable and efficient host infrastructure middleware like ACE. This flexibility is the core of ACE's success since you needn't commit to an entire middleware suite if you don't use all of it. Instead, you can combine just the essential ACE middleware classes you need to compose applications that are small, but as powerful as necessary. For this reason, I predict that ACE will still be widely used long after the influence of today's heavyweight middleware has waned.

ACE's tremendous flexibility also needn't lead to a sea of incompatible middleware implementations. For example, if you build an embedded system that speaks the CORBA Internet inter-ORB protocol (IIOP) to the outside world, you can use The ACE ORB (TAO), which is a CORBA-compliant, open-source, real-time object request broker (ORB) built using the ACE wrapper facades and frameworks. If CORBA is overkill for your application needs, however, you can build custom, yet interoperable, middleware using the appropriate ACE classes. Both solutions can be based on the same core structures and protocols, such as the ACE Common Data Representation (CDR) classes and its TCP/IP Socket wrapper facades. They can therefore communicate seamlessly with one another, just as you can take a train from Paris to Istanbul—the famous Orient Express—and travel through many European countries without having to change trains due to incompatible railroad networks.

As Steve Vinoski and I have pointed out, there are many similarities between high-quality mass transit systems and high-quality networking middleware. To me and thousands of other C++ developers around the world, ACE is *the* toolkit for building the latter! After saying so many good things about ACE, however, let's return to the main intent of this foreword: introducing the second volume (C++NPv2) of the *C++ Network Programming* series. As with all software technologies and middleware, the more you understand your tools, the better you'll be able to apply them. It turns out that using ACE in your applications is just one aspect of improving your networked software. To benefit significantly from ACE's many advantages, you therefore also need a sound understanding of the core concepts, patterns, and usage rules that underlie its powerful frameworks.

For years, a common way to learn ACE involved studying its code, comments, and example applications. Clearly, this process was time consuming and error prone. Moreover, even after managing to read the several hundred thousand lines of C++ code in ACE, it was easy to miss the forest for the trees. As the Greek philosopher Thucydides noted two millennia ago: "A man who has the knowledge but lacks the power to clearly express himself is no better off than if he had never any idea at all."

We're therefore fortunate that Doug and Steve found time in their busy schedules to create such a high-quality book on the ACE frameworks. C++NPv2 explains the ideas and concepts underlying the ACE frameworks in an easily accessible form using the popular concurrency and networking patterns from the POSA [POSA1, POSA2] and "Gang of Four" [GoF] patterns books. These patterns, in turn, reify thoughtful and time-proven solutions to common networking problems. For example, they tell you what the problems are, why these problems are hard, what the solutions to these problems are, and why these solutions applied to ACE are of high quality. If you want thorough coverage of the patterns and frameworks in ACE that are shaping the next generation of networked application software then read this book. I've learned much from it and I'm sure you will too.

Frank Buschmann
Senior Principal Engineer
Siemens Corporate Technology
Munich, Germany

About This Book

Software for networked applications must possess the following qualities to be successful in today's competitive, fast-paced computing industry:

- **Affordability,** to ensure that the total ownership costs of software acquisition and evolution are not prohibitively high

- **Extensibility,** to support successions of quick updates and additions to address new requirements and take advantage of emerging markets

- **Flexibility,** to support a growing range of multimedia data types, traffic patterns, and end-to-end quality of service (QoS) requirements

- **Portability,** to reduce the effort required to support applications on heterogeneous OS platforms and compilers

- **Predictability** and **efficiency,** to provide low latency to delay-sensitive real-time applications, high performance to bandwidth-intensive applications, and usability over low-bandwidth networks, such as wireless links

- **Reliability,** to ensure that applications are robust, fault tolerant, and highly available

- **Scalability,** to enable applications to handle large numbers of clients simultaneously

Writing high-quality networked applications that exhibit these qualities is hard—it's expensive, complicated, and error prone. The patterns, C++ language features, and object-oriented design principles presented in *C++ Network Programming, Volume 1: Mastering Complexity with ACE and Patterns* (C++NPv1) help to minimize complexity and mistakes in networked applications by refactoring common structure and functionality into reusable *wrapper facade* class libraries. The key benefits of reuse will be lost, however, if large parts of the application software that uses these class libraries—or worse, the class libraries themselves—must be rewritten for each new project.

Historically, many networked application software projects began by

1. Designing and implementing demultiplexing and dispatching infrastructure mechanisms that handle timed events and I/O on multiple socket handles
2. Adding service instantiation and processing mechanisms atop the demultiplexing and dispatching layer, along with message buffering and queueing mechanisms
3. Implementing large amounts of application-specific code using this *ad hoc* host infrastructure middleware

This development process has been applied many times in many companies, by many projects in parallel. Even worse, it's been applied by the same teams in a series of projects. Regrettably, this continuous rediscovery and reinvention of core concepts and code has kept costs unnecessarily high throughout the software development life cycle. This problem is exacerbated by the inherent diversity of today's hardware, operating systems, compilers, and communication platforms, which keep shifting the foundations of networked application software development.

Object-oriented frameworks [FJS99b, FJS99a] are one of the most flexible and powerful techniques that address the problems outlined above. A framework is a reusable, "semi-complete" application that can be specialized to produce custom applications [JF88]. Frameworks help to reduce the cost and improve the quality of networked applications by reifying proven software designs and patterns into concrete source code. By emphasizing the integration and collaboration of application-specific and application-independent classes, frameworks enable larger scale reuse of software than can be achieved by reusing individual classes or stand-alone functions.

In the early 1990s, Doug Schmidt started the open-source ACE project to bring the power and efficiency of patterns and frameworks to networked application development. As with much of Doug's work, ACE addressed many real-world problems faced by professional software developers. Over the following decade, his groups at the University of California, Irvine; Washington University, St. Louis; and Vanderbilt University, along with contributions from the ACE user community and Steve Huston at Riverace, yielded a C++ toolkit containing some of the most powerful and widely used concurrent object-oriented network programming frameworks in the world. By applying reusable software patterns and a lightweight OS portability layer, the frameworks in the ACE toolkit provide synchronous and asynchronous event processing; concurrency and synchronization; connection management; and service configuration, initialization, and hierarchical integration.

The success of ACE has fundamentally altered the way that networked applications and middleware are designed and implemented on the many operating systems outlined in Sidebar 2 (page 16). ACE is being used by thousands of development teams, ranging from large Fortune 500 companies to small startups to advanced research projects at universities and industry labs. Its open-source development model and self-supporting culture is similar in spirit and enthusiasm to that driving Linus Torvalds's popular Linux operating system.

This book describes how the ACE frameworks are designed and how they can help developers navigate between the limitations of

1. **Low-level native operating system APIs,** which are inflexible and nonportable
2. **High-level middleware,** such as *distribution middleware* and *common middleware services*, which often lacks the efficiency and flexibility to support networked applications with stringent QoS and portability requirements

The skills required to produce and use networked application frameworks have traditionally been locked in the heads of expert developers or buried deep within the source code of numerous projects that are spread throughout an enterprise or an industry. Neither of these locations is ideal, of course, since it's time consuming and error prone to reengineer this knowledge for each new application or project. To address this problem, this book illustrates the key patterns [POSA2, POSA1, GoF] that underlie the structure and functionality of the ACE frameworks. Our coverage of these patterns also makes it easier to understand the design, implementation, and effective use of the open-source ACE toolkit itself.

Intended Audience

This book is intended for "hands on" C++ developers or advanced students interested in understanding how to design object-oriented frameworks and apply them to develop networked applications. It builds upon material from C++NPv1 that shows how developers can apply patterns to master complexities arising from using native OS APIs to program networked applications. It's therefore important to have a solid grasp of the following topics covered in C++NPv1 before reading this book:

- **Networked application design dimensions,** including the alternative communication protocols and data transfer mechanisms discussed in Chapter 1 of C++NPv1
- **Internet programming mechanisms,** such as TCP/IP connection management and data transfer APIs [Ste98] discussed in Chapter 2 of C++NPv1
- **Concurrency design dimensions,** including the use of processes and threads, iterative versus concurrent versus reactive servers, and threading models [Ste99] discussed in Chapters 5 through 9 of C++NPv1
- **Synchronization techniques** necessary to coordinate the interactions of processes and threads on various OS platforms [KSS96, Lew95, Ric97] discussed in Chapter 10 of C++NPv1
- **Object-oriented design and programming techniques** [Boo94, Mey97] that can simplify OS APIs and avoid programming mistakes through the use of patterns, such as Wrapper Facade [POSA2] and Proxy [POSA1, GoF] discussed in Chapter 3 and Appendix A of C++NPv1

The ACE frameworks are highly flexible and powerful, due in large part to their use of C++ language features [Bja00]. You should therefore be familiar with C++ class inheritance and virtual functions (dynamic binding) as well as templates (parameterized types) and the mechanisms your compiler(s) offer to instantiate them. ACE provides a great deal of assistance in overcoming differences between C++ compilers. As always, however, you need to know the capabilities of your development tools and how to use them. Knowing your tools makes it easier to follow the source code examples in this book and to build and run them on your systems. Finally, as you read the examples in this book, keep in mind the points noted in Sidebar 7 (page 46) regarding UML diagrams and C++ code.

Structure and Content

Our C++NPv1 book addressed how to master certain complexities of developing networked applications, focusing on the use of ACE's wrapper facades to avoid problems with operating system APIs written in C. This book (which we call C++NPv2) elevates our focus to motivate and demystify the patterns, design techniques, and C++ features associated with developing and using the ACE frameworks. These frameworks help reduce the cost and improve the quality of networked applications by reifying proven software designs and patterns into frameworks that can be reused systematically across projects and enterprises. The ACE frameworks expand reuse technology far beyond what can be achieved by reusing individual classes or even class libraries.

This book presents numerous C++ applications to reinforce the design discussions by showing concrete examples of how to use the ACE frameworks. These examples provide step-by-step guidance that can help you apply key object-oriented techniques and patterns to your own networked applications. The book also shows how to enhance your design skills, focusing on the key concepts and principles that shape the design of successful object-oriented frameworks for networked applications and middleware.

The chapters in the book are organized as follows:

- Chapter 1 introduces the concept of an object-oriented framework and shows how frameworks differ from other reuse techniques, such as class libraries, components, patterns, and model-integrated computing. We then outline the frameworks in the ACE toolkit that are covered in subsequent chapters.

- Chapter 2 completes the domain analysis begun in C++NPv1, which covered the communication protocols and mechanisms, and the concurrency architectures used by networked applications. The focus in this book is on the service and configuration design dimensions that address key networked application properties, such as duration and structure, how networked services are identified, and the time at which they are bound together to form complete applications.

- Chapter 3 describes the design and use of the ACE Reactor framework, which implements the Reactor pattern [POSA2] to allow event-driven applications to demultiplex and dispatch service requests that are delivered to an application from one or more clients.

- Chapter 4 then describes the design and use of the most common implementations of the `ACE_Reactor` interface, which support a wide range of OS event demultiplexing mechanisms, including `select()`, `WaitForMultipleObjects()`, `XtAppMainLoop()`, and `/dev/poll`.

- Chapter 5 describes the design and use of the ACE Service Configurator framework. This framework implements the Component Configurator pattern [POSA2] to allow an application to link/unlink its component service implementations at run time without having to modify, recompile, or relink the application statically.

- Chapter 6 describes the design and effective use of the ACE Task framework. This framework can be used to implement key concurrency patterns, such as Active Object and Half-Sync/Half-Async [POSA2].

- Chapter 7 describes the design and effective use of the ACE Acceptor-Connector framework. This framework implements the Acceptor-Connector pattern [POSA2] to decouple the connection and initialization of cooperating peer services in a networked system from the processing they perform once connected and initialized.

- Chapter 8 describes the design and use of the ACE Proactor framework. This framework implements the Proactor and Acceptor-Connector patterns [POSA2] to allow event-driven applications to efficiently demultiplex and dispatch service requests triggered by the completion of asynchronously initiated operations.

- Chapter 9 describes the design and use of the ACE Streams framework. This framework implements the Pipes and Filters pattern [POSA1] to provide a structure for systems that process streams of data.

- The book concludes with a glossary of technical terms, a list of references for further study, and a general subject index.

The chapters are organized to build upon each other and to minimize forward references. We therefore recommend that you read the chapters in order.

Although this book illustrates the key capabilities of ACE's most important frameworks, we don't cover all uses and methods of those frameworks. For additional coverage of ACE, we refer you to *The ACE Programmer's Guide* [HJS] and the online ACE reference documentation, generated by Doxygen [Dim01]. ACE's reference documentation is available at `http://ace.ece.uci.edu/Doxygen/` and `http://www.riverace.com/docs/`.

Related Material

This book is based on ACE version 5.3, released in the fall of 2002. ACE 5.3 and all the sample applications described in our books are open-source software. Sidebar 3 (page 19) explains how you can obtain a copy of ACE so you can follow along, see the actual ACE classes and frameworks in complete detail, and run the code examples interactively as you read the book.

To learn more about ACE, or to report errors you find in the book, we recommend you subscribe to the ACE mailing list, `ace-users@cs.wustl.edu`. You can subscribe by sending a request to `ace-users-request@cs.wustl.edu`. Include the following command in the body of the e-mail (the subject is ignored):

```
subscribe ace-users [emailaddress@domain]
```

You must supply `emailaddress@domain` only if your message's `From` address is not the address you wish to subscribe. If you use this alternate address method, the list server will require an extra authorization step before allowing you to join the list.

Postings to the `ace-users` list are also forwarded to the `comp.soft-sys.ace` USENET newsgroup, along with postings to several other ACE-related mailing lists. Reading the messages via the newsgroup is a good way to keep up with ACE news and activity if you don't require immediate delivery of the 30 to 50 messages that are posted daily on the mailing lists.

Archives of postings to the `comp.soft-sys.ace` newsgroup are available at `http://groups.google.com/`. Enter `comp.soft-sys.ace` in the search box to go to a list of archived messages. Google has a complete, searchable archive of over 40,000 messages. You can also post a message to the newsgroup from Google's site.

Acknowledgments

Champion reviewing honors go to Alain Decamps, Don Hinton, Alexander Maack, Chris Uzdavinis, and Johnny Willemsen, who reviewed the book multiple times and provided extensive, detailed comments that improved its form and content substantially. Many thanks also to the official reviewers, Timothy Culp, Dennis Mancl, Phil Mesnier, and Jason Pasion, who read the entire book and gave us many helpful comments. Many other ACE users provided feedback on this book, including Marc M. Adkins, Tomer Amiaz, Vi Thuan Banh, Kevin Bailey, Stephane Bastien, John Dilley, Eric Eide, Andrew Finnell, Dave Findlay, Jody Hagins, Jon Harnish, Jim Havlicek, Martin Johnson, Christopher Kohlhoff, Alex Libman, Harald Mitterhofer, Llori Patterson, Nick Pratt, Dieter Quehl, Tim Rozmajzl, Irma Rastegayeva, Eamonn Saunders, Harvinder Sawhney, Christian Schuhegger, Michael Searles, Kalvinder Singh, Henny Sipma, Stephen Sturtevant, Leo Stutzmann, Tommy Svensson, Bruce Trask, Dominic Williams, and Vadim Zaliva.

We are deeply indebted to all the members, past and present, of the DOC groups at Washington University in St. Louis and the University of California, Irvine, as well as the team members at Riverace Corporation and Object Computing Inc., who developed, refined, and optimized many of the ACE capabilities presented in this book. This group includes Everett Anderson, Alex Arulanthu, Shawn Atkins, John Aughey, Luther Baker, Jaiganesh Balasubramanian, Darrell Brunsch, Don Busch, Chris Cleeland, Angelo Corsaro, Chad Elliot, Sergio Flores-Gaitan, Chris Gill, Pradeep Gore, Andy Gokhale, Priyanka Gontla, Myrna Harbibson, Tim Harrison, Shawn Hannan, John Heitmann, Joe Hoffert, James Hu, Frank Hunleth, Prashant Jain, Vishal Kachroo, Ray Klefstad, Kitty Krishnakumar, Yamuna Krishnamurthy, Michael Kircher, Fred Kuhns, David Levine, Chanaka Liyanaarachchi, Michael Moran, Ebrahim Moshiri, Sumedh Mungee, Bala Natarajan, Ossama Othman, Jeff Parsons, Kirthika Parameswaran, Krish Pathayapura, Irfan Pyarali, Sumita Rao, Carlos O'Ryan, Rich Siebel, Malcolm Spence, Marina Spivak, Naga Surendran, Steve Totten, Bruce Trask, Nanbor Wang, and Seth Widoff.

We also want to thank the thousands of C++ developers from over 50 countries who've contributed to ACE for over a decade. ACE's excellence and success is a testament to the skills and generosity of many talented developers and the forward-looking companies that had the vision to contribute their work to ACE's open-source code base. Without their support, constant feedback, and encouragement, we would never have written this book. In recognition of the efforts of the ACE open-source community, we maintain a list of all contributors at `http://ace.ece.uci.edu/ACE-members.html`.

We are also grateful for the support from colleagues and sponsors of our research on patterns and development of the ACE toolkit, notably the contributions of Ron Akers (Motorola), Steve Bachinsky (SAIC), John Bay (DARPA), Detlef Becker (Siemens), Frank Buschmann (Siemens), Dave Busigo (DARPA), John Buttitto (Sun), Becky Callison (Boeing), Wei Chiang (Nokia Inc.), Joe Cross (Lockheed Martin), Lou DiPalma (Raytheon), Bryan Doerr (Savvis), Karlheinz Dorn (Siemens), Scott Ellard (Madison), Matt Emerson (Escient Convergence Group, Inc.), Sylvester Fernandez (Lockheed Martin), Nikki Ford (DARPA), Andreas Geisler (Siemens), Helen Gill (NSF), Inc.), Jody Hagins (ATD), Andy Harvey (Cisco), Sue Kelly (Sandia National Labs), Gary Koob (DARPA), Petri Koskelainen (Nokia Inc.), Sean Landis (Motorola), Patrick Lardieri (Lockheed Martin), Doug Lea (SUNY Oswego), Joe Loyall (BBN), Kent Madsen (EO Thorpe), Ed Margand (DARPA), Mike Masters (NSWC), Major Ed Mays (U.S. Marine Corps), John Mellby (Raytheon), Jeanette Milos (DARPA), Stan Moyer (Telcordia), Ivan Murphy (Siemens), Russ Noseworthy (Object Sciences), Adam Porter (U. of Maryland), Dieter Quehl (Siemens), Vijay Raghavan (Vanderbilt U.), Lucie Robillard (U.S. Air Force), Craig Rodrigues (BBN), Rick Schantz (BBN), Andreas Schulke (Siemens), Steve Shaffer (Kodak), Tom Shields (Raytheon), Dave Sharp (Boeing), Naval Sodha (Ericsson), Paul Stephenson (Ericsson), Tatsuya Suda (UCI), Umar Syyid (Storetrax, Inc.), Janos Sztipanovits (Vanderbilt U.), Gautam Thaker (Lockheed Martin), Lothar Werzinger (Krones), and Don Winter (Boeing).

Very special thanks go to Susan Cooper, our copy editor, for enhancing our written material. In addition, we are grateful for the encouragement and patience of our editor, Debbie Lafferty, our production coordinator, Elizabeth Ryan, the series editor and inventor of C++, Bjarne Stroustrup, and everyone else at Addison-Wesley who made it possible to publish this book.

Finally, we would also like to acknowledge our gratitude and indebtedness to the late W. Richard Stevens, the father of network programming literature. The following poem by Samuel Butler sums up our view of Richard's enduring influence:

> Not on sad Stygian shore, nor in clear sheen
> Of far Elysian plain, shall we meet those
> Among the dead whose pupils we have been ...
> Yet meet we shall, and part, and meet again,
> Where dead men meet, on lips of living men.

Steve's Acknowledgments

Wow...C++NPv1 took almost 3 years to complete—this volume took roughly nine months. Thank you to my wife Jane who cheerfully endured this process. Your persistent exhortation to keep life in balance and "be the tortoise" really helped me stay the course, and without your infinite patience through many long days and nights, I would not have completed this—thank you! Thanks to Doug Schmidt for getting the bulk of this book down and organized in world-class time amidst a full-time job and his usual, amazing amount of work on ACE. Finally, thank you to Riverace's customers who supported this work so enthusiastically. It's a privilege to serve you.

Doug's Acknowledgments

I'd like to thank my wife Sonja and my parents for their love and support during the writing of this book. Now that it's done we'll have lots more time to have fun! Thanks also to Steve Huston, who time-shared his overloaded schedule to wrap up the book. I'd also like to thank my friends and colleagues at the College of William and Mary; Washington University, St. Louis; University of California, Irvine; Vanderbilt University; DARPA; and Siemens—as well as the thousands of ACE and TAO developers and users worldwide—who have greatly enriched my intellectual and interpersonal life over the past two decades. I look forward to working with all of you in the future.

CHAPTER 1

Object-Oriented Frameworks for Network Programming

CHAPTER SYNOPSIS

Object-oriented frameworks help reduce the cost and improve the quality of networked applications by reifying software designs and pattern languages that have proven effective in particular application domains. This chapter illustrates what frameworks are and compares them with other popular software development techniques, such as class libraries, components, patterns, and model-integrated computing. It then illustrates the process of applying frameworks to networked applications and outlines the ACE frameworks that are the focus of this book. These frameworks are based on a pattern language [POSA1, POSA2] that has been applied to thousands of production networked applications and middleware worldwide.

1.1 An Overview of Object-Oriented Frameworks

Even as computing power and network bandwidth increase dramatically, the development of networked application software remains expensive, time consuming, and error prone. The cost and effort stems from the growing demands placed on networked software, as well as the continual rediscovery and reinvention of core software design and implementation artifacts throughout the software industry. Moreover, the heterogeneity of hardware architectures, diversity of OS and network platforms, and stiff global competition makes it increasingly hard to build high-quality networked application software from scratch.

The key to building high-quality networked software in a time-to-market-driven environment is the ability to reuse successful software designs and implementations that have already been developed. Reuse has been a popular topic of debate and discussion for over 30 years in the software community [McI68]. There are two general types of reuse:

- **Opportunistic reuse,** in which developers cut and paste code from existing programs to create new ones. Opportunistic reuse works in a limited way for individual programmers or small groups. It doesn't scale up across business units or enterprises, however, and therefore doesn't significantly reduce development cycle time and cost or improve software quality. Worse, opportunistic reuse can actually impede development progress since cut-and-paste code often begins to diverge as it proliferates, forcing developers to fix the same bugs multiple times in multiple places.
- **Systematic reuse,** which is an intentional and concerted effort to create and apply multiuse software architectures, patterns, frameworks, and components throughout a product line [CN02]. In a well-honed systematic reuse process, each new project leverages time-proven designs and implementations, only adding new code that's specific to a particular application. This type of reuse is essential to increase software productivity and quality by breaking the costly cycle of rediscovering, reinventing, and revalidating common software artifacts.

Middleware [SS02] is a class of software that can increase systematic reuse levels significantly by functionally bridging the gap between the end-to-end functional requirements of networked applications and the underlying operating systems and network protocol stacks. Middleware provides capabilities that are critical to networked applications because they automate common network programming tasks. Developers who use middleware can therefore program their networked applications more like stand-alone applications, rather than wrestling with the many tedious and error-prone details associated with low-level OS event demultiplexing, message buffering and queueing, marshaling and demarshaling, and connection management mechanisms. Popular examples of middleware include Java virtual machines (JVMs), Enterprise JavaBeans (EJB), .NET, the Common Object Request Broker Architecture (CORBA), and the ADAPTIVE Communication Environment (ACE).

Systematically developing high-quality, reusable middleware for networked applications presents many hard technical challenges, including

- Detecting and recovering from transient and partial failures of networks and hosts in an application-independent manner
- Minimizing the impact of latency and jitter on end-to-end application performance
- Determining *how* to partition a distributed application into separate component services
- Deciding *where* and *when* to distribute and load balance services in a network

Since reusable middleware is inherently abstract, it's hard to validate its quality and to manage its production. Moreover, the skills required to develop, deploy, and support reusable networked application middleware have traditionally been a "black art," locked in the heads of expert developers and architects. These technical impediments to systematic reuse are often exacerbated by a myriad of nontechnical impediments [Hol97], such as organizational, economic, administrative, political, sociological, and psychological factors. It's therefore not surprising that significant levels of software reuse have been slow to materialize in many projects and organizations [Sch00].

While it's never easy to make reuse work universally, we've led the development of powerful *host infrastructure middleware* called ACE that's designed specifically with systematic reuse in mind. During the past decade, we've written hundreds of thousands of lines of C++ code while developing and applying ACE to networked applications as part of our work with dozens of telecommunication, aerospace, medical, and financial services companies. As a result of our experience, we've documented many patterns and pattern languages [POSA2, POS00] that have guided the design of reuseable middleware and applications. In addition, we've taught hundreds of tutorials and courses on reuse, middleware, and patterns to thousands of developers and students. Despite the many technical and nontechnical challenges, we've identified a solid body of work that combines advanced research, time-proven design knowledge, hands-on experience, and software artifacts that can significantly enhance the systematic reuse of networked application software.

At the heart of this body of work are object-oriented frameworks [FJS99b, FJS99a], which are a powerful technology for achieving systematic reuse of networked application software.[1] Below, we describe the three characteristics of frameworks [JF88] that help them to achieve the important networked application qualities listed on page xi. Figure 1.1 (page 4) illustrates how these characteristics work together.

A framework provides an integrated set of domain-specific structures and functionality. Systematic reuse of software depends largely on how well frameworks model the commonalities and variabilities [CHW98] in application domains, such as business data processing, telecom call processing, graphical user interfaces, or distributed object computing middleware. Since frameworks reify the key roles and relationships of classes in application domains, the amount of reusable code increases and the amount of code rewritten for each application decreases.

A framework exhibits "inversion of control" at run time via callbacks. A *callback* is an object registered with a dispatcher that calls back to a method on the object when a particular event occurs, such as a connection request or data arriving on a socket handle. Inversion of control decouples the canonical detection, demultiplexing, and dispatching steps within a framework from the application-defined *event handlers* managed by the framework. When events occur, the framework calls back to virtual *hook methods* in the registered event handlers, which then perform application-defined processing in response to the events.

Since frameworks exhibit inversion of control, they can simplify application design because the framework—rather than the application—runs the event loop to detect events, demultiplex events to event handlers, and dispatch hook methods on the handlers that process

---

[1] In the remainder of this book we use the term *framework* to mean *object-oriented framework*.

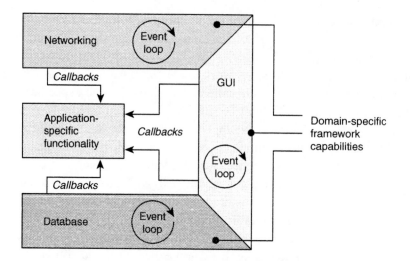

Figure 1.1: Synergy of Framework Capabilities

the events. The use of virtual hook methods in the handler classes decouples the application's classes from the framework, allowing each to be changed independently as long as the interface signature and interaction protocols aren't modified.

A framework is a "semi-complete" application that programmers can customize to form complete applications by inheriting from and instantiating classes in the framework. Inheritance enables the features of framework base classes to be shared selectively by subclasses. If a base class provides default implementations of its methods, application developers need only override those virtual methods whose default behavior doesn't meet their needs.

Since a framework is a semi-complete application, it enables larger-scale reuse of software than can be achieved by reusing individual classes or stand-alone functions. The amount of reuse increases due to a framework's ability to integrate application-defined and application-independent classes. In particular, a framework abstracts the canonical control flow of applications in a domain into families of related classes, which can collaborate to integrate customizable application-independent code with customized application-defined code.

1.2   Comparing Software Development and Reuse Techniques

Object-oriented frameworks don't exist in isolation. Class libraries, components, patterns, and model-integrated computing are other techniques that are being applied to reuse software and increase productivity. This section compares frameworks with these techniques to illustrate their similarities and differences, as well as to show how the techniques can be combined to enhance systematic reuse for networked applications.

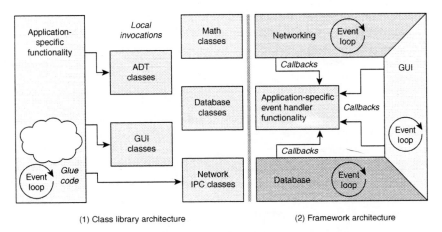

(1) Class library architecture   (2) Framework architecture

Figure 1.2: Class Library versus Framework Architectures

1.2.1   Comparing Frameworks and Class Libraries

A class is a general-purpose, reusable building block that specifies an interface and en-capsulates the representation of its internal data and the functionality of its instances. A library of classes was the most common first-generation object-oriented development tech-nique [Mey97]. Class libraries generally support reuse-in-the-small more effectively than function libraries since classes emphasize the cohesion of data and methods that operate on the data.

Although class libraries are often domain independent and can be applied widely, their effective scope of reuse is limited because they don't capture the canonical control flow, collaboration, and variability among families of related software artifacts. The total amount of reuse with class libraries is therefore relatively small, compared with the amount of application-defined code that must be rewritten for each application. The need to reinvent and reimplement the overall software architecture and much of the control logic for each new application is a prime source of cost and delay for many software projects.

The C++ standard library [Bja00] is a good case in point. It provides classes for strings, vectors, and other containers. Although these classes can be reused in many application domains, they are relatively low level. Application developers are therefore responsible for (re)writing much of the "glue code" that performs the bulk of the application control flow and class integration logic, as shown in Figure 1.2 (1).

Frameworks are a second-generation development technique [Joh97] that extends the benefits of class libraries in several ways. Most importantly, classes in a framework collab-orate to provide a reusable architecture for a family of related applications. Class collab-oration in a framework yields "semi-complete" applications that embody domain-specific object structures and functionality. Frameworks can be classified by various means, such as the blackbox and whitebox distinctions described in Sidebar 1 (page 6).

Sidebar 1: Overview of Whitebox and Blackbox Frameworks

Frameworks can be classified in terms of the techniques used to extend them, which range along a continuum from *whitebox frameworks* to *blackbox frameworks* [HJE95], as described below:

- **Whitebox frameworks.** Extensibility is achieved in a whitebox framework via object-oriented language features, such as inheritance and dynamic binding. Existing functionality can be reused and customized by inheriting from framework base classes and overriding predefined hook methods [Pre95] using patterns such as Template Method [GoF], which defines an algorithm with some steps supplied by a derived class. To extend a whitebox framework, application developers must have some knowledge of its internal structure.

- **Blackbox frameworks.** Extensibility is achieved in a blackbox framework by defining interfaces that allow objects to be plugged into the framework via composition and delegation. Existing functionality can be reused by defining classes that conform to a particular interface and then integrating these classes into the framework using patterns such as *Function Object* [Kuh97], *Bridge/Strategy* [GoF], and *Pluggable Factory* [Vli98b, Vli99, Cul99], which provide a blackbox abstraction for selecting one of many implementations. Blackbox frameworks can be easier to use than whitebox frameworks since application developers need less knowledge of the framework's internal structure. Blackbox frameworks can also be harder to design, however, since framework developers must define crisp interfaces that anticipate a range of use cases.

Another way that class libraries differ from frameworks is that the classes in a library are typically passive since they perform their processing by borrowing the thread from so-called self-directed applications that invoke their methods. As a result, developers must continually rewrite much of the control logic needed to bind the reusable classes together to form complete networked applications. In contrast, frameworks are active since they direct the flow of control within an application via various callback-driven event handling patterns, such as Reactor [POSA2] and Observer [GoF]. These patterns invert the application's flow of control using the *Hollywood Principle*: "Don't call us, we'll call you" [Vli98a]. Since frameworks are active and manage the application's control flow, they can perform a broader range of activities on behalf of applications than is possible with passive class libraries.

Frameworks and class libraries are complementary technologies in practice. Frameworks provide a foundational structure to applications. Since frameworks are focused on a specific domain, however, they aren't expected to satisfy the broadest range of application development needs. Class libraries are therefore often used in conjunction within frameworks and applications to implement commonly needed code artifacts, such as strings, files, and time/date classes.

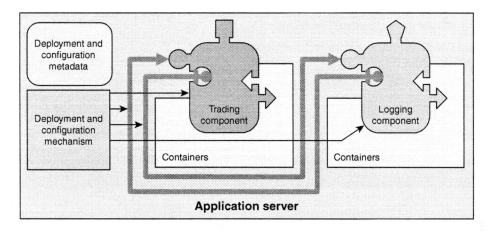

Figure 1.3: A Component Architecture

For example, the ACE frameworks use the ACE wrapper facade classes to ensure their portability. Likewise, applications can use the ACE container classes described in [HJS] to help implement their event handlers. Whereas the ACE container classes and wrapper facades are passive, the ACE frameworks are active and provide inversion of control at run time. The ACE toolkit provides both frameworks and a library of classes to help programmers address a range of challenges that arise when developing networked applications.

1.2.2   Comparing Frameworks and Components

A component is an encapsulated part of a software system that implements a specific service or set of services. A component has one or more interfaces that provide access to its services. Components serve as building blocks for the structure of an application and can be reused based solely upon knowledge of their interface protocols.

Components are a third-generation development technique [Szy98] that are widely used by developers of multitier enterprise applications. Common examples of components include ActiveX controls [Egr98] and COM objects [Box98], .NET web services [TL01], Enterprise JavaBeans [MH01], and the CORBA Component Model (CCM) [Obj01a]. Components can be plugged together or scripted to form complete applications, as shown in Figure 1.3.

Figure 1.3 also shows how a component implements the business application logic in the context of a container. A container allows its component to access resources and services provided by an underlying middleware platform. In addition, this figure shows how generic application servers can be used to instantiate and manage containers and execute the components configured into them. Metadata associated with components provide instructions that application servers use to configure and connect components.

Many interdependent components in enterprise applications can reside in multiple—possibly distributed—application servers. Each application server consists of some number of components that implement certain services for clients. These components in turn may include other *collocated* or remote services. In general, components help developers reduce their initial software development effort by integrating custom application components with reusable off-the-shelf components into generic application server frameworks. Moreover, as the requirements of applications change, components can help make it easier to migrate and redistribute certain services to adapt to new environments, while preserving key application properties, such as security and availability.

Components are generally less lexically and spatially coupled than frameworks. For example, applications can reuse components without having to subclass them from existing base classes. In addition, by applying common patterns, such as Proxy [GoF] and Broker [POSA1], components can be distributed to servers throughout a network and accessed by clients remotely. Modern application servers, such as JBoss and BEA Systems's Web-Logic Server, use these types of patterns to facilitate an application's use of components.

The relationship between frameworks and components is highly synergistic, with neither subordinate to the other [Joh97]. For example, the ACE frameworks can be used to develop higher-level application components, whose interfaces then provide a facade [GoF] for the internal class structure of the frameworks. Likewise, components can be used as pluggable strategies in blackbox frameworks [HJE95]. Frameworks are often used to simplify the development of middleware component models [TL01, MH01, Obj01a], whereas components are often used to simplify the development and configuration of networked application software.

1.2.3   Comparing Frameworks and Patterns

Developers of networked applications must address design challenges related to complex topics, such as connection management, service initialization, distribution, concurrency control, flow control, error handling, event loop integration, and dependability. Since these challenges are often independent of specific application requirements, developers can resolve them by applying the following types of patterns [POSA1]:

- **Design patterns** provide a scheme for refining the elements of a software system and the relationships between them, and describe a common structure of communicating elements that solves a general design problem within a particular context.

- **Architectural patterns** express the fundamental, overall structural organization of software systems and provide a set of predefined subsystems, specify their responsibilities, and include guidelines for organizing the relationships between them.

- **Pattern languages** define a vocabulary for talking about software development problems and provide a process for the orderly resolution of these problems.

Traditionally, patterns and pattern languages have been locked in the heads of expert developers or buried deep within the source code of software applications and systems. Allowing this valuable information to reside only in these locations is risky and expensive. Explicitly capturing and documenting patterns for networked applications helps to

- **Preserve important design information** for programmers who enhance and maintain existing software. This information will be lost if it isn't documented, which can increase software entropy and decrease software maintainability and quality.

- **Guide design choices** for developers who are building new applications. Since patterns document the common traps and pitfalls in their domain, they help developers to select suitable architectures, protocols, algorithms, and platform features without wasting time and effort (re)implementing solutions that are known to be inefficient or error prone.

Knowledge of patterns and pattern languages helps to reduce development effort and maintenance costs. Reuse of patterns alone, however, does not create flexible and efficient software. Although patterns enable reuse of abstract design and architecture knowledge, software abstractions documented as patterns don't directly yield reusable code. It's therefore essential to augment the study of patterns with the creation and use of frameworks. Frameworks help developers avoid costly reinvention of standard software artifacts by reifying common patterns and pattern languages and by refactoring common implementation roles.

ACE users can write networked applications quickly because the frameworks in ACE implement the core patterns associated with service access, event handling, concurrency, and synchronization [POSA2]. This knowledge transfer makes ACE more accessible and directly applicable compared to many other common knowledge transfer activities, such as seminars, conferences, or design and code reviews. Although these other activities are useful, they are limited because participants must learn from past work of others, and then try to apply it to their current and future projects. In comparison, ACE provides direct knowledge transfer by embodying framework usage patterns in a powerful toolkit containing both networked application domain experience *and* working code.

For example, JAWS [HS99] is a high-performance, open-source, adaptive Web server built using the ACE frameworks. Figure 1.4 (page 10) illustrates how the JAWS Web server is structured as a set of collaborating frameworks whose design is guided by the patterns listed along the borders of the figure. These patterns help resolve common design challenges that arise when developing concurrent servers, including encapsulating low-level operating system APIs, decoupling event demultiplexing and connection management from protocol processing, scaling up server performance via multithreading, minimizing server threading overhead, using asynchronous I/O effectively, and enhancing server configurability. More information on the patterns and design of JAWS appears in Chapter 1 of POSA2.

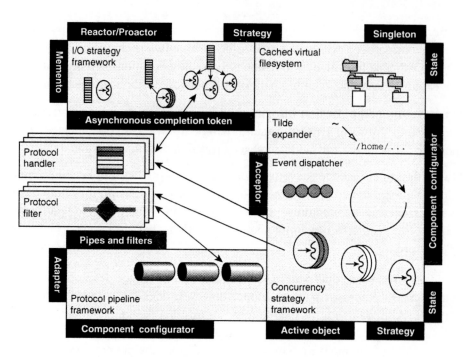

Figure 1.4: Patterns Forming the Architecture of JAWS

1.2.4   Comparing Frameworks and Model-Integrated Computing

Model-integrated computing (MIC) [SK97] is an emerging development paradigm that uses domain-specific modeling languages to systematically engineer software ranging from small-scale real-time embedded systems to large-scale enterprise applications. MIC development environments include domain-specific model analysis and model-based program synthesis tools. MIC models can capture the essence of a class of applications, as well as focus on a single, custom application. MIC also allows the modeling languages and environments themselves to be modeled by so-called *meta-models* [SKLN01], which help to synthesize domain-specific modeling languages that can capture subtle insights about the domains they are designed to model, making this knowledge available for reuse.

Popular examples of MIC being used today include the Generic Modeling Environment (GME) [LBM+01] and Ptolemy [BHLM94] (which are used primarily in the real-time and embedded domain) and UML/XML tools based on the OMG Model Driven Architecture (MDA) [Obj01b] (which are used primarily in the business domain thus far). When implemented properly, these MIC technologies help to

- Free application developers from dependencies on particular software APIs, which ensures that the models can be reused for a long time, even as existing software APIs are obsoleted by newer ones.

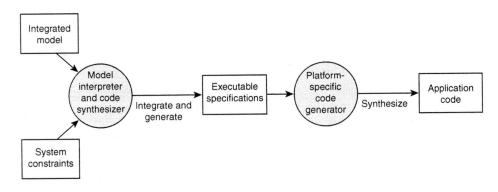

Figure 1.5: Steps in the Model-Integrated Computing Development Process

- Provide correctness proofs for various algorithms by analyzing the models automatically and offering refinements to satisfy various constraints.
- Generate code that's highly dependable and robust since the modeling tools themselves can be synthesized from meta-models using provably correct technologies.
- Rapidly prototype new concepts and applications that can be modeled quickly using this paradigm, compared to the effort required to prototype them manually.
- Reuse domain-specific modeling insights, saving significant amounts of time and effort, while also reducing application time-to-market and improving consistency and quality.

As shown in Figure 1.5, the MIC development process uses a set of tools to analyze the interdependent features of the application captured in a model and determine the feasibility of supporting different QoS requirements in the context of the specified constraints. Another set of tools then translates models into executable specifications that capture the platform behavior, constraints, and interactions with the environment. These executable specifications in turn can be used to synthesize application software.

Earlier efforts at model-based development and code synthesis attempted by CASE tools generally failed to deliver on their potential for the following reasons [All02]:

- They attempted to generate entire applications, including the infrastructure and the application logic, which led to inefficient, bloated code that was hard to optimize, validate, evolve, or integrate with existing code.
- Due to the lack of sophisticated domain-specific languages and associated modeling tools, it was hard to achieve round-trip engineering, that is, moving back and forth seamlessly between model representations and the synthesized code.
- Since CASE tools and early modeling languages dealt primarily with a restricted set of platforms (such as mainframes) and legacy programming languages (such as COBOL), they did not adapt well to the distributed computing paradigm that arose

from advances in PC and Internet technology and newer object-oriented programming languages, such as Java, C++, and C#.

Many of the limitations with model-integrated computing outlined above can be overcome by integrating MIC tools and processes with object-oriented frameworks [GSNW02]. This integration helps to overcome problems with earlier-generation CASE tools since it does not require the modeling tools to generate all the code. Instead, large portions of applications can be *composed* from reusable, prevalidated framework classes. Likewise, integrating MIC with frameworks helps address environments where application requirements and functionality change at a rapid pace by synthesizing and assembling newer extended framework classes and automating the configuration of many QoS-critical aspects, such as concurrency, distribution, transactions, security, and dependability.

The combination of model-integrated computing with frameworks, components, and patterns is an area of active research [Bay02]. In the DOC group, for example, there are R&D efforts underway to develop a MIC tool suite called the *Component Synthesis with Model-Integrated Computing* (CoSMIC) [GSNW02]. CoSMIC extends the popular GME modeling and synthesis tools [LBM+01] and the ACE ORB (TAO) [SLM98] to support the development, assembly, and deployment of QoS-enabled networked applications. To ensure the QoS requirements can be realized in the middleware layer, CoSMIC's model-integrated computing tools can specify and analyze the QoS requirements of application components in their accompanying metadata.

1.3   Applying Frameworks to Network Programming

One reason why it's hard to write robust, extensible, and efficient networked applications is that developers must master many complex networking programming concepts and mechanisms, including

- Network addressing and service identification/discovery
- Presentation layer conversions, such as marshaling, demarshaling, and encryption, to handle heterogeneous hosts with alternative processor byte orderings
- Local and remote interprocess communication (IPC) mechanisms
- Event demultiplexing and event handler dispatching
- Process/thread lifetime management and synchronization

Application programming interfaces (APIs) and tools have evolved over the years to simplify the development of networked applications and middleware. Figure 1.6 illustrates the IPC APIs available on OS platforms ranging from UNIX to many real-time operating systems. This figure shows how applications can access networking APIs for local and remote IPC at several levels of abstraction. We briefly discuss each level of abstraction below, starting from the lower-level kernel APIs to the native OS user-level networking APIs and the host infrastructure middleware.

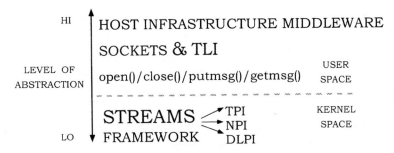

Figure 1.6: Levels of Abstraction for Network Programming

Kernel-level networking APIs.   Lower-level networking APIs are available in an OS kernel's I/O subsystem. For example, the UNIX `putmsg()` and `getmsg()` system functions can be used to access the *Transport Provider Interface* (TPI) [OSI92b] and the *Data Link Provider Interface* (DLPI) [OSI92a] available in System V STREAMS [Rit84]. It's also possible to develop network services, such as routers [KMC+00], network file systems [WLS+85], or even Web servers [JKN+01], that reside entirely within an OS kernel.

Programming directly to kernel-level networking APIs is rarely portable between different OS platforms, however. It's often not even portable across different versions of the same OS! Since kernel-level programming isn't used in most networked applications, we don't cover it any further in this book. See [Rag93], [SW95, MBKQ96], and [SR00] for coverage of these topics in the context of System V UNIX, BSD UNIX, and Windows 2000, respectively.

User-level networking APIs.   Networking protocol stacks in modern commercial operating systems reside within the protected address space of the OS kernel. Applications running in user space access protocol stacks in the OS kernel via IPC APIs, such as the Socket or TLI APIs. These APIs collaborate with an OS kernel to provide the capabilities shown in the following table:

Capability	Description
Local endpoint management	Create and destroy local communication endpoints, allowing access to available networking facilities.
Connection establishment and connection termination	Enable applications to establish connections actively or passively with remote peers and to shutdown all or part of the connections when transmissions are complete.
Options management	Negotiate and enable/disable protocol and endpoint options.
Data transfer mechanisms	Exchange data with peer applications.
Name/address translation	Convert human-readable names to low-level network addresses and vice versa.

These capabilities are covered in Chapter 2 of C++NPv1 in the context of the Socket API.

Many IPC APIs are modeled loosely on the UNIX file I/O API, which defines the
`open()`, `read()`, `write()`, `close()`, `ioctl()`, `lseek()`, and `select()` functions [Rit84]. Due to syntactic and semantic differences between file I/O and network I/O,
however, networking APIs provide additional functionality that's not supported directly by
the standard UNIX file I/O APIs. For example, the pathnames used to identify files on a
UNIX system aren't globally unique across hosts in a heterogeneous distributed environment. Different naming schemes, such as IP host addresses and TCP/UDP port numbers,
have therefore been devised to uniquely identify communication endpoints used by networked applications.

Host infrastructure middleware frameworks.   Many networked applications exchange
messages using synchronous and/or asynchronous request/response protocols in conjunction with host infrastructure middleware frameworks. Host infrastructure middleware encapsulates OS concurrency and IPC mechanisms to automate many low-level aspects of
networked application development, including

- Connection management and event handler initialization
- Event detection, demultiplexing, and event handler dispatching
- Message framing atop bytestream protocols, such as TCP
- Presentation conversion issues involving network byte ordering and parameter mar-
  shaling and demarshaling
- Concurrency models and synchronization of concurrent operations
- Networked application composition from dynamically configured services
- Hierarchical structuring of layered networked applications and services
- Management of quality of service (QoS) properties, such as scheduling access to
  processors, networks, and memory

The increasing availability and popularity of high-quality and affordable host infrastructure
middleware is helping to raise the level of abstraction at which developers of networked
applications can work effectively. For example, [C++NPv1, SS02] present an overview of
higher-level distributed object computing middleware, such as CORBA [Obj02] and The
ACE ORB (TAO) [SLM98], which is an implementation of CORBA built using the frameworks and classes in ACE. It's still useful, however, to understand how lower level IPC
mechanisms work to fully comprehend the challenges that arise when designing, porting,
and optimizing networked applications.

1.4   A Tour through the ACE Frameworks

1.4.1   An Overview of ACE

ACE is a highly portable, widely used, open-source host infrastructure middleware toolkit.
The source code is freely available from `http://ace.ece.uci.edu/` or `http://`

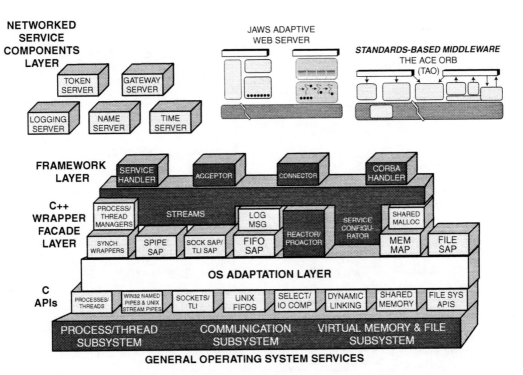

Figure 1.7: The Layered Architecture of ACE

www.riverace.com/. The core ACE library contains roughly a quarter million lines of C++ code that comprises approximately 500 classes. Many of these classes cooperate to form ACE's major frameworks. The ACE toolkit also includes higher-level components, as well as a large set of examples and an extensive automated regression test suite.

To separate concerns, reduce complexity, and permit functional subsetting, ACE is designed using a layered architecture [POSA1], shown in Figure 1.7. The capabilities provided by ACE span the session, presentation, and application layers in the OSI reference model [Bla91]. The foundation of the ACE toolkit is its combination of an OS adaptation layer and C++ wrapper facades, which together encapsulate core OS network programming mechanisms to run portably on all the OS platforms shown in Sidebar 2 (page 16). The higher layers of ACE build on this foundation to provide reusable frameworks, networked service components, and standards-based middleware.

1.4.2   A Synopsis of the ACE Frameworks

The ACE frameworks are an integrated set of classes that can be instantiated and customized to provide complete networked applications and service components. These frameworks help to transfer decades of accumulated knowledge directly from the ACE developers to

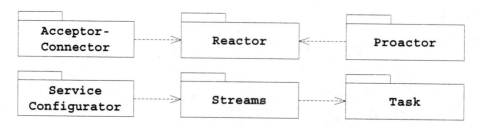

Figure 1.8: The Key Frameworks in ACE

Sidebar 2: OS Platforms Supported by ACE

ACE runs on a wide range of operating systems, including:

- PCs, for example, Windows (32- and 64-bit versions), WinCE, and Macintosh OS X
- Most versions of UNIX, for example, SunOS/Solaris, IRIX, HP-UX, Tru64 UNIX (Digital UNIX), AIX, DG/UX, Linux (Redhat, Debian, and SuSE), SCO OpenServer, UnixWare, NetBSD, and FreeBSD
- Real-time operating systems, for example, VxWorks, ChorusOS, LynxOS, Pharlap TNT, QNX Neutrino and RTP, RTEMS, and pSoS
- Large enterprise systems, for example, OpenVMS, MVS OpenEdition, Tandem NonStop-UX, and Cray UNICOS.

ACE can be used with all of the major C++ compilers on these platforms. The ACE Web site at `http://ace.ece.uci.edu` contains a complete, up-to-date list of platforms, along with instructions for downloading and building ACE.

ACE users in the form of expertise embodied in well-tested and reusable C++ software artifacts. The ACE frameworks implement a pattern language for programming concurrent object-oriented networked applications. Figure 1.8 illustrates the ACE frameworks. To illustrate how the ACE frameworks rely on and use each other, the lines between boxes represent a dependency in the direction of the arrow. Each framework is outlined below.

ACE Reactor and Proactor frameworks. These frameworks implement the Reactor and Proactor patterns [POSA2], respectively. Both are architectural patterns that allow applications to be driven by events that are delivered to the application from one or more event sources, the most important of which are I/O endpoints. The Reactor framework facilitates a *reactive I/O* model, with events signaling the ability to begin a synchronous I/O operation. The Proactor framework is designed for a *proactive I/O* model where one or more asynchronous I/O operations are initiated and the completion of each operation triggers an event. Proactive I/O models can achieve the performance benefits of concurrency without incurring many of its liabilities. The Reactor and Proactor frameworks automate the detection, demultiplexing, and dispatching of application-defined handlers in response to many types of events. Chapters 3 and 4 describe the ACE Reactor framework and Chapter 8 describes the ACE Proactor framework.

ACE Service Configurator framework. This framework implements the Component Configurator pattern [POSA2], which is a design pattern that allows an application to link and unlink its component implementations without having to modify, recompile, or relink the application statically. The ACE Service Configurator framework supports the configuration of applications whose services can be assembled late in the design cycle, such as at installation time and/or run time. Applications with high availability requirements, such as mission-critical systems that perform online transaction processing or real-time industrial process automation, often require such flexible configuration capabilities. Chapter 2 describes the design dimensions associated with configuring networked services and Chapter 5 describes the ACE Service Configurator framework.

ACE Task framework. This framework implements various concurrency patterns, such as Active Object and Half-Sync/Half-Async [POSA2]. Active Object is a design pattern that decouples the thread that executes a method from the thread that invoked it. Its purpose is to enhance concurrency and simplify synchronized access to objects that reside in their own threads of control. Half-Sync/Half-Async is an architectural pattern that decouples asynchronous and synchronous processing in concurrent systems, to simplify programming without reducing performance unduly. This pattern incorporates two intercommunicating layers, one for asynchronous and one for synchronous service processing. A queueing layer mediates communication between services in the asynchronous and synchronous layers. Chapter 5 of C++NPv1 describes the design dimensions associated with concurrent networked applications and Chapter 6 of this book describes the ACE Task framework.

ACE Acceptor-Connector framework. This framework leverages the Reactor framework and reifies the Acceptor-Connector pattern [POSA2]. This design pattern decouples the connection and initialization of cooperating peer services in a networked system from the processing they perform once connected and initialized. The Acceptor-Connector framework decouples the active and passive initialization roles from application-defined service processing performed by communicating peer services after initialization is complete. Chapter 7 describes this framework.

ACE Streams framework. This framework implements the Pipes and Filters pattern, which is an architectural pattern that provides a structure for systems that process a stream of data [POSA1]. The ACE Streams framework simplifies the development and composition of hierarchically layered services, such as user-level protocol stacks and network management agents [SS94]. Chapter 9 describes this framework.

When used together, the ACE frameworks outlined above enable the development of networked applications that can be updated and extended without the need to modify, re-

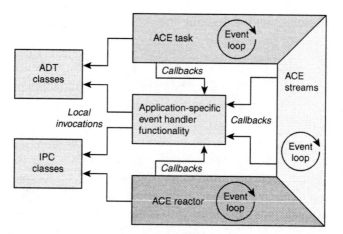

Figure 1.9: Applying Class Libraries to Develop and Use ACE Frameworks

compile, relink, or restart running applications. ACE achieves this unprecedented flexibility and extensibility by combining

- **OS mechanisms,** such as event demultiplexing, IPC, dynamic linking, multithreading, multiprocessing, and synchronization [Ste99]
- **C++ language features,** such as templates, inheritance, and dynamic binding [Bja00]
- **Patterns,** such as Component Configurator [POSA2], Strategy [GoF], and Handler/Callback [Ber95]

The ACE frameworks provide inversion of control via callbacks, as shown below:

ACE Framework	Inversion of Control
Reactor and Proactor	Calls back to application-supplied event handlers to perform processing when events occur synchronously and asynchronously.
Service Configurator	Calls back to application-supplied service objects to initialize, suspend, resume, and finalize them.
Task	Calls back to an application-supplied hook method to perform processing in one or more threads of control.
Acceptor-Connector	Calls back to service handlers to initialize them after they're connected.
Streams	Calls back to initialize and finalize tasks when they are pushed and popped from a stream.

The callback methods in ACE's framework classes are defined as C++ virtual methods. This use of dynamic binding allows networked applications to freely implement and extend interface methods without modifying or rebuilding existing framework classes. In contrast, the ACE wrapper facades rarely use callbacks or virtual methods, so they aren't as extensible as the ACE frameworks. The ACE wrapper facades do support a broad range of use cases, however, and can be integrated together via generic programming [Ale01] techniques based on the C++ *traits* and *traits classes idioms* outlined in Sidebar 40 (page 165).

Figure 1.9 illustrates how the class libraries and frameworks in ACE are complementary technologies. The ACE toolkit simplifies the implementation of its frameworks via its class libraries of containers, which include lists, queues, hash tables, strings, and other reusable data structures. Likewise, application-defined code invoked by event handlers in the ACE Reactor framework can use the ACE wrapper facades and the C++ standard library classes [Jos99] to perform IPC, synchronization, file management, and string processing operations. Sidebar 3 describes how to build the ACE library so that you can experiment with the examples we present in this book.

Sidebar 3: Building ACE and Programs that Use ACE

ACE is open-source software that you can download from `http://ace.ece.uci. edu` or `http://www.riverace.com` and build yourself. These sites contain a wealth of other material on ACE, such as tutorials, technical papers, and an overview of other ACE wrapper facades and frameworks that aren't covered in this book. You can also purchase a prebuilt version of ACE from Riverace at a nominal cost. See `http://www.riverace.com` for a list of the prebuilt compiler and OS platforms supported by Riverace.

If you want to build ACE yourself, you should download and unpack the ACE distribution into an empty directory. The top-level directory in the distribution is named `ACE_wrappers`. We refer to this top-level directory as "ACE_ROOT." You should create an environment variable by that name containing the full path to the top-level ACE directory. The ACE source and header files reside in `$ACE_ROOT/ace`.

The `$ACE_ROOT/ACE-INSTALL.html` file has complete instructions for building ACE, including how to configure it for your OS and compiler. This book's networked logging service example source and header files reside in `$ACE_ROOT/examples/ C++NPv2` and are ready to build on all platforms that ACE supports. To build your own programs, the `$ACE_ROOT` directory must be added to your compiler's file include path. For command-line compilers, this can be done with the `-I` or `/I` compiler option. Graphical IDEs provide similar options, such as MSVC++'s "Preprocessor, Additional include directories" section of the C/C++ tab on the Project Settings dialog box.

1.5   Example: A Networked Logging Service

It's been our experience that the principles, methods, and skills required to develop and use reusable networked application software cannot be learned solely by generalities or toy examples. Instead, programmers must learn concrete technical skills and gain hands-on experience by developing and using real frameworks and applications. We therefore illustrate key points and ACE capabilities throughout this book by extending and enhancing the networked logging service example introduced in C++NPv1, which collects and records diagnostic information sent from one or more client applications.

The logging service in C++NPv1 used many of ACE's wrapper facades in a two-tier client/server architecture. This book's logging service examples use a more powerful architecture that illustrates a broader complement of capabilities and patterns, and demonstrates how ACE's frameworks can help achieve efficient, predictable, and scalable networked applications. This service also helps to demonstrate key design and implementation considerations and solutions that will arise when you develop your own concurrent object-oriented networked applications.

Figure 1.10 illustrates the application processes and daemons in our networked logging service, which we outline below.

Client application processes (such as P_1, P_2, and P_3) run on client hosts and generate log records ranging from debugging messages to critical error messages. The logging information sent by a client application contains the time the log record was created, the process identifier of the application, the priority level of the log record, and a variable-sized string containing the log record text message. Client applications send these log records to a *client logging daemon* running on their local host.

Client logging daemons run on every host machine participating in the networked logging service. Each client logging daemon receives log records from that host's client applications via some form of local IPC mechanism, such as shared memory, pipes, or sockets. The client logging daemon uses a remote IPC mechanism, such as TCP/IP, to forward log records to a *server logging daemon* running on a designated host.

Server logging daemons collect and output the incoming log records they receive from client applications via client logging daemons. A server logging daemon[2] can determine which client host sent each message by using addressing information it obtains from the underlying Socket API. There's generally one server logging daemon per system configuration, though they could be replicated to avoid a single point of failure.

Figure 1.11 (page 22) shows the progression of networked application servers that we'll develop and use in this book. These client and server logging daemons will illustrate how to use the ACE frameworks and wrapper facades with the following concurrency models.

Concurrency Model	Section
Reactive	3.5, 4.2, 5.4
Thread pool	4.3, 4.4, 6.3
Thread-per-connection	7.2, 7.3
Producer/consumer	6.2, 7.4, 9.2
Proactive	8.2 – 8.5

---

[2]We use the terms *server logging daemon* and *logging server* interchangeably throughout this book.

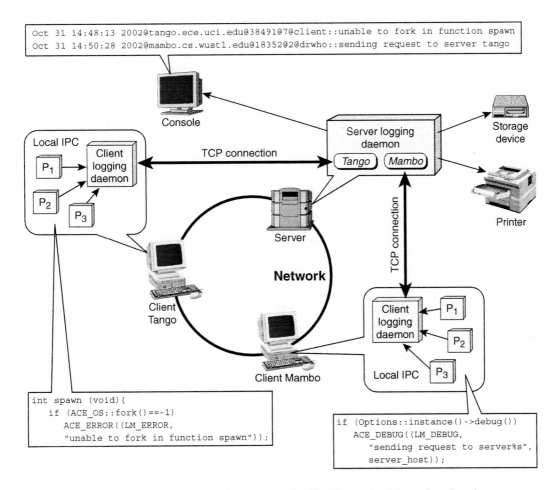

Figure 1.10: Processes and Daemons in the Networked Logging Service

1.6   Summary

Networked application software has been developed manually from scratch for decades. The continual rediscovery and reinvention of core concepts and capabilities associated with this process has kept the costs of engineering and evolving networked applications too high for too long. Improving the quality and quantity of systematic software reuse is essential to resolve this problem.

Middleware is a class of software that's particularly effective at providing systematically reusable artifacts for networked applications. Developing and using middleware is therefore an important way to increase reuse. There are many technical and nontechnical challenges that make middleware development and reuse hard, however. This chapter described how object-oriented frameworks can be applied to overcome many of these chal-

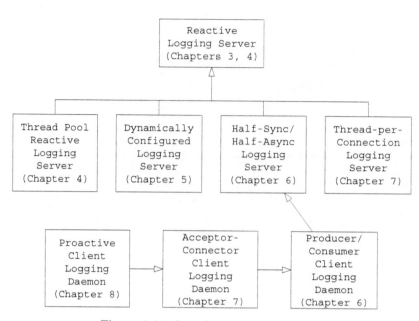

Figure 1.11: Logging Server Examples

lenges. To make the most appropriate choice of software development technologies, we also described the differences between frameworks and class libraries, components, patterns, and model-integrated computing. Each technology plays a part in reducing software development costs and life cycles and increasing software quality, functionality, and performance.

The result of applying framework development principles and patterns to the domain of networked applications has yielded the ACE frameworks. These frameworks handle common network programming tasks and can be customized via C++ language features to produce complete networked applications. When used together, the ACE frameworks simplify the creation, composition, configuration, and porting of networked applications without incurring significant performance overhead. The rest of this book explains how and why the ACE frameworks were developed and shows many examples of how ACE uses C++ features to achieve its goals.

An intangible, but valuable, benefit of ACE is its transfer of decades of accumulated knowledge from ACE framework developers to ACE framework users in the form of expertise embodied in well-tested C++ classes that implement time-proven networked application software development strategies. These frameworks took scores of person-years to develop, optimize, and mature. Fortunately, you can take advantage of the expertise embodied in these frameworks without having to independently rediscover or reinvent the patterns and classes that underlie them.

CHAPTER 2

Service and Configuration Design Dimensions

CHAPTER SYNOPSIS

A service is a set of functionality offered to a client by a server. Common services available on the Internet today include

- Web content retrieval services, such as Apache and Google
- Software distribution services, such as Castanet, Citrix, or Softricity
- Electronic mail and network news transfer services
- File access on remote machines
- Network time synchronization
- Payment processing services
- Streaming audio/video services, such as RealPlayer and QuickTime

Networked applications can be created by configuring their constituent services together at various points of time, such as compile time, static link time, installation time, or run time.

Chapters 1 and 5 of C++NPv1 provided a domain analysis of the communication protocols and mechanisms and the concurrency architectures used by networked applications. This chapter expands that coverage to analyze other design dimensions that address key networked application properties. These properties include service duration and structure, how networked services are identified, and the time at which they are bound together to form complete applications. These design dimensions are important in any networked application, and of particular importance to the ACE Service Configurator framework (Chapter 5). If you're already familiar with these design dimensions, however, you may want to skip ahead to Chapter 3, which begins the coverage of the ACE frameworks.

2.1 Service and Server Design Dimensions

When designing networked applications, it's important to recognize the difference between a *service*, which is a capability offered to clients, and a *server*, which is the mechanism by which the service is offered. The design decisions regarding services and servers are easily confused, but should be considered separately. This section covers the following service and server design dimensions:

- Short- versus long-duration services
- Internal versus external services
- Stateful versus stateless services
- Layered/modular versus monolithic services
- Single- versus multiservice servers
- One-shot versus standing servers

2.1.1 Short-Duration versus Long-Duration Services

The services offered by network servers can be classified as short duration or long duration. These time durations reflect how long a service holds system resources. The primary trade-off in this design dimension involves holding system resources when they may be better used elsewhere versus the overhead of restarting a service when it's needed. In a networked application, this dimension is closely related to protocol selection because setup requirements for different protocols can vary significantly.

Short-duration services execute in brief, often fixed, amounts of time and usually handle a single request at a time. Examples of short-duration services include computing the current time of day, resolving the Ethernet number of an IP address, and retrieving a disk block from the cache of a network file server. To minimize the amount of time spent setting up a connection, short-duration services are often implemented using connectionless protocols, such as UDP/IP [Ste94].

Long-duration services run for extended, often variable, lengths of time and may handle numerous requests during their lifetime. Examples of long-duration services include transferring large software releases via FTP, downloading MP3 files from a Web server using HTTP, streaming audio and video from a server using RTSP, accessing host resources remotely via TELNET, and performing remote file system backups over a network. Services that run for longer durations allow more flexibility in protocol selection. For example, to improve efficiency and reliability, these services are often implemented with connection-oriented protocols, such as TCP/IP [Ste94], or session-oriented protocols, such as RTSP [SRL98] or SCTP [SX01].

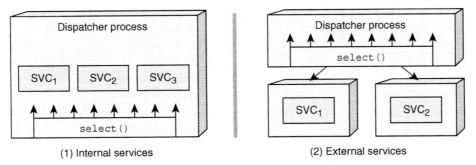

Figure 2.1: Internal versus External Services

Logging service $\Rightarrow$ From the standpoint of an individual log record, our server logging daemon seems like a short-duration service. Each log record is limited to a maximum length of 4K bytes, though in practice most are much smaller. The actual time spent handling a log record is relatively short. Since a client may transmit many log records, however, we optimize performance by designing client logging daemons to establish connections with their peer server logging daemons. We then reuse these connections for subsequent logging requests. It would be wasteful and time consuming to set up and tear down a socket connection for each logging request, particularly when small requests are sent frequently. We therefore model our client and server logging daemons as long-duration services.

2.1.2   Internal versus External Services

Services can be classified as internal or external. The primary tradeoffs in this dimension are service initialization time, isolation of one service from another, and simplicity.

Internal services execute in the same address space as the server that receives the request, as shown in Figure 2.1 (1). As described in Chapter 5 of C++NPv1, an internal service can run iteratively, concurrently, or reactively in relation to other internal services. Internal services usually have low initialization latency and their context switch time is generally shorter than that of services residing in separate processes.

   Internal services may also reduce application robustness, however, since separate services within a process aren't protected from one another. One faulty service can therefore corrupt data shared with other internal services in the process, which may produce incorrect results, crash the process, or cause the process to hang indefinitely. As a result, internal services should be reserved for code that can be trusted to operate correctly when run in the context of other services in an application's address space.

External services execute in different process address spaces. For instance, Figure 2.1 (2) illustrates a master service process that monitors a set of network ports. When a connection request arrives from a client, the master accepts the connection and then spawns a new process to perform the requested service externally. External services may be more robust than internal services since the failure of one need not cause the failure of another. To increase robustness, therefore, mission-critical application services are often isolated in separate processes. The price for this robustness, however, can be a reduction in performance due to process management and IPC overhead.

Some server frameworks support both internal and external services. For example, the INETD *superserver* [Ste98] is a daemon that listens for connection requests or messages on certain ports and runs programs to perform the services associated with those ports. System administrators can choose between internal and external services in INETD by modifying the `inetd.conf` configuration file as follows:

- INETD can be configured to execute short-duration services, such as ECHO and DAY-TIME, *internally* via calls to statically linked functions in the INETD program.
- INETD can also be configured to run longer-duration services, such as FTP and TEL-NET, *externally* by spawning separate processes.

Sidebar 4 (page 31) describes this and other service provisioning mechanisms that use both internal and external services.

Logging service ⇒ All logging server implementations in this book are designed as internal services. As long as only one type of service is configured into our logging server, we needn't isolate it from harmful side effects of other services. There are valid reasons to protect the processing of different client sessions from each other, however, particularly if services are linked dynamically using the Component Configurator pattern [POSA2]. Chapter 8 in C++NPv1 therefore illustrates how to implement a logging server as an external service using the `ACE_Process` and `ACE_Process_Manager` classes.

2.1.3 Stateful versus Stateless Services

Services can be classified as stateful or stateless. The amount of state, or context, that a service maintains between requests impacts the complexity and resource consumption of clients and servers. Stateful and stateless services trade off efficiency for reliability, with the right choice depending on a variety of factors, such as the probability and impact of host and network failures.

Stateful services cache certain information, such as session state, authentication keys, identification numbers, and I/O handles, in a server to reduce communication and computation overhead. For instance, Web cookies enable a Web server to preserve state across multiple page requests.

Stateless services retain no volatile state within a server. For example, the Network File System (NFS) [Ste94] provides distributed data storage and retrieval services that don't maintain volatile state information within a server's address space. Each request sent from

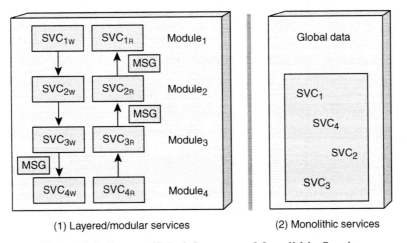

Figure 2.2: Layered/Modular versus Monolithic Services

a client is completely self-contained with the information needed to carry it out, such as the file handle, byte count, starting file offset, and user credentials.

Some common network applications, such as FTP and TELNET, don't require retention of persistent application state information between consecutive service invocations. These stateless services are generally fairly simple to configure and reconfigure reliably. Conversely, the CORBA Naming Service [Obj98] is a common middleware service that manages various bindings whose values may need to be retained even if the server containing the service crashes. If preserving state across failures is paramount to system correctness, you may need to use a transaction monitor [GR93] or some type of active replication [BvR94].

Logging service ⇒ Our networked logging service exhibits both stateful and stateless characteristics. The state maintained by the server process resides largely in the OS kernel (e.g., connection blocks) and the file system (e.g., the log records). Both client and server logging daemon services in this book are stateless, however, since they process each record individually without requiring or using any information from, or expectation of, any previous or possible future request. The need to handle any possible request ordering is not a factor since we use TCP/IP, which provides an ordered, reliable communication byte stream.

2.1.4   Layered/Modular versus Monolithic Services

Service implementations can be classified as layered/modular or monolithic. The primary tradeoffs in this dimension are service reusability, extensibility, and efficiency.

Layered/modular services can be decomposed into a series of partitioned and hierarchically related tasks. For instance, application families can be specified and implemented as layered/modular services, as shown in Figure 2.2 (1). Each layer can handle a self-contained portion of the overall service, such as input and output, event analysis, event filtering, and service processing. Interconnected services can collaborate by exchanging control and data messages for incoming and outgoing communication.

Powerful communication frameworks have emerged over the years to simplify and automate the development and configuration of layered/modular services [SS93]. Examples include System V STREAMS [Rit84], the x-kernel [HP91], the Conduits+ framework [HJE95], and the ACE Streams framework (Chapter 9). These frameworks decouple the service functionality from the following service design aspects:

- **Compositional strategies**, such as the time and/or order in which services and protocols are composed together (described in Chapters 5 and 9 of this book)
- **Concurrency and synchronization strategies**, such as task- and message-based architectures (described in Chapter 5 of C++NPv1) that execute services at run time
- **Communication strategies**, such as the protocols and messaging mechanisms (described in Chapters 1–3 of C++NPv1) that interconnect services together [SS95b]

Monolithic services are tightly coupled clumps of functionality that aren't organized hierarchically. They may contain separate modules of functionality that vaguely resemble layers, but are most often tightly coupled via shared, global variables, as shown in Figure 2.2 (2) (page 27). They are also often tightly coupled functionally, with control flow diagrams that look like spaghetti. Monolithic services are therefore hard to understand, maintain, and extend. While they may sometimes be appropriate in short-lived, "throw away" prototypes [FY00], they are rarely suitable for software that must be maintained and enhanced by multiple developers over longer amounts of time.[1]

Developers can often select either layered or monolithic service architectures to structure their networked applications. The ACE Task and Streams frameworks, discussed in Chapters 6 and 9, provide efficient and extensible ways to build modular services. The advantages of designing layered/modular services are

- Layering enhances reuse since multiple higher-layer application services can share lower-layer services.
- Implementing applications via an interconnected series of layered services enables transparent, incremental enhancement of their functionality.
- A layered/modular architecture facilitates macro-level performance improvements by allowing the selective omission of unnecessary service functionality or selective configuration of contextually optimal service functionality.
- Modular designs generally improve the implementation, testing, and maintenance of networked applications and services.

---

[1]After you become proficient with the ACE toolkit, you'll find it's usually *much* faster to build a properly layered prototype than to hack together a monolithic one.

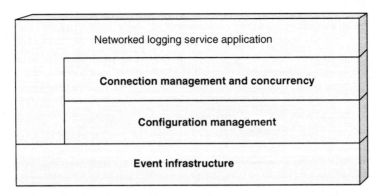

Figure 2.3: Networked Logging Service Architecture Layers

There can also be some disadvantages, however, with using a layered/modular architecture to develop networked applications:

- The modularity of layered implementations can cause excessive overhead. For example, layering may be inefficient if buffer sizes don't match in adjacent layers, thereby causing additional segmentation, reassembly, and transmission delays.
- Communication between layers must be designed and implemented properly, which can introduce another source of errors.
- Information hiding within layers can make it hard to manage resources predictably in applications with stringent real-time requirements.

Logging service ⇒ By carefully separating design concerns, our client and server logging daemons are designed using the layered/modular architecture depicted in Figure 2.3 and described below.

1. **Event infrastructure layer,** which detects and demultiplexes events and dispatches them to their associated event handlers. Chapters 3 and 4 describe how the Reactor pattern and ACE Reactor framework can be applied to implement a generic event infrastructure layer. Likewise, Chapter 8 describes how the Proactor pattern and ACE Proactor framework can be applied for a similar purpose.
2. **Configuration management layer,** which installs, initializes, controls, and shuts service components down. Chapter 5 describes how the Component Configurator pattern and ACE Service Configurator framework can be applied to implement a generic configuration management layer.
3. **Connection management and concurrency layer,** which performs connection and initialization services that are independent of application functionality. Chapters 6 and 7 describe how the Acceptor-Connector and Half-Sync/Half-Async patterns and the ACE Acceptor-Connector and Task frameworks can implement a generic connection management layer.

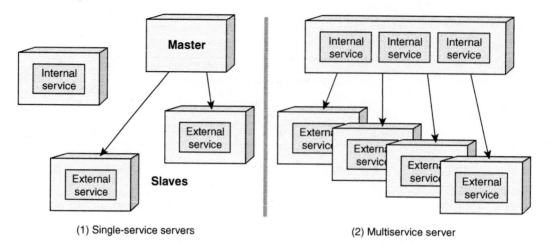

(1) Single-service servers   (2) Multiservice server

Figure 2.4: Single-service versus Multiservice Servers

4. **Application layer,** which customizes the application-independent classes provided by the other layers to create concrete objects that configure applications, handle events, establish connections, exchange data, and perform logging-specific process-ing. Throughout this book, we illustrate how to implement these application-level capabilities using the ACE frameworks and the ACE wrapper facade classes.

2.1.5   Single-Service versus Multiservice Servers

Protocols and services rarely operate in isolation, but instead are accessed by applications within the context of a server. Servers can be designed either as single service or multiser-vice. The tradeoff in this dimension is between resource consumption versus robustness.

Single-service servers offer only one service. As shown in Figure 2.4 (1), a service can be internal or external, but there's only a single service per process. Examples of single-service servers include

- The RWHO daemon (RWHOD), which reports the identity and number of active users, as well as host workloads and host availability
- Early versions of UNIX standard network services, such as FTP and TELNET, that ran as distinct single-service daemons initiated at OS boot time [Ste98]

Each instance of these single-service servers executed externally in a separate process. As the number of system servers increased, however, this statically configured, single-service-per-process approach incurred the following limitations:

- It consumed excessive OS resources, such as virtual memory and process table slots.

- It caused redundant initialization and networking code to be written separately for each service program.
- It required running processes to be shut down and restarted manually to install new service implementations.
- It led to *ad hoc* and inconsistent administrative mechanisms' being used to control different types of services.

Multiservice servers address the limitations with single-service servers by integrating a collection of single-service servers into a single administrative unit, as shown in Figure 2.4 (2). Examples of multiservice servers include INETD (which originated with BSD UNIX [MBKQ96, Ste98]), LISTEN (which is the System V UNIX network listener service [Rag93]), and the Service Control Manager (SCM) (which originated with Windows NT [SR00]). Sidebar 4 compares and contrasts these multiservice servers.

Sidebar 4: Comparing Multiservice Server Frameworks

This sidebar compares the multiservice server frameworks supported by various versions of UNIX and Windows.

- INETD's internal services, such as ECHO and DAYTIME, are fixed at static link time. The master INETD daemon permits dynamic reconfiguration of its external services, such as FTP or TELNET. For instance, when the INETD daemon is sent the SIGHUP signal, it reads its `inetd.conf` file and performs the `socket()`/`bind()`/`listen()` sequence for all services listed in that file. Since INETD does not support dynamic reconfiguration of internal services, however, any newly listed services must still be processed by spawning slave daemons via `fork()` and the `exec*()` family of system functions.

- The System V UNIX LISTEN port monitoring facility is similar to INETD, though it only supports connection-oriented protocols accessed via TLI and System V STREAMS, and doesn't provide internal services. Unlike INETD, however, LISTEN supports standing servers by passing initialized file descriptors via STREAMS pipes from the LISTEN process to a previously registered standing server.

- Unlike INETD and LISTEN, the Windows SCM is not a port monitor since it doesn't provide built-in support for listening to a set of I/O ports and dispatching server processes on demand when client requests arrive. Instead, it provides an RPC-based interface that allows a master SCM process to automatically initiate and control (i.e., pause, resume, or terminate) administrator-installed services (such as FTP and TELNET) that typically run as separate threads within either a single-service or a multiservice daemon process. Each installed service is individually responsible for configuring the service and monitoring any communication endpoints. These endpoints may be more general than TCP or UDP sockets, for example, they can be Windows named pipes.

A multiservice server can yield the following benefits:

- It can reduce OS resource consumption by spawning servers on demand.
- It simplifies server development and reuses common code by automatically daemonizing a server process (described in Sidebar 5), initializing transport endpoints, monitoring ports, and demultiplexing/dispatching client requests to service handlers.
- It can allow external services to be updated without modifying existing source code or terminating running server processes.
- It consolidates network service administration via a uniform set of configuration management utilities. For example, the INETD superserver provides a uniform interface for coordinating and initiating external services, such as FTP and TELNET, and internal services, such as DAYTIME and ECHO.

Logging service ⇒ Implementations of the networked logging service in C++NPv1 all used single-service servers. Starting in Chapter 5 of this book, various entities in the networked logging service will be configured via the ACE Service Configurator framework, which can be used to configure multiservice superservers similar to INETD.

Sidebar 5: Daemons and Daemonizing

A daemon is a long-running server process that executes in the "background" performing various services on behalf of clients [Ste98]. A daemon is not associated with an interactive user or controlling terminal. It's therefore important to ensure a daemon is designed robustly to recover from errors and to manage its resources carefully.

Daemonizing a UNIX process involves spawning a new server process, closing all unnecessary I/O handles, changing the current filesystem directory away from the initiating user's, resetting the file access creation mask, disassociating from the controlling process group and controlling terminal, and ignoring terminal I/O-related events and signals. An ACE server can convert itself into a daemon on UNIX by invoking the static method ACE::daemonize() or passing the '-b' option to ACE_Service_Config::open() (page 141). A Windows Service [Ric97] is a form of daemon and can be programmed in ACE using the ACE_NT_Service class.

2.1.6 One-shot versus Standing Servers

In addition to being single service or multiservice, networked servers can be designed as either one shot or standing. The primary tradeoffs in this dimension involve how long the server runs and uses system resources. When evaluating choices in this dimension, consider anticipated usage frequency for the service(s) offered by the server, as well as requirements for startup speed and configuration flexibility.

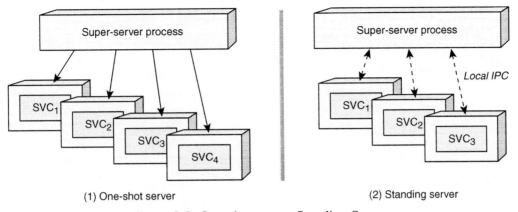

Figure 2.5: One-shot versus Standing Servers

One-shot servers are spawned on demand, for example, by an INETD superserver. They perform service requests in a separate thread or process, as shown in Figure 2.5 (1). A one-shot server terminates after the completion of the request or session that triggered its creation. An example of a one-shot server is a UNIX FTP server. When an FTP client connects to the server, a new process is spawned to handle the FTP session, including user authentication and file transfers. The FTP server process exits when the client session ends.

A one-shot server doesn't remain in system memory when it's idle. Therefore, this design strategy can consume fewer system resources, such as virtual memory and process table slots. This advantage is clearly more pronounced for services that are seldom used.

Standing servers continue to run beyond the lifetime of any particular service request or session they process. Standing servers are often initiated at boot time or by a superserver after the first client request. They may receive connection and/or service requests via local IPC channels, such as named pipes or sockets, that are attached to a superserver, as shown in Figure 2.5 (2). Alternatively, a standing server may take ownership of, or inherit, an IPC channel from the original service invocation.

An example of a standing server is the Apache Web server [HMS98]. Apache's initial parent process can be configured to pre-spawn a pool of child processes that service client HTTP requests. Each child process services a tunable number of client requests before it exits. The parent process can spawn new child processes as required to support the load on the Web server.

Compared with one-shot servers, standing servers can improve service response time by amortizing the cost of spawning a server process or thread over a series of client requests. As in Apache's case, they can also be tuned adaptively to support differing types of load. The ability of a standing server design to terminate and respawn service processes periodically can also guard against OS or application problems, such as memory leaks, that degrade performance over time or become security holes.

Logging service ⇒ We implement the client and server logging daemons in our networked logging service as standing servers to improve performance of the overall system. We justify the tradeoff of occupying process slots and system resources since logging is a service that's used frequently. Thus, restarting a logging server for each client would delay the client making the request and degrade overall system performance.

The choice between one-shot or standing servers is orthogonal to the choice between short- or long-duration services described in Section 2.1.1. The former design alternative usually reflects OS resource management constraints, whereas the latter design alternative is a property of a service. For example, we could easily change to a short-duration service without changing the standing nature of the server itself. Likewise, if the logging service is lightly used in some environments, it could easily be changed to a one-shot server, with or without revisiting the duration of each service request.

2.2   Configuration Design Dimensions

This section covers the following configuration design dimensions:

- Static versus dynamic naming
- Static versus dynamic linking
- Static versus dynamic configuration

2.2.1   Static versus Dynamic Naming

Applications can be categorized according to whether their services are named statically or dynamically. The primary tradeoff in this dimension involves run-time efficiency versus flexibility.

Statically named services associate the name of a service with object code that exists at compile time and/or static link time. For example, INETD's internal services, such as ECHO and DAYTIME, are bound to statically named functions stored internally in the INETD program. A statically named service can be implemented in either static or dynamic libraries.

Dynamically named services defer the association of a service name with the object code that implements the service. Code therefore needn't be identified—nor even be written, compiled, and linked—until an application begins executing the corresponding service at run time. A common example of dynamic naming is demonstrated by INETD's handling of TELNET, which is an external service. External services can be updated by modifying the `inetd.conf` configuration file and sending the SIGHUP signal to the INETD process. When INETD receives this signal, it rereads `inetd.conf` and dynamically rebinds the services it offers to their new executables.

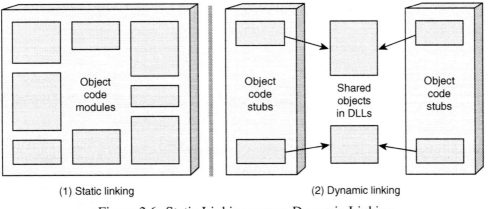

(1) Static linking   (2) Dynamic linking

Figure 2.6: Static Linking versus Dynamic Linking

2.2.2   Static versus Dynamic Linking

Applications can also be categorized according to whether their services are linked into a process address space statically or dynamically. The primary tradeoffs in this dimension involve extensibility, security, reliability, and efficiency.

Static linking creates a complete executable program by binding together all its object files at compile time and/or static link time, as shown in Figure 2.6 (1).

Dynamic linking loads object files into and unloads object files from the address space of a process when a program is invoked initially or updated at run time, as shown in Figure 2.6 (2). The OS run-time linker updates external symbol addresses for each process that the object file is loaded into to reflect the memory region the file is loaded into. Operating systems generally support two types of dynamic linking:

- **Implicit dynamic linking** loads referenced object files during program execution without explicit action by the program itself. Many platforms offer the option to defer address resolution and relocation operations until a method is first referenced. This lazy evaluation strategy minimizes link editing overhead during application initialization. Implicit dynamic linking is used to implement *dynamically linked libraries* (DLLs) [SR00], also known as *shared libraries* [GLDW87].

- **Explicit dynamic linking** allows an application to obtain, use, and remove the runtime address bindings of certain function- or data-related symbols defined in DLLs. Explicit dynamic linking mechanisms supported by popular operating systems include UNIX functions (`dlopen()`, `dlsym()`, and `dlclose()`) and Windows functions (`LoadLibrary()`, `GetProcAddress()`, and `FreeLibrary()`).

Dynamic linking can help to reduce the memory consumption of both a process in memory and its program image stored on disk. Ideally, only one copy of DLL code will exist, regardless of the number of processes that execute the DLL code simultaneously.

When choosing between dynamic and static linking, developers must carefully weigh tradeoffs between flexibility, security, and robustness against the potential benefits of time and space efficiency. The following are some downsides to using dynamic linking:

- **Security and robustness problems.** A dynamically linked application may be less secure and robust than a statically linked application. It may be less secure because *trojan horses* can be interposed in DLLs. It may be less robust because a faulty DLL can corrupt the state of other code or data in the same application process.

- **Run-time overhead.** Dynamic linking can incur more run-time overhead compared with static linking. In addition to opening and mapping multiple files, external symbol addresses in DLLs must be adjusted based on the memory locations the files are loaded into. Although lazy linking can ameliorate this effect, it can be noticeable, especially the first time a DLL is loaded into memory. Moreover, compilers that generate position-independent code often use extra levels of indirection to resolve method invocations and access global variables within DLLs [GLDW87].

- **Excessive jitter.** Time-critical applications may be unable to tolerate the latency of linking DLLs into a process and resolving method addresses dynamically.

Naturally, you should empirically evaluate the impact of dynamic linking to determine whether it's really an issue for your applications.

2.2.3   Static versus Dynamic Configuration

As described in Section 2.1, networked applications often offer or use a variety of services. By combining the naming and linking dimensions described in Sections 2.2.1 and 2.2.2, we can classify networked application services as being either statically or dynamically configured. As with static versus dynamic linking, the primary tradeoffs in this dimension involve extensibility, security, reliability, and efficiency.

Static configuration refers to the activities associated with initializing an application that contains statically named services (i.e., developing each service as a separate function or class) and then compiling, linking, and executing them in a separate OS process. In this case, the services in the application cannot be extended at run time. This design may be necessary for secure applications that only contain trusted services. Statically configured applications can also benefit from the more aggressive compiler optimizations applicable to statically linked programs.

However, there are several problems with statically configuring networked applications and services:

- They can yield nonextensible applications and software architectures that tightly couple the implementation and the configuration of a particular service with respect to other services in an application.

- Static configuration limits the ability of system administrators to change the parameters or configuration of applications to suit local operating conditions or variations in network and hardware configurations.
- Large-scale statically configured applications may be impractical due to their executable size, which can be hard to deliver, take excessive time to load, and can cause thrashing in systems if sufficient memory isn't available.

Dynamic configuration refers to the activities associated with initializing an application that offers dynamically named services. When combined with explicit dynamic linking and process/thread creation mechanisms, the services offered by applications configured dynamically can be extended at installation or boot time, or even during run time. This extensibility can yield the following configuration-related optimizations:

- **Dynamic service reconfiguration.** Highly available networked applications, such as online transaction processing or telecom call processing systems, may require flexible dynamic reconfiguration management capabilities. For example, it may be necessary to phase a new version of a service into a server without disrupting other services that it's already executing. Reconfiguration protocols based on explicit dynamic linking mechanisms can enhance the functionality and flexibility of networked applications since they enable services to be inserted, deleted, or modified at run time without first stopping and restarting the underlying process or thread(s) [SS94].

- **Functional subsetting.** Dynamic configuration simplifies the steps necessary to produce subsets of functionality for application families developed to run on a range of OS platforms. Explicit dynamic linking enables the fine-grain addition, removal, or modification of services. This in turn allows the same framework to be used for space-efficient embedded applications and for large enterprise distributed applications. For example, a Web browsing application may be able to run on PDAs, PCs, and/or workstations by dynamically configuring subsets, such as image rendering, Java capability, printing, or direct phone number dialing.

- **Application workload balancing.** It's often hard to determine the processing characteristics of application services in advance since workloads can vary considerably at run time. It may therefore be necessary to use dynamic configuration to support load balancing techniques [OOS01] and system partitionings that locate application services on different host machines throughout a network. For example, developers may have the opportunity to collocate or distribute certain services, such as image processing, on either side of a client/server boundary. Bottlenecks may result if many services are configured into a server application and too many active clients access these services simultaneously. Conversely, configuring many services into clients can result in a bottleneck if clients execute on cheaper, less powerful machines.

Logging service ⇒ Our networked logging service implementations in C++NPv1 and in Chapters 3 and 4 of this book are configured statically. In Chapter 5 of this book, we describe ACE_DLL, which is a portable wrapper facade that encapsulates the ability to load/unload shared libraries (DLLs) dynamically and find symbols in them. We also describe the ACE Service Configurator framework, which can configure application services dynamically. From Chapter 5 onward most of our examples are configured dynamically.

2.3 Summary

This chapter described two groups of design dimensions related to the successful development and deployment of networked applications. *Service design dimensions* affect the ways in which application services are structured, developed, and instantiated. *Service configuration dimensions* affect user or administrator abilities to vary the run-time placement and configuration of networked services after delivery and deployment.

Service design dimensions have a significant impact on how effectively applications use system and network resources. Efficient resource usage is closely linked to application response time, as well as to overall system performance and scalability. Performance is an important factor that's visible to end users. Though a coherent and modular design is less visible to end users, it's critical to a product's long-term success.

Good design simplifies maintenance and allows application functionality to evolve in response to market changes and competitive pressures without losing quality or performance. Fortunately, performance and modularity needn't be an either/or proposition. By carefully considering service design dimensions and applying ACE judiciously, you'll be able to create highly efficient *and* well-designed networked applications.

Even well-designed services and applications may need to adapt to a variety of deployment environments and user demands. Service configuration dimensions involve tradeoffs between design decisions associated with identifying a particular set of services and linking these services into the address space of one or more applications. To produce successful solutions, a networked application's flexibility must be weighed against its security, packaging, and complexity concerns.

When developing networked applications, the two sets of design dimensions in this chapter should be considered along with the dimensions described in Chapters 1 and 5 of C++NPv1. The ACE frameworks described in this book offer powerful tools to implement flexible and extensible designs with many combinations of tradeoffs and capabilities.

CHAPTER 3

The ACE Reactor Framework

CHAPTER SYNOPSIS

This chapter describes the design and use of the ACE Reactor framework. This framework implements the Reactor pattern [POSA2], which allows event-driven applications to react to events originating from a number of disparate sources, such as I/O handles, timers, and signals. Applications override framework-defined *hook methods*, which the framework then dispatch to process events. We show how to implement a logging server using a reactor that (1) detects and demultiplexes different types of connection and data events from various event sources and (2) then dispatches the events to application-defined handlers that process the events.

3.1   Overview

The ACE Reactor framework simplifies the development of event-driven programs, which characterize many networked applications. Common sources of events in these applications include activity on an IPC stream for I/O operations, POSIX signals, Windows handle signaling, and timer expirations. In this context, the ACE Reactor framework is responsible for

- Detecting the occurrence of events from various event sources
- Demultiplexing the events to their preregistered event handlers
- Dispatching to hook methods defined by the handlers to process the events in an application-defined manner

This chapter describes the following ACE Reactor framework classes that networked applications can use to detect the occurrence of events and then demultiplex and dispatch the events to their event handlers:

ACE Class	Description
ACE_Time_Value	Provides a portable, normalized representation of time and duration that uses C++ operator overloading to simplify time-related arithmetic and relational operations.
ACE_Event_Handler	An abstract class whose interface defines the hook methods that are the target of ACE_Reactor callbacks. Most application event handlers developed with ACE are descendants of ACE_Event_Handler.
ACE_Timer_Queue	An abstract class defining the capabilities and interface for a timer queue. ACE contains a variety of classes derived from ACE_Timer_Queue that provide flexible support for different timing requirements.
ACE_Reactor	Provides the interface for managing event handler registrations and executing the event loop that drives event detection, demultiplexing, and dispatching in the Reactor framework.

The most important relationships between the classes in the ACE Reactor framework are shown in Figure 3.1. These classes play the following roles in accordance with the Reactor pattern [POSA2]:

- **Event infrastructure layer classes** provide application-independent strategies for synchronously detecting and demultiplexing events to event handlers and then dispatching the associated event handler hook methods. The infrastructure layer components in the ACE Reactor framework include ACE_Time_Value, ACE_Event_Handler, the ACE timer queue classes, and the various implementations of the ACE_Reactor.

- **Application layer classes** define event handlers to perform application-defined processing in their hook methods. In the ACE Reactor framework, application layer classes are descendants of ACE_Event_Handler.

The power of the ACE Reactor framework comes from encapsulating the differences between event demultiplexing mechanisms available on various operating systems and maintaining a separation of concerns between framework classes and application classes. By separating application-independent event demultiplexing and dispatching *mechanisms* from application-dependent event processing *policies*, the ACE Reactor framework provides the following benefits:

- **Broad portability.** The framework can be configured to use many OS event demultiplexing mechanisms, such as select() (available on UNIX, Windows, and many real-time operating systems), /dev/poll (available on certain UNIX platforms), and WaitForMultipleObjects() (available only on Windows).

- **Automates event detection, demultiplexing, and dispatching.** By eliminating reliance on nonportable native OS event demultiplexing APIs, the ACE Reactor framework provides applications with a uniform object-oriented event detection, demulti-

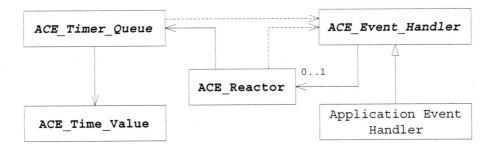

Figure 3.1: The ACE Reactor Framework Classes

plexing, and dispatching mechanism. Event handler objects can be registered with the ACE_Reactor to process various types of events.

- **Transparent extensibility.** The framework employs hook methods via inheritance and dynamic binding to decouple *lower-level event mechanisms*, such as detecting events on multiple I/O handles, expiring timers, and demultiplexing and dispatching methods of the appropriate event handler to process these events, from *higher-level application event processing policies*, such as connection establishment strategies, data marshaling and demarshaling, and processing of client requests. This design allows the ACE Reactor framework to be extended transparently without modifying existing application code.

- **Increase reuse and minimize errors.** Developers who write programs using native OS event demultiplexing operations must reimplement, debug, and optimize the same low-level code for each application. In contrast, the ACE Reactor framework's event detection, demultiplexing, and dispatching mechanisms are generic and can therefore be reused by many networked applications. This separation of concerns allows developers to focus on high-level application-defined event handler policies, rather than wrestling repeatedly with low-level mechanisms.

- **Efficient event demultiplexing.** The ACE Reactor framework performs its event demultiplexing and dispatching logic efficiently. For instance, the ACE_Select_ Reactor presented in Section 4.2 uses the ACE_Handle_Set_Iterator wrapper facade class described in Chapter 7 of C++NPv1. This wrapper facade uses an optimized implementation of the Iterator pattern [GoF] to avoid examining fd_set bitmasks one bit at a time. This optimization is based on a sophisticated algorithm that uses the C++ exclusive-or operator to reduce run-time complexity from *O(number of total bits)* to *O(number of enabled bits)*, which can improve the run-time performance of large-scale applications substantially.

The remainder of this chapter motivates and describes the capabilities of each class in the ACE Reactor framework. We illustrate how this framework can be used to enhance the design of our networked logging server. If you aren't familiar with the Reactor pattern from POSA2, we recommend that you read about it first before delving into the detailed examples in this chapter. Chapter 4 then describes the design and use of the most common implementations of the `ACE_Reactor` interface presented here. That chapter also describes the various concurrency models supported by these `ACE_Reactor` implementations.

3.2   The ACE_Time_Value Class

Motivation

Different operating systems provide different functions and data to access and manipulate the time and date. For example, UNIX platforms define the `timeval` structure as follows:

```
struct timeval {
  long secs;
  long usecs;
};
```

Different date and time representations are used on other OS platforms, such as POSIX, Windows, and proprietary real-time operating systems. Time values are used in a number of situations, including timeout specifiers. As described in Sidebar 6 (page 45), ACE specifies timeouts in absolute time for some situations, such as the concurrency and synchronization wrapper facades in C++NPv1, and in relative time for other situations, such as the `ACE_Reactor` I/O timeouts and timer settings. The wide range of uses and different representations across platforms makes addressing these portability differences in each application unnecessarily tedious and costly, which is why the ACE Reactor framework provides the `ACE_Time_Value` class.

Class Capabilities

`ACE_Time_Value` applies the Wrapper Facade pattern [POSA2] and C++ operator overloading to simplify the use of portable time and duration related operations. This class provides the following capabilities:

- It provides a standardized representation of time that's portable across OS platforms.
- It can convert between different platform time representations, such as `timespec_t` and `timeval` on UNIX, and FILETIME and `timeval` on Windows.
- It uses operator overloading to simplify time-based comparisons by permitting standard C++ syntax for time-based arithmetic and relational expressions.

- Its constructors and methods normalize time quantities by converting the fields in a `timeval` structure into a canonical format that ensures accurate comparisons between `ACE_Time_Value` instances.
- It can represent either a duration, such as 5 seconds and 310,000 microseconds, or an absolute date and time, such as 2001-09-11-08.46.00. Note that some methods, such as `operator*=()`, are meaningless with absolute times.

The interface for `ACE_Time_Value` is shown in Figure 3.2 (page 44). As you read this book, keep in mind the points noted in Sidebar 7 (page 46) regarding UML diagrams and C++ code. The key methods of `ACE_Time_Value` are outlined in the following table:

Method	Description
`ACE_Time_Value()` `set()`	Overloaded constructors and methods that convert from various time formats, such as `timeval`, `FILETIME`, `timespec_t`, or `long`, to a normalized `ACE_Time_Value`.
`sec()`	An accessor that returns the seconds portion of an `ACE_Time_Value`.
`usec()`	An accessor that returns the microseconds portion of an `ACE_Time_Value`.
`msec()`	Converts the `sec()`/`usec()` `ACE_Time_Value` format into millisecond format.
`operator+=()` `operator-=()` `operator*=()`	Arithmetic methods that add, subtract, and multiply an `ACE_Time_Value`.

In addition to the methods shown above, the following binary operators are friends of the `ACE_Time_Value` class that define arithmetic and relational operations:

Method	Description
`operator+()` `operator-()`	Arithmetic methods that add and subtract two `ACE_Time_Values`.
`operator==()` `operator!=()`	Methods that compare two `ACE_Time_Values` for equality and inequality.
`operator<()` `operator>()` `operator<=()` `operator>=()`	Methods that determine relationships between two `ACE_Time_Values`.

All `ACE_Time_Value` constructors and methods normalize the time values they operate on. Normalization reduces microsecond quantities equivalent to one second or more by transferring the seconds value to the `secs` member, leaving the remaining microseconds value in `usecs`. For example, normalizing the quantity `ACE_Time_Value(1, 1000000)` will compare equal to the normalized `ACE_Time_Value(2)` quantity. In contrast, a bitwise comparison of non-normalized objects won't detect their equivalence.

```
                              ACE_Time_Value
+ zero : ACE_Time_Value
+ max_time : ACE_Time_Value
- tv_ : timeval
+ ACE_Time_Value (sec : long, usec : long = 0)
+ ACE_Time_Value (t : const struct timeval &)
+ ACE_Time_Value (t : const timespec_t  &)
+ ACE_Time_Value (t : const FILETIME &)
+ set (sec : long, usec : long)
+ set (t : const struct timeval &)
+ set (t : const timespec_t  &)
+ set (t : const FILETIME &)
+ sec () : long
+ usec () : long
+ msec () : long
+ operator+= (tv : const ACE_Time_Value &) : ACE_Time_Value &
+ operator-= (tv : const ACE_Time_Value &) : ACE_Time_Value &
+ operator*= (d : double) : ACE_Time_Value &
```

Figure 3.2: The ACE_Time_Value Class

Sidebar 6 describes the differences in the interpretation of ACE_Time_Value when used to represent timeout values for various classes in ACE.

Example

The following example creates two ACE_Time_Value objects whose values can be set via command-line arguments. It then performs range checking to ensure the values are reasonable.

```
 1 #include "ace/OS.h"
 2
 3 const ACE_Time_Value max_interval (60 * 60); // 1 hour.
 4
 5 int main (int argc, char *argv[]) {
 6   ACE_Time_Value expiration = ACE_OS::gettimeofday ();
 7   ACE_Time_Value interval;
 8
 9   ACE_Get_Opt opt (argc, argv, "e:i:"));
10   for (int c; (c = opt ()) != -1;)
11     switch (c) {
12     case 'e': expiration += ACE_Time_Value (atoi (opt.opt_arg ()));
13               break;
14     case 'i': interval = ACE_Time_Value (atoi (opt.opt_arg ()));
15               break;
16     }
```

Sidebar 6: Absolute versus Relative ACE_Time_Value Timeouts

Some ACE classes use relative timeouts, whereas others use absolute timeouts:

- **Relative time semantics**
  - ACE IPC wrapper facade I/O methods (Chapter 3 in C++NPv1), as well as higher level framework classes that use them, such as those in the ACE Acceptor-Connector framework (Chapter 7)
  - ACE_Reactor and ACE_Proactor event loop and timer scheduling methods (Chapters 3 and 8)
  - ACE_Process and ACE_Process_Manager wait() methods (Chapter 8 in C++NPv1) and
  - Time slice quantum for ACE_Sched_Params (Chapter 9 in C++NPv1).

- **Absolute time semantics**
  - ACE synchronizer wrapper facades, such as ACE_Condition_Thread_Mutex and ACE_Thread_Semaphore (Chapter 10 in C++NPv1)
  - ACE timer queue scheduling methods (Chapter 3)
  - ACE_Task methods (Chapter 6) and
  - ACE_Message_Queue methods (Chapter 6), as well as classes based on or that use ACE_Message_Queue, such as those in the ACE Streams framework (Chapter 9) ACE_Activation_Queue, ACE_Future, and ACE_Future_Set [HJS] and
  - The ACE_Thread_Manager::wait() method (Chapter 9 in C++NPv1).

Relative timeouts are often used where the operation (such as an ACE_Process_Manager::wait() operation) may delay before being able to proceed, but will be called only once. Conversely, absolute timeouts are often used where the operation (such as an ACE_Condition_Thread_Mutex::wait() operation) may be called multiple times via a loop. Use of absolute time avoids the need to recompute the timeout value for each loop iteration [KSS96].

```
17    if (interval > max_interval)
18      cout << "interval must be less than "
19           << max_interval.sec () << endl;
20    else if (expiration > (ACE_Time_Value::max_time - interval))
21      cout << "expiration + interval must be less than "
22           << ACE_Time_Value::max_time.sec () << endl;
23    return 0;
24  }
```

Lines 3–7   Initialize the ACE_Time_Value objects. By default, an ACE_Time_Value object is initialized to zero.

Lines 9–16   Parse the command-line arguments using the ACE_Get_Opt class described in Sidebar 8 (page 47).

Lines 17–22   Perform range checking to ensure the values are reasonable.

Sidebar 7: Displaying ACE Classes and C++ Code

We generally provide a UML diagram and a table that describe the key methods for each ACE C++ class used in this book. Complete class interfaces are available online at `http://ace.ece.uci.edu` and `http://www.riverace.com/docs/`. We recommend you keep a copy of the ACE source code handy for quick reference. Complete class implementations and networked logging service examples are available in the ACE source distribution's `$ACE_ROOT/ace` and `$ACE_ROOT/examples/C++NPv2` directories, respectively.

To save space in the book, our UML class diagrams focus on attributes and operations that are used in our code examples. Class diagrams don't show an attributes section when no attributes are directly pertinent to our discussions. We use *italics* to denote an abstract class or method as follows:

- A method name set in italics indicates a C++ virtual method that you can reimplement in a derived class.

- A class name set in italics indicates that you probably need to reimplement one or more of the class's virtual methods to use the class effectively.

If you need a UML overview, we recommend *UML Distilled* [wKS00].

To further save space, we use some programming shortcuts that aren't used in ACE, such as omitting much of the error-handling code in our C++ examples. Naturally, ACE always checks for error conditions and takes the appropriate action, just as your application software should. Some of our C++ examples also implement methods within the class definition, which we don't do in ACE itself since it clutters class interfaces and slows down compilation. To learn more about ACE's programming guidelines, please see `$ACE_ROOT/docs/ACE-guidelines.html`.

3.3   The ACE_Event_Handler Class

Motivation

Networked applications are often based on a *reactive* model, in which they respond to various types of events, such as I/O activity, expired timers, or signals. Application-independent mechanisms that detect events and dispatch them to event-handling code should be reused across applications, while application-defined code that responds to the events should reside in the event handlers. To reduce coupling and increase reuse, a framework separates the reuseable mechanisms and provides the means to incorporate application-defined event handlers. This separation of concerns is the basis of the ACE Reactor framework's inversion of control. Its event detection and dispatching mechanisms control execution flow and invoke event-handling callback hook methods when there's application processing to perform.

Sidebar 8: The ACE_Get_Opt Class

`ACE_Get_Opt` is an iterator for parsing options from command-line arguments. Options passed in an `optstring` are preceded by '-' for short options or '--' for long options. `ACE_Get_Opt` can be used to parse argc/argv arguments, such as those passed as a program's `main()` command line or to an `init()` hook method. This class provides the following capabilities:

- A thin C++ wrapper facade for the standard POSIX `getopt()` function. Unlike `getopt()`, however, each instance of `ACE_Get_Opt` maintains its own state, so it can be used reentrantly. `ACE_Get_Opt` is also easier to use than `getopt()` since the `optstring` and argc/argv arguments are only passed once to its constructor, rather than to each iterator call.
- It can be told to start processing the command line at an arbitrary point specified by the `skip_args` parameter, which allows it to skip the program name when parsing a command line passed to `main()` or continue processing where it left off at a later time.
- It can regroup all the option arguments at the beginning of the command line, while maintaining their relative order, which simplifies option and nonoption argument processing. After all the options are scanned, it returns EOF and `opt_ind()` points to the first nonoption argument, so the program can continue processing the remaining arguments.
- Multiple argument ordering modes: PERMUTE_ARGS, REQUIRE_ORDER, and RETURN_IN_ORDER.
- A colon following a short option character in the `optstring` signifies that the option takes an argument. The argument is taken from the remaining characters of the current `argv`-element or the next `argv`-element as needed. If an `argv`-element of '--' is encountered, this signifies the end of the option section and EOF is returned.
- Short options that don't take arguments can be grouped together on the command line after the leading '-', but in that case, only the last short option in the group can take an argument. A '?' is returned if the short option is not recognized.
- Long option formats are similar to the GNU `getopt_long()` function. Long options can be defined with corresponding short options. When `ACE_Get_Opt` finds a long option with a corresponding short option, it returns the short option making it much easier for the caller to handle it in a `switch` statement. Many examples in the book illustrate the use of both long and short options.
- Since short options are defined as integers, long options that wouldn't normally have a meaningful short option equivalent can designate nonalphanumeric values for the corresponding short option. These nonalphanumeric cannot appear in the argument list or in the `optstring` parameter, but can be returned and processed efficiently in a `switch` statement.

```
┌────────────────────────────────────────────────────────────────────┐
│                      ACE_Event_Handler                               │
├────────────────────────────────────────────────────────────────────┤
│ - priority_ : int                                                    │
│ - reactor_  : ACE_Reactor *                                          │
├────────────────────────────────────────────────────────────────────┤
│ # ACE_Event_Handler (r : ACE_Reactor * = 0,                          │
│                         prio : int = LO_PRIORITY)                     │
│ + ~ACE_Event_Handler ()                                              │
│ + handle_input (h : ACE_HANDLE = ACE_INVALID_HANDLE) : int           │
│ + handle_output (h : ACE_HANDLE = ACE_INVALID_HANDLE) : int          │
│ + handle_exception (h : ACE_HANDLE = ACE_INVALID_HANDLE) : int       │
│ + handle_timeout (now : ACE_Time_Value &, act : void * = 0) : int    │
│ + handle_signal (signum : int, info : siginfo_t * = 0,               │
│                    ctx : ucontext_t * = 0) : int                     │
│ + handle_close (h : ACE_HANDLE, mask : ACE_Reactor_Mask) : int       │
│ + get_handle () : ACE_HANDLE                                         │
│ + reactor () : ACE_Reactor *                                         │
│ + reactor (r : ACE_Reactor *)                                        │
│ + priority () : int                                                  │
│ + priority (prio : int)                                              │
└────────────────────────────────────────────────────────────────────┘
```

Figure 3.3: The ACE_Event_Handler Class

To maintain this separation of concerns, there must be a way to invoke callbacks. One way to implement callbacks is to define a separate function for each type of event. This approach can become unwieldy for application developers, however, since they must:

1. Keep track of which functions correspond to which events
2. Design a way to associate data with callback functions
3. Use a procedural model of programming since there's no object interface involved

To resolve these problems and support an object-oriented callback model, the ACE Reactor framework defines the ACE_Event_Handler base class.

Class Capabilities

ACE_Event_Handler is the base class of all reactive event handlers in ACE. This class provides the following capabilities:

- It defines hook methods for input events, output events, exception events, timer events, and signal events.[1]

---

[1]On Windows, an ACE_Event_Handler can also handle synchronization events, such as transitioning from the nonsignaled to signaled state with Windows event objects, mutexes, or semaphores [SR00], which we discuss in Section 4.4.

- Its hook methods allow applications to extend event handler subclasses in many ways without changing the framework.
- Its use of object-oriented callbacks simplifies the association of data with hook methods that manipulate the data.
- Its use of objects also automates the binding of an event source (or set of sources) with data the event source is associated with, such as a network session.
- It centralizes how event handlers can be destroyed when they're not needed.
- It holds a pointer to the ACE_Reactor that manages it, making it simple for an event handler to manage its event (de)registration correctly.

The interface for ACE_Event_Handler is shown in Figure 3.3 and its key methods are outlined in the following table:

Method	Description
ACE_Event_Handler()	Assigns the ACE_Reactor pointer that can be associated with an event handler.
~ACE_Event_Handler()	Calls purge_pending_notifications() (page 77) to remove itself from the reactor's notification mechanism.
handle_input()	Hook method called when input events occur, for example, connection or data events.
handle_output()	Hook method called when output events are possible, for example, when flow control abates or a nonblocking connection completes.
handle_exception()	Hook method called when an exceptional event occurs, for example, the arrival of TCP urgent data.
handle_timeout()	Hook method called when a timer expires.
handle_signal()	Hook method called when signaled by the OS, either via POSIX signals or when a Windows synchronization object transitions to the signaled state.
handle_close()	Hook method that performs user-defined termination activities when one of the other handle_*() hook methods returns −1 or when ACE_Reactor::remove_handler() is called explicitly to unregister an event handler (page 73).
get_handle()	Returns the underlying I/O handle. This method can be left as a no-op if an event handler only handles time-driven events.
reactor()	Accessors to get/set the ACE_Reactor pointer that can be associated with an ACE_Event_Handler.
priority()	Accessors to get/set the priority of the event handler, as used by the ACE_Priority_Reactor (mentioned in Chapter 4).

Applications can inherit from ACE_Event_Handler to create *event handlers* that have the following properties:

- They override one or more of the ACE_Event_Handler class's handle_*() hook methods to perform application-defined processing in response to the corresponding types of events.

- They are registered or scheduled with an `ACE_Reactor`, which then dispatches hook methods on the handlers to process events that occur.
- Since event handlers are objects, not functions, it's straightforward to associate data with a handler's hook methods to hold state across multiple reactor callbacks.

Below, we discuss three aspects of programming `ACE_Event_Handler` hook methods.

1. Types of events and event handler hook methods. When an application registers an event handler with a reactor, it must indicate what type(s) of event(s) the event handler should process. ACE designates these event types via the following enumerators defined in `ACE_Event_Handler`:

Event Type	Description
READ_MASK	Indicates input events, such as data on a socket or file handle. A reactor dispatches the `handle_input()` hook method to process input events.
WRITE_MASK	Indicates output events, such as when flow control abates. A reactor dispatches the `handle_output()` hook method to process output events.
EXCEPT_MASK	Indicates exceptional events, such as urgent data on a socket. A reactor dispatches the `handle_exception()` hook method to process exceptional events.
ACCEPT_MASK	Indicates passive-mode connection events. A reactor dispatches the `handle_input()` hook method to process connection events.
CONNECT_MASK	Indicates a nonblocking connection completion. A reactor dispatches the `handle_output()` hook method to process nonblocking connection completion events.

These values can be combined ("or'd" together) to efficiently designate a set of events. This set of events can populate the `ACE_Reactor_Mask` parameter that's passed to the `ACE_Reactor::register_handler()` methods (page 73).

Event handlers used for I/O events can provide a handle, such as a socket handle, via their `get_handle()` hook method. When an application registers an event handler with a reactor, the reactor calls back to the handler's `get_handle()` method to retrieve its handle. This handle is then included in the handle set a reactor uses to detect I/O events.

2. Event handler hook method return values. When registered events occur, the reactor dispatches the appropriate event handler's `handle_*()` hook methods to process them. Sidebar 9 describes some idioms to apply when implementing these hook methods. When a `handle_*()` method finishes its processing, it must return a value that's interpreted by the reactor as follows:

- **Return value 0** indicates that the reactor should continue to detect and dispatch the registered event for this event handler (and handle if it's an I/O event). This behavior is common for event handlers that process multiple instances of an event, for example, reading data from a socket as it becomes available.

Sidebar 9: Idioms for Designing ACE Event Handlers

The following are some idioms for designing event handlers for use with the ACE Reactor framework:

- To prevent starvation, keep the execution time of an event handler's `handle_*()` hook methods short, ideally shorter than the average interval between event occurrences. If a hook method may run for a long time processing a request, consider queueing the request in an `ACE_Message_Queue` and processing it later. The *Example* portion of Section 6.3 illustrates this approach by combining the ACE Task framework with the ACE Reactor framework to implement a concurrent logging server based on the Half-Sync/Half-Async pattern.
- Consolidate an event handler's cleanup activities in its `handle_close()` hook method, rather than dispersing them throughout its other methods. This idiom is particularly important when dealing with dynamically allocated event handlers that are deallocated via `delete this`, because it's easier to check whether there are potential problems with deleting nondynamically allocated memory.
- Only call `delete this` in an event handler's `handle_close()` method, and only after the handler's *final* registered event has been removed from the reactor. This idiom avoids dangling pointers that can otherwise occur if an event handler that registered with a reactor for multiple events is deleted prematurely. Sidebar 10 (page 53) illustrates one way to keep track of this information.

- **Return value greater than 0** also indicates that the reactor should continue to detect and dispatch the registered event for this event handler. Additionally, if a value > 0 is returned after processing an I/O event, the reactor will dispatch this event handler on the handle again *before* the reactor blocks on its event demultiplexer. This feature enhances overall system fairness for cooperative I/O event handlers by allowing one event handler to perform a limited amount of computation, then relinquish control to allow other event handlers to be dispatched before it regains control again.

- **Return value -1** instructs the reactor to stop detecting the registered event for this event handler (and handle if it's an I/O event). Before the reactor removes this event handler/handle from its internal tables, it invokes the handler's `handle_close()` hook method, passing it the `ACE_Reactor_Mask` value of the event that's now unregistered. This event handler may remain registered for other events on the same, or a different, handle; it's the handler's responsibility to track which event(s) it's still registered for, as shown in Sidebar 10 (page 53).

3. Cleaning up an event handler.   An event handler's `handle_close()` method is called when one of its other hook methods decides that cleanup is required. The `handle_close()` method can then perform user-defined shutdown activities, such as releasing memory allocated by the object, closing IPC objects or log files, etc. The ACE Reactor framework ignores the return value of the `handle_close()` method itself.

ACE_Reactor only calls `handle_close()` when a hook method returns a negative value, as described above, or when a handler is removed from the reactor explicitly (page 74). It will *not* call `handle_close()` automatically when an IPC mechanism reaches end-of-file or an I/O handle is closed by either the local application or a remote peer. Applications must therefore detect when an I/O handle has closed and take steps to ensure an ACE_Reactor calls `handle_close()`. For example, when a `recv()` or `read()` call returns 0, the event handler should return −1 from the `handle_*()` method or call the ACE_Reactor::remove_handler() method (page 74).

In addition to the event types shown in the table on page 50, a reactor can pass the following enumerators defined in ACE_Event_Handler to `handle_close()`:

Event Type	Description
TIMER_MASK	Indicates time-driven events and is passed by a reactor when a `handle_timeout()` hook method returns −1.
SIGNAL_MASK	Indicates signal-based events (or handle-based events on Windows) and is passed by a reactor when a `handle_signal()` hook method returns −1. ACE's signal-handling facilities are described in [HJS].

Example

We implement our logging server by inheriting from ACE_Event_Handler and driving its processing via the ACE_Reactor's event loop. We handle two types of events:

1. **Data events,** which indicate the arrival of log records from connected client logging daemons
2. **Accept events,** which indicate the arrival of new connections from client logging daemons

We therefore define two types of event handlers in our logging server:

1. Logging_Event_Handler—This class processes log records received from a connected client logging daemon. It uses the ACE_SOCK_Stream class from Chapter 3 in C++NPv1 to read log records from a connection.
2. Logging_Acceptor—This class is a factory that allocates a Logging_Event_Handler dynamically and initializes it when a client logging daemon connects. It uses the ACE_SOCK_Acceptor class from Chapter 3 of C++NPv1 to initialize the ACE_SOCK_Stream contained in Logging_Event_Handler.

Both event handlers inherit from ACE_Event_Handler, which enables a reactor to dispatch their `handle_input()` methods. The relationship between ACE_Reactor,

Sidebar 10: Tracking Dynamic Event Handler Event Registrations

Applications are responsible for determining when a dynamically allocated event handler can be deleted. For example, the following class shows an idiom in which an event handler keeps track of when all events it's registered for have been removed from its associated reactor.

```
class My_Event_Handler : public ACE_Event_Handler {
private:
  // Keep track of the events the handler's registered for.
  ACE_Reactor_Mask mask_;
public:
  // ... class methods shown below ...
```

The class constructor initializes the `mask_` data member for READ and WRITE events and then registers `this` object with its reactor parameter to handle both types of events, as follows:

```
My_Event_Handler (ACE_Reactor *r): ACE_Event_Handler (r) {
  ACE_SET_BITS (mask_,
                ACE_Event_Handler::READ_MASK
                | ACE_Event_Handler::WRITE_MASK);
  reactor ()->register_handler (this, mask_);
}
```

The `handle_input()` and `handle_output()` methods must return −1 when they're finished processing READ and WRITE events, respectively. Each time a `handle_*()` method returns −1 the reactor dispatches the `handle_close()` hook method, passing it the `ACE_Reactor_Mask` value of the event that's being unregistered. This hook method clears the corresponding bit from `mask_`, as follows:

```
virtual int handle_close (ACE_HANDLE, ACE_Reactor_Mask mask) {
  if (mask == ACE_Event_Handler::READ_MASK) {
    ACE_CLR_BITS (mask_, ACE_Event_Handler::READ_MASK);
    // Perform READ_MASK cleanup logic...
  }
  if (mask == ACE_Event_Handler::WRITE_MASK) {
    ACE_CLR_BITS (mask_, ACE_Event_Handler::WRITE_MASK);
    // Perform WRITE_MASK cleanup logic.
  }
  if (mask_ == 0) delete this;
  return 0;
}
```

Only when `mask_` is zero does `handle_close()` call `delete this`.

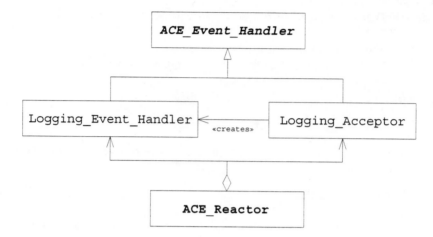

Figure 3.4: ACE_Reactor-based Logging Server Classes

ACE_Event_Handler, Logging_Acceptor, and Logging_Event_Handler is shown in Figure 3.4.

We start by creating the Logging_Acceptor.h file that includes the necessary headers:

```
#include "ace/Event_Handler.h"
#include "ace/INET_Addr.h"
#include "ace/Log_Record.h"
#include "ace/Reactor.h"
#include "ace/SOCK_Acceptor.h"
#include "ace/SOCK_Stream.h"
#include "Logging_Handler.h"
```

All but one of these headers are defined in ACE. The exception is Logging_Handler.h, which contains the Logging_Handler class defined in Chapter 4 of C++NPv1.

The Logging_Acceptor class inherits from ACE_Event_Handler and defines a private instance of the ACE_SOCK_Acceptor factory, as shown below:

```
class Logging_Acceptor : public ACE_Event_Handler {
private:
  // Factory that connects <ACE_SOCK_Stream>s passively.
  ACE_SOCK_Acceptor acceptor_;

protected:
  virtual ~Logging_Acceptor () {} // No-op destructor.
```

We declare the no-op destructor in the protected access control section to ensure dynamic allocation of Logging_Acceptor. Sidebar 11 explains why event handlers should generally be allocated dynamically.

Sidebar 11: Strategies for Managing Event Handler Memory

Event handlers should generally be allocated dynamically for the following reasons:

- **Simplify memory management.** For example, deallocation can be localized in an event handler's `handle_close()` method, using the event handler event registration tracking idiom shown in Sidebar 10 (page 53).

- **Avoid "dangling handler" problems.** For example, the lifecycle of an event handler instantiated on the stack or as a member of another class is controlled externally while its reactor registrations are controlled internally. If the handler is destroyed while it's still registered with a reactor, there will be unpredictable problems later if the reactor tries to dispatch the nonexistent handler.

- **Avoid portability problems.** For example, dynamic allocation alleviates subtle problems stemming from the delayed event handler cleanup semantics of the `ACE_WFMO_Reactor` (page 107).

Certain types of applications, such as real-time systems, avoid or minimize the use of dynamic memory to improve their predictability. If you must allocate event handlers statically for such applications, here are some conventions to follow:

1. Don't call `delete this` in `handle_close()`.

2. Unregister all events from reactors in the class destructor, at the latest.

3. Ensure that the lifetime of a registered event handler is longer than the reactor it's registered with if it can't be unregistered for some reason.

4. Avoid the use of the `ACE_WFMO_Reactor` since it defers the removal of event handlers, thereby making it hard to enforce convention 3.

5. If using `ACE_WFMO_Reactor`, pass the `DONT_CALL` flag to `ACE_Reactor::remove_handler()` and carefully manage shutdown activities without the benefit of the reactor's `handle_close()` callback.

We next show the interface and portions of the `Logging_Acceptor` method implementations. Although we don't show much error handling code in this example, a production implementation (such as the logging server in the ACE network service components library) should take appropriate corrective action if failures occur.

```
public:
  // Simple constructor.
  Logging_Acceptor (ACE_Reactor *r = ACE_Reactor::instance ())
    : ACE_Event_Handler (r) {}

  // Initialization method.
  virtual int open (const ACE_INET_Addr &local_addr);
```

```
// Called by a reactor when there's a new connection to accept.
virtual int handle_input (ACE_HANDLE = ACE_INVALID_HANDLE);

// Called when this object is destroyed, e.g., when it's
// removed from a reactor.
virtual int handle_close (ACE_HANDLE = ACE_INVALID_HANDLE,
                          ACE_Reactor_Mask = 0);

// Return the passive-mode socket's I/O handle.
virtual ACE_HANDLE get_handle () const
  { return acceptor_.get_handle (); }

// Returns a reference to the underlying <acceptor_>.
ACE_SOCK_Acceptor &acceptor () { return acceptor_; }
};
```

The `Logging_Acceptor::open()` method initializes a passive-mode acceptor socket to listen for connections at `local_addr`. The `Logging_Acceptor` then registers itself with the reactor to handle ACCEPT events.

```
int Logging_Acceptor::open (const ACE_INET_Addr &local_addr) {
  if (acceptor_.open (local_addr) == -1) return -1;
  return reactor ()->register_handler
          (this, ACE_Event_Handler::ACCEPT_MASK);
}
```

Since the passive-mode socket in the `ACE_SOCK_Acceptor` becomes active when a new connection can be accepted, the reactor dispatches the `Logging_Acceptor::handle_input()` method automatically. We'll show this method's implementation on page 58 after first defining the following `Logging_Event_Handler` class:

```
class Logging_Event_Handler : public ACE_Event_Handler
{
protected:
  // File where log records are written.
  ACE_FILE_IO log_file_;

  // Connection to remote peer.
  Logging_Handler logging_handler_;
```

This class inherits from `ACE_Event_Handler` and adapts the `Logging_Handler` defined in Chapter 4 of C++NPv1 for use with the ACE Reactor framework. In addition to a `Logging_Handler`, each `Logging_Event_Handler` contains an `ACE_FILE_IO` object to keep a separate log file for each connected client.

The public methods in the `Logging_Event_Handler` class are shown below.

```
public:
  // Initialize the base class and logging handler.
  Logging_Event_Handler (ACE_Reactor *reactor)
    : ACE_Event_Handler (reactor),
      logging_handler_ (log_file_) {}

  virtual ~Logging_Event_Handler () {} // No-op destructor.
  virtual int open (); // Activate the object.

  // Called by a reactor when logging events arrive.
  virtual int handle_input (ACE_HANDLE = ACE_INVALID_HANDLE);

  // Called when this object is destroyed, e.g., when it's
  // removed from a reactor.
  virtual int handle_close (ACE_HANDLE = ACE_INVALID_HANDLE,
                            ACE_Reactor_Mask = 0);

  // Return socket handle of the contained <Logging_Handler>.
  virtual ACE_HANDLE get_handle () const;

  // Get a reference to the contained <ACE_SOCK_Stream>.
  ACE_SOCK_Stream &peer () { return logging_handler_.peer (); }

  // Return a reference to the <log_file_>.
  ACE_FILE_IO &log_file () const { return log_file_; }
};
```

The `Logging_Event_Handler::get_handle()` method is defined as follows:

```
ACE_HANDLE Logging_Event_Handler::get_handle (void) const {
  Logging_Handler &h =
      ACE_const_cast (Logging_Handler &, logging_handler_);
  return h.peer ().get_handle ();
}
```

Since `get_handle()` is a const method, we use the `ACE_const_cast` macro to call the nonconst `Logging_Handler::peer()` method. This is safe since we call the const `get_handle()` method using it. Sidebar 17 (page 176) of C++NPv1 explains the various macros ACE provides to support portable casting on all C++ compilers. You don't need to use these macros if your applications use only compilers that support the standard C++ cast operators.

Now that we've outlined Logging_Event_Handler, we'll implement Logging_Acceptor::handle_input(), which is dispatched by a reactor whenever a new connection can be accepted. This factory method creates, connects, and activates a Logging_Event_Handler, as shown below:

```
 1 int Logging_Acceptor::handle_input (ACE_HANDLE) {
 2    Logging_Event_Handler *peer_handler = 0;
 3    ACE_NEW_RETURN (peer_handler,
 4                         Logging_Event_Handler (reactor ()), -1);
 5    if (acceptor_.accept (peer_handler->peer ()) == -1) {
 6      delete peer_handler;
 7      return -1;
 8    } else if (peer_handler->open () == -1) {
 9      peer_handler->handle_close ();
10      return -1;
11    }
12    return 0;
13 }
```

Lines 2–4   Create a new Logging_Event_Handler that will process the new client's logging session. Sidebar 12 (page 60) describes the ACE_NEW_RETURN macro and other ACE memory management macros. The new Logging_Event_Handler receives this object's ACE_Reactor pointer, which ensures that the new handler registers with the reactor that dispatched this hook method, thereby joining the logging server's event loop.

Lines 5–7   Accept the new connection into the socket handle of the Logging_Event_Handler, deleting the peer_handler and returning −1 if an error occurs. As discussed on page 51, when −1 is returned from an event handler's handle_input() the reactor will automatically invoke the handler's handle_close() hook method, which is defined as follows for the Logging_Acceptor:

```
int Logging_Acceptor::handle_close (ACE_HANDLE,
                                          ACE_Reactor_Mask) {
  acceptor_.close ();
  delete this;
  return 0;
}
```

Since we always use our Logging_Acceptor class in circumstances that require it to delete itself, we allocate it dynamically in the various examples in the book.

Lines 8–10   Activate the connected peer_handler by calling its open() method. If this method returns −1 we close the peer_handler, which deletes itself in Logging_Event_Handler::handle_close() (page 60). The open() method is shown on the following page.

```
 1 int Logging_Event_Handler::open () {
 2   static const char LOGFILE_SUFFIX[] = ".log";
 3   char filename[MAXHOSTNAMELEN + sizeof (LOGFILE_SUFFIX)];
 4   ACE_INET_Addr logging_peer_addr;
 5
 6   logging_handler_.peer ().get_remote_addr (logging_peer_addr);
 7   logging_peer_addr.get_host_name (filename, MAXHOSTNAMELEN);
 8   ACE_OS_String::strcat (filename, LOGFILE_SUFFIX);
 9
10   ACE_FILE_Connector connector;
11   connector.connect (log_file_,
12                      ACE_FILE_Addr (filename),
13                      0, // No timeout.
14                      ACE_Addr::sap_any, // Ignored.
15                      0, // Don't try to reuse the addr.
16                      O_RDWR|O_CREAT|O_APPEND,
17                      ACE_DEFAULT_FILE_PERMS);
18
19   return reactor ()->register_handler
20           (this, ACE_Event_Handler::READ_MASK);
21 }
```

Lines 3–8   Determine the connected client's hostname and use this as the logfile's name.

Lines 10–17   Create or open the file that stores log records from a connected client.

Lines 19–20   Use the ACE_Reactor::register_handler() method (page 73) to register this event handler for READ events with the Logging_Acceptor's reactor.

When log records arrive from clients, the reactor will automatically dispatch the following Logging_Event_Handler::handle_input() method:

```
int Logging_Event_Handler::handle_input (ACE_HANDLE)
{ return logging_handler_.log_record (); }
```

This method processes a log record by calling Logging_Handler::log_record(), which reads the record from the socket and writes it to the log file associated with the client connection. Since logging_handler_ maintains its own socket handle, the handle_input() method simply ignores its ACE_HANDLE parameter.

Whenever an error occurs or a client closes a connection to the logging server, the log_record() method returns −1, which the handle_input() method then passes back to the reactor that dispatched it (Sidebar 13 on page 61 discusses strategies for handling peers that simply stop communicating). This value causes the reactor to dispatch the Logging_Event_Handler::handle_close() hook method, which closes both the socket to the client and the log file and then deletes itself, as follows:

Sidebar 12: The ACE Memory Management Macros

C++NPv1 and this book solve many problems related to differences between OS APIs. Another problem area is differences between C++ compilers. The C++ `operator new()` dynamic memory allocator is a good example. Early C++ runtimes returned a NULL pointer when an allocation failed, whereas newer runtimes throw an exception. ACE defines macros that unify the behavior and return a NULL pointer regardless of the compiler's behavior. ACE uses these macros to ensure consistent, portable behavior; your applications can use them as well.

If memory allocation fails, all of the ACE memory management macros set the specified pointer to NULL and set `errno` to ENOMEM. The ACE_NEW_RETURN macro returns a specified value from the current method on failure, whereas the ACE_NEW macro simply returns and the ACE_NEW_NORETURN macro continues to execute in the current method. These macros enable applications to work portably, regardless of the C++ compiler memory allocation error handling policies. For example, the ACE_NEW_RETURN macro is defined as follows for compilers that throw the `std::bad_alloc` C++ exception when `new` fails:

```
#define ACE_NEW_RETURN(POINTER,CTOR,RET_VAL) \
  do { try { POINTER = new CTOR; } catch (std::bad_alloc) \
    { errno = ENOMEM; POINTER = 0; return RET_VAL; } \
  } while (0)
```

In contrast, ACE_NEW_RETURN is defined as follows for compiler configurations that offer a `nothrow` variant of `operator new`:

```
#define ACE_NEW_RETURN(POINTER,CTOR,RET_VAL) \
  do { POINTER = new (ACE_nothrow) CTOR; \
    if (POINTER == 0) { errno = ENOMEM; return RET_VAL; } \
  } while (0)
```

```
int Logging_Event_Handler::handle_close (ACE_HANDLE,
                                         ACE_Reactor_Mask) {
  logging_handler_.close ();
  log_file_.close ();
  delete this;
  return 0;
}
```

This method can safely `delete this` since the `Logging_Event_Handler` object is allocated dynamically and won't be used by the reactor or any other part of the program. The *Example* in Section 3.5 illustrates this method in the context of the complete Reactor framework.

Sidebar 13: Handling Silent Peers

If a client disconnects, either gracefully or abruptly, its socket will become readable. A reactor can detect this event and dispatch the `handle_input()` hook method on the event handler that's associated with the socket handle. The handler will then determine that the connection has closed, which is usually revealed by a `recv()` or `read()` call returning 0 or −1. If the client simply stops communicating altogether, however, there could be a number of causes, including

- An Ethernet cable's being pulled out of its connector, which may be plugged back in shortly and the connection continues or
- The host crashed without the opportunity to close any connections, so the local endpoint of the connection is stranded and will never continue.

In these cases there are no events for a reactor to detect.

Depending on the needs of your application services and the application-level protocol(s) used, there are several ways to handle a silent peer. These include:

- Wait until the TCP keepalive mechanism abandons the peer and closes the connection, which will trigger an event on the socket that can be handled just as if the client closed the connection. Unfortunately, this may take a long time—maybe hours—as described in [SW95].
- Implement an application-level policy or protocol, such as a "heartbeat" message or periodic "are you there?" message. If the peer fails to send a heartbeat message or answer the "are you there?" message within an application defined period of time, abort the connection unilaterally. The application may then attempt to reopen the connection at a later time.
- Implement a policy that if the peer does not send any data for some determined amount of time, the connection will be abandoned. This type of policy is used by the `Logging_Event_Handler_Ex` class (page 68).

3.4   The ACE Timer Queue Classes

Motivation

Many networked applications perform activities periodically or must be notified when specified time periods have elapsed. For example, Web servers require watchdog timers that release resources if clients don't send an HTTP GET request shortly after they connect.

Native OS timer capabilities vary, but many platforms share the following problems:

- **Limited number of timers.** Many platforms allow applications to set a limited number of timers. For example, the POSIX `alarm()` and `ualarm()` system functions each reset a single "alarm clock" timer on each call. Managing multiple timer periods therefore often involves developing a timer queue mechanism that keeps track of the next scheduled expiration. Scheduling a new "earliest" timer can (re)set the alarm clock if necessary.

- **Timer expiration raises a signal.** For example, the alarm() system function raises the SIGALRM signal when the timer expires. Programming timer signals is hard because application actions are restricted in signal context. Applications can minimize processing in signal context on UNIX platforms by using the sleep() system function or using the sigsuspend() system function. These solutions are nonportable, however, and they block the calling thread, which can impede concurrency and complicate programming.

One way to avoid these problems is to manage timers in the normal course of event handling, as follows:

1. Develop a timer queue mechanism that orders timers and associates each timer with an action to perform when a timer expires

2. Integrate the timer queue with the application's use of a synchronous event demultiplexer, such as select() or WaitForMultipleObjects(), to integrate the handling of timer expirations with other event processing.

It's hard to develop this type of timer facility portably across OS platforms, however, due to the wide range of capabilities and restrictions. Moreover, this capability is often redeveloped for many projects due to tight coupling between the timer queue mechanism and the synchronous event demultiplexing mechanism. To alleviate the need for application developers to rewrite efficient, scalable, and portable time-driven dispatchers in an *ad hoc* manner, the ACE Reactor framework defines a family of reusable timer queue classes.

Class Capabilities

The ACE timer queue classes allow applications to register time-driven event handlers derived from ACE_Event_Handler. These classes provide the following capabilities:

- They allow applications to schedule event handlers whose handle_timeout() hook methods will be dispatched efficiently and scalably at caller-specified times in the future, either once or at periodic intervals.

- They allow applications to cancel a timer associated with a particular event handler or all timers associated with an event handler.

- They allow applications to configure a timer queue's time source, such as ACE_OS:: gettimeofday() or ACE_High_Res_Timer::gettimeofday_hr(), described in Sidebar 14 (page 65).

The interfaces and relationships of all the ACE timer queue classes are shown in Figure 3.5 (page 64). The key methods in these classes are outlined in the following table:

Method	Description
`schedule()`	Schedule an event handler whose `handle_timeout()` method will be dispatched at a caller-specified time in the future and, optionally, at periodic intervals.
`cancel()`	Cancel a timer associated with a particular event handler or all timers associated with an event handler.
`expire()`	Dispatch the `handle_timeout()` method of all event handlers whose expiration time is less than or equal to the current time of day, which is represented as an absolute value, for example, 2001-09-11-09.37.00.
`gettimeofday()`	A pair of overloaded methods that allow applications to (1) set the method used to control the timer queue's source of the current time value and (2) call that method to return the current absolute time value.

The `schedule()` method of an ACE timer queue must be passed two parameters:

- A pointer to an event handler that will be the target of the subsequent `handle_timeout()` dispatching and

- A reference to an `ACE_Time_Value` indicating the absolute future time when the `handle_timeout()` hook method should be invoked on the event handler.

This method can optionally be passed the following parameters:

- A `void` pointer that's stored internally by the timer queue and passed back unchanged when the `handle_timeout()` method is dispatched. This pointer can be used as an *asynchronous completion token* (ACT) in accordance with the Asynchronous Completion Token pattern [POSA2]. This pattern allows an application to efficiently demultiplex and process the responses of asynchronous operations it invokes on services. By using an ACT, the same event handler can be registered with a timer queue at multiple future dispatching times.

- A reference to a second `ACE_Time_Value` that designates the interval at which the event handler should be dispatched periodically. If this parameter is omitted, the event handler's `handle_timeout()` method is dispatched only once. When specifying very short timer values, keep in mind that the actual timer resolution will be limited to that of the timer queue's time source clock update frequency, which varies by platform.

When a timer queue dispatches an event handler's `handle_timeout()` method, it passes as parameters the current time and the `void` pointer ACT passed to the `schedule()` method when the event handler was scheduled originally.

    The return value of `schedule()` uniquely identifies each timer event that's scheduled with a timer queue. Applications can pass the unique timer identifier to the `cancel()` method to remove a particular timer event before it expires. Applications can also pass the

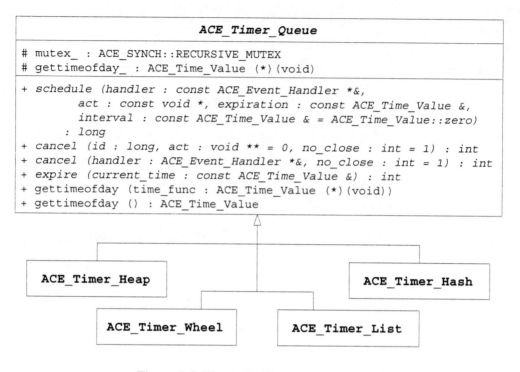

Figure 3.5: The ACE Timer Queue Classes

address of the handler to `cancel()` to remove all timers associated with a particular event handler. If a non-NULL pointer to a `void` pointer is passed to `cancel()`, it's assigned the ACT passed by the application when the timer was scheduled originally, which makes it possible to allocate an ACT dynamically without leaking memory.

The ACE timer queue classes combine design patterns, hook methods, and template arguments to provide the following timer queue implementations:

- `ACE_Timer_Heap`, which is a partially ordered, almost complete binary tree implemented in an array [Rob99]. Its average- and worst-case performance for scheduling, canceling, and expiring an event handler is $O(\lg n)$, which is why it's the default timer queue mechanism in the ACE Reactor framework. Heap-based timer queues are useful for operating systems [BL88] and middleware [SLM98] whose applications require predictable and low-latency time-driven dispatching. Sidebar 15 (page 66) describes some issues that developers of real-time applications should consider when using the ACE timer queue mechanisms in their code.

- `ACE_Timer_Wheel`, which uses a *timing wheel* [VL97] that contains a circular buffer designed to schedule, cancel, and dispatch timers in $O(1)$ time in the average case, but $O(n)$ in the worst case.

Sidebar 14: ACE Time Sources

Figure 3.5 shows that `ACE_Timer_Queue::gettimeofday()` can be changed to use any static method that returns an `ACE_Time_Value` value. The returned time value is expected to be absolute, but it need not be the current date and time (commonly known as "wall clock" time). The primary requirement of the time-returning static method is that it provides an accurate basis for timer scheduling and expiration decisions. ACE provides two mechanisms that fit this requirement:

- `ACE_OS::gettimeofday()`, which is a static method that returns an `ACE_Time_Value` containing the current absolute date and time as reported by the operating system.

- `ACE_High_Res_Timer::gettimeofday_hr()`, which is a static method that returns the value of an OS-specific high-resolution timer, converted to `ACE_Time_Value` units. These timers are often based on the number of CPU clock ticks since boot time, rather than the actual wall clock time.

The granularity of these timers can differ by three to four orders of magnitude. When they're used to time out event demultiplexing mechanisms, however, the resolution is usually similar due to the intricacies of clocks, timer interrupt servicing, and OS scheduling. In the context of the Reactor's timer queue, they differ mainly in their behavior when the system's date and/or time is changed, where the values reported by `ACE_OS::gettimeofday()` will change but the values reported by `ACE_High_Res_Timer::gettimeofday_hr()` won't be affected—they'll keep increasing at a constant rate. If an application's timer behavior must remain constant—even if the wall clock time changes—the default time source should be replaced with `ACE_High_Res_Timer::gettimeofday_hr()`, as shown in the *Example* portion of Section 3.4.

- `ACE_Timer_Hash`, which uses a hash table to manage the queue. Like the timing wheel implementation, the average-case time required to schedule, cancel, and expire timers is $O(1)$ and its worst-case is $O(n)$.

- `ACE_Timer_List`, which is implemented as a linked list of absolute timers ordered by increasing deadline. Although its average and worst-case performance for scheduling and canceling timers is $O(n)$, it uses the least amount of memory of the ACE timer queue implementations.

The ACE Reactor framework allows developers to use any of these timer queue implementations to achieve the functionality needed by their applications, without burdening them with a "one size fits all" implementation. Since the methods in the `ACE_Timer_Queue` base class are virtual, applications can also integrate their own implementations of other timer queue mechanisms.

Sidebar 15: Using Timers in Networked Real-time Applications

Networked real-time applications are becoming increasingly widespread and important [GSC02]. Common examples include telecommunication networks (e.g., wireless phone services), telemedicine (e.g., remote surgery), manufacturing process automation (e.g., hot rolling mills), and defense applications (e.g., avionics mission computing systems). These types of applications typically have one thing in common: *the right answer delivered too late becomes the wrong answer.*

If one reactor is used to dispatch both I/O and timer queue handlers, variations in the amount of time spent handling I/O can cause the timer queue processing to "drift," which can wreak havoc on the scheduling analysis and predictability of networked real-time applications. Moreover, the event demultiplexing and synchronization mechanisms used to integrate I/O and timer dispatching in implementations of the ACE Reactor framework can incur more overhead than some real-time applications can afford.

Developers of networked real-time applications may therefore want to use separate ACE timer queues running in different threads to handle timer dispatching. Depending on the relative importance of timers versus I/O, different thread priorities can be used for the different threads. The ACE_Thread_Timer_Queue_Adapter is a useful class that can simplify the design of these networked real-time applications.

Example

Although the Logging_Acceptor and Logging_Event_Handler event handlers in Section 3.3 implement the logging server functionality correctly, they may consume system resources unnecessarily. For example, clients can connect to a server and then not send log records for long periods of time. In the example below, we illustrate how to apply the ACE timer queue mechanisms to reclaim resources from those event handlers whose clients log records infrequently. Our design is based on the *Evictor* pattern [HV99], which describes how and when to release resources, such as memory and I/O handles, in order to optimize system resource management.

We use the Evictor pattern in conjunction with the ACE Reactor framework's timer queue mechanisms to check periodically when each registered event handler has received its last client log record. If the time the last log record was received exceeds a designated threshold (one hour), the following actions occur:

1. The event handler is disconnected from its client.
2. Its resources are returned to the OS.
3. It is removed from the reactor.

Clients must detect these closed connections and reestablish them when they need to send more log records, as shown in the *Example* portions of Sections 6.2 and 7.4.

This example uses `ACE_Timer_Queue::gettimeofday()` to obtain all time-of-day values. This method allows us to change the program's time source at run time as described in Sidebar 14 (page 65). For example, if changes to the system's time-of-day clock should neither delay nor hasten client evictions, the following code can be added to `main()` before any timer-related work is done:

```
ACE_Reactor *r = ACE_Reactor::instance ();
ACE_High_Res_Timer::global_scale_factor ();
r->timer_queue ()->
  gettimeofday (&ACE_High_Res_Timer::gettimeofday_hr);
```

The `ACE_High_Res_Timer::global_scale_factor()` call performs any initialization needed to obtain accurate timer values before the program starts doing real work.

To implement the Evictor pattern, we extend `Logging_Acceptor` and `Logging_Event_Handler` in Section 3.3 to create `Logging_Acceptor_Ex` and `Logging_Event_Handler_Ex`. We then register a timer for every instance of `Logging_Event_Handler_Ex`. Since the default ACE timer queue (`ACE_Timer_Heap`) is highly scalable and efficient, its scheduling, cancellation, and dispatching overhead is low, even if there are thousands of timers and instances of `Logging_Event_Handler_Ex`.

We start by creating a new header file called `Logging_Acceptor_Ex.h` that contains the new `Logging_Acceptor_Ex` class. The changes to this class are minor. We simply override and modify its `handle_input()` method to create a `Logging_Event_Handler_Ex` rather than a `Logging_Event_Handler`, as shown below:

```
#include "ace/INET_Addr.h"
#include "ace/Reactor.h"
#include "Logging_Acceptor.h"
#include "Logging_Event_Handler_Ex.h"

class Logging_Acceptor_Ex : public Logging_Acceptor {
public:
  typedef ACE_INET_Addr PEER_ADDR;

  // Simple constructor to pass <ACE_Reactor> to base class.
  Logging_Acceptor_Ex (ACE_Reactor *r = ACE_Reactor::instance ())
    : Logging_Acceptor (r) {}

  int handle_input (ACE_HANDLE) {
    Logging_Event_Handler_Ex *peer_handler = 0;
    ACE_NEW_RETURN (peer_handler,
                    Logging_Event_Handler_Ex (reactor ()), -1);
    // ... same as Logging_Acceptor::handle_input()
  }
};
```

In Chapter 7, we'll illustrate how the ACE Acceptor-Connector framework uses C++ features (such as templates, inheritance, and dynamic binding) and design patterns (such as Template Method and Strategy [GoF]) to add new behavior to an event handler without copying or modifying existing code.

The `Logging_Event_Handler_Ex` class involves more substantial additions, so we create both a `Logging_Event_Handler_Ex.h` file and a `Logging_Event_Handler_Ex.cpp` file. In `Logging_Event_Handler_Ex.h` we extend `Logging_Event_Handler` to create the following `Logging_Event_Handler_Ex` class:

```cpp
class Logging_Event_Handler_Ex : public Logging_Event_Handler {
private:
  // Time when a client last sent a log record.
  ACE_Time_Value time_of_last_log_record_;

  // Maximum time to wait for a client log record.
  const ACE_Time_Value max_client_timeout_;
```

We implement the Evictor pattern by adding an `ACE_Time_Value` that keeps track of the time when a client last sent a log record. The methods in the public interface of `Logging_Event_Handler_Ex` are shown below:

```cpp
public:
  typedef Logging_Event_Handler PARENT;

  // 3600 seconds == one hour.
  enum { MAX_CLIENT_TIMEOUT = 3600 };

  Logging_Event_Handler_Ex
      (ACE_Reactor *reactor,
       const ACE_Time_Value &max_client_timeout
         = ACE_Time_Value (MAX_CLIENT_TIMEOUT))
    : Logging_Event_Handler (reactor),
      time_of_last_log_record (0),
      max_client_timeout_ (max_client_timeout) {}

  virtual ~Logging_Event_Handler_Ex () { /* no-op */ }
  virtual int open (); // Activate the event handler.

  // Called by a reactor when logging events arrive.
  virtual int handle_input (ACE_HANDLE);

  // Called when a timeout expires to check if the client has
  // been idle for an excessive amount of time.
  virtual int handle_timeout (const ACE_Time_Value &tv,
                              const void *act);
```

```
      // Called when this object is destroyed, e.g., when it's
      // removed from a reactor.
      virtual int handle_close (ACE_HANDLE = ACE_INVALID_HANDLE,
                                ACE_Reactor_Mask = 0);
};
```

The `Logging_Event_Handler_Ex::handle_input()` method notes the time when a log record is received from the connected client. We get the time from the timer queue's time source to ensure that all comparisons are consistent. After recording the time, this method forwards to its parent's `handle_input()` method to process the log record, as shown below:

```
int Logging_Event_Handler_Ex::handle_input (ACE_HANDLE h) {
  time_of_last_log_record_ =
    reactor ()->timer_queue ()->gettimeofday ();
  return PARENT::handle_input (h);
}
```

The `open()` method is shown next:

```
 1 int Logging_Event_Handler_Ex::open () {
 2   int result = PARENT::open ();
 3   if (result != -1) {
 4     ACE_Time_Value reschedule (max_client_timeout_.sec () / 4);
 5     result = reactor ()->schedule_timer
 6                    (this, 0,
 7                     max_client_timeout_,   // Initial timeout.
 8                     reschedule);           // Subsequent timeouts.
 9   }
10   return result;
11 }
```

Line 2   Forward to the parent's `open()` method (page 59).

Lines 4–8   Call `ACE_Reactor::schedule_timer()` (page 76) to schedule this event handler to be dispatched by the reactor periodically to check whether its client sent it a log record recently. We schedule the initial timer to expire in `max_client_timeout_` seconds (which defaults to one hour) and also request that it then expire periodically every `max_client_timeout_` / 4 seconds (i.e., check every 15 minutes).

When a timer expires, the reactor uses its timer queue mechanism to dispatch the following `handle_timeout()` hook method automatically:

```
int Logging_Event_Handler_Ex::handle_timeout
      (const ACE_Time_Value &now, const void *) {
  if (now - time_of_last_log_record_ >= max_client_timeout_)
    reactor ()->remove_handler (this,
                                ACE_Event_Handler::READ_MASK);
  return 0;
}
```

When an ACE timer queue dispatches `handle_timeout()`, it sets the `now` parameter to the absolute time (from `ACE_Timer_Queue::gettimeofday()`) when the queue expires the timer. `Logging_Event_Handler_Ex::handle_timeout()` checks if the time elapsed between `now` and the time when this event handler received its last log record is greater than the designated `max_client_timeout_` threshold. If so, it calls `ACE_Reactor::remove_handler()`, which triggers the reactor to call the following hook method to remove the event handler from the reactor:

```
int Logging_Event_Handler_Ex::handle_close (ACE_HANDLE,
                                            ACE_Reactor_Mask) {
    reactor ()->cancel_timer (this);
    return PARENT::handle_close ();
}
```

This method cancels the handler's timer and calls its parent's `handle_close()` method (page 60), which closes the log file and socket to the client, and then deletes itself.

3.5   The ACE_Reactor Class

Motivation

Event-driven networked applications have historically been programmed using native OS mechanisms, such as the Socket API and the `select()` synchronous event demultiplexer. Applications developed this way, however, are not only nonportable, they are inflexible because they tightly couple low-level event detection, demultiplexing, and dispatching code together with application event processing code. Developers must therefore rewrite all this code for each new networked application, which is tedious, expensive, and error prone. It's also unnecessary because much of event detection, demultiplexing, and dispatching can be generalized and reused across many networked applications.

One way to address these problems is to combine skilled object-oriented design with networked application domain experience to produce a set of framework classes that separates application event handling code from the reusable event detection, demultiplexing, and dispatching code in the framework. Sections 3.2 through 3.4 laid the groundwork for this framework by describing reusable time value and timer queue classes, and by defining the interface between framework and application event processing code with the `ACE_Event_Handler` class. This section describes how the `ACE_Reactor` class at the heart of the ACE Reactor framework defines how applications can register for, and be notified about, events from multiple sources.

Class Capabilities

`ACE_Reactor` implements the Facade pattern [GoF] to define an interface that applications can use to access the various ACE Reactor framework features. This class provides the following capabilities:

- It centralizes event loop processing in a reactive application.
- It detects events via an event demultiplexer, such as `select()` or `WaitForMultipleObjects()`, provided by the OS and used by the reactor implementation.
- It demultiplexes events to event handlers when the event demultiplexer indicates the occurrence of the designated events.
- It dispatches the appropriate hook methods on registered event handlers to perform application-defined processing in response to the events.
- It ensures that any thread can change a Reactor's event set or queue a callback to an event handler and expect the Reactor to act on the request promptly.

The interface for `ACE_Reactor` is shown in Figure 3.6 (page 72). This class has a rich interface that exports all the features in the ACE Reactor framework. We therefore group its method descriptions into the six categories described below.

1. Reactor initialization and destruction methods.   The following methods initialize and destroy an `ACE_Reactor`:

Method	Description
`ACE_Reactor()` `open()`	These methods create and initialize instances of a reactor.
`~ACE_Reactor()` `close()`	These methods clean up the resources allocated when a reactor was initialized.

The `ACE_Reactor` class isolates a variety of demultiplexing mechanisms behind the stable interface discussed in this chapter. To partition the different mechanisms in an easy-to-use and easy-to-maintain way, the `ACE_Reactor` class uses the Bridge pattern [GoF] to separate its implementations from its class interface. This design allows users to substitute a specific reactor implementation when the default isn't appropriate.

The `ACE_Reactor` constructor can optionally be passed a pointer to the implementation used to detect and demultiplex events and to dispatch the methods on the appropriate event handlers. The `ACE_Select_Reactor` described in Section 4.2 is the default implementation of the `ACE_Reactor` on most platforms. The exception is Windows, which defaults to `ACE_WFMO_Reactor` for the reasons described in Sidebar 25 (page 105).

The `ACE_Reactor::open()` method can be passed:

- The number of I/O handles and event handlers managed by the reactor. The default varies according to the reactor implementation, as described in Sidebar 20 (page 92).
- The type of timer queue implementation the reactor will use. The default is the `ACE_Timer_Heap` described in Section 3.4 (page 64).

Although ACE offers "full-featured" class constructors, they're best used in error-free or prototype situations where error checking is not important (see Item 10 in [Mey96]). The preferred usage in ACE is a separate call to `open()` (and `close()` in the case of object cleanup) methods. This preference stems from the ability of `open()` and `close()`

ACE_Reactor
<u>reactor_</u> : ACE_Reactor *   # implementation_ : ACE_Reactor_Impl *

+ ACE_Reactor (implementation : ACE_Reactor_Impl * = 0,
                delete_implementation : int = 0)
 + open (max_handles : int, restart : int = 0,
        sig_handler : ACE_Sig_Handler * = 0,
        timer_queue : ACE_Timer_Queue * = 0) : int
 + close () : int
 + register_handler (handler : ACE_Event_Handler *,
                   mask : ACE_Reactor_Mask) : int
 + register_handler (io : ACE_HANDLE, handler : ACE_Event_Handler *,
                   mask : ACE_Reactor_Mask) : int
 + remove_handler (handler : ACE_Event_Handler *,
                  mask : ACE_Reactor_Mask) : int
 + remove_handler (io : ACE_HANDLE, mask : ACE_Reactor_Mask) : int
 + remove_handler (hs : const ACE_Handle_Set&, m : ACE_Reactor_Mask) : int
 + suspend_handler (handler : ACE_Event_Handler *) : int
 + resume_handler (handler : ACE_Event_Handler *) : int
 + mask_ops (handler : ACE_Event_handler *,
            mask : ACE_Reactor_Mask, ops : int) : int
 + schedule_wakeup (handler : ACE_Event_Handler *,
                   masks_to_be_added : ACE_Reactor_Mask) : int
 + cancel_wakeup (handler : ACE_Event_Handler *,
                 masks_to_be_cleared : ACE_Reactor_Mask) : int
 + handle_events (max_wait_time : ACE_Time_Value * = 0) : int
 + run_reactor_event_loop (event_hook : int (*)(void *) = 0) : int
 + end_reactor_event_loop () : int
 + reactor_event_loop_done () : int
 + schedule_timer (handler : ACE_Event_Handler *, arg : void *,
             delay : ACE_Time_Value &,
             repeat : ACE_Time_Value & = ACE_Time_Value::zero) : int
 + cancel_timer (handler : ACE_Event_Handler *,
               dont_call_handle_close : int = 1) : int
 + cancel_timer (timer_id : long, arg : void ** = 0,
               dont_call_handle_close : int = 1) : int
 + notify (handler : ACE_Event_Handler * = 0,
          mask : ACE_Reactor_Mask = ACE_Event_Handler::EXCEPT_MASK,
          timeout : ACE_Time_Value * = 0) : int
 + max_notify_iterations (iterations : int) : int
 + purge_pending_notifications (handler : ACE_Event_Handler *,
                   mask : ACE_Reactor_Mask = ALL_EVENTS_MASK) : int
 + <u>instance</u> () : ACE_Reactor *
 + owner (new_owner : ACE_thread_t, old_owner : ACE_thread_t * = 0) : int

Figure 3.6: The ACE_Reactor Class

to return error indications, whereas ACE constructors and destructors don't throw native C++ exceptions. The motivation for avoiding native C++ exceptions in ACE's design is discussed in Section A.6 of C++NPv1. The `ACE_Svc_Handler` class discussed in Section 7.2 of this book closes the underlying socket handle automatically.

The `ACE_Reactor` destructor and `close()` methods release all the resources used by a reactor. This shutdown process involves calling the `handle_close()` hook method on all event handlers associated with handles that remain registered with a reactor. Any scheduled timers are deleted without notice and any notifications that are buffered in the reactor's notification mechanism (page 77) are lost when a reactor is closed.

2. Event handler management methods.   The following methods register and remove event handlers from an `ACE_Reactor`:

Method	Description
register_handler()	Register an event handler for I/O- and signal-based events.
remove_handler()	Remove an event handler from I/O-based and signal-based event dispatching.
suspend_handler()	Temporarily prevent dispatching events to an event handler.
resume_handler()	Resume event dispatching for a previously suspended handler.
mask_ops()	Get, set, add, or clear the event type(s) associated with an event handler and its dispatch mask.
schedule_wakeup()	Add the designated masks to an event handler's entry, which must have been registered previously via register_handler().
cancel_wakeup()	Clear the designated masks from an event handler's entry, but don't remove the handler from the reactor.

The `ACE_Reactor`'s registration and removal methods offer multiple overloaded signatures to facilitate their use in many different situations. For example, the `register_handler()` methods can be used with any of the following signatures:

- `(ACE_Event_Handler *, ACE_Reactor_Mask)`—In this version, the first parameter identifies the application's event handler and the second indicates the type of event(s) the handler is prepared to process. The method's implementation uses *double-dispatching* [GoF] to obtain a handle via the handler's `get_handle()` method. The advantage of this design is that application code need not obtain nor expose an I/O handle explicitly, which prevents accidental association of the wrong handle with an event handler. Most examples in this book therefore use this variant of `register_handler()`.

- `(ACE_HANDLE, ACE_Event_Handler *, ACE_Reactor_Mask)`—In this version, a new first parameter is added to explicitly specify the I/O handle associated with the application's event handler. This design is potentially more error-prone than the two-parameter version above since callers can accidentally pass an I/O handle that doesn't match the event handler. However, it allows an application to register multiple I/O handles for the same event handler, which is necessary for handlers that must be associated with multiple IPC objects. This method can also be used to conserve memory if a single event handler can process events from many unrelated I/O streams that don't require maintenance of per-handle state. The client logging daemon example in the *Example* portion of Section 6.2 illustrates the three parameter variant of register_handler().

- (const ACE_Sig_Set &sigset, ACE_Event_Handler *new_sh, ACE_Sig_Action *new_disp)—In this version, a new event handler (new_sh) is specified to handle a set of POSIX signals. When any signal in sigset is raised, the reactor will call the handle_signal() hook method on the associated event handler. Unlike other callbacks from the reactor, handle_signal() is called in signal context. Its actions are therefore restricted to a subset of available system calls. Developers are advised to check their OS platform documentation for details.

The ACE_Reactor::remove_handler() methods can be used to remove event handlers from a reactor so that they are no longer registered for one or more types of I/O events or signals. There are variants with and without an explicit handle specification (just like the first two register_handler() method variants described above). One variant accepts an ACE_Handle_Set to remove a number of handles at once; the other accepts an ACE_Sig_Set to remove signals from reactor handling. The ACE_Reactor::cancel_timer() method (page 76) must be used to remove event handlers that are scheduled for timer events.

When an application calls one of the ACE_Reactor::remove_handler() methods for I/O event removal, it can pass a bit mask consisting of the enumeration literals defined in the table on page 50. This bit mask indicates which I/O event types are no longer of interest. The event handler's handle_close() method is subsequently called to notify it of the removal. After handle_close() returns and the event handler is no longer registered to handle any I/O events, the ACE_Reactor removes the event handler from its internal I/O event demultiplexing data structures.

An application can prevent handle_close() from being called back by adding the ACE_Event_Handler::DONT_CALL flag to remove_handler()'s mask parameter. This flag instructs a reactor not to dispatch the handle_close() method when removing an event handler, as shown in the Service_Reporter::fini() method (page 135). To ensure a reactor won't invoke handle_close() in an infinite recursion, the DONT_CALL flag should *always* be passed to remove_handler() when it's called from within the handle_close() hook method itself.

By default, the handle_close() hook method is not called when canceling timers via the cancel_timer() method. However, an optional final argument can be supplied to request that handle_close() be called. The handle_close() method is not called when removing an event handler from signal handling.

The `suspend_handler()` method can be used to remove a handler or set of handlers temporarily from the reactor's handle-based event demultiplexing activity. The `resume_handler()` method reverts the actions of `suspend_handler()` so that the handle(s) are included in the set of handles waited upon by the reactor's event demultiplexer. Since `suspend_handler()` and `resume_handler()` affect only I/O handle-based dispatching, they have no effect on timers, signal handling, or notifications.

The `mask_ops()` method performs operations that get, set, add, or clear the event type(s) associated with an event handler's dispatch mask. The `mask_ops()` method assumes that an event handler is already present and doesn't try to register or remove it. It's therefore more efficient than using `register_handler()` and `remove_handler()`. The `schedule_wakeup()` and `cancel_wakeup()` methods are simply "syntactic sugar" for common operations involving `mask_ops()`. They help prevent subtle errors, however, such as replacing a mask when adding bits was intended. For example, the following `mask_ops()` calls enable and disable the `ACE_Event_Handler::WRITE_MASK`:

```
ACE_Reactor::instance ()->mask_ops
   (handler, ACE_Event_Handler::WRITE_MASK, ACE_Reactor::ADD_MASK);
// ...
ACE_Reactor::instance ()->mask_ops
   (handler, ACE_Event_Handler::WRITE_MASK, ACE_Reactor::CLR_MASK);
```

These calls can be replaced by the following more concise and informative method calls:

```
ACE_Reactor::instance ()->schedule_wakeup
   (handler, ACE_Event_Handler::WRITE_MASK);
// ...
ACE_Reactor::instance ()->cancel_wakeup
   (handler, ACE_Event_Handler::WRITE_MASK);
```

3. Event-loop management methods.   Inversion of control is a key capability offered by the ACE Reactor framework. Similar to other frameworks, such as the X Windows Toolkit or Microsoft Foundation Classes (MFC), `ACE_Reactor` implements the event loop that controls when application event handlers are dispatched. After registering its initial event handlers, an application can manage its event loop via methods in the following table:

Method	Description
`handle_events()`	Waits for an event to occur and then dispatches the associated event handler(s). A timeout parameter can limit the time spent waiting for an event.
`run_reactor_event_loop()`	Calls the `handle_events()` method repeatedly until it fails, `reactor_event_loop_done()` returns 1, or an optional timeout occurs.
`end_reactor_event_loop()`	Instructs a reactor to shut down its event loop.
`reactor_event_loop_done()`	Returns 1 when the reactor's event loop has been ended via a call to `end_reactor_event_loop()`.

The handle_events() method gathers the handles of all registered event handlers, passes them to the reactor's event demultiplexer, and blocks for up to an application-specified time interval awaiting the occurrence of an event, such as I/O activity or timer expiration. When an event occurs, this method dispatches the appropriate preregistered event handlers by invoking their handle_*() hook method(s) defined by the application to process the event(s). If more than one event occurs, they are all dispatched before returning. The return value indicates the number of events processed, 0 if no events occurred before the caller-specified timeout, or −1 if an error occurred.

The run_reactor_event_loop() method is a simple wrapper around handle_events(). It runs the event loop continually, calling handle_events() until either

- An error occurs
- The time designated in the optional ACE_Time_Value elapses
- The end_reactor_event_loop() method is called—possibly from within one of the event handling callbacks—to end the event loop

Applications without specialized event handling needs often use run_reactor_event_loop() and end_reactor_event_loop() to handle their event loops because these methods detect and handle errors automatically.

Many networked applications run a reactor's event loop in a single thread of control. Sections 4.3 and 4.4 describe how the ACE_TP_Reactor and ACE_WFMO_Reactor classes allow multiple threads to call their event loop methods concurrently.

4. Timer management methods. By default, ACE_Reactor uses the ACE_Timer_Heap timer queue mechanism described in Section 3.4 to schedule and dispatch event handlers in accordance to their timeout deadlines. The timer management methods exposed by the ACE_Reactor include:

Method	Description
schedule_timer()	Registers an event handler that will be executed after a user-specified amount of time.
cancel_timer()	Cancels one or more timers that were previously registered.

The ACE_Reactor codifies the proper usage of the ACE timer queue functionality in the context of handling a range of event types including I/O and timers. In fact, most users interact with the ACE timer queues only via the ACE_Reactor, which integrates the ACE timer queue functionality into the Reactor framework as follows:

- The schedule_timer() method allows users to specify timers using relative time, which is generally easier to work with than the absolute times the ACE timer queues use. This method uses the timer queue's gettimeofday() mechanism to adjust user-specified times automatically to the time method used by the timer queue.
- The handle_events() method queries the timer queue to find the expiration time of the earliest timer. It then uses this value to limit the amount of time the event demultiplexer waits for I/O events.

- The `handle_events()` method will call the timer queue methods to expire timers when the event demultiplexer times out after the time for the earliest timer arrives.

Together, these actions effectively integrate timers into the ACE Reactor framework in an easy-to-use way that allows applications to reuse the ACE timer queue capabilities without interacting with timer queue methods directly. Sidebar 16 describes how to minimize dynamic memory allocations in ACE timer queues.

Sidebar 16: Minimizing Memory Allocations in ACE Timer Queues

The `ACE_Timer_Queue` base class depicted in Figure 3.5 (page 64) offers no method to set the size of a timer queue. This omission is deliberate because there's no uniform meaning for "size" at that level of the class hierarchy. Each timer queue subclass has a different meaning for "size" that's related to its underlying data structures. The timer queue subclasses therefore offer size-related parameters in their constructors. These parameters are hints instructing the timer queue implementation how large to make its initial internal data structures. Although the timer queues resize automatically to accomodate arbitrarily large numbers of timers, resizing involves dynamic memory allocation, which can introduce overhead that's prohibitive for some applications.

In addition to sizing the queue, the `ACE_Timer_Heap` and `ACE_Timer_Wheel` classes offer the ability to preallocate timer queue entries so the queue can avoid any subsequent dynamic memory allocation. To make the `ACE_Reactor` use a custom-tuned queue for its timer operations you simply need to do the following:

1. Instantiate the desired ACE timer queue class, specifying the desired size and preallocation argument, if applicable.
2. Instantiate an ACE reactor implementation object, specifying the timer queue from step 1.
3. Instantiate a new `ACE_Reactor` object, supplying the implementation object from step 2.

---

5. Notification methods.   A reactor has a notification mechanism that applications can use to insert events and event handlers into a reactor's dispatching engine. The following methods manage various aspects of a reactor's notification mechanism:

Method	Description
`notify()`	Inserts an event (and an optional event handler) into the reactor's event detector, which causes it to be processed when the reactor next waits for events.
`max_notify_iterations()`	Sets the maximum number of handlers a reactor will dispatch from its notification mechanism.
`purge_pending_notifications()`	Purges a specified event handler or all event handlers from the reactor's notification mechanism.

The ACE_Reactor::notify() method can be used for several purposes:

- The reactor notification mechanism enables other threads to wake up a reactor's owner thread whose event demultiplexer function is blocked waiting for I/O events to occur. For example, since mask_ops(), schedule_wakeup(), and cancel_wakeup() don't cause the reactor to reexamine its set of handles and handlers, any new masks will only be noticed the next time a reactor's handle_events() method is called. If no other activity is expected shortly, or if the wait masks should be reexamined immediately, ACE_Reactor::notify() can be called to force a reactor to reexamine its set of handles and handlers.

- The notify() method can be passed an event handler pointer and one of the ACE_Reactor_Mask values, such as READ_MASK, WRITE_MASK, or EXCEPT_MASK. These parameters trigger the reactor to dispatch the corresponding event handler hook method (outlined in the table on page 50) *without* needing to associate the handler with I/O handles or timer events. This feature enables the reactor to scale to an open-ended number of event handlers since there's no requirement that a handler whose pointer is passed to ACE_Reactor::notify() has ever been, or ever will be, registered with that reactor.

By default, a reactor dispatches all event handlers in its notification mechanism after detecting a notification event. The max_notify_iterations() method can change the number of event handlers dispatched. Setting a low value improves fairness and prevents starvation, though it increases dispatching overhead somewhat.

Sidebar 17: Avoiding Reactor Notification Mechanism Deadlock

By default, the reactor notification mechanism is implemented with a bounded buffer and notify() uses a blocking send call to insert notifications into the queue. A deadlock can therefore occur if the buffer is full and notify() is called by a handle_*() method of an event handler. There are several ways to avoid such deadlocks:

- Pass a timeout to the notify() method. This solution pushes the responsibility for handling buffer overflow to the thread that calls notify().
- Design the application so that it doesn't generate calls to notify() faster than a reactor can process them. This is ultimately the best solution, though it requires careful analysis of program behavior.

Sidebar 22 (page 94) describes a way to avoid ACE_Select_Reactor deadlocks.

Notifications to the reactor are queued internally while waiting for the reactor to dispatch them (Sidebar 17 discusses how to avoid deadlock on a queue). If an event handler associated with a notification is invalidated before the notification is dispatched, a catastrophic failure can occur when the reactor tries to dispatch an invalid event handler pointer. The purge_pending_notifications() method can therefore be used to remove any notifications associated with an event handler from the queue. The ACE Reactor framework assists users by calling `purge_pending_notifications()` from the `ACE_Event_Handler` destructor. This behavior is inherited by all application event handlers because the destructor is declared `virtual`.

Notifications remain in a queue until they are dispatched or purged by an event handler, which ensures that a notification will be processed even if the reactor is busy processing other events at the time that `notify()` is called. However, if the reactor ceases to detect and dispatch events (e.g., after `run_reactor_event_loop()` returns), any queued notifications remain and will not be dispatched unless and until the reactor is directed to detect and dispatch events again. Notifications will therefore be lost if the reactor is closed or deleted before dispatching the queued notifications. Applications are responsible for deciding when to terminate event processing, and no events from any source will be detected, demultiplexed, or dispatched after that time.

6. Utility methods.   The `ACE_Reactor` class also defines the following utility methods:

Method	Description
`instance()`	A static method that returns a pointer to a singleton `ACE_Reactor`, which is created and managed by the Singleton pattern [GoF] combined with the Double-Checked Locking Optimization pattern [POSA2].
`owner()`	Assigns a thread to "own" a reactor's event loop.

The `ACE_Reactor` can be used in two ways:

- **As a singleton** [GoF] via the `instance()` method shown in the table above.
- **By instantiating one or more instances.** This capability can be used to support multiple reactors within a process. Each reactor is often associated with a thread running at a particular priority [Sch98].

Some reactor implementations, such as the `ACE_Select_Reactor` described in Section 4.2, only allow one thread to run their `handle_events()` method. The `owner()` method changes the identity of the thread that owns the reactor to allow this thread to run the reactor's event loop. Sidebar 18 (page 80) describes how to avoid deadlock when using a reactor in multithreaded applications.

Figure 3.8 (page 85) presents a sequence diagram of the interactions among classes in the ACE Reactor framework. Additional coverage of the ACE Reactor framework's design appears in the Reactor pattern's *Implementation* section in Chapter 3 of POSA2.

Example

Before we show the rest of the reactive networked logging server, let's quickly review the external behavior of the logging server and client developed in C++NPv1. The logging server listens on a TCP port number specified on the command line, defaulting to the port

---

Sidebar 18: Avoiding Reactor Deadlock in Multithreaded Applications

Although reactors are often used in single-threaded applications, they can also be used in multithreaded applications. In this context, it's important to avoid deadlock between multiple threads that are sharing an `ACE_Reactor`. For example, an `ACE_Reactor` holds a *recursive mutex* when it dispatches a callback to an event handler. If the dispatched callback method directly or indirectly calls back into the reactor *within the same thread of control*, the recursive mutex's `acquire()` method detects this automatically and simply increases its count of the lock recursion nesting depth, rather than deadlocking the thread.

Even with recursive mutexes, however, it's still possible to incur deadlock under the following circumstances:

- The original callback method calls a second method that blocks trying to acquire a mutex that's held by a second thread executing the same method.
- The second thread directly or indirectly calls into the same reactor.

In this case, deadlock can occur since the reactor's recursive mutex doesn't realize that the second thread is calling on behalf of the first thread where the callback method was dispatched originally.

One way to avoid `ACE_Reactor` deadlock in a multithreaded application is to not make blocking calls to other methods from callbacks if those methods are executed concurrently by competing threads that directly or indirectly call back into the same reactor. It may be necessary to use an `ACE_Message_Queue` described in Section 6.2 to exchange information asynchronously if a `handle_*()` callback method must communicate with another thread that accesses the same reactor.

---

number specified as `ace_logger` in the OS network services file. For example, the following line might appear in the UNIX `/etc/services` file:

```
ace_logger      9700/tcp     # Connection-oriented Logging Service
```

Client applications can optionally specify the TCP port and the IP host name or address where the client application and logging server should rendezvous to exchange log records. If this information isn't specified, however, the port number is located in the services database, and the hostname is assumed to be the ACE_DEFAULT_SERVER_HOST, which is defined as "`localhost`" on most OS platforms.

The version of the logging server shown below offers the same capabilities as the `Reactive_Logging_Server_Ex` version in Chapter 7 of C++NPv1. Both servers run in a single thread of control in a single process, handling log records from multiple clients reactively. The main difference is that the version described here reuses the event detection, demultiplexing, and dispatching capabilities from the ACE Reactor framework. This refactoring removes the following application-independent code from the original `Reactive_Logging_Server_Ex` implementation:

Handle-to-object mapping.   Two data structures in `Reactive_Logging_Server_ Ex` performed the following mappings:

1. An `ACE_Handle_Set` contained all the socket handles for connected clients and the `ACE_SOCK_Acceptor` handle for accepting new client connections.
2. An `ACE_Hash_Map_Manager` mapped socket handles to loosely associated `ACE_ FILE_IO` objects, which write log records to the appropriate output file.

Since the ACE Reactor framework now provides and maintains the code that manages handle-to-object mappings, the resulting application is smaller, faster, and makes much better use of the reusable software artifacts available in ACE.

Event detection, demultiplexing, and dispatching.   To detect both connection and data events, the `Reactive_Logging_Server_Ex` server used the `ACE::select()` synchronous event demultiplexer method. This design had the following drawbacks, however:

1. It worked only as long as the OS provided `select()`.
2. It worked *well* only as long as the OS implemented `select()` efficiently.
3. The code that called `ACE::select()` and processed the resulting handle sets was hard to reuse for other applications.

The new logging server reuses the ACE Reactor framework's ability to portably and efficiently detect, demultiplex, and dispatch I/O- and time-based events. This framework also allows the application to integrate signal handling if the need arises.

With the application-independent code described above removed, an important maintenance problem with the original code is revealed. Although the code worked correctly, the `Reactive_Logging_Server_Ex`, `Logging_Handler`, handle-to-`ACE_FILE_IO` map and `ACE_FILE_IO` objects were loosely cohesive and tightly coupled. Changing the event handling mechanism therefore also required changes to all of the application-specific event handling code, which illustrates the negative effects of tangling application-specific code with (what should be) application-independent code. This resulted in a design that was hard to extend and maintain, which would add considerable cost to the logging server as it evolved over time.

In contrast, the `Logging_Event_Handler` class (page 56) shows how the new reactive logging server separates concerns more effectively by combining `ACE_FILE_IO` with a `Logging_Handler` and registering the socket's handle with the reactor. This example show the following steps that developers can use to integrate applications with the ACE Reactor framework:

1. Create event handlers by inheriting from the `ACE_Event_Handler` base class and overriding its virtual methods to handle various types of events.
2. Register event handlers with an instance of `ACE_Reactor`.
3. Run an event loop that demultiplexes and dispatches events to the event handlers.

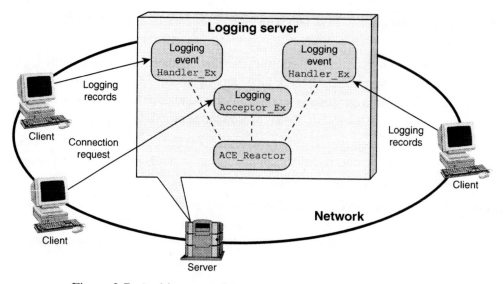

Figure 3.7: Architecture of the ACE_Reactor Logging Server

Figure 3.7 illustrates the reactive logging server architecture that builds on our earlier implementations from C++NPv1. This architecture enhances reuse and extensibility by decoupling the following aspects of the logging server:

- **ACE Reactor framework classes.** These classes encapsulate the lower-level OS mechanisms that perform event detection and the demultiplexing and dispatching of events to event handler hook methods.

- **ACE Socket wrapper facade classes.** The ACE_SOCK_Acceptor and ACE_ SOCK_Stream classes presented in Chapter 3 of C++NPv1 are used in this version of the logging server. As in previous versions, the ACE_SOCK_Acceptor accepts network connections from remote clients and initializes ACE_SOCK_Stream objects. An initialized ACE_SOCK_Stream object then processes data exchanged with its connected client.

- **Logging event handler classes.** These classes implement the capabilities specific to the networked logging service. As shown in the *Example* portion of Section 3.4, the Logging_Acceptor_Ex factory uses an ACE_SOCK_Acceptor to accept client connections. Likewise, the Logging_Event_Handler_Ex uses an ACE_ SOCK_Stream to receive log records from connected clients. Both Logging_* classes are descendants of ACE_Event_Handler, so their handle_input() methods can receive callbacks from an ACE_Reactor.

Our implementation begins in a header file called Reactor_Logging_Server.h, which includes several header files that provide the various capabilities we'll use in our ACE_Reactor-based logging server.

```
#include "ace/ACE.h"
#include "ace/Reactor.h"
```

We next define the `Reactor_Logging_Server` class, which forms the basis for many subsequent logging server examples in this book:

```
template <class ACCEPTOR>
class Reactor_Logging_Server : public ACCEPTOR {
public:
  Reactor_Logging_Server (int argc, char *argv[], ACE_Reactor *);
};
```

This class inherits from its `ACCEPTOR` template parameter. To vary certain aspects of `Reactor_Logging_Server`'s connection establishment and logging behavior, subsequent examples will instantiate it with various types of acceptors, such as the `Logging_Acceptor_Ex` (pages 67, 96, and 101), the `Logging_Acceptor_WFMO` (page 113), the `TP_Logging_Acceptor` (page 193), and the `TPC_Logging_Acceptor` (page 227). `Reactor_Logging_Server` also contains a pointer to the `ACE_Reactor` that it uses to detect, demultiplex, and dispatch I/O- and time-based events to their event handlers.

   `Reactor_Logging_Server` differs from the `Logging_Server` class defined in Chapter 4 of C++NPv1 since `Reactor_Logging_Server` uses the `ACE_Reactor::handle_events()` method to process events via callbacks to instances of `Logging_Acceptor` and `Logging_Event_Handler`. Thus, the `handle_connections()`, `handle_data()`, and `wait_for_multiple_events()`, hook methods used in the reactive logging servers from C++NPv1 are no longer needed.

   The `Reactor_Logging_Server` template implementation resides in `Reactor_Logging_Server_T.cpp`. Its constructor performs the steps necessary to initialize the reactive logging server:

```
 1 template <class ACCEPTOR>
 2 Reactor_Logging_Server<ACCEPTOR>::Reactor_Logging_Server
 3   (int argc, char *argv[], ACE_Reactor *reactor)
 4   : ACCEPTOR (reactor) {
 5   u_short logger_port = argc > 1 ? atoi (argv[1]) : 0;
 6   ACE_TYPENAME ACCEPTOR::PEER_ADDR server_addr;
 7   int result;
 8
 9   if (logger_port != 0)
10     result = server_addr.set (logger_port, INADDR_ANY);
11   else
12     result = server_addr.set ("ace_logger", INADDR_ANY);
13   if (result != -1)
14     result = ACCEPTOR::open (server_addr);
15   if (result == -1) reactor->end_reactor_event_loop ();
16 }
```

Line 5   Set the port number that we'll use to listen for client connections.

Line 6   Use the PEER_ADDR trait class that's part of the ACCEPTOR template parameter to define the type of server_addr. The use of traits simplifies the wholesale replacement of IPC classes and their associated addressing classes. Sidebar 19 explains the meaning of the ACE_TYPENAME macro.

Lines 9–12   Set the local server address server_addr.

Line 14   Pass server_addr to ACCEPTOR::open() to initialize the passive-mode endpoint and register this object with the reactor for ACCEPT events.

Line 15   If an error occured, instruct the reactor to shut its event loop down so the main() function doesn't hang.

Sidebar 19: The C++ typename Keyword and ACE_TYPENAME Macro

The C++ typename keyword tells the compiler that a symbol (such as PEER_ADDR) is a type. This keyword is necessary when the qualifier is a template type argument (such as ACCEPTOR) because the compiler won't have a concrete class to examine until templates are instantiated, which could be much later in the build process. Since typename is a relatively recent addition to C++, ACE provides a portable way to specify it. The ACE_TYPENAME macro expands to the typename keyword on C++ compilers that support it and to nothing on compilers that don't.

We conclude with the logging server's main() function, which resides in Reactor_Logging_Server.cpp:

```
 1 typedef Reactor_Logging_Server<Logging_Acceptor_Ex>
 2         Server_Logging_Daemon;
 3
 4 int main (int argc, char *argv[]) {
 5   ACE_Reactor reactor;
 6   Server_Logging_Daemon *server = 0;
 7   ACE_NEW_RETURN (server,
 8                   Server_Logging_Daemon (argc, argv, &reactor),
 9                   1);
10
11   if (reactor.run_reactor_event_loop () == -1)
12     ACE_ERROR_RETURN ((LM_ERROR, "%p\n",
13                        "run_reactor_event_loop()"), 1);
14   return 0;
15 }
```

Lines 1–2   Instantiate the Reactor_Logging_Server template with the Logging_Acceptor_Ex class (page 67) to create the Server_Logging_Daemon typedef.

Lines 6–9   Dynamically allocate a Server_Logging_Daemon object.

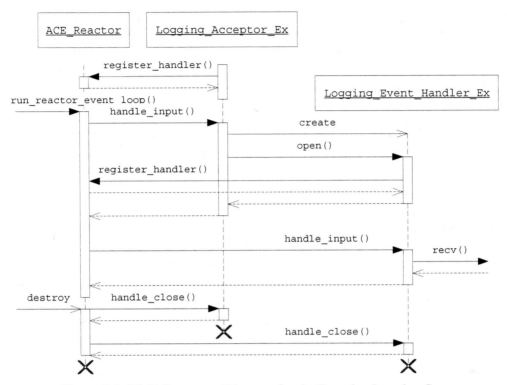

Figure 3.8: UML Sequence Diagram for the Reactive Logging Server

Lines 11–13   Use the local instance of ACE_Reactor to drive all subsequent connection and data event processing until an error occurs. The ACE_ERROR_RETURN macro and other ACE debugging macros are described in Sidebar 10 on page 93 of C++NPv1.

Line 15   When the local reactor's destructor runs at the end of main() it calls the Logging_Acceptor::handle_close() method (page 58) to delete the dynamically allocated Server_Logging_Daemon object. The destructor also calls Logging_Event_Handler_Ex::handle_close() (page 70) for each registered event handler to clean up the handler and shut the server down gracefully.

Figure 3.8 illustrates the interactions in the example above. Since all event detection, demultiplexing, and dispatching is handled by the ACE Reactor framework, the reactive logging server implementation is much shorter than the equivalent ones in C++NPv1. In fact, the work involved in moving from the C++NPv1 reactive servers to the current server largely involves deleting code that's no longer needed, such as handle set and handle set management, handle-to-ACE_FILE_IO mapping, synchronous event demultiplexing, and event dispatching. The remaining application-defined functionality is isolated in classes inherited from the ACE Reactor framework.

3.6   Summary

This chapter showed how the ACE Reactor framework can simplify the development of concise, correct, portable, and efficient event-driven networked applications by encapsulating OS event demultiplexing mechanisms within an object-oriented C++ interface. Likewise, it showed how the ACE Reactor framework enhances reuse, improves portability, and enables the extensibility of event handlers by separating event detection, demultiplexing, and dispatching *mechanisms* from application-defined event processing *policies*.

Since reusable classes in the ACE Reactor framework perform the lower-level event detection, demultiplexing, and event handler dispatching, a relatively small amount of application-defined code must be written. For example, the logging service in Sections 3.3 and 3.4 is mostly concerned with application-defined processing activities, such as receiving client log records. Any applications that reuse the ACE_Reactor class described in Section 3.5 can therefore leverage the knowledge and experience of its skilled middleware developers, as well as its future enhancements and optimizations.

The ACE Reactor framework uses dynamic binding extensively since the dramatic improvements in clarity, extensibility, and modularity it provides usually compensate for any decrease in efficiency resulting from its indirect virtual table dispatching [HLS97]. The ACE Reactor framework is often used to develop networked applications, where the major sources of overhead result from caching, latency, network/host interface hardware, presentation-level formatting, dynamic memory allocation and copying, synchronization, and concurrency management. The additional indirection caused by dynamic binding is often insignificant by comparison [Koe92]. In addition, good C++ compilers can eliminate virtual method overhead completely via the use of "adjustor thunk" optimizations [Lip96].

One of the most powerful properties of the ACE Reactor framework design is its ability to enhance extensibility both above and below its public interface. The Reactor implementations provide a good example of how applying patterns can provide a set of classes that take advantage of unique platform capabilities, while maintaining the ability for networked applications to run unchanged across diverse computing platforms. The next chapter studies the techniques that ACE uses to achieve this flexibility.

CHAPTER 4

ACE Reactor Implementations

CHAPTER SYNOPSIS

This chapter describes the design and use of several implementations of the `ACE_Reactor`
interface described in Chapter 3. These implementations support a diverse collection of
operating system synchronous event demultiplexing mechanisms, including `select()`,
`WaitForMultipleObjects()`, `XtAppMainLoop()`, and `/dev/poll`. We explain
the motivations for, and capabilities provided by, the most common reactor implementations
available in the ACE Reactor framework. We also illustrate how to use three different implementations of the `ACE_Reactor` to improve our logging server example. In addition,
we show the range of concurrency models supported by these `ACE_Reactor` implementations.

4.1 Overview

The ACE Reactor framework discussed in Chapter 3 presents a real-world example of a
framework that's designed for extensibility. The original `ACE_Reactor` implementation
was based solely on the `select()` synchronous event demultiplexing mechanism. As
application requirements and ACE platform support evolved, however, the internal design
of the ACE Reactor framework changed to support new application needs and new OS
platform capabilities. Fortunately, the `ACE_Reactor` interface has remained relatively
consistent. This stability is important since it simultaneously helps to

- Ensure compatibility with applications written for previous ACE versions
- Allow each application to take advantage of new reactor capabilities as the need arises

This chapter focuses on the most common implementations of the ACE Reactor framework, which are listed in the following table:

ACE Class	Description
ACE_Select_Reactor	Uses the select() synchronous event demultiplexer function to detect I/O and timer events; incorporates orderly handling of POSIX signals.
ACE_TP_Reactor	Uses the Leader/Followers pattern [POSA2] to extend ACE_Select_Reactor event handling to a pool of threads.
ACE_WFMO_Reactor	Uses the Windows WaitForMultipleObjects() event demultiplexer function to detect socket I/O, timeouts, and Windows synchronization events.

ACE also offers other more specialized reactor implementations that are outlined in Section 4.5. The variety of reactor requirements motivating all these reactors grew out of the popular reactive model of networked application design, coupled with:

- The growing popularity and availability of multithreaded systems

- The addition of Windows to ACE's set of supported platforms

- High performance I/O, CPU, and synchronous multiprocessing hardware

- The desire to integrate event handling with GUI frameworks, such as Microsoft Windows, X11 Windows, Trolltech AS's Qt, the Fast Light Toolkit, and TCL/Tk

Newer reactor implementations began by subclassing ACE_Reactor and overriding methods to implement the new capabilities. In 1997, during ACE version 4.4 development, however, the design was changed when ACE user Thomas Jordan suggested use of the Bridge pattern [GoF] for the following reasons:

- The ACE_Reactor interface needed to remain constant to preserve backward compatibility, yet the implementation needed to be flexible and selectable at run time.

- The reactor implementations needed to take advantage of related capability by subclassing where it made sense, yet avoid it completely where it didn't. For example, ACE_TP_Reactor is derived from ACE_Select_Reactor, but ACE_WFMO_Reactor is completely different.

- The expanding set of reactor implementations indicated the need for flexibility to allow further enhancements without changing the ACE_Reactor interface.

Application of the Bridge pattern to the reactor implementations led to the design depicted in Figure 4.1, which shows the major reactor implementations that this chapter discusses. The ACE_Reactor class, which was the original implementation, now plays the *Abstraction* role in the Bridge pattern. The ACE_Reactor_Impl class plays the *Implementor* role, and the various user-visible reactor implementations each play a *ConcreteImplementor* role. The Bridge pattern allows considerable freedom in implementation and allows applications to choose different reactors at run time with minimal impact to existing code.

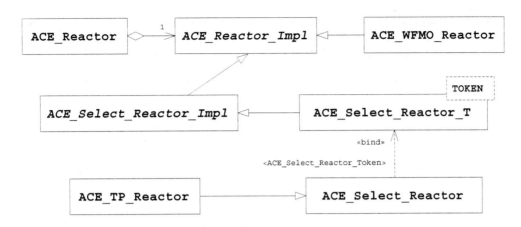

Figure 4.1: Implementations of the ACE_Reactor Interface

The remainder of this chapter motivates and describes the capabilities of the most common implementations of the ACE_Reactor interface: ACE_Select_Reactor, ACE_TP_Reactor, and ACE_WFMO_Reactor. It explores the detailed design issues associated with these implementations to illustrate the subtleties involved in developing extensible and efficient object-oriented frameworks. It also shows how these reactor implementations can be used to enhance the design of our networked logging server.

4.2   The ACE_Select_Reactor Class

Motivation

As discussed in Chapter 5 of C++NPv1, a reactive server responds to events from one or more sources. Ideally, response to events is quick enough so that all requests appear to be processed simultaneously, although event processing is usually handled by a single thread. A synchronous event demultiplexer is at the heart of each reactive server. This demultiplexer mechanism detects and reacts to events originating from a number of sources, making the events available to the server synchronously, as part of its normal execution path.

The select() function is the most common synchronous event demultiplexer. This system function waits for specified events to occur on a set of I/O handles.[1] When one or more of the I/O handles become active, or after a designated amount of time elapses, select() returns. Its return value indicates the number of handles that are active, that the caller-specified time elapsed before an event occurred, or an error occurred. The caller can then take appropriate action. Additional coverage of select() is available in Chapter 6 of C++NPv1 and in [Ste98].

---

[1]The Windows version of select() works only on socket handles.

Although `select()` is available on most OS platforms, programming to the native `select()` C API requires developers to wrestle with many low-level details, such as

- Setting and clearing `fd_sets`
- Detecting events and responding to signal interrupts
- Managing internal locks
- Demultiplexing events to associated event handlers
- Dispatching functions that process I/O, signal, and timer events

Chapter 7 of C++NPv1 discussed several wrapper facade classes that can be used to master many complexities associated with these low-level details. It's also useful, however, to use `select()` in environments where it's necessary to

- Allow multiple threads to change the I/O handle sets used by the `select()` thread
- Interrupt the `select()` function before events occur
- Remove thread support overhead entirely, either because it isn't needed or because the platform or application configuration doesn't support multithreading

To address these issues systematically, the ACE Reactor framework defines the `ACE_Select_Reactor` class, which provides all the capabilities outlined above.

Class Capabilities

`ACE_Select_Reactor` is an implementation of the `ACE_Reactor` interface that uses the `select()` synchronous event demultiplexer function to detect I/O and timer events. In addition to supporting all the features of the `ACE_Reactor` interface, the `ACE_Select_Reactor` class provides the following capabilities:

- It supports reentrant reactor invocations, where applications can call the `handle_events()` method from event handlers that are being dispatched by the same reactor.
- It can be configured to be either synchronized or nonsynchronized, which trades off thread safety for reduced overhead.
- It preserves fairness by dispatching all active handles in its handle sets before calling `select()` again.

The `ACE_Select_Reactor` is the default implementation of `ACE_Reactor` on all platforms except Windows, which uses the `ACE_WFMO_Reactor` for the reasons described in Sidebar 25 (page 105).

Implementation overview. `ACE_Select_Reactor` descends from `ACE_Reactor_Impl`, as shown in Figure 4.1 (page 89). It therefore serves as a concrete implementation of the `ACE_Reactor`. As shown in Figure 4.2, `ACE_Select_Reactor` is actually a `typedef` of the `ACE_Select_Reactor_T` template (the *Concurrency considerations*

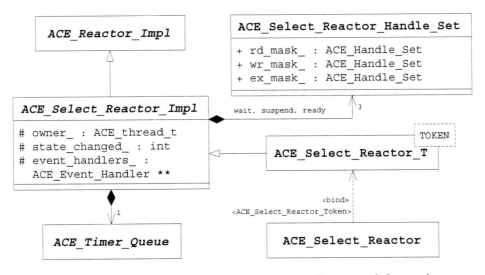

Figure 4.2: The ACE_Select_Reactor Framework Internals

section on page 93 discusses this implementation aspect further). The ACE_Select_
Reactor_Impl class contains the data and methods that are independent of the template argument to ACE_Select_Reactor_T, which isolates them from the template
argument-dependent factors and prevents them from being duplicated in each template instantiation. Sidebar 20 (page 92) explains how to change the number of event handlers
managed by an instance of ACE_Select_Reactor.

The ACE Reactor framework's notification mechanism (page 77) enables a reactor to
process an open-ended number of event handlers and can be used to unblock a reactor from
its event loop. By default, ACE_Select_Reactor implements its notification mechanism via an ACE_Pipe, which is a bidirectional IPC mechanism whose semantics are
described in Sidebar 21 (page 93). The two ends of the pipe play the following roles:

- **The writer role.** The ACE_Select_Reactor::notify() method exposes the
  writer end of the pipe to application threads, which use the notify() method to
  pass event handler pointers to an ACE_Select_Reactor via its notification pipe.

- **The reader role.** The ACE_Select_Reactor registers the reader end of the pipe
  internally with a READ_MASK. When the reactor detects an event in the reader end
  of its notification pipe it wakes up and dispatches its notify handler to process a
  user-configurable number of event handlers from the pipe. The number of handlers
  dispatched is controlled by the max_notify_iterations() method (page 77).

Sidebar 17 (page 78) explains how to avoid deadlocks that can result from the fact that the
buffer size of an ACE_Pipe is bounded. In addition to those application design tips, Sidebar 22 (page 94) describes another potential problem related to notifications; its solution
also provides a way to enlarge the notification mechanism, which helps avoid deadlocks.

Sidebar 20: Controlling the Size of an ACE_Select_Reactor

The number of event handlers that can be managed by an `ACE_Select_Reactor` defaults to the value of the `FD_SETSIZE` macro. `FD_SETSIZE` is generally used by the OS to size the `fd_set` structures discussed in Chapter 7 of C++NPv1. Since the internals of `ACE_Select_Reactor` rely on `fd_set`, and `FD_SETSIZE` controls its size, `FD_SETSIZE` can play an important role in increasing the number of possible event handlers in `ACE_Select_Reactor`. This value can be controlled as follows:

- To create an `ACE_Select_Reactor` that's *smaller* than the default size of `FD_SETSIZE`, simply pass in the value to the `ACE_Select_Reactor::open()` method. This does not require recompilation of the ACE library.

- To create an `ACE_Select_Reactor` that's *larger* than the default size of `FD_SETSIZE`, you'll need to change the value of `FD_SETSIZE` in your `$ACE_ROOT/ace/config.h` file and recompile the ACE library (and possibly your OS kernel and C library on some platforms). After recompiling and reinstalling the necessary libraries, you can then pass in the desired number of event handlers to the `ACE_Select_Reactor::open()` method. You should be fine as long as this value is less than or equal to the new `FD_SETSIZE` and the maximum number of handles supported by the OS.

Although the steps described above make it possible to handle a large number of I/O handles per `ACE_Select_Reactor`, it's not necessarily a good idea since performance may suffer due to deficiencies with `select()` [BM98]. To handle a large numbers of handles, you might therefore consider using the `ACE_Dev_Poll_Reactor` (page 114) that's available on certain UNIX platforms. An alternative choice could be a design using asynchronous I/O based on the ACE Proactor framework discussed in Chapter 8 (available on Windows and certain UNIX platforms). Avoid the temptation to divide a large number of handles between multiple instances of `ACE_Select_Reactor` since one of the deficiencies stems from the need for `select()` to scan large `fd_set` structures, not ACE's use of `select()`.

Unlike the event handlers registered with a reactor, the handlers passed via a reactor's notification mechanism needn't be associated with I/O-based or timer-based events, which helps improve the flexibility and scalability of `ACE_Select_Reactor`. Likewise, this mechanism allows all event handler processing to be serialized in the reactor's main thread, which simplifies event handler implementations since they needn't be thread-safe. Figure 4.3 illustrates how `ACE_Pipe` is used within `ACE_Select_Reactor`.

With events originating in numerous sources, both application-supplied (timers and I/O handles) and internal (notification pipe), it's important for an `ACE_Select_Reactor` to dispatch events to event handlers in an effective order. Years of experimentation and refinement resulted in the following order for event handler dispatching in the `ACE_Select_Reactor::handle_events()` method:

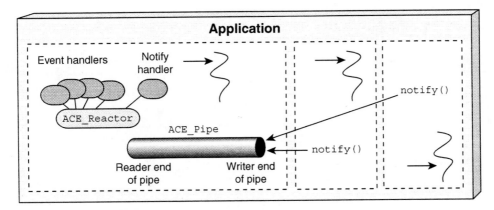

Figure 4.3: The ACE_Select_Reactor Notification Mechanism

Sidebar 21: The ACE_Pipe Class

The ACE_Select_Reactor's notification mechanism is implemented via the ACE_Pipe class, which provides a portable, bidirectional IPC mechanism that transfers data within an OS kernel. This wrapper facade class is implemented using a STREAMS pipe on modern UNIX platforms, a socketpair() on legacy UNIX platforms, or a connected TCP/IP socket on Windows platforms. After initializing an ACE_Pipe, applications can obtain its "read" and "write" handles via access methods and invoke I/O operations to receive and send data. These handles can also be included in ACE_Handle_Set objects passed to ACE::select() or to any reactor based on select(), such as the ACE_Select_Reactor or ACE_Priority_Reactor.

---

1. Time-driven events
2. Notifications
3. Output I/O events
4. Exception I/O events
5. Input I/O events

Applications should generally not rely on the order in which the different types of events are dispatched since not all reactor implementations guarantee the same order. For example, the ACE_Dev_Poll_Reactor (page 114) might not dispatch notifications before I/O events. There are situations, however, where knowing the dispatching order of events is useful. For example, an event handler's handle_output() callback method may encounter an error writing to a socket because the peer application aborts the connection. In this case, it's likely that the socket is also ready for input and the handler's handle_input() callback will be invoked shortly, where common socket and handler cleanup can take place.

Sidebar 22: Enlarging ACE_Select_Reactor's Notification Mechanism

In some situations, it's possible that a notification queued to an `ACE_Select_Reactor` won't be delivered until after the desired event handler is destroyed. This delay stems from the time window between when the `notify()` method is called and the time when the reactor reacts to the notification pipe, reads the notification information from the pipe, and dispatches the associated callback. Although application developers can often work around this scenario and avoid deleting an event handler while notifications are pending, it's not always possible to do so.

ACE offers a way to change the `ACE_Select_Reactor` notification queueing mechanism from an `ACE_Pipe` to a user-space queue that can grow arbitrarily large. This alternate mechanism offers the following benefits:

- Greatly expands the queueing capacity of the notification mechanism, also helping to avoid deadlock (see Sidebar 17 on page 78)
- Allows the `ACE_Reactor::purge_pending_notifications()` method to scan the queue and remove desired event handlers

To enable this feature, add `#define ACE_HAS_REACTOR_NOTIFICATION_QUEUE` to your `$ACE_ROOT/ace/config.h` file and rebuild ACE. This option is not enabled by default because the additional dynamic memory allocation required may be prohibitive for high-performance or embedded systems.

Concurrency considerations. The `ACE_Select_Reactor` is an instantiation of the `ACE_Select_Reactor_T` class template shown in Figure 4.2 (page 91). This template uses the Strategized Locking pattern [POSA2] to allow application developers to configure the necessary level of synchronization. The `TOKEN` template argument is always an instantiation of `ACE_Select_Reactor_Token_T` with one of the following types:

- `ACE_Token`—This produces a synchronized reactor, allowing multiple threads to invoke event handler registration, removal, and management methods on a single `ACE_Reactor` that's shared by all threads in a process. The `ACE_Token` recursive locking mechanism is described in Sidebar 23.

- `ACE_Noop_Token`—This produces an unsynchronized reactor that minimizes the overhead of event handling for single-threaded applications. `ACE_Noop_Token` exports the same interface as `ACE_Token`, but performs no synchronization. This type of token is the default when ACE is built without multithreading support.

Only one thread (called the *owner*) can invoke `ACE_Select_Reactor::handle_events()` at a time. By default, the owner of an `ACE_Reactor` is the identity of the thread that initialized it. The `ACE_Select_Reactor::owner()` method is used to change ownership of the `ACE_Select_Reactor` to a particular thread id. This method is useful when the thread running the reactor's event loop differs from the thread that initialized the reactor. The `event_loop()` function on page 97 illustrates this use case.

Sidebar 23: The ACE_Token Class

ACE_Token is a lock whose interface is compatible with other ACE synchronization wrapper facades, such as ACE_Thread_Mutex or ACE_RW_Mutex from Chapter 10 of C++NPv1, but whose implementation has the following capabilities:

- It implements *recursive mutex* semantics; that is, a thread that owns the token can reacquire it without deadlocking. Before a token can be acquired by a different thread, however, its release() method must be called the same number of times that acquire() was called.
- Each ACE_Token maintains two ordered lists that are used to queue high- and low-priority threads waiting to acquire the token. Threads requesting the token using ACE_Token::acquire_write() are kept in the high-priority list and take precedence over threads that call ACE_Token::acquire_read(), which are kept in the low-priority list. Within a priority list, threads that are blocked awaiting to acquire a token are serviced in either FIFO or LIFO order according to the current queueing strategy as threads release the token.
- The ACE_Token queueing strategy can be obtained or set via calls to ACE_Token::queueing_strategy() and defaults to FIFO, which ensures the fairness among waiting threads. In contrast, UNIX International and Pthreads mutexes don't strictly enforce any particular thread acquisition ordering. For applications that don't require strict FIFO ordering, the ACE_Token LIFO strategy can improve performance by maximizing CPU cache affinity [SOP+00].
- The ACE_Token::sleep_hook() hook method is invoked if a thread can't acquire a token immediately. This method allows a thread to release any resources it's holding before it waits to acquire the token, thereby avoiding deadlock, starvation, and unbounded priority inversion.

ACE_Select_Reactor uses an ACE_Token-derived class named ACE_Select_Reactor_Token to synchronize access to a reactor. Requests to change the internal states of a reactor use ACE_Token::acquire_write() to ensure other waiting threads see the changes as soon as possible. ACE_Select_Reactor_Token overrides its sleep_hook() method to notify the reactor of pending threads via its notification mechanism described in Sidebar 21 (page 93).

Example

Since the reactive logging server on page 84 runs continuously there's no way to shut it down gracefully, other than to terminate it abruptly. For example, an administrator can send its process a "kill –9" from a UNIX login console or end the process via the Windows Task Manager. Abruptly terminating a process via these mechanisms prevents it from performing cleanup activities, such as flushing log records to disk, releasing synchronization locks, and closing TCP/IP connections. In this example, we show how to use the ACE_Select_Reactor::notify() mechanism to shut down the logging server cleanly.

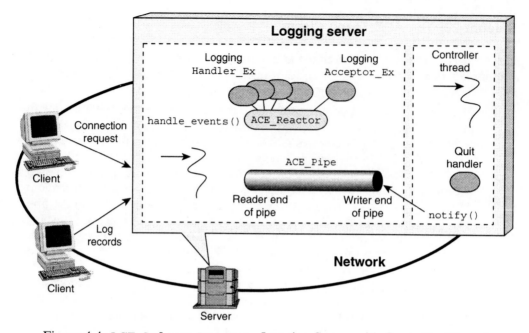

Figure 4.4: ACE_Select_Reactor Logging Server with Controller Thread

Figure 4.4 shows the architecture of our solution, which uses the ACE_Select_Reactor's notification mechanism to shut down our Reactor_Logging_Server via the following steps:

1. We'll spawn a controller thread that waits for an administrator to pass it commands via its standard input.
2. When the "quit" command is received, the controller thread passes a special event handler to the reactor via its notify() method and then exits the thread.
3. The reactor invokes this event handler's handle_exception() method, which calls end_reactor_event_loop() and then deletes itself.
4. When ACE_Reactor::run_reactor_event_loop() next checks the result of the reactor_event_loop_done() method, it will be true, causing the reactor event loop to exit, and the main server thread to exit gracefully.

The C++ code below illustrates these four steps. It's in Select_Reactor_Logging_Server.cpp and the revised main() function is shown first:

```
1 #include "ace/streams.h"
2 #include "ace/Reactor.h"
3 #include "ace/Select_Reactor.h"
4 #include "ace/Thread_Manager.h"
5 #include "Reactor_Logging_Server.h"
6 #include <string>
```

```
 7 // Forward declarations.
 8 ACE_THR_FUNC_RETURN controller (void *);
 9 ACE_THR_FUNC_RETURN event_loop (void *);
10
11 typedef Reactor_Logging_Server<Logging_Acceptor_Ex>
12         Server_Logging_Daemon;
13
14 int main (int argc, char *argv[]) {
15   ACE_Select_Reactor select_reactor;
16   ACE_Reactor reactor (&select_reactor);
17
18   Server_Logging_Daemon *server = 0;
19   ACE_NEW_RETURN (server,
20                    Server_Logging_Daemon (argc, argv, &reactor),
21                    1);
22   ACE_Thread_Manager::instance()->spawn (event_loop, &reactor);
23   ACE_Thread_Manager::instance()->spawn (controller, &reactor);
24   return ACE_Thread_Manager::instance ()->wait ();
25 }
```

Lines 1–12   Include the header files, define some forward declarations, and instantiate the `Reactor_Logging_Server` template with the `Logging_Acceptor_Ex` class (page 67) to create the `Server_Logging_Daemon` type definition. `ACE_THR_FUNC_RETURN` portably specifies the thread function's return type.

Lines 15–16   Set the implementation of the local `ACE_Reactor` instance to be an `ACE_Select_Reactor`.

Lines 20–21   Dynamically create an instance of `Server_Logging_Daemon`.

Line 22   Use the `ACE_Thread_Manager` singleton from Chapter 9 of C++NPv1 to spawn a thread that runs the following `event_loop()` function:

```
static ACE_THR_FUNC_RETURN event_loop (void *arg) {
  ACE_Reactor *reactor = ACE_static_cast (ACE_Reactor *, arg);

  reactor->owner (ACE_OS::thr_self ());
  reactor->run_reactor_event_loop ();
  return 0;
}
```

Note how we set the owner of the reactor to the identity of the thread that runs the event loop. The *Concurrency considerations* discussion (page 94) explains the use of thread ownership for `ACE_Select_Reactor`.

Line 23   Spawn a thread to run the `controller()` function, which waits for an administrator to shut down the server via a command on its standard input.

Line 24   Wait for the other two threads to exit before returning from the `main()` function. `ACE_Thread_Manager::wait()` also reaps the exit status of the two threads to avoid memory leaks. Sidebar 42 (page 186) describes the conventions to follow to ensure memory isn't leaked when threads exit.

Line 25   At this point, the event loop isn't running, but the `Server_Logging_Daemon` and existing client connections are still open. The `reactor` and `select_reactor` objects are about to go out of scope, however. Since the `ACE_Reactor` plays the Abstraction role in the Bridge pattern, the only important field in `reactor` is a pointer to its implementation object, `select_reactor`. By default, the `ACE_Reactor` destructor only destroys the implementation object if the `ACE_Reactor` created it. Since `select_reactor` was created on the stack and passed to `reactor`, `select_reactor` is not destroyed by the `ACE_Reactor` destructor. Instead, it's destroyed when it goes out of scope. Its destruction triggers callbacks to `Logging_Acceptor::handle_close()` (page 58) and the `Logging_Event_Handler_Ex::handle_close()` (page 70) hook methods for each logging handler and logging event handler, respectively, that are still registered with the `reactor`.

The `controller()` function can be implemented as follows:

```
 1  static ACE_THR_FUNC_RETURN controller (void *arg) {
 2    ACE_Reactor *reactor = ACE_static_cast (ACE_Reactor *, arg);
 3    Quit_Handler *quit_handler = 0;
 4    ACE_NEW_RETURN (quit_handler, Quit_Handler (reactor), 0);
 5
 6    for (;;) {
 7      std::string user_input;
 8      std::getline (cin, user_input, '\n');
 9      if (user_input == "quit") {
10        reactor->notify (quit_handler);
11        break;
12      }
13    }
14    return 0;
15  }
```

Lines 2–4   After casting the `void` pointer argument back into an `ACE_Reactor` pointer, we create a special event handler called `Quit_Handler`. Its `handle_exception()` and `handle_close()` methods simply shut down the `ACE_Select_Reactor`'s event loop and delete the event handler, respectively, as shown below:

```
class Quit_Handler : public ACE_Event_Handler {
public:
  Quit_Handler (ACE_Reactor *r): ACE_Event_Handler (r) {}

  virtual int handle_exception (ACE_HANDLE) {
    reactor ()->end_reactor_event_loop ();
    return -1; // Trigger call to handle_close() method.
  }

  virtual int handle_close (ACE_HANDLE, ACE_Reactor_Mask)
  { delete this; return 0; }
```

```
private:

  // Private destructor ensures dynamic allocation.
  virtual ~Quit_Handler () {}
};
```

Lines 6–13   Go into a loop that waits for an administrator to type `"quit"` on the standard input stream. When this occurs, we pass the `quit_handler` to the reactor via its `notify()` method and exit the controller thread.

The implementation shown above is portable to all ACE platforms that support threads. Section 4.4 illustrates how to take advantage of Windows-specific features to accomplish the same behavior.

4.3   The ACE_TP_Reactor Class

Motivation

Although the `ACE_Select_Reactor` is flexible, it's somewhat limited in multithreaded applications because only the owner thread can call its `handle_events()` method. `ACE_Select_Reactor` therefore serializes processing at the event demultiplexing layer, which may be overly restrictive and nonscalable for certain networked applications. One way to solve this problem is to spawn multiple threads and run the event loop of a separate instance of `ACE_Select_Reactor` in each of them. This design can be hard to program, however, since it requires developers to implement a proxy that partitions event handlers evenly between the reactors to divide the load evenly across threads. Often, a more effective way to address the limitations with `ACE_Select_Reactor` is to use the ACE Reactor framework's `ACE_TP_Reactor` class, where "TP" stands for "thread pool."

Class Capabilities

`ACE_TP_Reactor` is another implementation of the `ACE_Reactor` interface. This class implements the Leader/Followers architectural pattern [POSA2], which provides an efficient concurrency model where multiple threads take turns calling `select()` on sets of I/O handles to detect, demultiplex, dispatch, and process service requests that occur. In addition to supporting all the features of the `ACE_Reactor` interface, the `ACE_TP_Reactor` provides the following capabilities:

- It enables a pool of threads to call its `handle_events()` method, which can improve scalability by handling events on multiple handles concurrently. As a result, the `ACE_TP_Reactor::owner()` method is a no-op.

- It prevents multiple I/O events from being dispatched to the same event handler simultaneously in different threads. This constraint preserves the I/O dispatching behavior of ACE_Select_Reactor, alleviating the need to add synchronization locks to a handler's I/O processing.
- After a thread obtains a set of active handles from select(), the other reactor threads dispatch from that handle set instead of calling select() again.

Implementation overview. ACE_TP_Reactor is a descendant of ACE_Reactor_ Impl, as shown in Figure 4.1 (page 89). It also serves as a concrete implementation of the ACE_Reactor interface, just like ACE_Select_Reactor. In fact, ACE_TP_ Reactor derives from ACE_Select_Reactor and reuses much of its internal design.

Concurrency considerations. Multiple threads running an ACE_TP_Reactor event loop can process events concurrently on different handles. They can also dispatch timeout and I/O callback methods concurrently on the same event handler. The only serialization in the ACE_TP_Reactor occurs when I/O events occur concurrently on the *same* handle. In contrast, the ACE_Select_Reactor serializes all its dispatching to handlers whose handles are active in the handle set.

Compared to other thread pool models, such as the half-sync/half-async model in Chapter 5 of C++NPv1 and Section 6.3 of this book, the leader/followers implementation in ACE_TP_Reactor keeps all event processing local to the thread that dispatches the handler. This design provides the following performance enhancements:

- It enhances CPU cache affinity and eliminates the need to allocate memory dynamically and share data buffers between threads.
- It minimizes locking overhead by not exchanging data between threads.
- It minimizes priority inversion since no extra queueing is used.
- It doesn't require a context switch to handle each event, which reduces latency.

These performance enhancements are discussed further in the Leader/Followers pattern description in POSA2.

Given the added capabilities of the ACE_TP_Reactor, you may wonder why anyone would ever use the ACE_Select_Reactor. There are two primary reasons:

1. **Less overhead**—Although the ACE_Select_Reactor is less powerful than the ACE_TP_Reactor it also incurs less time and space overhead. Moreover, single-threaded applications can instantiate the ACE_Select_Reactor_T template with an ACE_Noop_Token-based token to eliminate the internal overhead of acquiring and releasing tokens completely.
2. **Implicit serialization**—The ACE_Select_Reactor is particularly useful when explicitly writing serialization code at the application-level is undesirable. For example, application programmers who are unfamiliar with synchronization techniques may prefer to let the ACE_Select_Reactor serialize their event handling, rather than using threads and adding locks in their application code.

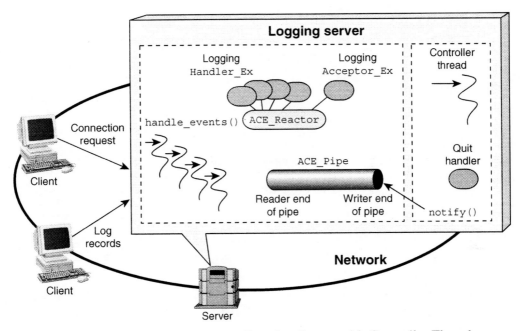

Figure 4.5: ACE_TP_Reactor Logging Server with Controller Thread

Example

To illustrate the power of the ACE_TP_Reactor, we'll revise the main() function from page 96 to spawn a pool of threads that share the Reactor_Logging_Server's I/O handles. Figure 4.5 illustrates the architecture of this server. This architecture is nearly identical to the one in Figure 4.4 (page 96), with the only difference being the pool of threads that call ACE_Reactor::handle_events(). This example is in the TP_Reactor_Logging_Server.cpp file. The C++ code for main() is shown below.

```
 1 #include "ace/streams.h"
 2 #include "ace/Reactor.h"
 3 #include "ace/TP_Reactor.h"
 4 #include "ace/Thread_Manager.h"
 5 #include "Reactor_Logging_Server.h"
 6 #include <string>
 7 // Forward declarations
 8 ACE_THR_FUNC_RETURN controller (void *);
 9 ACE_THR_FUNC_RETURN event_loop (void *);
10
11 typedef Reactor_Logging_Server<Logging_Acceptor_Ex>
12         Server_Logging_Daemon;
13
14 int main (int argc, char *argv[]) {
15   const size_t N_THREADS = 4;
16   ACE_TP_Reactor tp_reactor;
```

```
17    ACE_Reactor reactor (&tp_reactor);
18    auto_ptr<ACE_Reactor> delete_instance
19      (ACE_Reactor::instance (&reactor));
20
21    Server_Logging_Daemon *server = 0;
22    ACE_NEW_RETURN (server,
23                     Server_Logging_Daemon (argc, argv,
24                        ACE_Reactor::instance ()), 1);
25    ACE_Thread_Manager::instance ()->spawn_n
26      (N_THREADS, event_loop, ACE_Reactor::instance ());
27    ACE_Thread_Manager::instance ()->spawn
28      (controller, ACE_Reactor::instance ());
29    return ACE_Thread_Manager::instance ()->wait ();
30  }
```

Lines 1–12   Include the header files, define some forward declarations, and instantiate the `Reactor_Logging_Server` template with the `Logging_Acceptor_Ex` (page 67) to create the `Server_Logging_Daemon` type definition.

Lines 16–19   Create a local instance of `ACE_TP_Reactor` and use it as the implementation of a local `ACE_Reactor` object. For variety, we then set the singleton `ACE_Reactor` to the address of the local reactor. Subsequent uses of `ACE_Reactor::instance ()` will now use our local reactor. When reassigning the singleton reactor, the caller becomes responsible for managing the lifetime of the previous singleton. In this case, we assign it to an `auto_ptr` so it's deleted automatically if the program ends.

Lines 21–24   Dynamically allocate an instance of `Server_Logging_Daemon`.

Lines 25–26   Spawn `N_THREADS`, each of which runs the `event_loop ()` function (page 97). The new singleton reactor's pointer is passed to `event_loop ()` (`ACE_TP_Reactor` ignores the `owner ()` method called in that function).

Lines 27–28   Spawn a single thread to run the `controller ()` function (page 98).

Line 29   Wait for the other threads to exit and save the status as `main ()`'s return value.

Line 30   When the `main ()` function returns, the `tp_reactor` destructor triggers calls to the `Logging_Acceptor::handle_close ()` (page 58) and `Logging_Event_Handler_Ex::handle_close ()` (page 70) hook methods for each logging handler and logging event handler, respectively, that are still registered with it. By default, the `ACE_Object_Manager` (Sidebar 23 on page 218 of C++NPv1) deletes the singleton `ACE_Reactor` during shutdown. Since we replaced the original singleton with our local `reactor` object, however, ACE won't delete either the original instance (because we assumed ownership of it on line 18) or our local one (because ACE won't delete a reactor it didn't create, unless specifically directed to).

The primary difference between this example and the example on page 96 is the number of threads executing the event loop. Although multiple threads can dispatch events to `Logging_Event_Handler` and `Logging_Acceptor_Ex` objects, the `ACE_TP_`

`Reactor` ensures that the same handler won't be invoked from multiple threads concurrently. Since the event handling classes in the logging server are completely self-contained, there's no chance for race conditions involving access from multiple threads. We therefore needn't make any changes to them to ensure thread safety.

4.4   The ACE_WFMO_Reactor Class

Motivation

Although the `select()` function is available on most operating systems, it's not always the most efficient or most powerful event demultiplexer on any given OS platform. In particular, `select()` has the following limitations:

- On UNIX platforms, it only supports demultiplexing of I/O handles, such as files, terminal devices, FIFOs, and pipes. It does not portably support demultiplexing of synchronizers, threads, or System V Message Queues.
- On Windows, `select()` only supports demultiplexing of socket handles.
- It can only be called by one thread at a time for a particular set of I/O handles, which can degrade potential parallelism.

Windows defines the `WaitForMultipleObjects()` system function, described in Sidebar 24 (page 104), to alleviate these problems. This function works with many Windows handle types that can be signaled. Although it doesn't work directly with I/O handles, it can be used to demultiplex I/O-related events in two ways:

1. Event handles used in overlapped I/O operations
2. Event handles associated with socket handles via `WSAEventSelect()`

Moreover, multiple threads can call `WaitForMultipleObjects()` concurrently on the same set of handles, thereby enhancing potential parallelism.

`WaitForMultipleObjects()` is tricky to use correctly, however, for the following reasons [SS95a]:

- `WaitForMultipleObjects()` returns an index to the first handle array slot with a signaled handle. It does not, however, indicate the number of handles that are signaled, and there is no simple way to scan the handles and check which are. `WaitForMultipleObjects()` must therefore be invoked numerous times to find all signaled handles. In contrast, `select()` returns a set of active I/O handles and a count of how many are active.
- `WaitForMultipleObjects()` doesn't guarantee a fair distribution of notifications, that is, the lowest active handle in the array is always returned, regardless of how long other handles further back in the array may have had pending events.

To shield programmers from these low-level details, preserve demultiplexing fairness, and leverage the power of `WaitForMultipleObjects()` on Windows platforms, the ACE Reactor framework provides the `ACE_WFMO_Reactor` class.

Sidebar 24: The Windows WaitForMultipleObjects() Function

The Windows `WaitForMultipleObjects()` event demultiplexer function is similar to `select()`. It blocks on an array of up to 64 handles until one or more of them become *active* (which is known as being "signaled" in Windows terminology) or until the interval in its timeout parameter elapses. It can be programmed to return to its caller when either any one or more of the handles becomes active or all the handles become active. In either case, it returns the index of the lowest active handle in the caller-specified array of handles. Unlike the `select()` function, which only demultiplexes I/O handles, `WaitForMultipleObjects()` can wait for many types of Windows objects, including a thread, process, synchronizer (e.g., event, semaphore, or mutex), change notification, console input, and timer.

Class Capabilities

`ACE_WFMO_Reactor` is yet another implementation of the `ACE_Reactor` interface, which uses the `WaitForMultipleObjects()` function to wait for events to occur on a set of event sources. In addition to supporting all the features of the `ACE_Reactor` interface, the `ACE_WFMO_Reactor` class provides the following capabilities:

- It enables a pool of threads to call its `handle_events()` method concurrently (as a result, the `ACE_WFMO_Reactor::owner()` method is a no-op). This facility is more powerful than that of `ACE_TP_Reactor`. In `ACE_WFMO_Reactor`, all of the event handling threads can dispatch events concurrently instead of taking turns in a leader/followers arrangement. We'll discuss this aspect of `ACE_WFMO_Reactor` in more detail in the *Concurrency considerations* section on page 106.

- It allows applications to wait for socket I/O events and scheduled timers, similar to the `select()`-based reactors. `ACE_WFMO_Reactor` also integrates event demultiplexing and dispatching for all event types that `WaitForMultipleObjects()` supports, as outlined in Sidebar 24.

- Each call to `handle_events()` waits for a handle to become active. Starting from that handle, it iterates through all other active handles before returning. This design prevents an active handle from starving handles further down in the handle set array.

- Using the `ACE_Msg_WFMO_Reactor` subclass, applications can process all the events above plus window messages.

`ACE_WFMO_Reactor` is the default `ACE_Reactor` implementation on Windows for the reasons described in Sidebar 25. Note that `ACE_WFMO_Reactor` dispatches events in the same order as the `ACE_Select_Reactor` (page 92).

Implementation overview. As shown in Figure 4.1 (page 89), `ACE_WFMO_Reactor` inherits from `ACE_Reactor_Impl`. It therefore serves as a concrete implementation

---

Sidebar 25: Why ACE_WFMO_Reactor Is the Default on Windows

The ACE_WFMO_Reactor is the default implementation of the ACE_Reactor on Windows platforms for the following reasons:

- It lends itself more naturally to multithreaded processing, which is common on Windows (ACE_WFMO_Reactor was developed before ACE_TP_Reactor and was the first reactor to support multithreaded event handling).
- Applications often use signalable handles in situations where a signal may have been used on POSIX (e.g., child process exit) and these events can be dispatched by ACE_WFMO_Reactor.
- It can handle a wider range of events than the ACE_Select_Reactor, which can only handle socket and timer events on Windows.
- It's easily integrated with ACE_Proactor event handling, discussed in Sidebar 58 (page 290).

---

of the ACE_Reactor interface. Just as ACE_Select_Reactor leverages the capabilities of the select() function, ACE_WFMO_Reactor leverages the capabilities of WaitForMultipleObjects(), as shown in Figure 4.6 (page 106).

ACE_WFMO_Reactor's most significant differences from ACE_Select_Reactor and ACE_TP_Reactor include the following:

- **Limited number of handles.** Unlike ACE_Select_Reactor and ACE_TP_Reactor, which can be configured to demultiplex hundreds or thousands of handles, ACE_WFMO_Reactor can process no more than 62 handles. This limitation stems from the fact that Windows only allows WaitForMultipleObjects() to wait for 64 handles per thread. ACE_WFMO_Reactor uses two of these handles internally: one for its notification mechanism and another for synchronizing concurrent handler updates. If more than 64 handles must be demultiplexed, you can use multiple ACE_WFMO_Reactor objects in multiple threads, use the ACE_Proactor (Chapter 8), or use the ACE_Select_Reactor and increase its size via the mechanisms described in Sidebar 20 (page 92).

- **WRITE_MASK semantics different from** select(). When a socket can send more data, select() detects a WRITE condition. It will continue to detect this condition as long as the socket remains writeable, that is, until it becomes flow controlled. In contrast, the Windows WSAEventSelect() function only sets the WRITE event when the socket is first connected, whether passively or actively, and when the socket transitions from flow-controlled to writeable. When relying on WRITE events using the ACE_WFMO_Reactor, you must therefore continue to write until the connection closes or the socket becomes flow controlled and a send() fails with EWOULDBLOCK. If this behavior is undesirable, you might consider choosing the ACE_Select_Reactor as the ACE_Reactor implementation on Windows since it has the same WRITE_MASK semantics as on UNIX platforms.

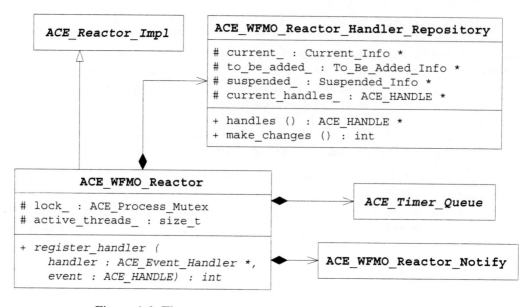

Figure 4.6: The ACE_WFMO_Reactor Framework Internals

• **Different notification mechanism.** The ACE_Select_Reactor's notification mechanism is implemented using the ACE_Pipe mechanism described in Sidebar 21 (page 93). In contrast, the ACE_WFMO_Reactor's notification mechanism is implemented using a synchronized version of the ACE_Message_Queue described in Section 6.2. As a result, the queue can be configured to have a user-defined size that can help avoid the deadlock problems discussed in Sidebar 17 (page 78). The default maximum number of queued notifications for ACE_WFMO_Reactor is 1,024. To change this value:

- Create a new ACE_WFMO_Reactor_Notify object, specifying the desired maximum number of queued notifications to its constructor.
- Create a new ACE_WFMO_Reactor object, passing a pointer to the new ACE_WFMO_Reactor_Notify object to the ACE_WFMO_Reactor constructor.

Concurrency considerations. The ACE_WFMO_Reactor allows multiple threads to call its handle_events() method concurrently. This capability complicates its design, however, and introduces some subtle behavioral differences from select()-based reactors, as discussed below:

• **Coordination of registration changes.** Each change to the set of registered handles will affect all threads executing the event loop. Allowing these changes to occur without synchronization would cause errors ranging from missed events to incorrect or invalid handlers being dispatched. To handle registration changes properly in the presence of multiple threads, ACE_WFMO_Reactor maintains three sets of handler information objects:

1. *Current handlers*, which are the handlers used for event detection and demultiplexing

2. *New handlers*, which are awaiting addition to the set of current handlers

3. *Suspended handlers*, which are handlers suspended from the current handler set

When registration changes are requested (such as registering, removing, suspending, or resuming an event handler), the handle, event handler, and event type information are remembered and the need for changing the associated information is noted. The next thread that completes its pass through `handle_events()` will notice the need for a change, obtain the reactor's lock, and wait for all other threads running `handle_events()` to complete. To ensure that they complete in a timely fashion, the waiting thread signals an internal event that's part of the dispatch handle set, causing all threads blocked in `WaitForMultipleObjects()` to awake. At this point, all event-handling threads will block waiting for changes to occur. When the original thread completes the necessary information and handle changes, the reactor lock is released, and all event-handling threads restart their event waiting, demultiplexing, and dispatching with the updated handle set.

• **Deferred event handler cleanup.** `ACE_WFMO_Reactor`'s registration change delay introduces a subtle behavioral difference compared to `select()`-based reactors. When a `handle_*()` method returns −1 or `ACE_Reactor::remove_handler()` is called on an event handler, the `ACE_WFMO_Reactor` defers the handler removal and callback to the handler's `handle_close()` hook until the registration changes can take place as described above. An application therefore can't delete an event handler immediately after requesting an `ACE_WFMO_Reactor` to remove it since the reactor's later call to the `handle_close()` method will dispatch through an invalid pointer.

The differences between `ACE_WFMO_Reactor` and the `select()`-based reactors can be masked in practice by adhering to the idiom of performing all cleanup in an event handler's `handle_close()` hook method, as described in Sidebar 9 (page 51). This idiom prevents premature deletion of the event handler object. In cases where this idiom doesn't apply (for example if an event handler is an automatic object whose destruction cannot be deferred), the `ACE_Event_Handler::DONT_CALL` flag must be passed to `ACE_Reactor::remove_handler()` to prevent `ACE_WFMO_Reactor` from invoking the `handle_close()` hook method later. It's therefore advisable to allocate event handlers dynamically, as advocated in Sidebar 11 (page 55), which avoids the need to manage the lifetime of event handlers outside the `ACE_Reactor` handler management scheme.

• **Multithreaded dispatch to same handler.** Unlike those using `select()`-based reactors, multithreaded applications can demultiplex and dispatch events concurrently using the `ACE_WFMO_Reactor::handle_events()` method.[2] In the multithreaded case it's therefore possible that different threads will dispatch events simultaneously to the same

---

[2] Although multiple threads can *call* `ACE_TP_Reactor::handle_events()` concurrently, only one thread at a time (the leader) actually runs `select()`.

event handler. This can happen, for example, when a handler-scheduled timer expires while I/O is being processed. It can also occur in the following situation:

1. $Thread_1$ dispatches a socket input event to a handler.
2. $Thread_1$ calls ACE_SOCK_Stream::recv() to read data.
3. More data are available on the socket, due to a limited receive in step 2 or the arrival of more data.
4. $Thread_2$ dispatches the input event on the same handle, resulting in a race condition between $thread_1$ and $thread_2$.

Event handlers must therefore explicitly protect against race conditions when the handle_events() event loop is executed by multiple threads on the same ACE_WFMO_Reactor object. The ACE_TP_Reactor avoids these race conditions by implementing an internal protocol that automatically suspends a handle before dispatching its event handler. Any follower thread that subsequently becomes the leader doesn't dispatch events on the affected handle until the callback is complete and the handle is resumed. Sidebar 26 explains why this handler suspension protocol can't be used with the ACE_WFMO_Reactor.

Example

This example illustrates how to use a signalable handle with the ACE_WFMO_Reactor. It also illustrates one technique for properly serializing I/O handling in a thread pool running the ACE_WFMO_Reactor event loop. Figure 4.7 (page 110) illustrates the architecture of this server. It's similar to the one in Figure 4.4 (page 96), with the difference being the *pool* of threads that call ACE_Reactor::handle_events(). Since this example explicitly specifies an instance of ACE_WFMO_Reactor, it works only on Windows.

This example is in the WFMO_Reactor_Logging_Server.cpp file. We start by defining a Quit_Handler class:

```
class Quit_Handler : public ACE_Event_Handler {
private:
  ACE_Manual_Event quit_seen_; // Keep track of when to shutdown.
public:
```

Although this class inherits from ACE_Event_Handler, it's used quite differently from the Quit_Handler defined on page 98. The Quit_Handler constructor illustrates some of the differences below:

```
 1 Quit_Handler (ACE_Reactor *r): ACE_Event_Handler (r) {
 2    SetConsoleMode (ACE_STDIN, ENABLE_LINE_INPUT
 3                              | ENABLE_ECHO_INPUT
 4                              | ENABLE_PROCESSED_INPUT);
 5    if (reactor ()->register_handler
 6        (this, quit_seen_.handle ()) == -1
 7        || ACE_Event_Handler::register_stdin_handler
 8            (this, r, ACE_Thread_Manager::instance ()) == -1)
 9      r->end_reactor_event_loop ();
10 }
```

Sidebar 26: Why ACE_WFMO_Reactor Doesn't Suspend Handles

The `ACE_WFMO_Reactor` doesn't implement a handler suspension protocol internally to minimize the amount of policy imposed on application classes. In particular, multithreaded applications can process events more efficiently when doing so doesn't require interevent serialization, as is the case when receiving UDP datagrams. This behavior isn't possible in the `ACE_TP_Reactor` because of the semantic differences in the functionality of the following OS event demultiplexing mechanisms:

- `WaitForMultipleObjects()`. When demultiplexing a socket handle's I/O event, one `ACE_WFMO_Reactor` thread will obtain the I/O event mask from `WSAEnumNetworkEvents()`, and the OS atomically clears that socket's internal event mask. Even if multiple threads demultiplex the socket handle simultaneously, only one obtains the I/O event mask and will dispatch the handler. The dispatched handler must take some action that reenables demultiplexing for that handle before another thread will dispatch it.

- `select()`. There's no automatic OS serialization for `select()`. If multiple threads were allowed to see a ready-state socket handle, they would all dispatch it, yielding unpredictable behavior at the `ACE_Event_Handler` layer and reduced performance due to multiple threads all working on the same handle.

It's important to note that the handler suspension protocol can't be implemented in the application event handler class when it's used in conjunction with the `ACE_WFMO_Reactor`. This is because suspension requests are queued and aren't acted on immediately, as described on page 107. A handler could therefore receive upcalls from multiple threads until the handler was actually suspended by the `ACE_WFMO_Reactor`. The `Logging_Event_Handler_WFMO` class (page 111) illustrates how to use mutual exclusion to avoid race conditions in upcalls.

Lines 2–4   Simplify input handling by setting the console to read a whole line of text (not small pieces at a time) without including control characters, such as Ctl-C.

Lines 5–6   We illustrate how to register an event handle with the reactor. We will signal this event when the `quit` command is entered. Sidebar 27 (page 111) outlines the capabilities of the `ACE_Manual_Event` class.

Lines 7–8   Use `ACE_Event_Handler::register_stdin_handler()` to establish the input mechanism, which causes the `Quit_Handler::handle_input()` hook method to be called repeatedly until it returns −1. On Windows, all these calls will be made from a thread other than the event loop thread(s), which removes the requirement for the input-handling method to serialize its processing.

Line 9   If either registration fails, we immediately mark the reactor event loop as ended, which forces an immediate end to the loop when the main program starts it.

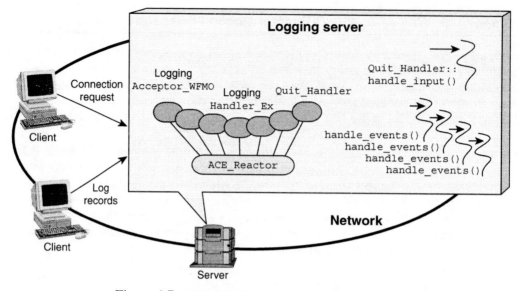

Figure 4.7: ACE_WFMO_Reactor Logging Server

The Quit_Handler::handle_input() method is shown below:

```
virtual int handle_input (ACE_HANDLE h) {
  CHAR user_input[BUFSIZ];
  DWORD count;
  if (!ReadFile (h, user_input, BUFSIZ, &count, 0)) return -1;
  user_input[count] = '\0';
  if (ACE_OS_String::strncmp (user_input, "quit", 4) == 0)
    return -1;
  return 0;
}
```

When the "quit" command is seen, handle_input() returns −1, which triggers ACE_WFMO_Reactor to dispatch Quit_Handler::handle_close():

```
virtual int handle_close (ACE_HANDLE, ACE_Reactor_Mask)
{ quit_seen_.signal (); return 0; }
```

The manual event handle from quit_seen_ was registered with the reactor in the Quit_ Handler constructor (page 108). When the event is signaled in the handle_close() method, the ACE_WFMO_Reactor will then demultiplex the event and call the Quit_ Handler::handle_signal() method shown below.

```
virtual int handle_signal (int, siginfo_t *, ucontext_t *)
{ reactor ()->end_reactor_event_loop (); return 0; }
```

This hook method calls the reactor's end_reactor_event_loop() method, which causes all of the event-handling threads to stop. It's possible to call end_reactor_ event_loop() directly from handle_close(). We moved the call to handle_signal() to illustrate how to use a signalable handle with ACE_WFMO_Reactor.

When the Quit_Handler object is destroyed, its destructor behaves as follows:

```
1  ~Quit_Handler () {
2    ACE_Event_Handler::remove_stdin_handler
3      (reactor (), ACE_Thread_Manager::instance ());
4    reactor ()->remove_handler (quit_seen_.handle (),
5                                ACE_Event_Handler::DONT_CALL);
6  }
```

Lines 2–3   Cancel the effects of the previous register_stdin_handler() call.

Lines 4–5   Unregister the event handle from the reactor. The DONT_CALL flag prevents the reactor from calling back to handle_close(), so the cleanup is complete at this point and we needn't worry about a later callback through an invalid object pointer.

Sidebar 27: The ACE_Manual_Event and ACE_Auto_Event Classes

ACE provides two synchronization wrapper facade classes that should be familiar to Windows programmers: ACE_Manual_Event and ACE_Auto_Event. These classes allow threads in a process to wait on an event or inform other threads about the occurrence of a specific event in a thread-safe manner. On Windows these classes are wrapper facades around native event objects, whereas on other platforms ACE emulates the Windows event object facility.

Events are similar to condition variables in the sense that a thread can use them to either signal the occurrence of an application-defined event or wait for that event to occur. Unlike stateless condition variables, however, a signaled event remains set until a class-specific action occurs. For example, an ACE_Manual_Event remains set until it is explicitly reset and an ACE_Auto_Event remains set until a single thread waits on it. These two classes allow users to control the number of threads awakened by signaling operations, and allows an event to indicate a state transition, even if no threads are waiting at the time the event is signaled.

Events are more expensive than mutexes, but provide better control over thread scheduling. Events provide a simpler synchronization mechanism than condition variables. Condition variables are more useful for complex synchronization activities, however, since they enable threads to wait for arbitrary condition expressions.

Due to concurrency differences between ACE_WFMO_Reactor and the select()-based reactors (shown in Sections 4.2 and 4.3), we also derive a new Logging_Event_Handler_WFMO class to add protection against race conditions. We need only override the handle_input() hook method of Logging_Event_Handler_Ex (page 68) and add a mutex to explicitly serialize access of threads in the thread pool to a client logging daemon connection, as follows:

```
class Logging_Event_Handler_WFMO
    : public Logging_Event_Handler_Ex {
public:
  Logging_Event_Handler_WFMO (ACE_Reactor *r)
    : Logging_Event_Handler_Ex (r) {}

protected:
  int handle_input (ACE_HANDLE) {
    ACE_GUARD_RETURN (ACE_SYNCH_MUTEX, monitor, lock_, -1);
    return logging_handler_.log_record ();
  }

  ACE_Thread_Mutex lock_; // Serialize threads in thread pool.
};
```

Since Logging_Acceptor_Ex (page 67) instantiates a new Logging_Event_
Handler_Ex object for each new client connection, our use of a different event handler class also mandates a new acceptor class. The following subclass of Logging_
Acceptor_Ex instantiates the correct type of event handler when a new client connection
arrives:

```
class Logging_Acceptor_WFMO : public Logging_Acceptor_Ex {
public:
  Logging_Acceptor_WFMO
    (ACE_Reactor *r = ACE_Reactor::instance ())
    : Logging_Acceptor_Ex (r) {}

protected:
  virtual int handle_input (ACE_HANDLE) {
    Logging_Event_Handler_WFMO *peer_handler = 0;
    ACE_NEW_RETURN (peer_handler,
                    Logging_Event_Handler_WFMO (reactor ()), -1);
    if (acceptor_.accept (peer_handler->peer ()) == -1)
    { delete peer_handler; return -1; }
    else if (peer_handler->open () == -1)
    { peer_handler->handle_close (); return -1; }
    return 0;
  }
};
```

The handle_input () method doesn't require protection against race conditions since
it only operates on objects local to the method. In fact, except for the type of event handler
that's instantiated for each new connection, Logging_Acceptor_WFMO is identical to
Logging_Acceptor_Ex (page 67). The ACE Acceptor-Connector framework in Chapter 7 shows how to factor out the event handler type into a reusable acceptor class.

Our `ACE_WFMO_Reactor` logging server's `main()` function is shown below:

```
#include "ace/Reactor.h"
#include "ace/Synch.h"
#include "ace/WFMO_Reactor.h"
#include "ace/Thread_Manager.h"
#include "Reactor_Logging_Server.h"

ACE_THR_FUNC_RETURN event_loop (void *); // Forward declaration.

typedef Reactor_Logging_Server<Logging_Acceptor_WFMO>
        Server_Logging_Daemon;

int main (int argc, char *argv[]) {
  const size_t N_THREADS = 4;
  ACE_WFMO_Reactor wfmo_reactor;
  ACE_Reactor reactor (&wfmo_reactor);

  Server_Logging_Daemon *server = 0;
  ACE_NEW_RETURN
    (server, Server_Logging_Daemon (argc, argv, &reactor), 1);
  Quit_Handler quit_handler (&reactor);
  ACE_Thread_Manager::instance ()->spawn_n
    (N_THREADS, event_loop, &reactor);
  return ACE_Thread_Manager::instance ()->wait ();
}
```

The main differences between this `main()` and the one shown on page 101 are

- `Reactor_Logging_Server` is instantiated with `Logging_Acceptor_WFMO` rather than `Logging_Acceptor_Ex`.
- The `ACE_WFMO_Reactor` is used instead of `ACE_TP_Reactor`.
- The controller thread dedicated to shutdown processing is replaced by an instance of `Quit_Handler`, described above.
- The calls to the `WaitForMultipleObjects()` event demultiplexer can actually run concurrently in different threads, rather than having calls to `select()` be serialized using the Leader/Followers pattern, as is the case with the `ACE_TP_Reactor`.
- The program will only run on Windows platforms, instead of all ACE platforms.
- We don't use the singleton reactor API, but instead use a local reactor instance again.

4.5   Summary

This chapter described how the most common `ACE_Reactor` implementations are designed and illustrated some subtle nuances of their different capabilities. In addition to giving some guidelines on when to use each, our discussions emphasized two points:

1. Different implementations of OS event demultiplexing mechanisms can present significant challenges, as well as important opportunities.
2. A well-designed framework can be extended to use OS capabilities effectively while isolating complex design issues in the framework, rather than in application code.

An intelligently designed framework can significantly improve the portability and extensibility of both applications and the framework itself. The ACE Reactor framework implementations are good examples of how applying *patterns,* such as Wrapper Facade, Facade, and Bridge, and *C++ features,* such as inheritance and dynamic binding, can yield a high-quality, highly reusable framework with these elusive qualities. The ACE Reactor framework implementations described in this chapter encapsulate many complex capabilities, allowing networked application developers to focus on application-specific concerns.

One of the most powerful properties of the ACE Reactor framework design is its ability to enhance extensibility at the following variation points:

- **Customized event handlers.** It's straightforward to extend application functionality by inheriting from the `ACE_Event_Handler` class or one of its pre-defined ACE subclasses (such as `ACE_Service_Object`, `ACE_Task`, or `ACE_Svc_Handler`) and selectively implementing the necessary virtual method(s). For example, Chapter 7 illustrates how event handlers in our client and server logging daemons can be customized transparently to support authentication.

- **Customized `ACE_Reactor` implementations.** It's straightforward to modify the underlying event demultiplexing mechanism of an `ACE_Reactor` without affecting existing application code. For example, porting a reactive logging server from a UNIX platform to a Windows platform requires no visible changes to application code. In contrast, porting a C implementation of the server from `select()` to `WaitForMultipleObjects()` is tedious and error-prone.

Over the previous decade, ACE's use in new environments has yielded new requirements for event-driven application support. For example, GUI integration is an important area due to new GUI toolkits and event loop requirements. The following new Reactor implementations were made easier due to the ACE Reactor framework's modular design:

ACE Class	Description
`ACE_Dev_Poll_Reactor`	Uses the `/dev/poll` or `/dev/epoll` demultiplexer. It's designed to be more scalable than `select()`-based reactors.
`ACE_Priority_Reactor`	Dispatches events in developer-assigned priority order.
`ACE_XtReactor`	Integrates ACE with the X11 Toolkit.
`ACE_FlReactor`	Integrates ACE with the Fast Light (FL) GUI framework.
`ACE_QtReactor`	Integrates ACE with the Qt GUI toolkit.
`ACE_TkReactor`	Integrates ACE with the TCL/Tk GUI toolkit.
`ACE_Msg_WFMO_Reactor`	Adds Windows message handling to `ACE_WFMO_Reactor`.

You can read about these reactors in the ACE documentation at `http://ace.ece.uci.edu/Doxygen/` or `http://www.riverace.com/docs/`.

CHAPTER 5

The ACE Service Configurator Framework

CHAPTER SYNOPSIS

This chapter describes the design and use of the ACE Service Configurator framework, which is an implementation of the Component Configurator pattern [POSA2]. This pattern helps increase application extensibility and flexibility by decoupling the behavior of services from the point of time when implementations of these services are configured into application processes. The chapter concludes by illustrating how the ACE Service Configurator framework can help to improve the extensibility of our networked logging server.

5.1 Overview

Section 2.2 described the naming and linking design dimensions that developers need to consider when configuring networked applications. An extensible strategy for addressing these design dimensions is to apply the *Component Configurator* design pattern [POSA2]. This pattern allows an application to reconfigure its services at run time without having to modify, recompile, or relink the program itself, or shut down and restart the application.

The ACE Service Configurator framework is a portable implementation of the Component Configurator pattern that allows applications to defer configuration and implementation decisions about their services until late in the design cycle—as late as installation time or even at run time. The ACE Service Configurator framework supports the ability to activate services selectively at run time regardless of whether they are

- **Static services,** which are linked statically into an application program
- **Dynamic services,** which are linked from one or more shared libraries (DLLs)

Each service can also be passed `argc`/`argv`-style arguments to set certain information at run time. Due to ACE's integrated framework design, services using the ACE Service Configurator framework can also be dispatched by the ACE Reactor framework.

This chapter examines the following ACE Service Configurator framework classes:

ACE Class	Description
`ACE_Service_Object`	Defines a uniform interface that the ACE Service Configurator framework uses to configure and control a service implementation. Control operations include initializing, suspending, resuming, and terminating a service.
`ACE_Service_Repository`	A central repository for all services managed using the ACE Service Configurator framework. It provides methods for locating, reporting on, and controlling all of an application's configured services.
`ACE_Service_Repository_Iterator`	A portable mechanism for iterating through all the services in a repository.
`ACE_Service_Config`	Provides an interpreter that parses and executes scripts specifying which services to (re)configure into an application (e.g., by linking and unlinking DLLs) and which services to suspend and resume.

The most important relationships between the classes in the ACE Service Configurator framework are shown in Figure 5.1. These classes play the following roles in accordance with the Component Configurator pattern [POSA2]:

- **Configuration management layer classes** perform application-independent strategies to install, initialize, control, and shut down service objects. The classes in the configuration management layer in the ACE Service Configurator framework include `ACE_Service_Config`, `ACE_Service_Repository`, and `ACE_Service_Repository_Iterator`.

- **Application layer classes** implement concrete services to perform an application's processing. In the ACE Service Configurator framework, application layer classes are descendants of `ACE_Service_Object`, which in turn inherits from `ACE_Event_Handler` (Chapter 3), thereby enabling service objects to be linked and unlinked dynamically, and to participate in the ACE Reactor framework.

The ACE Service Configurator framework provides the following benefits:

- **Flexibility.** The framework allows developers to offer multiple services, and a choice of different implementations of services, that can be assembled at run time. The choices concerning which services to execute on which network node(s) can be made (and changed) at any point, ranging from application build time to the actual point

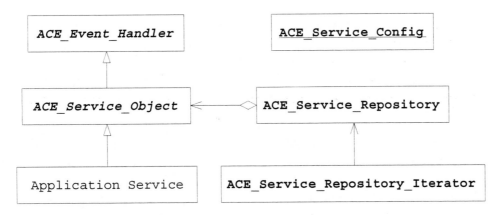

Figure 5.1: The ACE Service Configurator Framework Classes

when services start running. Developers can also limit choices (e.g., by not offering dynamically linkable services) where desired.

- **Configurability.** Developers can customize and configure application data for nearly any aspect of a service and for each deployment. Services can be developed to read traditional configuration data, such as port numbers, network addresses, and file system locations. Moreover, services can allow tuning and performance decisions to be deferred until the right information is available to guide them. For example, depending on the run-time platform's available multithreading facilities and available CPUs, it may be either more or less efficient to run multiple services in separate threads or separate processes. The ACE Service Configurator framework enables applications to be configured by site-knowledgable administrators, or they can select and tune these behaviors flexibly at run time, when there's enough information to help match client demands with available system processing resources.

- **Managability.** All configuration information can be stored in a configuration script file, known as `svc.conf`. The framework uses these scripts to load and configure services. An application's installation procedure can record settings in an `svc.conf` file. Administrators can also edit and tune this information as needed, without rebuilding the application itself. Applications can form their own configuration directives and pass them directly to the ACE Service Configurator framework. The framework groups an application's services into one administrative unit and enables an application to report on its services and their states.

- **Consistency.** The framework imposes a uniform interface for initializing, suspending, resuming, and terminating a service. This uniformity provides consistency to framework users and allows services to be treated as building blocks that can be assembled flexibly to form complete applications.

- **Maintainability.** The framework's decoupling of service implementation from configuration into networked applications allows service implementations to evolve over time, independently of which networked applications they're included in. Each service can be developed and tested independently, which simplifies subsequent service composition and increases reuse.

- **Enhanced dynamism and control.** The framework enables a service to be reconfigured dynamically without modifying, recompiling, or statically relinking existing code. Each service can also be reconfigured without affecting other services or stopping and restarting the server process itself. These reconfiguration capabilities are often required for high-availability applications, such as mission-critical systems that perform online transaction processing or telecom call processing.

The remainder of this chapter motivates and describes the capabilities of each class in the ACE Service Configurator framework. We also illustrate how this framework can be used to enhance the extensibility of our networked logging server. If you aren't familiar with the Component Configurator pattern from POSA2 we recommend that you read about it first before delving into the detailed examples in this chapter.

5.2   The ACE_Service_Object Class

Motivation

Service configuration and life cycle management involves the following aspects that we've alluded to briefly above:

- **Initialization.** A service must be initialized, which may involve creating one or more objects or invoking a factory method. Configuration parameters are passed to the service at this time.

- **Execution control.** Certain applications require the ability to suspend and resume services. Offering this capability therefore requires a mechanism by which a management application can locate the desired services and then contact the services to request or force the suspend/resume operation.

- **Reporting.** Mission-critical services often require the ability to respond to requests for information concerning their status and availability in a uniform way.

- **Termination.** Orderly shutdown processes are required to ensure that a service's resources are released properly, any necessary status information is updated, and that service shutdown is ordered properly to avoid improper service interactions.

Designing and implementing these capabilities in an *ad hoc* manner often produces tightly coupled data structures and classes, which are hard to evolve and reuse in future projects.

Moreover, if multiple projects or development groups undertake similar efforts, the primary benefits of service configuration will be lost because it's highly unlikely that multiple designs will interoperate at either the service or management level.

Since service configuration and management are largely application-independent they are good candidates to incorporate into a framework. Enforcing a uniform interface across all networked services makes it easier to configure and manage them consistently. In turn, this consistency simplifies application development and deployment by mitigating key challenges inherent in creating reusable administrative configuration tools. To provide a uniform interface between the ACE Service Configurator framework and the application-defined services, each service must be a descendant of a common base class called `ACE_Service_Object`.

Class Capabilities

`ACE_Service_Object` provides a uniform interface that allows service implementations to be configured and managed by the ACE Service Configurator framework. This class provides the following capabilities:

- It provides hook methods that initialize a service (e.g., allocating its resources) and shut a service down (e.g., cleaning up its resources).
- It provides hook methods to suspend service execution temporarily and to resume execution of a suspended service.
- It provides a hook method that reports key service information, such as its purpose, current status, and the port number where it listens for client connections.

These methods are generally invoked as callbacks from the ACE Service Configurator framework when it interprets the configuration directives described on page 141.

The interface for `ACE_Service_Object` is shown in Figure 5.2 (page 120). By inheriting from `ACE_Event_Handler` and `ACE_Shared_Object`, subclasses of `ACE_Service_Object` can be dispatched by the ACE Reactor framework and can be linked and unlinked from a DLL dynamically, respectively. The key configuration-related hook methods of `ACE_Service_Object` are outlined in the following table:

Method	Description
`init()`	Used by the framework to instruct a service to initialize itself. "argc/argv"-style arguments can be passed to `init()` to control service initialization.
`fini()`	Used by the framework to instruct a service to shut itself down. This method typically performs termination operations that release a service's resources, such as memory, synchronization locks, or I/O handles.
`suspend()` `resume()`	Used by the framework to instruct a service to suspend and resume execution.
`info()`	Used to query a service for certain information about itself, such as its name, purpose, and network address. Clients can query a server to retrieve this information and use it to contact a particular service running in a server.

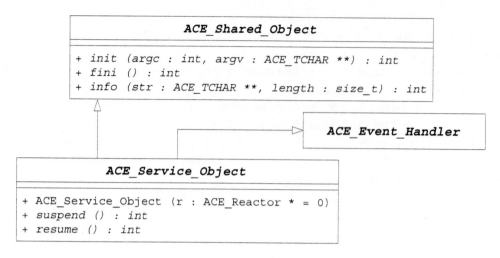

Figure 5.2: The ACE_Service_Object Class

These hook methods collectively impose a uniform interface between the ACE Service Configurator framework and the application-defined services that it manages.

Application services that inherit from ACE_Service_Object can selectively override its hook methods, which are called back at the appropriate time by the ACE Service Configurator framework in response to specific events. For example, a service object's init() hook method is called when the Service Configurator framework executes a directive to activate the service (both the dynamic and static directives activate a service, as shown on page 141). The init() hook method must return 0 if initialization succeeds and −1 if it fails. If (and only if) init() succeeds, the corresponding fini() method will be called on the service object when the ACE Service Configurator framework executes the remove directive for the service, or shuts down all services.

The Service Configurator is the first ACE framework we've studied that has extensive interaction with administrators or applications. These interactions introduce the need to operate with local character sets. Figure 5.2 shows the ACE_TCHAR type, which helps ACE deal with non-ASCII character sets portably. ACE's facilities for handling wide-character and Unicode characters are described in Sidebar 28. We'll use this facility to handle character strings in the remainder of this book.

Example

To illustrate the ACE_Service_Object class, we reimplement our reactive logging server from the *Example* portion of Section 3.5. This revision can be configured dynamically by the ACE Service Configurator framework, rather than configured statically into the main() program shown on page 84. To accomplish this, we'll apply the Adapter pat-

Sidebar 28: How ACE Deals with Narrow and Wide Characters

Developers outside the United States are acutely aware that many character sets in use today require more than one byte, or octet, to represent each character. Characters that require more than one octet are referred to as "wide characters." The most popular multiple octet standard is ISO/IEC 10646, the Universal Multiple-Octet Coded Character Set (UCS). Unicode is a separate standard, but is essentially a restricted subset of UCS that uses two octets for each character (UCS-2). Many Windows programmers are familiar with Unicode.

C++ represents wide characters with the `wchar_t` type, which enables methods to offer multiple signatures that are differentiated by their character type. Wide characters have a separate set of C string manipulation functions, however, and existing C++ code, such as string literals, requires change for wide-character usage. As a result, programming applications to use wide-character strings can become expensive, especially when applications written initially for U.S. markets must be internationalized for other countries. To improve portability and ease of use, ACE uses C++ method overloading and the macros described below to use different character types without changing APIs:

Macro	Usage
ACE_HAS_WCHAR	Configuration setting to build ACE with its wide-character methods
ACE_USES_WCHAR	Configuration setting that directs ACE to use wide characters internally
ACE_TCHAR	Defined as either `char` or `wchar_t`, to match ACE's internal character width
ACE_TEXT(str)	Defines the string literal `str` correctly based on ACE_USES_WCHAR
ACE_TEXT_CHAR_TO_TCHAR(str)	Converts a `char *` string to ACE_TCHAR format, if needed
ACE_TEXT_ALWAYS_CHAR(str)	Converts an ACE_TCHAR string to `char *` format, if needed

ACE must be built with the ACE_HAS_WCHAR configuration setting for applications to use wide characters. Moreover, ACE must be built with the ACE_USES_WCHAR setting if ACE should also use wide characters internally. The ACE_TCHAR and ACE_TEXT macros are illustrated in examples throughout this book.

ACE also supplies two string classes, ACE_CString and ACE_WString, which hold narrow and wide characters, respectively. These classes are analogous to the standard C++ `string` class, but can be configured to use custom memory allocators and are more portable. ACE_TString is a `typedef` for one of the two string types depending on the ACE_USES_WCHAR configuration setting.

tern [GoF] to create the following template class in the Reactor_Logging_Server_
Adapter.h header file:

```
template <class ACCEPTOR>
class Reactor_Logging_Server_Adapter : public ACE_Service_Object {
public:
  // Hook methods inherited from <ACE_Service_Object>.
  virtual int init (int argc, ACE_TCHAR *argv[]);
  virtual int fini ();
  virtual int info (ACE_TCHAR **, size_t) const;
  virtual int suspend ();
  virtual int resume ();

private:
  Reactor_Logging_Server<ACCEPTOR> *server_;
};
```

This template inherits from the ACE_Service_Object class and contains a pointer to
a Reactor_Logging_Server object (page 83). We instantiated this template with the
ACCEPTOR class parameter to defer our choice of the acceptor factory until later in the
design cycle. The Adapter pattern is a good choice here because it allows reuse of our
existing Reactor_Logging_Server class. If we were designing this example from
scratch with the ability to be configured as a service, however, a more direct approach would
be to derive Reactor_Logging_Server from ACE_Service_Object instead of
from ACE_Event_Handler. In that case, the adapter class would not be needed, and we
could still defer the choice of the acceptor factory until later.

   Figure 5.3 illustrates the lifecycle of the objects in this example when an instance of
Reactor_Logging_Server_Adapter is configured dynamically. When this service
is configured into the address space of an application, the ACE Service Configurator framework creates an instance of Reactor_Logging_Server_Adapter and invokes the
following init() hook method automatically:

```
 1 template <class ACCEPTOR> int
 2 Reactor_Logging_Server_Adapter<ACCEPTOR>::init
 3   (int argc, ACE_TCHAR *argv[])
 4 {
 5   int i;
 6   char **array = 0;
 7   ACE_NEW_RETURN (array, char*[argc], -1);
 8   ACE_Auto_Array_Ptr<char *> char_argv (array);
 9
10   for (i = 0; i < argc; ++i)
11     char_argv[i] = ACE::strnew (ACE_TEXT_ALWAYS_CHAR(argv[i]));
```

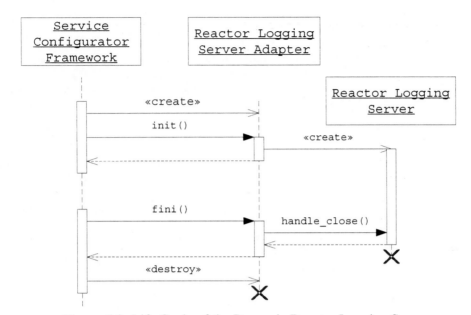

Figure 5.3: Life Cycle of the Dynamic Reactor Logging Server

```
12   ACE_NEW_NORETURN (server_, Reactor_Logging_Server<ACCEPTOR>
13                                (i, char_argv.get (),
14                                ACE_Reactor::instance ())));
15   for (i = 0; i < argc; ++i) ACE::strdelete (char_argv[i]);
16   return server_ == 0 ? -1 : 0;
17 }
```

Lines 5–11   The ACE Service Configurator framework passes `argv` as an array of `ACE_`
`TCHAR` pointers, but the `Reactor_Logging_Server` constructor accepts a `char *`
array. The `init()` method therefore uses the `ACE_TEXT_ALWAYS_CHAR` macro to convert to the `char` format where needed. This macro creates a temporary object with the
transformed string, which is then copied via `ACE::strnew()` to preserve it through the
`Reactor_Logging_Server` constructor. Sidebar 29 (page 125) describes the `ACE::`
`strnew()` and `ACE::strdelete()` methods.

Lines 12–14   Dynamically allocate an instance of the `Reactor_Logging_Server`
that contains the desired reactor, acceptor, and handlers.

Line 15   Free the memory used for the converted `argv` strings.

When instructed to remove the dynamically configured logging service, the ACE Service Configurator framework invokes the `Reactor_Logging_Server_Adapter::`
`fini()` hook method shown below:

```
template <class ACCEPTOR> int
Reactor_Logging_Server_Adapter<ACCEPTOR>::fini ()
{ server_->handle_close (); server_ = 0; return 0; }
```

This method calls `Reactor_Logging_Server::handle_close()`, which deletes the `Reactor_Logging_Server` object allocated by `init()`. The ACE Service Configurator framework uses the "gobbler" function (page 137) to delete a service object after calling its `fini()` hook method. We therefore must not call `delete this` in `fini()`.

The `info()` hook method reports service-specific information when the framework requests it. Our `info()` method formats a string containing the TCP port it's listening on:

```
 1 template <class ACCEPTOR> int
 2 Reactor_Logging_Server_Adapter<ACCEPTOR>::info
 3     (ACE_TCHAR **bufferp, size_t length) const {
 4   ACE_TYPENAME ACCEPTOR::PEER_ADDR local_addr;
 5   server_->acceptor ().get_local_addr (local_addr);
 6
 7   ACE_TCHAR buf[BUFSIZ];
 8   ACE_OS::sprintf (buf,
 9                     ACE_TEXT ("%hu"),
10                     local_addr.get_port_number ());
11   ACE_OS_String::strcat
12     (buf, ACE_TEXT ("/tcp # Reactive logging server\n"));
13   if (*bufferp == 0) *bufferp = ACE::strnew (buf);
14   else ACE_OS_String::strncpy (*bufferp, buf, length);
15   return ACE_OS_String::strlen (*bufferp);
16 }
```

Lines 4–5 Obtain the network address from the instance of `ACE_SOCK_Acceptor` that's used by the `Reactor_Logging_Server`.

Lines 7–12 Format a message that explains what the service does and how to contact it.

Line 13 If the caller didn't supply a buffer to hold the formatted message, allocate a buffer and copy the message into it using `ACE::strnew()`. In this case, the caller must use `ACE::strdelete()` to free the buffer. ACE does not specify how an implementation of `info()` must allocate memory. Developers writing an implementation of `info()` must therefore define and clearly document the policy for their implementations. It's strongly recommended that developers use `ACE::strnew()` to allocate the string, and require their users to call `ACE::strdelete()` to free the memory. Sidebar 29 describes the motivation for these methods.

Line 14 If the caller did supply a buffer for the message, copy the formatted message into it, limited to the `length` passed by the caller.

Line 15 Return the length of the message.

Sidebar 29: Portable Heap Operations with ACE

Library functions and classes, such as `Reactor_Logging_Server_Adapter::info()` (page 124), often allocate memory dynamically. Memory allocated dynamically in C++ programs should eventually be freed. To write portable C++ programs, it's important to match these allocate and free operations to avoid corrupting the heap (also known as the freestore).

A surprisingly common misconception is that simply ensuring the proper matching of calls to `operator new()` and `operator delete()` (or calls to `malloc()` and `free()`) is sufficient for correct heap management. This strategy relies on the implicit assumption that there's one universal heap per process. In practice, however, a heap is simply a memory area managed by some run-time component, such as the C or C++ run-time library. If an executing program is exposed to multiple run-time library instances, it's likely there will be multiple heaps as well.

For example, Windows supplies multiple variants of the C/C++ run-time library, such as Debug versus Release and Multithreaded versus Single-threaded. Each of these variants maintains its own heap. Memory allocated from one heap *must* be released back to the same heap. Thus, correct heap management requires not only matching the proper method/function calls, but also making them through the same run-time library. It's easy to violate these requirements when code from one subsystem or provider frees memory allocated by another.

To assist in managing dynamic memory portably, ACE offers matching allocate and free methods listed in the table below:

Method	Usage
`ACE::strnew()`	Allocates memory for a copy of a character string and copies the string into it.
`ACE::strdelete()`	Releases memory allocated by `strnew()`.
`ACE_OS_Memory::malloc()`	Allocates a memory block of specified size.
`ACE_OS_Memory::calloc()`	Allocates a memory block to hold a specified number of objects, each of a given size. The memory contents are explicitly initialized to 0.
`ACE_OS_Memory::realloc()`	Changes the size of a memory block allocated via `ACE_OS_Memory::malloc()`.
`ACE_OS_Memory::free()`	Releases memory allocated via any of the above three `ACE_OS_Memory` methods.

As long as developers match the correct ACE allocation and deallocation methods, ACE ensures the correct run-time library functions will be called on the correct heaps on all platforms. For complete details on these methods, see the online ACE reference documentation at `http://ace.ece.uci.edu/Doxygen/` and `http://www.riverace.com/docs/`.

Unlike the other `ACE_Service_Object` hook methods shown in Figure 5.2 (page 120), an `info()` method isn't always invoked by the ACE Service Configurator framework, though it can be. Instead, it's often called directly by a server program, as shown in the `Service_Reporter::handle_input()` method (page 133). Moreover, application developers can determine the most useful content of the message since `info()` doesn't mandate a particular format.

The `suspend()` and `resume()` hook methods are similar to each other:

```
template <class ACCEPTOR> int
Reactor_Logging_Server_Adapter<ACCEPTOR>::suspend ()
{ return server_->reactor ()->suspend_handler (server_); }

template <class ACCEPTOR> int
Reactor_Logging_Server_Adapter<ACCEPTOR>::resume ()
{ return server_->reactor ()->resume_handler (server_); }
```

Since the `Reactor_Logging_Server` class descends from `ACE_Event_Handler`, the `server_` object can be passed to the singleton reactor's `suspend_handler()` and `resume_handler()` methods (page 73). Both methods *double-dispatch* to `Reactor_Logging_Server::get_handle()` to extract the underlying passive-mode socket handle. This socket handle is then temporarily removed from or replaced in the list of socket handles handled by the singleton reactor. The *Example* portion of Section 5.4 shows how the `Reactor_Logging_Server_Adapter` can be configured into and out of a generic server application dynamically.

5.3 The ACE_Service_Repository Classes

Motivation

The ACE Service Configurator framework supports the configuration of both single-service and multiservice servers. Section 5.2 explained why the goals of initialization, execution control, reporting, and termination require application services to be based on a common framework class. For the framework to leverage the accessibility provided by `ACE_Service_Object` effectively, it must store service information in a well-known repository and be able to access and control these service objects individually or collectively.

Application services in multiservice servers also may require access to each other. To avoid tightly coupling these services, and to preserve the benefits of delayed configuration decisions, services should be able to locate each other at run time. Therefore, to satisfy the needs of the framework and applications *without* requiring developers to provide these capabilities in an *ad hoc* way, the ACE Service Configurator framework provides the `ACE_Service_Repository` and `ACE_Service_Repository_Iterator` classes.

Class Capabilities

`ACE_Service_Repository` implements the *Manager pattern* [Som98] to control the life cycle of, and the access to, service objects configured by the ACE Service Configurator framework. This class provides the following capabilities:

- It keeps track of all service implementations that are configured into an application and maintains each service's status, such as whether it's active or suspended.
- It provides the mechanism by which the ACE Service Configurator framework inserts, manages, and removes services.
- It provides a convenient mechanism to terminate all services, in reverse order of their initialization.
- It allows an individual service to be located by its name.

The interface for `ACE_Service_Repository` is shown in Figure 5.4 (page 128) and its key methods are outlined in the following table:

Method	Description
`ACE_Service_Repository()` `open()`	Initialize the repository and allocate its dynamic resources.
`~ACE_Service_Repository()` `close()`	Close down the repository and release its dynamically allocated resources.
`insert()`	Add a new service into the repository.
`find()`	Locate an entry in the repository.
`remove()`	Remove an existing service from the repository.
`suspend()`	Suspend a service in the repository.
`resume()`	Resume a suspended service in the repository.
`instance()`	A static method that returns a pointer to a singleton `ACE_Service_Repository`.

The `ACE_Service_Repository` binds the following entities together:
- The name of a service, which is represented as a character string, and
- An instance of `ACE_Service_Type`, which is the class used by the ACE Service Configurator framework to link, initialize, suspend, resume, remove, and unlink services from a server statically or dynamically.

The `ACE_Service_Type` class provides the framework with the operations necessary to act on the configured services. The ACE Service Configurator framework can be used to configure dynamic and static services, as well as the `ACE_Module` and `ACE_Stream` capabilities covered in Sections 9.2 and 9.3, respectively.

The `ACE_Service_Type` class uses the Bridge pattern to allow type-specific data and behavior in service types to evolve without impacting the class. The `ACE_Service_Type` class plays the *Abstraction* role in this pattern and the `ACE_Service_Type_Impl` class plays the *Implementor* role. The following classes each play the *ConcreteImplementor* role, representing the types of services that can be recorded in the service repository:

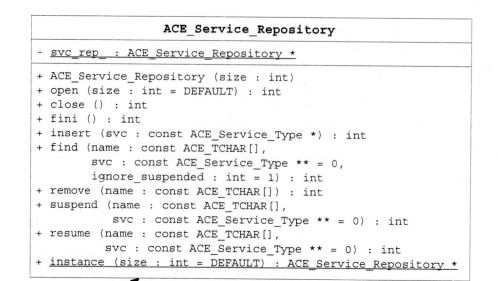

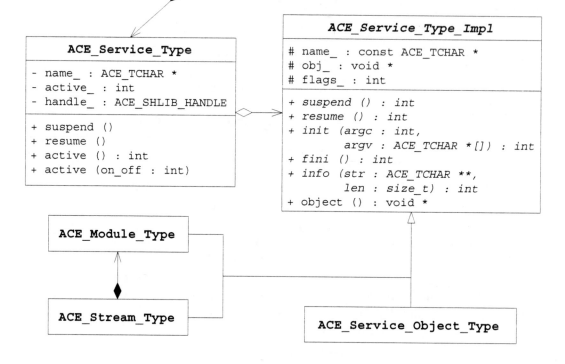

Figure 5.4: The ACE_Service_Repository Class

1. ACE_Service_Object_Type—The object() method returns a pointer to the associated ACE_Service_Object described in Section 5.2.
2. ACE_Module_Type—The object() method returns a pointer to the associated ACE_Module described in Section 9.2.
3. ACE_Stream_Type—The object() method returns a pointer to the associated ACE_Stream described in Section 9.3.

For dynamically linked service objects, ACE_Service_Type also stores the handle of the DLL that contains the service's executable code. The ACE Service Configurator framework uses this handle to unlink and unload a service object from a running server when the service it offers is no longer needed. Sidebar 30 (page 131) shows how a program can use ACE_Dynamic_Service and ACE_Service_Type to retrieve services from ACE_Service_Repository programmatically.

ACE_Service_Repository_Iterator implements the Iterator pattern [GoF] to provide applications with a way to sequentially access the ACE_Service_Type items in an ACE_Service_Repository without exposing its internal representation. The interface for ACE_Service_Repository_Iterator is shown in Figure 5.5 (page 130) and its key methods are outlined in the following table:

Method	Description
ACE_Service_Repository_Iterator()	Initialize the iterator.
next()	Pass back a pointer to the next ACE_Service_Type in the repository.
done()	Returns 1 when all items have been seen.
advance()	Move ahead one item in the repository.

Never delete entries from an ACE_Service_Repository that's being iterated over since the ACE_Service_Repository_Iterator is not a *robust iterator* [Kof93].

Example

This example illustrates how the ACE_Service_Repository and ACE_Service_Repository_Iterator classes can be used to implement a Service_Reporter class. This class provides a "meta-service" that clients can use to obtain information on all services that the ACE Service Configurator framework has configured into an application statically or dynamically. A client interacts with a Service_Reporter as follows:

- The client establishes a TCP connection to the Service_Reporter object.
- The Service_Reporter returns a list of all the server's services to the client.
- The Service_Reporter closes the TCP/IP connection.

Sidebar 31 (page 132) describes ACE_Service_Manager, which is a class bundled with the ACE toolkit that provides a superset of Service_Reporter features.

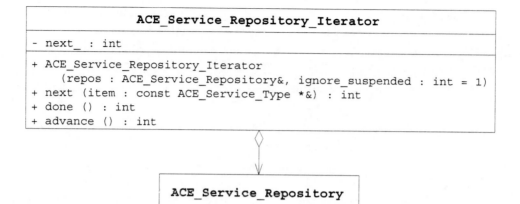

Figure 5.5: The ACE_Service_Repository_Iterator Class

The Service_Reporter class is described below. We first create a file called
Service_Reporter.h that contains the following class definition:

```
class Service_Reporter : public ACE_Service_Object {
public:
  Service_Reporter (ACE_Reactor *r = ACE_Reactor::instance ())
    : ACE_Service_Object (r) {}

  // Hook methods inherited from <ACE_Service_Object>.
  virtual int init (int argc, ACE_TCHAR *argv[]);
  virtual int fini ();
  virtual int info (ACE_TCHAR **, size_t) const;
  virtual int suspend ();
  virtual int resume ();

protected:
  // Reactor hook methods.
  virtual int handle_input (ACE_HANDLE);
  virtual ACE_HANDLE get_handle () const
  { return acceptor_.get_handle (); }

private:
  ACE_SOCK_Acceptor acceptor_; // Acceptor instance.
  enum { DEFAULT_PORT = 9411 };
};
```

Since Service_Reporter inherits from ACE_Service_Object, it can be configured by the ACE Service Configurator framework. The ACE Service Configurator framework will create an instance of this class at run time, so the constructor must be public.

Sidebar 30: The ACE_Dynamic_Service Template

The ACE_Dynamic_Service class template provides a type-safe way to access the ACE_Service_Repository programmatically. An application process can use this template to retrieve services registered with its local ACE_Service_Repository. As shown below, the TYPE template parameter ensures that a pointer to the appropriate type of service is returned from the static instance() method:

```
template <class TYPE>
class ACE_Dynamic_Service {
public:
  // Use <name> to search the <ACE_Service_Repository>.
  static TYPE *instance (const ACE_TCHAR *name) {
    const ACE_Service_Type *svc_rec;
    if (ACE_Service_Repository::instance ()->find
          (name, &svc_rec) == -1) return 0;
    const ACE_Service_Type_Impl *type = svc_rec->type ();
    if (type == 0) return 0;
    ACE_Service_Object *obj =
      ACE_static_cast (ACE_Service_Object *, type->object ());
    return ACE_dynamic_cast (TYPE *, obj);
  }
};
```

If an instance of the Server_Logging_Daemon service has been linked dynamically and initialized by the ACE Service Configurator framework, an application can use the ACE_Dynamic_Service template to access the service programmatically as shown below:

```
typedef Reactor_Logging_Server_Adapter<Logging_Acceptor>
        Server_Logging_Daemon;

Server_Logging_Daemon *logging_server =
  ACE_Dynamic_Service<Server_Logging_Daemon>::instance
    (ACE_TEXT ("Server_Logging_Daemon"));

ACE_TCHAR *service_info = 0;
logging_server->info (&service_info);
ACE_DEBUG ((LM_DEBUG, "%s\n", service_info));
ACE::strdelete (service_info);
```

Note that this example assumes info() allocates string memory via the ACE:: strnew() method discussed in Sidebar 29 (page 125).

Sidebar 31: The ACE_Service_Manager Class

ACE_Service_Manager provides clients with access to administrative commands to access and manage the services currently offered by a network server. These commands "externalize" certain internal attributes of the services configured into a server. During server configuration, an ACE_Service_Manager is typically registered at a well-known communication port, for example, port 9411. Clients can connect to an ACE_Service_Manager at that port and issue one of the following commands.

- help—a list of all services configured into an application via the ACE Service Configurator framework is returned to the client.
- reconfigure—a reconfiguration is triggered to reread the local service configuration file.

If a client sends anything other than these two commands, its input is passed to ACE_Service_Config::process_directive() (page 141), which enables remote configuration of servers via command-line instructions such as

```
% echo "suspend My_Service" | telnet hostname 9411
```

It's therefore important to use the ACE_Service_Manager only if your application runs in a trusted environment since a malicious attacker can use it to deny access to legitimate services or configure rogue services in a Trojan Horse manner. For this reason, ACE_Service_Manager is a static service that ACE disables by default.

An application can direct ACE to load its static services, including the ACE_Service_Manager, with the ACE_Service_Config::open() method (page 141) in either of two ways:

1. At compile time, by passing a 0 for the ignore_static_svcs argument
2. At run time, by including the '-y' option with the argc/argv pair; this overrides the ignore_static_svcs value.

The implementations of the Service_Reporter hook methods are placed into the Service_Reporter.cpp file. The ACE Service Configurator framework calls the following Service_Reporter::init() hook method when a Service_Reporter is configured into an application:

```
1  int Service_Reporter::init (int argc, ACE_TCHAR *argv[]) {
2    ACE_INET_Addr local_addr (Service_Reporter::DEFAULT_PORT);
3    ACE_Get_Opt get_opt (argc, argv, ACE_TEXT ("p:"), 0);
4    get_opt.long_option (ACE_TEXT ("port"),
5                         'p', ACE_Get_Opt::ARG_REQUIRED);
6    for (int c; (c = get_opt ()) != -1;)
7      if (c == 'p') local_addr.set_port_number
8                    (ACE_OS::atoi (get_opt.opt_arg ()));
9    acceptor_.open (local_addr);
10   return reactor ()->register_handler
```

```
11              (this,
12               ACE_Event_Handler::ACCEPT_MASK);
13 }
```

Line 2   Initialize `local_addr` to the `Service_Reporter`'s default TCP port number.

Lines 3–8   Parse the service configuration options using the `ACE_Get_Opt` class described in Sidebar 8 (page 47). We start parsing at `argv[0]` rather than `argv[1]`, which is the default. If the `-p`, or the long version `--port`, option is passed into `init()`, the `local_addr` port number is reset to that value. Since `ACE_Get_Opt` always returns the corresponding short option for any long options it encounters, it's sufficient to test only for `'p'` in the loop iterator.

Lines 9–12   Initialize the `ACE_SOCK_Acceptor` to listen on the `local_addr` port number and register the instance of `Service_Reporter` with the reactor for ACCEPT events. When a connection request arrives from a client, the reactor dispatches the following `Service_Reporter::handle_input()` hook method:

```
 1 int Service_Reporter::handle_input (ACE_HANDLE) {
 2   ACE_SOCK_Stream peer_stream;
 3   acceptor_.accept (peer_stream);
 4
 5   ACE_Service_Repository_Iterator iterator
 6     (*ACE_Service_Repository::instance (), 0);
 7
 8   for (const ACE_Service_Type *st;
 9        iterator.next (st) != 0;
10        iterator.advance ()) {
11     iovec iov[3];
12     iov[0].iov_base = ACE_const_cast (char *, st->name ());
13     iov[0].iov_len =
14       ACE_OS_String::strlen (st->name ()) * sizeof (ACE_TCHAR);
15     const ACE_TCHAR *state = st->active () ?
16           ACE_TEXT (" (active) ") : ACE_TEXT (" (paused) ");
17     iov[1].iov_base = ACE_const_cast (char *, state);
18     iov[1].iov_len =
19       ACE_OS_String::strlen (state) * sizeof (ACE_TCHAR);
20     ACE_TCHAR *report = 0;    // Ask info() to allocate buffer.
21     int len = st->type ()->info (&report, 0);
22     iov[2].iov_base = ACE_static_cast (char *, report);
23     iov[2].iov_len = ACE_static_cast (size_t, len);
24     iov[2].iov_len *= sizeof (ACE_TCHAR);
25     peer_stream.sendv_n (iov, 3);
26     ACE::strdelete (report);
27   }
```

```
28
29   peer_stream.close ();
30   return 0;
31 }
```

Lines 2–3   Accept a new client connection. The `Service_Reporter` is an iterative service that only handles one client at a time.

Lines 5–6   Initialize an `ACE_Service_Repository_Iterator`, which we'll use to report all the active and suspended services offered by the server. Passing a 0 as the second argument to this constructor instructs it to also return information on suspended services, which are ignored by default.

Lines 8–27   For each service, invoke its `info()` method to obtain a descriptive synopsis of the service, and send this information back to the client via the connected socket. The `sendv_n()` gather-write method transfers all data buffers in the array of `iovec` structures efficiently using a single system function call, as discussed by Sidebar 6 in Chapter 3 of C++NPv1. Since there are no record boundaries in a TCP stream, the client may not be able to find the end of each line of text. It's therefore polite to code `info()` methods to include a newline at the end of the message. Note that this code can work with either narrow or wide characters, as discussed in Sidebar 28 (page 121). The text received by the client will be in the character set and width of the `Service_Reporter`. Designing a mechanism to handle this properly is left as an exercise for the reader.

Line 29   Close down the connection to the client and release the socket handle.

The `Service_Reporter::info()` hook method passes back a string that tells which TCP port number it's listening on and what the service does:

```
int Service_Reporter::info (ACE_TCHAR **bufferp,
                               size_t length) const {
  ACE_INET_Addr local_addr;
  acceptor_.get_local_addr (local_addr);

  ACE_TCHAR buf[BUFSIZ];
  ACE_OS::sprintf
    (buf, ACE_TEXT ("%hu"), local_addr.get_port_number ());
  ACE_OS_String::strcat
    (buf, ACE_TEXT ("/tcp # lists services in daemon\n"));
  if (*bufferp == 0) *bufferp = ACE::strnew (buf);
  else ACE_OS_String::strncpy (*bufferp, buf, length);
  return ACE_OS_String::strlen (*bufferp);
}
```

As with the `Reactor_Logging_Server_Adapter::info()` method (page 124), the caller must delete the dynamically allocated buffer using `ACE::strdelete()`.

The `Service_Reporter`'s `suspend ()` and `resume ()` hook methods forward to the corresponding methods in the reactor singleton, as follows:

```
int Service_Reporter::suspend ()
{ return reactor ()->suspend_handler (this); }

int Service_Reporter::resume ()
{ return reactor ()->resume_handler (this); }
```

The `Service_Reporter::fini ()` method is shown below:

```
int Service_Reporter::fini () {
  reactor ()->remove_handler
    (this,
     ACE_Event_Handler::ACCEPT_MASK
     | ACE_Event_Handler::DONT_CALL);
  return acceptor_.close ();
}
```

This method closes the `ACE_SOCK_Acceptor` endpoint and removes the `Service_Reporter` from the singleton reactor. The ACE Service Configurator framework is responsible for deleting a service object after calling its `fini ()` hook method. We therefore don't need to `delete this` object in `handle_close ()`, so we pass the DONT_CALL flag to prevent the reactor from invoking this callback.

Finally, we must supply the ACE Service Configurator framework with some "book-keeping" information regarding this new service. Although the code for this service will be statically linked into the example program, we want the framework to instantiate a `Service_Reporter` object to execute the service when it's activated. We therefore add the necessary ACE service macros to the `Service_Reporter` implementation file. These macros create a `Service_Reporter` and register it with the `ACE_Service_Repository`, as described in Sidebar 32 (page 136).

```
 1 ACE_FACTORY_DEFINE (ACE_Local_Service, Service_Reporter)
 2
 3 ACE_STATIC_SVC_DEFINE (
 4   Reporter_Descriptor,
 5   ACE_TEXT ("Service_Reporter"),
 6   ACE_SVC_OBJ_T,
 7   &ACE_SVC_NAME (Service_Reporter),
 8   ACE_Service_Type::DELETE_THIS
 9   | ACE_Service_Type::DELETE_OBJ,
10   0 // This object is not initially active.
11 )
12
13 ACE_STATIC_SVC_REQUIRE (Reporter_Descriptor)
```

Sidebar 32: The ACE Service Factory Macros

Applications can use the following macros defined in `ace/OS.h` to simplify the creation and use of factory functions and static service registration. With the exception of `ACE_STATIC_SVC_REGISTER`, these macros should be used at file scope, rather than in a namespace, class, or method.

Factory and gobbler function macros. Static and dynamic services must supply a factory function to create the service object and a "gobbler" function to delete it. ACE provides the following three macros to help generate and use these functions:

- `ACE_FACTORY_DEFINE(LIB, CLASS)`—Used in an implementation file to define the factory and gobbler functions for a service. `LIB` is the ACE export macro prefix (see Sidebar 37 on page 150) used with the library containing the factory function. It can be `ACE_Local_Service` if the function needn't be exported from a DLL. `CLASS` is the type of service object the factory must create.

- `ACE_FACTORY_DECLARE(LIB, CLASS)`—Declares the factory function defined by the `ACE_FACTORY_DEFINE` macro. Use this macro to generate a reference to the factory function from a compilation unit other than the one containing the `ACE_FACTORY_DEFINE` macro.

- `ACE_SVC_NAME(CLASS)`—Generates the name of the factory function defined via the `ACE_FACTORY_DEFINE` macro. The generated name can be used to get the function address at compile time, such as for the `ACE_STATIC_SVC_DEFINE` macro, below.

Static service information macro. ACE provides the following macro to generate static service registration information. It defines the service name, type, and a pointer to the factory function the framework calls to create a service instance:

- `ACE_STATIC_SVC_DEFINE(REG, NAME, TYPE, FUNC_ADDR, FLAGS, ACTIVE)`—Used in an implementation file to define static service information. `REG` forms the name of the information object, which must match the parameter passed to `ACE_STATIC_SVC_REQUIRE` and `ACE_STATIC_SVC_REGISTER`. Other parameters set `ACE_Static_Svc_Descriptor` attributes.

Static service registration macros. The static service registration information must be passed to the ACE Service Configurator framework at program startup. The following two macros cooperate to perform this registration:

- `ACE_STATIC_SVC_REQUIRE(REG)`—Used in the service implementation file to define a static object whose constructor will add the static service registration information to the framework's list of known static services.

- `ACE_STATIC_SVC_REGISTER(REG)`—Used at the start of the main program to ensure the object defined in `ACE_STATIC_SVC_REQUIRE` registers the static service no later than the point this macro appears.

Line 1   The ACE_FACTORY_DEFINE macro generates the following functions:

```
void _gobble_Service_Reporter (void *arg) {
  ACE_Service_Object *svcobj =
    ACE_static_cast (ACE_Service_Object *, arg);
  delete svcobj;
}

extern "C" ACE_Service_Object *
_make_Service_Reporter (void (**gobbler) (void *)) {
  if (gobbler != 0) *gobbler = _gobble_Service_Reporter;
  return new Service_Reporter;
}
```

The ACE_FACTORY_DEFINE macro simplifies the use of the ACE Service Configurator framework as follows:

- **It generates compiler-independent factory functions.** This macro generates the _make_Service_Reporter() factory function with extern "C" linkage, allowing the framework to locate this function in a DLL's symbol table without knowing the C++ compiler's *name-mangling* scheme.
- **It manages dynamic memory consistently.** To ensure correct behavior across platforms, it's important that memory allocated in a DLL be deallocated in the same DLL, as described in Sidebar 29 (page 125). The gobbler function passed to _make_Service_Reporter() therefore enables the ACE Service Configurator framework to ensure memory is allocated and deleted within the same heap.

Lines 3–11   The ACE_STATIC_SVC_DEFINE macro is used to initialize an instance of ACE_ Static_Svc_Descriptor. This object stores the information needed to describe the statically configured service reporter service. Service_Reporter is the service object's class name and "Service_Reporter" is the name used to identify the service in the ACE_Service_Repository. ACE_SVC_OBJ_T is the type of the service object container. We use the ACE_SVC_NAME macro in conjunction with the C++ "address-of" operator to obtain the address of the _make_Service_Reporter() factory function that creates an instance of Service_Reporter. DELETE_THIS and DELETE_OBJ are enumerated literals defined in the ACE_Service_Types class that effect processing after the service's fini() hook method is called, as follows:

- DELETE_THIS directs ACE to delete the ACE_Service_Object_Type object representing the service and
- DELETE_OBJ causes the gobbler function to be called so the Service_Reporter object can be cleaned up.

Line 13   The ACE_STATIC_SVC_REQUIRE macro defines an object that registers the instance of the Service_Reporter's ACE_Static_Svc_Descriptor object with the ACE_Service_Repository. On many platforms, this macro also ensures the object is instantiated. Some platforms, however, also require the ACE_STATIC_SVC_REGISTER macro in the main() function of the program this service is linked into.

The *Example* portion of Section 5.4 shows how a Service_Reporter can be configured statically into a server application.

5.4   The ACE_Service_Config Class

Motivation

Before a service can execute, it must be configured into an application's address space. One way to configure services into a networked application is to statically link the functionality provided by its various classes and functions into separate OS processes, and then manually instantiate or initialize them at run time. We used this approach in the logging server examples in Chapters 3 and 4 and throughout C++NPv1, where the logging server program runs in a process that handles log records from client applications. Although our use of the ACE Reactor framework in earlier chapters improved the networked logging server's modularity and portability, the following drawbacks arose from statically configuring the Reactor_Logging_Server class with its main() program:

- **Service configuration decisions are made prematurely in the development cycle,** which is undesirable if developers don't know the best way to collocate or distribute services in advance. Moreover, the "best" configuration may change as the computing context changes. For example, an application may write log records to a local file when it's running on a disconnected laptop computer. When the laptop is connected to a LAN, however, it may forward log records to a centralized logging server. Forcing networked applications to commit prematurely to a particular service configuration impedes their flexibility and can reduce their performance and functionality. It can also force costly redesign and reimplementation later in a project's life cycle.

- **Modifying a service may affect other services adversely** if the implementation of a service is coupled tightly with its initial configuration. To enhance reuse, for example, a logging server may initially reside in the same program as other services, such as a name service. If the other services change, however, for example if the name service lookup algorithm changes, all existing code in the server would require modification, recompilation, and static relinking. Moreover, terminating a running process to change some of its service code would also terminate the collocated logging service. This disruption in service may not be acceptable for highly available systems, such as telecommunication switches or customer care call centers [SS94].

- **System performance may scale poorly** since associating a separate process with each service ties up OS resources, such as I/O handles, virtual memory, and process table slots. This design is particularly wasteful if services are often idle. Moreover, processes can be inefficient for many short-lived communication tasks, such as asking a time service for the current time or resolving a host address request via the Domain Name Service (DNS).

To address the drawbacks of purely static configurations, the ACE Service Configurator framework defines the `ACE_Service_Config` class.

Class Capabilities

`ACE_Service_Config` implements the Facade pattern [GoF] to integrate other classes in the ACE Service Configurator framework and coordinate the activities necessary to manage the services in an application. This class provides the following capabilities:

- It interprets a scripting language that allows applications or administrators to provide the ACE Service Configurator framework with commands, called *directives*, to locate and initialize a service's implementation at run time, as well as to suspend, resume, reinitialize, and/or shut down a component after it's been initialized. Directives can be specified to `ACE_Service_Config` in either of two ways:

  1. Using configuration files (named `svc.conf` by default) that contain one or more directives

  2. Programmatically, by passing individual directives as strings

- It supports the management of services located in the application (the so-called *static services*), as well as those that must be linked dynamically (the so-called *dynamic services*) from separate shared libraries (DLLs).

- It allows service reconfiguration at run time using the following mechanisms:

  1. On POSIX platforms, `ACE_Service_Config` can be integrated with the ACE Reactor framework to reprocess its configuration files upon receipt of a SIGHUP signal or any other user-specified signal, such as SIGINT.

  2. By passing the `"reconfigure"` command via `ACE_Service_Manager`, as described in Sidebar 31 (page 132).

  3. An application can request its `ACE_Service_Config` to reprocess its configuration files at any time. For example, a Windows directory change notification event can be used to help a program learn when its configuration file changes. This change event can then trigger reprocessing of the configuration.

  4. An application can also specify individual directives for its `ACE_Service_Config` to process at any time via the `process_directive()` method.

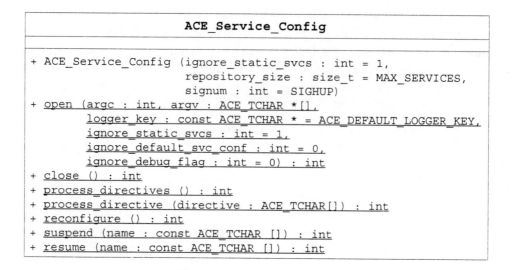

Figure 5.6: The ACE_Service_Config Class

The interface for ACE_Service_Config is shown in Figure 5.6. This class has a rich interface since it exports all the features in the ACE Service Configurator framework. We therefore group the description of its methods into the three categories described below.

1. Service Configurator life cycle management methods. The following methods initialize and shut down the ACE_Service_Config:

ACE Class	Description
ACE_Service_Config() open()	These methods create and initialize the ACE_Service_Config.
close()	This method shuts down and finalizes all the configured services and deletes the resources allocated when the ACE_Service_Config was initialized.

There's only one instance of ACE_Service_Config's state in a process. This class is a variant of the Monostate pattern [CB97], which ensures a unique state for its instances by declaring all data members to be static. Moreover, the ACE_Service_Config methods are also declared as static. The ACE_Service_Config constructor, however, is the only way to set the maximum size of the ACE_Service_Repository. It's also the only programmatic way to change the signal number that can be registered with the reactor to trigger reconfigurations. Instantiating an instance of ACE_Service_Config therefore simply sets these parameters for the underlying monostate object and does not create a separate configuration object. Thus, the ACE_Service_Config destructor is a no-op.

The open() method is the common way of initializing the ACE_Service_Config. It parses arguments passed in the argc and argv parameters, skipping the first parameter (argv[0]) since that's the name of the program. The options recognized by ACE_Service_Config are outlined in the following table:

Option	Description
'-b'	Turn the application process into a *daemon* (see Sidebar 5 on page 32).
'-d'	Display diagnostic information as directives are processed.
'-f'	Supply a file containing directives other than the default svc.conf file. This argument can be repeated to supply multiple configuration files.
'-n'	Don't process static directives, which eliminates the need to initialize the ACE_Service_Repository statically.
'-s'	Designate the signal to be used to cause the ACE_Service_Config to reprocess its configuration file. By default, SIGHUP is used.
'-S'	Supply a directive to the ACE_Service_Config directly. This argument can be repeated to process multiple directives.
'-y'	Process static directives, which requires the static initialization of the ACE_Service_Repository.

2. Service configuration methods. After parsing all its argc/argv arguments, the ACE_Service_Config::open() method calls one or both of the following methods to configure the application:

Method	Description
process_directives()	Process a sequence of directives that are stored in the designated script file(s). This method allows multiple directives to be stored persistently and processed iteratively in batch mode. Each service configuration directive in each configuration file is executed in the order they are specified.
process_directive()	Process a single directive passed as a string.This method allows directives to be created dynamically and processed interactively, such as via a GUI or a network connection.

The following table summarizes the service configuration directives that can be processed by these two ACE_Service_Config methods:

Directive	Description
dynamic	Dynamically link a service and initialize it by calling its init() hook method.
static	Call the init() hook method to initialize a service that was linked statically.
remove	Remove a service completely, that is, call its fini() hook method and unlink it from the application process when it's no longer used.
suspend	Call a service's suspend() hook method to pause it without removing it.
resume	Call a service's resume() hook method to continue processing a service that was suspended earlier.
stream	Initialize an ordered list of hierarchically related modules.

We describe the syntax and semantics for the tokens in each of these directives below.

- **Dynamically link and initialize a service:** dynamic *svc-name svc-type*
  DLL-name:factory_func() [*"argc/argv options"*]

  The dynamic directive instructs the ACE Service Configurator framework to dynamically link and initialize a service object. The *svc-name* is the name assigned to the service. The *svc-type* designates the type of the service, which can be a Service_Object *, Module *, or Stream *. *DLL-name* is the name of the dynamic link library that contains the *factory_func()* symbol. This symbol is the entry point for an extern "C" function that the ACE_Service_Config interpreter invokes to create an instance of a service. If the *svc-type* is Service_Object * then *factory_func()* must return a pointer to an object derived from ACE_Service_Object. The *factory_func()* symbol should have a leading underscore character since linkers add that character to externally visible symbols.

  DLL-name can be either a full pathname or a filename without a suffix. If it's a full pathname, the ACE_DLL::open() method described in Sidebar 33 is used to dynamically link the designated file into the application process. If it's a filename, however, ACE_DLL::open() uses ACE::ldfind() (also described in Sidebar 33) to locate the DLL and dynamically link it into the address space of the process via ACE_DLL::open(). The dynamic directive can be used portably across operating systems since ACE encapsulates these platform details.

  The *argc/argv options* are an optional list of parameters that can be supplied to initialize a service object via its init() hook method. The ACE Service Configurator framework uses the ACE_ARGV class described in Sidebar 35 (page 148) to separate the string into arguments and substitute the values of environment variables that are included in the string.

- **Initialize a statically linked service:** static *svc-name* [*"argc/argv options"*]

  Although ACE_Service_Config is commonly used to configure services dynamically, it can also be used to configure services statically via the static directive. The *svc-name* and optional *argc/argv options* are the same as those in the dynamic directive. The syntax is simpler, however, since the service object must already be linked into the executable program image statically. Thus, there's no need to either locate and link a DLL or call a factory function to create a service object. Static configuration trades flexibility for increased security, which may be useful for certain types of servers that must contain only trusted, statically linked services. Recall from Sidebar 31 (page 132) that static service loading is disabled by default. Static service loading must therefore be enabled explicitly to use them, or else the static directive will have no effect.

Sidebar 33: The ACE_DLL Class

Applications that link and unlink DLLs explicitly can encounter the following problems:

- **A nonuniform programming interface** that's even less portable than the Socket API described in Chapter 3 of C++NPv1
- **Unsafe types that invite errors and misuse** because the native OS DLL APIs return weakly typed handles that are passed to DLL functions, such as those used to locate symbols and unlink the DLL
- **Potential resource leaks,** since it's possible to forget to release DLL handles

To address these problems, ACE defines the ACE_DLL wrapper facade class to encapsulate explicit linking/unlinking functionality. This class eliminates the need for applications to use error-prone, weakly typed handles and also ensures that resources are released properly by its destructor. In addition, it uses the ACE::ldfind() method to locate DLLs via the following algorithms:

- **DLL filename expansion**—ACE::ldfind() determines the name of the DLL by adding the appropriate prefix and suffix. For example, it adds the lib prefix and .so suffix for Solaris and the .dll suffix for Windows.
- **DLL search path**—ACE::ldfind() will also search for the designated DLL using the platform's DLL search path environment variable. For example, it searches for DLLs using LD_LIBRARY_PATH on many UNIX systems and PATH on Windows.

The key methods in the ACE_DLL class are outlined in the following table.

ACE Class	Description
ACE_DLL() open()	Opens and dynamically links a designated DLL
~ACE_DLL() close()	Closes and optionally unlinks the DLL
symbol()	Returns a pointer to a function or object in the DLL
error()	Returns a string explaining which failure occurred

The interface of ACE_DLL is shown in the figure below.

```
                        ACE_DLL
    - handle_  : ACE_SHLIB_HANDLE

    + open (name : const ACE_TCHAR *,
            mode : int = ACE_DEFAULT_SHLIB_MODE,
            close_on_destruct : int = 1) : int
    + close () : int
    + symbol (name : const ACE_TCHAR *) : void *
    + error (void) : ACE_TCHAR *
```

- **Remove a service completely:** `remove` *svc-name*

  The `remove` directive causes the `ACE_Service_Config` interpreter to query the `ACE_Service_Repository` for the named service. If this service is located, the interpreter invokes its `fini()` hook method, which performs the activities needed to clean up resources when the service shuts down. If a service destruction function pointer is associated with the service object, it's called to destroy the service object itself (the `ACE_FACTORY_DEFINE` macro defines this function automatically). Finally, if the service was linked dynamically from a DLL, it's unlinked via the `ACE_DLL::close()` method. Since a DLL can be linked multiple times in a process, `ACE_DLL::close()` ensures that the DLL is only unlinked when it's no longer in use.

- **Suspend a service without removing it:** `suspend` *svc-name*

  The `suspend` directive causes the `ACE_Service_Config` interpreter to query the `ACE_Service_Repository` for the designated *svc-name* service. If this service is located, its `suspend()` hook method is invoked. A service can override this method to implement the appropriate actions needed to suspend its processing.

- **Resume a previously suspended service:** `resume` *svc-name*

  The `resume` directive causes the `ACE_Service_Config` interpreter to query the `ACE_Service_Repository` for the designated *svc-name* service. If this service is located, its `resume()` hook method is invoked. A service can override this method to implement the appropriate actions needed to resume its processing, which typically reverse the effects of the `suspend()` method.

- **Initialize an ordered list of hierarchically related modules:** `stream` *svc-name* '{' *module-list* '}'

  The `stream` directive causes the `ACE_Service_Config` interpreter to initialize an ordered list of hierarchically related modules. Each module consists of a pair of services that are interconnected and communicate by passing `ACE_Message_Block` objects. The implementation of the `stream` directive uses the ACE Streams framework described in Chapter 9.

The complete *Backus/Naur Format* (BNF) syntax for `svc.conf` files parsed by the `ACE_Service_Config` is shown in Figure 5.7. Sidebar 34 (page 146) describes how to specify `svc.conf` files using the optional XML syntax.

3. Utility methods. `ACE_Service_Config` defines the following utility methods:

Method	Description
`reconfigure()`	Reprocess the current configuration file(s).
`suspend()`	Suspend a service, identified by name.
`resume()`	Resume a suspended service, identified by name.

```
<svc-conf-entries> ::= <svc-conf-entries> <svc-conf-entry> | NULL
<svc-conf-entry>   ::= <dynamic> | <static> | <suspend> |
                      <resume> | <remove> | <stream>
<dynamic> ::= dynamic <svc-location> <parameters-opt>
<static> ::= static <svc-name> <parameters-opt>
<suspend> ::= suspend <svc-name>
<resume> ::= resume <svc-name>
<remove> ::= remove <svc-name>
<stream> ::= stream <streamdef> '{' <module-list> '}'
<streamdef> ::= <svc-name> | dynamic | static
<module-list> ::= <module-list> <module> | NULL
<module> ::= <dynamic> | <static> | <suspend> |
             <resume> | <remove>
<svc-location> ::= <svc-name> <svc-type> <svc-factory> <status>
<svc-type> ::= Service_Object '*' | Module '*' | Stream '*' | NULL
<svc-factory> ::= PATHNAME ':' FUNCTION '(' ')'
<svc-name> ::= STRING
<status> ::= active | inactive | NULL
<parameters-opt> ::= '"' STRING '"' | NULL
```

Figure 5.7: BNF for the ACE_Service_Config Scripting Language

The reconfigure() method can be used to force the ACE_Service_Config interpreter to reprocess the service configuration files. This capability is useful if your application monitors the service configuration files for changes. When changes are noticed, they can be processed using the reconfigure() method. This method is the recommended way to make run-time changes on Windows since there's no equivalent to the common UNIX practice of sending a signal, such as SIGHUP, to a process.

The suspend() and resume() methods enable the suspension and resumption of a service if its name is known. It's a shortcut to the methods defined in the ACE_Service_Repository singleton.

Example

This example shows how to apply the ACE Service Configurator framework to create a server whose initial configuration behaves as follows:

- It statically configures an instance of Service_Reporter.
- It dynamically links and configures the Reactor_Logging_Server_Adapter template from the *Example* portion of Section 5.2 into the server's address space.

We then show how to dynamically reconfigure the server to support a different implementation of a reactive logging service.

Sidebar 34: Using XML to Configure Services

The `ACE_Service_Config` class can be configured to interpret an XML-based scripting language. The Document Type Definition (DTD) for this language is shown below:

```
<!ELEMENT ACE_Svc_Conf (dynamic|static|suspend|resume
                        |remove|stream|streamdef)*>
<!ELEMENT streamdef ((dynamic|static),module)>
<!ATTLIST streamdef id IDREF #REQUIRED>
<!ELEMENT module (dynamic|static|suspend|resume|remove)+>
<!ELEMENT stream (module)>
<!ATTLIST stream id IDREF #REQUIRED>
<!ELEMENT dynamic (initializer)>
<!ATTLIST dynamic id ID #REQUIRED
                  status (active|inactive) "active"
                  type (module|service_object|stream)
                  #REQUIRED>
<!ELEMENT initializer EMPTY>
<!ATTLIST initializer init CDATA #REQUIRED
                      path CDATA #IMPLIED
                      params CDATA #IMPLIED>
<!ELEMENT static EMPTY>
<!ATTLIST static id ID #REQUIRED
                 params CDATA #IMPLIED>
<!ELEMENT suspend EMPTY>
<!ATTLIST suspend id IDREF #REQUIRED>
<!ELEMENT resume EMPTY>
<!ATTLIST resume id IDREF #REQUIRED>
<!ELEMENT remove EMPTY>
<!ATTLIST remove id IDREF #REQUIRED>
```

The syntax of this XML-based configuration language is different from the one in Figure 5.7, but its semantics are the same. Although it's more verbose to compose, the ACE XML-based configuration file format is more flexible. For example, users can plug in customized XML event handlers to extend the behavior of the ACE Service Configurator framework without modifying the underlying ACE implementation.

The XML configuration file format is relatively new (it was introduced in ACE 5.3). It's therefore not yet the default used by the ACE Service Configurator framework. Users can choose the XML-based Service Configurator by compiling ACE with the `ACE_HAS_XML_SVC_CONF` macro enabled. ACE provides the `svcconf-convert.pl` perl script to translate original format files into the new XML format. The script is located in the `$ACE_ROOT/bin/` directory.

Initial server configuration.   We start by writing the following generic main() program in Configurable_Logging_Server.cpp. This program configures the Service_ Reporter and Reactor_Logging_Server_Adapter services into an application process and then runs the reactor's event loop.

```
 1 #include "ace/OS.h"
 2 #include "ace/Service_Config.h"
 3 #include "ace/Reactor.h"
 4
 5 int ACE_TMAIN (int argc, ACE_TCHAR *argv[]) {
 6   ACE_STATIC_SVC_REGISTER (Reporter);
 7
 8   ACE_Service_Config::open
 9     (argc, argv, ACE_DEFAULT_LOGGER_KEY, 0);
10
11   ACE_Reactor::instance ()->run_reactor_event_loop ();
12   return 0;
13 }
```

Lines 1–3   There are no service-specific header files (or code) in the main() program. It's therefore completely generic, and can be reused for many programs that are configured using the ACE Service Configurator and Reactor frameworks.

Line 5   Replace the main() entry point name with the ACE_TMAIN macro. This macro uses the alternate wmain() entry point on Windows when Unicode is enabled, and the usual main() in all other situations.

Line 6   Register the static Reporter service with the ACE Service Configurator framework. Although the framework now knows of the service, it is not activated unless a service configuration directive causes it to be.

Lines 8–9   Call ACE_Service_Config::open() to configure the application. All decisions about which service(s) to load, and all of the service parameters, are located in the service configuration file, which is external to the binary application program. We then run the reactor's event loop to handle I/O events from clients.

Since we know that our program will activate the static Service_Reporter service, we added the fourth argument (and by necessity, the third) to ACE_Service_Config:: open() to explicitly enable static service loading. If we instead decided to leave this decision to the user or administrator, that argument would not be supplied, and the user would choose to enable or disable static services by supplying the -y option on the command line.

When ACE_Service_Config::open() is called, it uses the ACE_Service_ Config::process_directives() method to interpret the svc.conf file below:

```
1 static Service_Reporter "-p $SERVICE_REPORTER_PORT"
2
3 dynamic Server_Logging_Daemon Service_Object *
4 SLD:_make_Server_Logging_Daemon()
5   "$SERVER_LOGGING_DAEMON_PORT"
```

Line 1 The `Service_Reporter` code, registration information, and factory function were all statically linked into the executable program. This directive therefore simply causes the Service Configurator framework to activate the service by calling `Service_Reporter::init()` (page 132). The `argc/argv` arguments passed to `init()` are the string `"-p"` and an expansion of the `SERVICE_REPORTER_PORT` environment variable. The Service Configurator framework expands this environment variable automatically using the `ACE_ARGV` class described in Sidebar 35. `ACE_ARGV` recognizes `SERVICE_REPORTER_PORT` as an environment variable by its leading $ character and substitutes its associated value. The `ACE_STATIC_SVC_REQUIRE` macro used in `Service_Reporter.cpp` (page 135) ensures the `Service_Reporter` is registered with `ACE_Service_Repository` before the `ACE_Service_Config::open()` method is called.

Sidebar 35: The ACE_ARGV Class

The `ACE_ARGV` class is a useful utility class that can
  1. Transform a string into an `argc/argv`-style vector of strings
  2. Incrementally assemble a set of strings into an `argc/argv` vector
  3. Transform an `argc/argv`-style vector into a string

During the transformation, the class can substitute environment variable values for each $-delimited environment variable name encountered. `ACE_ARGV` provides an easy and efficient mechanism to create arbitrary command-line arguments. Consider its use whenever command-line processing is required, especially when environment variable substitution is desirable. ACE uses `ACE_ARGV` extensively, particularly in its Service Configurator framework.

Lines 3–5 This code configures the server logging daemon via the following steps:

1. Dynamically link the `SLD` DLL into the address space of the process.

2. Use the `ACE_DLL` class described in Sidebar 33 (page 143) to extract the `_make_Server_Logging_Daemon()` factory function from the `SLD` DLL symbol table.

3. The factory function is called to allocate a `Server_Logging_Daemon` object.

4. The Service Configurator framework calls the service object's `Server_Logging_Daemon::init()` hook method, passing as its `argc/argv` arguments an expansion of the `SERVER_LOGGING_DAEMON_PORT` environment variable that designates the port number where the server logging daemon listens for client connection requests.

5. If `init()` succeeds, the `Server_Logging_Daemon` pointer is stored in the `ACE_Service_Repository` under the name `"Server_Logging_Daemon"`.

Sidebar 36 illustrates an XML version of the `svc.conf` file shown above.

Sidebar 36: An XML svc.conf File Example

The XML representation of the `svc.conf` file shown on page 147 is shown below:

```
1  <ACE_Svc_Conf>
2    <static id='Service_Reporter'
3            params='-p $SERVICE_REPORTER_PORT'/>
4
5    <dynamic id='Server_Logging_Daemon'
6             type='service_object'>
7      <initializer path='SLD'
8                   init='_make_Server_Logging_Daemon'
9                   params='$SERVER_LOGGING_DAEMON_PORT'/>
10   </dynamic>
11 </ACE_Svc_Conf>
```

The XML `svc.conf` file is more verbose than the original format since it specifies field names explicitly. However, the XML format allows `svc.conf` files to express expanded capabilities, since new sections and fields can be added without affecting existing syntax. There's also no threat to backwards compatibility, as might occur if fields were added to the original format or the field order changed.

The SLD DLL is generated from the following SLD.cpp file:

```
#include "Reactor_Logging_Server_Adapter.h"
#include "Logging_Acceptor.h"
#include "SLD_export.h"

typedef Reactor_Logging_Server_Adapter<Logging_Acceptor>
        Server_Logging_Daemon;

ACE_FACTORY_DEFINE (SLD, Server_Logging_Daemon)
```

The SLD.cpp file contains the Server_Logging_Daemon type definition that instantiates the Reactor_Logging_Server_Adapter template with the Logging_Acceptor class (page 54). The ACE_FACTORY_DEFINE macro generates the _make_Server_Logging_Daemon() factory function in the DLL containing the service code. If code outside the service DLL needs to refer to the factory function, it can use the ACE_FACTORY_DECLARE macro to declare the _make_Server_Logging_Daemon() factory function with the proper import declaration.

ACE's import/export helper macros are described in Sidebar 37 (page 150). These macros help to ensure that a DLL's externally visible symbols are exported properly from the DLL on all supported platforms, as well as allowing the DLL's users to import them properly. Applying the export macros within the ACE service macros allow the ACE Service Configurator framework to look up the factory function's entry point symbol when activating a service.

Sidebar 37: The ACE DLL Import/Export Macros

Windows has specific rules for explicitly importing and exporting symbols in DLLs. Developers with a UNIX background may not have encountered these rules in the past, but they are important for managing symbol usage in DLLs on Windows. ACE makes it easy to conform to these rules by supplying a script that generates the necessary import/export declarations and a set of guidelines for using them successfully. To ease porting, the following procedure can be used on all platforms that ACE runs on:

1. Select a concise mnemonic for each DLL to be built.
2. Run the `$ACE_ROOT/bin/generate_export_file.pl` Perl script, specifying the DLL's mnemonic on the command line. The script will generate a platform-independent header file and write it to the standard output. Redirect the output to a file named `<mnemonic>_export.h`
3. `#include` the generated file in each DLL source file that declares a globally visible class or symbol.
4. To use in a class declaration, insert the keyword `<mnemonic>_Export` between `class` and the class name.
5. When compiling the source code for the DLL, define the macro `<mnemonic>_BUILD_DLL`.

Following this procedure results in the following behavior on Windows:

- Symbols decorated using the above guidelines will be declared using `__declspec(dllexport)` when built in their DLL
- When referenced from components outside the DLL, the symbols will be declared `__declspec(dllimport)`.

If you choose a separate mnemonic for each DLL and use them consistently, it will be straightforward to build and use DLLs across all OS platforms.

The UML sequence diagram in Figure 5.8 illustrates the steps involved in configuring the server logging daemon based on the `svc.conf` file shown above. At program start time, the object generated by the ACE_STATIC_SVC_REQUIRE macro registers the `Service_Reporter` information created using the ACE_STATIC_SVC_DEFINE macro into `ACE_Service_Config`. When the `ACE_Service_Config::open()` method is called it uses the specified factory function to instantiate a `Service_Reporter` object, but doesn't activate it. The `open()` method then calls `process_directives()`, which interprets the directives in the `svc.conf` file. The first directive activates the static `Service_Reporter` service. The second directive triggers the following actions:

1. The SLD DLL is linked dynamically.
2. The `_make_Server_Logging_Daemon` factory function is called to create an instance of `Reactor_Logging_Server_Adapter`.
3. The new service object's `init()` method is called to activate the service.

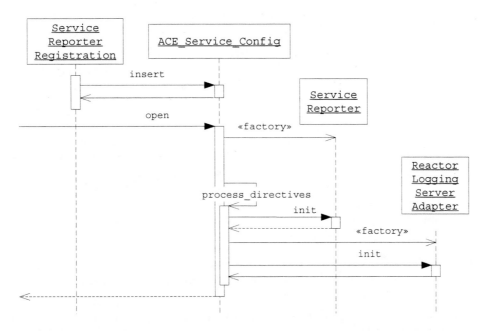

Figure 5.8: UML Sequence Diagram for Configuring the Logging Server

When all configuration activities are done, the `main()` program calls `ACE_Reactor::run_reactor_event_loop()`. At that point, the services are running, just like the objects that were configured statically in previous examples.

Reconfiguring the server.   The ACE Service Configurator framework can reconfigure a server at run time in response to external events, such as signals or commands. At this point, the framework rereads its `svc.conf` file(s) and performs the designated directives, such as inserting or removing service objects into or from a server, and suspending or resuming existing service objects. We now illustrate how to use these features to reconfigure our server logging daemon dynamically.

The initial configuration of the logging server has the following limitations:

- It uses the `Logging_Acceptor` implementation from Section 3.3 (page 54), which doesn't time out logging handlers that remain idle for long periods of time.

- There is no way to shut down the `run_reactor_event_loop()` method called on the `ACE_Reactor` singleton.

We can add these capabilities without affecting existing code or the `Service_Reporter` service in the process by defining a new `svc.conf` file and instructing the server to reconfigure itself by sending it a signal, such as SIGHUP or SIGINT.

```
1 remove Server_Logging_Daemon
2
3 dynamic Server_Logging_Daemon Service_Object *
4 SLDex:_make_Server_Logging_Daemon_Ex()
5    "$SERVER_LOGGING_DAEMON_PORT"
6
7 dynamic Server_Shutdown Service_Object *
8 SLDex:_make_Server_Shutdown()
```

This `svc.conf` file assumes the server process is currently running with the `Server_Logging_Daemon` already configured. The ACE Service Configurator framework provides configuration mechanisms and assumes the policies that determine when and what to reconfigure are handled by an administrator or another application.

Line 1   Remove the existing server logging daemon from the ACE service repository and unlink it from the application's address space.

Lines 3–5   Dynamically configure a different instantiation of the `Reactor_Logging_Server_Adapter` template into the address space of the server logging daemon. In particular, the `_make_Server_Logging_Daemon_Ex()` factory function is created by the ACE_FACTORY_DEFINE macro shown below in the `SLDex.cpp` file, which is used to generate the `SLDex` DLL.

```
typedef Reactor_Logging_Server_Adapter<Logging_Acceptor_Ex>
        Server_Logging_Daemon_Ex;

ACE_FACTORY_DEFINE (SLDEX, Server_Logging_Daemon_Ex)
```

This macro instantiates the `Reactor_Logging_Server_Adapter` template with the `Logging_Acceptor_Ex` (page 67).

Lines 7–8   Dynamically configure a `Server_Shutdown` service object that uses the `controller()` function (page 98) and `Quit_Handler` class (page 98) to wait for an administrator to shut down the server via a command on its standard input. The `Server_Shutdown` class shown below inherits from `ACE_Service_Object` so that we can manage its life cycle via the ACE Service Configurator framework.

```
class Server_Shutdown : public ACE_Service_Object {
public:
```

`Server_Shutdown::init()` spawns a thread to run the `controller()` function:

```
  virtual int init (int, ACE_TCHAR *[]) {
    reactor_ = ACE_Reactor::instance ();
    return ACE_Thread_Manager::instance ()->spawn
          (controller, reactor_, THR_DETACHED);
  }
```

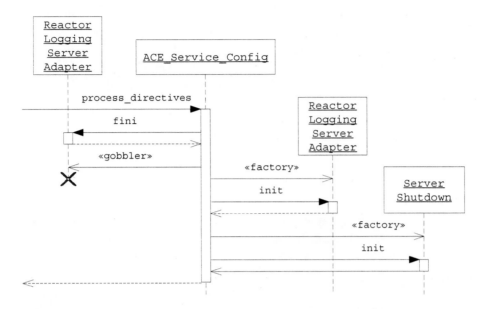

Figure 5.9: UML Sequence Diagram for Reconfiguring the Logging Server

We pass the THR_DETACHED flag to spawn so that the controller's thread identifier and other resources are reclaimed by the OS automatically after the thread terminates.

The Server_Shutdown::fini() method notifies the reactor to shut down:

```
virtual int fini () {
  Quit_Handler *quit_handler = 0;
  ACE_NEW_RETURN (quit_handler,
                  Quit_Handler (reactor_), -1);
  return reactor_->notify (quit_handler);
}

// ... Other method omitted ...
private:
  ACE_Reactor *reactor_;
};
```

We use ACE_FACTORY_DEFINE to generate the _make_Server_Shutdown() factory function needed by the ACE Service Configurator framework.

```
ACE_FACTORY_DEFINE (SLDEX, Server_Shutdown)
```

The UML sequence diagram in Figure 5.9 illustrates the steps involved in reconfiguring the server logging daemon based on the svc.conf file shown above.

The dynamic reconfiguration mechanism in the ACE Service Configurator framework enables developers to modify server functionality or fine-tune performance without extensive redevelopment and reinstallation effort. For example, debugging a faulty implementation of the logging service simply involves the dynamic reconfiguration of a functionally equivalent service that contains additional instrumentation to help identify the erroneous behavior. This reconfiguration process may be performed without modifying, recompiling, relinking, or restarting the currently executing server logging daemon. In particular, this reconfiguration doesn't affect the `Service_Reporter` that was configured statically.

5.5 Summary

Traditional software development techniques that statically link and configure a networked application's services together can be limiting. For example, the effort and time needed to rebuild an entire program for each new or modified service increases development and maintenance costs substantially. Moreover, making these changes in the field is inefficient and error prone, and can cause support costs to soar and customer satisfaction to plummet.

This chapter described the ACE Service Configurator framework, which implements the Component Configurator pattern [POSA2] to provide a portable way to statically and/or dynamically link services and then initiate, suspend, resume, and shut them down dynamically at run time. This framework helps to improve the extensibility of networked software by allowing applications to defer the selection of a particular service implementation until late in the software life cycle—as late as installation time or even run time. This flexibility yields the following important advantages:

- Applications can be composed and (re)configured at run time using mix-and-match, independently developed services.
- Developers can concentrate on a service's functionality and other key design dimensions without committing prematurely to a particular service configuration.
- Applications are composed of multiple services that are developed independently, so they don't require advanced global knowledge of each other, yet can still collaborate.

This chapter explained the origin and usage of each of the ACE Service Configurator framework's classes and helper macros. We also used these capabilities to separate parts of the previous chapter's logging servers into independently linkable and configurable services. The result was a networked logging service that can be configured and deployed in various ways. The extensibility afforded by the ACE Service Configurator framework allows operators and administrators to select the features and alternative implementation strategies that make the most sense in a particular context, as well as make localized decisions on how best to initialize and evolve them.

CHAPTER 6

The ACE Task Framework

CHAPTER SYNOPSIS

This chapter describes the design and use of the ACE Task framework. This framework helps to enhance the modularity and extensibility of concurrent object-oriented networked applications. The ACE Task framework forms the basis of common concurrency patterns, such as Active Object and Half-Sync/Half-Async [POSA2]. After discussing the motivation and usage of the framework's classes, we apply the ACE Task framework to enhance the concurrency and scalability of our networked logging service.

6.1 Overview

The ACE Task framework provides powerful and extensible object-oriented concurrency capabilities that can spawn threads in the context of an object, as well as transfer and queue messages between objects executing in separate threads. This framework can be applied to implement key concurrency patterns [POSA2], such as:

- The *Active Object* pattern, which decouples the thread that invokes a method from the thread that executes the method. This pattern enhances concurrency and simplifies synchronized access to objects executing in the context of one or more threads.
- The *Half-Sync/Half-Async* pattern, which decouples asynchronous and synchronous processing in concurrent systems to simplify programming without unduly reducing performance. This pattern introduces three layers: one for asynchronous (or reactive) processing, one for synchronous service processing, and a queueing layer that mediates communication between the asynchronous/reactive and synchronous layers.

This chapter shows how these patterns, and the ACE Task framework that reifies them, can be applied to develop concurrent object-oriented applications at a higher level of abstraction than existing C operating system APIs and C++ wrapper facades. The ACE Task framework consists of the following classes that networked applications can use to spawn and manage threads and pass messages between one or more threads within a process:

ACE Class	Description
`ACE_Message_Block`	Implements the Composite pattern [GoF] to enable efficient manipulation of fixed- and variable-sized messages
`ACE_Message_Queue`	Provides an intraprocess message queue that enables applications to pass and buffer messages between threads in a process
`ACE_Thread_Manager`	Allows applications to portably create and manage the lifetime, synchronization, and properties of one or more threads
`ACE_Task`	Allows applications to create passive or active objects that decouple different units of processing; use messages to communicate requests, responses, data, and control information; and can queue and process messages sequentially or concurrently

The most important relationships between the classes in the ACE Task framework are shown in Figure 6.1. This framework provides the following benefits:

- **Improves the consistency of programming style** by enabling developers to use C++ and object-oriented techniques throughout their concurrent networked applications. For example, the `ACE_Task` class provides an object-oriented programming abstraction that associates OS-level threads with C++ objects.

- **Manages a group of threads as a cohesive collection.** Multithreaded networked applications often require multiple threads to start and end as a group. The `ACE_Task` class therefore provides a *thread group* capability that allows other threads to wait for an entire group of threads to exit before continuing their processing.

- **Decouples producer and consumer threads** that run concurrently and collaborate by passing messages via a synchronized message queue.

- **Integrates concurrent processing,** such as the Half-Sync/Half-Async pattern's synchronous layer, with the ACE Reactor framework discussed in Chapter 3 or the ACE Proactor framework discussed in Chapter 8.

- **Facilitates dynamic configuration** of *tasks* via integration with the ACE Service Configurator framework discussed in Chapter 5. Developers therefore need not commit prematurely to concurrency decisions at design time or even at run time. Tasks can instead be designed to run according to configurations that may change as deployment site resources and dynamic conditions dictate.

The `ACE_Message_Block` and `ACE_Thread_Manager` classes were described in Chapters 4 and 9 of C++NPv1, respectively. This chapter therefore focuses largely on describing the capabilities provided by the `ACE_Message_Queue` and `ACE_Task` classes. However, we illustrate how all the classes in the ACE Task framework can be used to enhance the concurrency of our client and server logging daemons. If you aren't familiar with the Active Object and Half-Sync/Half-Async patterns from POSA2 we recommend that you read about them first before delving into the detailed examples in this chapter.

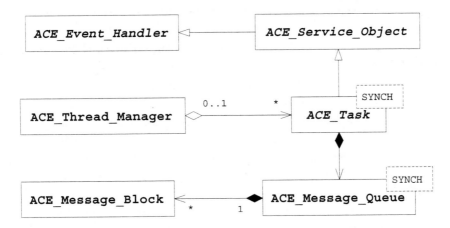

Figure 6.1: The ACE Task Framework Classes

6.2   The ACE_Message_Queue Class

Motivation

As discussed in Section 2.1.4 on page 27, networked applications whose services are layered/modular are often composed of a set of collaborating tasks within a process. To simplify interfaces and design, minimize maintenance costs, and maximize reuse, these tasks should have the following properties:

- **Low intertask coupling**, that is, separate task objects should have minimal dependencies on each other's data and methods.
- **High intratask cohesion**, that is, the methods and data in a task should focus on a related set of functionality.

To achieve these properties, tasks often communicate by passing messages via a generic method, such as push() or put(), rather than calling specific statically typed methods directly. Messages can represent work requests, work results, or other types of data to process. They can also represent control requests that direct tasks to alter their processing, for example, to shut down or reconfigure themselves.

When producer and consumer tasks are collocated in the same process, tasks often exchange messages via an intraprocess message queue. In this design, producer task(s) insert messages into a *synchronized message queue* serviced by consumer task(s) that remove and process the messages. If the queue is full, producers can either block or wait a bounded amount of time to insert their messages. Likewise, if the queue is empty, consumers can either block or wait a bounded amount of time to remove messages.

Although some operating systems supply intraprocess message queues natively, this capability isn't available on all platforms. Moreover, when it is offered, it's often either highly platform specific, such as VxWorks message queues, and/or inefficient, tedious, and error prone to use, such as System V IPC message queues [Ste99]. Examples of how to create wrapper facade classes to handle these problems appear in C++NPv1. Wrapper facades could encapsulate the spectrum of available intraprocess message queue mechanisms behind a common interface, emulating missing capabilities where needed. ACE takes a different approach, however, for the following reasons:

- **To avoid unnecessary complexity.** Native message queueing mechanisms, where they exist, can be hard to program correctly since they use low-level C APIs. They can also impose constraints on system administration that reflect poorly on a product's operational procedures, which can increase product support costs. For example, System V IPC message queues can persist after a program finishes execution if not cleaned up properly. These remnants may prevent an application from restarting, or contribute to resource leaks and often require a system administrator's intervention to repair the system manually. Likewise, System V IPC message queues offer interprocess queueing that incurs more overhead than the intraprocess queueing that's the target use case for many networked applications.

- **To avoid a matrix of increasing complexity.** Each native message queueing mechanism has its own message format. Properly encapsulating message queues with wrapper facades therefore requires a corresponding encapsulation of messages. Reconciling two wrappers' desired feature sets with the matrix of message queues and types complicates the design and development effort for the wrappers many times over. This problem would only get worse as ACE is ported to new platforms.

- **ACE already has a powerful message class.** ACE_Message_Block is a convenient, efficient, and powerful message class described in Chapter 4 of C++NPv1. It offers more capability than many platform-specific message formats, and also works portably across all ACE platforms.

Due to these factors, ACE defines the ACE_Message_Queue class, which is a portable and efficient intraprocess message queueing mechanism that leverages the advanced capabilities of ACE_Message_Block.

Class Capabilities

ACE_Message_Queue is a portable, lightweight intraprocess message queueing mechanism that provides the following capabilities:

- It allows messages (which are instances of ACE_Message_Block) to be enqueued at the front of the queue, the rear of the queue, or in priority order based on the message's priority. Messages can be dequeued from the front or back of the queue.

- It uses ACE_Message_Block to provide an efficient message buffering mechanism that minimizes dynamic memory allocation and data copying.

- It can be instantiated for either multithreaded or single-threaded configurations, allowing programmers to trade off strict synchronization for lower overhead when concurrent access to a queue isn't required.

- In multithreaded configurations, it supports configurable *flow control*, which prevents fast message producer thread(s) from swamping the processing and memory resources of slower message consumer thread(s).

- It allows timeouts to be specified on both enqueue and dequeue operations to avoid indefinite blocking.

- It can be integrated with the ACE Reactor framework's event handling mechanism.

- It provides allocators that can be strategized so the memory used by messages can be obtained from various sources, such as shared memory, heap memory, static memory, or thread-specific memory.

Figure 6.2 (page 160) shows the interface for ACE_Message_Queue. Since this class has a wide range of features, we divide its description into the four categories below.

1. Initialization and flow control methods.   The following methods can be used to initialize and manage flow control in an ACE_Message_Queue:

Method	Description
ACE_Message_Queue() open()	Initialize the queue, optionally specifying watermarks and a notification strategy (see Sidebar 38 on page 163).
high_water_mark() low_water_mark()	Set/get the high and low watermarks that determine when flow control starts and stops.
notification_strategy()	Set/get the notification strategy.

An ACE_Message_Queue contains a pair of watermarks that implement flow control to prevent a fast sender from overrunning the buffering and computing resources of a slower receiver. To reflect the total resource usage of messages in the queue, the watermarks are measured in bytes. Each ACE_Message_Queue maintains a count of the payload bytes in each queued ACE_Message_Block to keep track of the number of bytes in the queue. A new message can be enqueued if the total number of bytes in the queue *before* queueing the new message is less than or equal to the high watermark. Otherwise, ACE_Message_Queue flow control works as follows:

- If the queue is "synchronized," the calling thread will block until the total number of bytes in the queue falls below the low watermark or until a timeout occurs.

- If the queue is "unsynchronized," the call will return −1 with errno set to EWOULD-BLOCK.

The ACE_MT_SYNCH or ACE_NULL_SYNCH traits classes (page 163) can be used to designate whether a queue is synchronized or not, respectively. As ACE_Message_Block

```
┌──────────────────────────────────────────────────────┐   ┌ ─ ─ ─ ─ ─ ─ ─ ─ ─ ┐
│                    ACE_Message_Queue                  │     SYNCH_STRATEGY
│                                                       │   └ ─ ─ ─ ─ ─ ─ ─ ─ ─ ┘
├──────────────────────────────────────────────────────┤
│ # head_  : ACE_Message_Block *                        │
│ # tail_  : ACE_Message_Block *                        │
│ # high_water_mark_  : size_t                          │
│ # low_water_mark_  : size_t                           │
├──────────────────────────────────────────────────────┤
│ + ACE_Message_Queue (high_water_mark : size_t = DEFAULT_HWM,
│                      low_water_mark : size_t = DEFAULT_LWM,
│                      notify : ACE_Notification_Strategy * = 0)
│ + open (high_water_mark : size_t = DEFAULT_HWM,
│         low_water_mark : size_t = DEFAULT_LWM,
│         notify : ACE_Notification_Strategy * = 0) : int
│ + flush () : int
│ + notification_strategy (s : ACE_Notification_Strategy *) : void
│ + is_empty () : int
│ + is_full () : int
│ + enqueue_tail (item : ACE_Message_Block *,
│                 timeout : ACE_Time_Value * = 0) : int
│ + enqueue_head (item : ACE_Message_Block *,
│                 timeout : ACE_Time_Value * = 0) : int
│ + enqueue_prio (item : ACE_Message_Block *,
│                 timeout : ACE_Time_Value * = 0) : int
│ + dequeue_head (item : ACE_Message_Block *&,
│                 timeout : ACE_Time_Value * = 0) : int
│ + dequeue_tail (item : ACE_Message_Block *&,
│                 timeout : ACE_Time_Value * = 0) : int
│ + high_water_mark (new_hwm : size_t) : void
│ + high_water_mark (void) : size_t
│ + low_water_mark (new_lwm : size_t) : void
│ + low_water_mark (void) : size_t
│ + close () : int
│ + deactivate () : int
│ + activate () : int
│ + pulse () : int
│ + state () : int
└──────────────────────────────────────────────────────┘
```

Figure 6.2: The ACE_Message_Queue Class

objects are removed from a message queue, the count of queued bytes is decremented accordingly. The low watermark indicates the number of queued bytes at which a previously flow-controlled ACE_Message_Queue no longer considers itself full.

The default high and low watermarks are both 16K. The default watermark values cause an ACE_Message_Queue to flow control when more than 16K are queued and to cease flow control when the number of queued bytes drops below 16K. These defaults are appropriate for applications in which the average ACE_Message_Block size is considerably less than 1K.

Depending on load and design constraints, applications may require different settings for either or both of the watermarks. The default watermark values can be reset in the ACE_ Message_Queue's constructor or open() method, as well as by its high_water_ mark() and low_water_mark() mutator methods. One approach is to specify watermarks using the ACE Service Configurator framework described in Chapter 5, with defaults determined from application benchmarks measured during development and testing. The *Example* portions of Sections 6.3 and 7.4 illustrate how to set and use a message queue's high watermark to exert flow control within multithreaded networked applications.

2. Enqueue/dequeue methods and message buffering.   The following methods perform the bulk of the work in an ACE_Message_Queue:

Method	Description
is_empty() is_full()	The is_empty() method returns true when the queue contains no message blocks. The is_full() method returns true when the number of bytes in the queue is greater than the high watermark.
enqueue_tail()	Insert a message at the back of the queue.
enqueue_head()	Insert a message at the front of the queue.
enqueue_prio()	Insert a message according to its priority.
dequeue_head()	Remove and return the message at the front of the queue.
dequeue_tail()	Remove and return the message at the back of the queue.

The design of the ACE_Message_Queue class is based on the message buffering and queueing facilities in System V STREAMS [Rag93]. Messages passed to a message queue are instances of ACE_Message_Block and can be classified as either simple or composite messages. Simple messages contain a single ACE_Message_Block. Composite messages contain multiple ACE_Message_Block objects that are linked together in accordance with the Composite pattern [GoF], which provides a structure for building recursive aggregations. A composite message often contains the following message types:

- A **control message** that contains bookkeeping information, such as destination addresses and length fields, followed by
- One or more **data messages** that contain the actual contents of a composite message

Messages in a queue are linked bidirectionally via a pair of pointers that can be obtained using their next() and prev() accessor methods. This design optimizes enqueueing and dequeueing at the head and tail of a queue. Priority-based queueing with the ACE_Message_Queue::enqueue_prio() method uses the ACE_Message_ Block::msg_priority() accessor method to enqueue a message block ahead of all lower-priority message blocks already in the queue. Message blocks at the same priority are enqueued in first-in, first-out (FIFO) order.

Each message block in a composite message is chained together unidirectionally via a continuation pointer, which can be obtained via the cont() accessor method. Figure 6.3 (page 162) illustrates how three messages can be linked together to form an ACE_

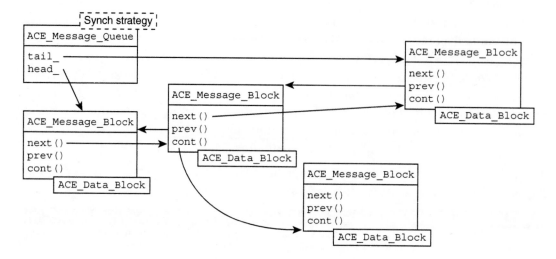

Figure 6.3: The Structure of an ACE_Message_Queue

Message_Queue. The head and tail messages in the queue are simple messages, whereas the middle one is a composite message with one message block chained via its continuation pointer.

Sidebar 39 (page 164) describes ACE_Message_Queue_Ex, which is a variant of ACE_Message_Queue that exchanges strongly typed messages.

3. Parameterized synchronization strategies. If you examine Figure 6.2 (page 160) carefully you'll see the ACE_Message_Queue template is parameterized by a SYNCH_STRATEGY traits class. This design is based on the Strategized Locking pattern [POSA2], which parameterizes the synchronization mechanisms that a class uses to protect its critical sections from concurrent access. Internally, the ACE_Message_Queue class uses the following traits from its SYNCH_STRATEGY traits class template parameter:

```
template <class SYNCH_STRATEGY>
class ACE_Message_Queue {
  // ...
protected:
  // C++ traits that coordinate concurrent access.
  ACE_TYPENAME SYNCH_STRATEGY::MUTEX lock_;
  ACE_TYPENAME SYNCH_STRATEGY::CONDITION notempty_;
  ACE_TYPENAME SYNCH_STRATEGY::CONDITION notfull_;
};
```

Sidebar 40 (page 165) describes the C++ traits and traits class idioms. These idioms enable application developers to customize an ACE_Message_Queue's synchronization strategy to suit their particular needs. The ACE_Message_Queue class fragment above shows how the following traits in its traits class template parameter are used:

Sidebar 38: Integrating an ACE_Message_Queue with an ACE_Reactor

Some platforms offer a way to integrate native message queue events with synchronous event demultiplexing. For example, AIX's version of `select()` can demultiplex events generated by System V message queues. Although this use of `select()` is nonportable, the ability to integrate a message queue with a reactor is useful in applications in which one thread must respond to both I/O events and items enqueued to a message queue. The `ACE_Message_Queue` class therefore offers a portable way to integrate event queueing with the ACE Reactor framework presented in Chapter 3.

The constructor of the `ACE_Message_Queue` class, as well as its `open()` and `notification_strategy()` methods, can be used to set a notification strategy for the `ACE_Message_Queue`. This design is an example of the Strategy pattern [GoF], which allows various algorithms to be substituted without changing the client (which is the `ACE_Message_Queue` class in this case). The notification strategy must be derived from `ACE_Notification_Strategy`, which allows the flexibility to insert any strategy necessary for your application. One such subclass strategy is `ACE_Reactor_Notification_Strategy`, whose constructor associates it with an `ACE_Reactor`, an `ACE_Event_Handler`, and an event mask. After the strategy object is associated with an `ACE_Message_Queue`, each queued message triggers the following sequence of actions:

1. `ACE_Message_Queue` calls the strategy's `notify()` method.
2. The `ACE_Reactor_Notification_Strategy::notify()` method notifies the associated reactor using the reactor notification mechanism (page 77).
3. The reactor dispatches the notification to the specified event handler using the designated mask.

- The `lock_` member serializes access to the queue's state and
- `notempty_` and `notfull_` are condition variables that enable callers to wait efficiently for a message to arrive or to insert a message, respectively.

The `SYNCH_STRATEGY` traits class used to parameterized `ACE_Message_Queue` allows these members to adapt to a synchronized or unsynchronized queue at compile time.

Sets of ACE's synchronization wrapper facades can be combined to form traits classes that define customized synchronization strategies. ACE provides the following two traits classes that prepackage the most common synchronization traits:

- `ACE_NULL_SYNCH`—The traits in this class are implemented in terms of "null" locking mechanisms, as shown below.

```
class ACE_NULL_SYNCH {
public:
  typedef ACE_Null_Mutex MUTEX;
  typedef ACE_Null_Mutex NULL_MUTEX;
  typedef ACE_Null_Mutex PROCESS_MUTEX;
  typedef ACE_Null_Mutex RECURSIVE_MUTEX;
```

Sidebar 39: The ACE_Message_Queue_Ex Class

The `ACE_Message_Queue` class enqueues and dequeues `ACE_Message_Block` objects, which provide a dynamically extensible way to represent messages. For programs requiring strongly typed messaging, ACE provides the `ACE_Message_Queue_Ex` class, which enqueues and dequeues messages that are instances of a `MESSAGE_TYPE` template parameter, rather than an `ACE_Message_Block`.

ACE_Message_Queue_Ex offers the same capabilities as `ACE_Message_Queue`. Its primary advantage is that application-defined data types can be queued without the need to type cast on enqueue and dequeue or copy objects into the data portion of an `ACE_Message_Block`. Since `ACE_Message_Queue_Ex` is not derived from `ACE_Message_Queue`, however, it can't be used with the `ACE_Task` class described in Section 6.3.

```
    typedef ACE_Null_Mutex RW_MUTEX;
    typedef ACE_Null_Condition CONDITION;
    typedef ACE_Null_Semaphore SEMAPHORE;
    typedef ACE_Null_Semaphore NULL_SEMAPHORE;
};
```

The `ACE_NULL_SYNCH` class is an example of the Null Object pattern [Woo97], which simplifies applications by defining a "no-op" placeholder that removes conditional statements in a class implementation. `ACE_NULL_SYNCH` is often used in single-threaded applications or in applications in which the need for interthread synchronization has either been eliminated via careful design or implemented via some other mechanism. The client logging daemon examples in Section 7.4 (page 238) illustrate the use of the `ACE_NULL_SYNCH` traits class.

- `ACE_MT_SYNCH`—The traits in this predefined class are implemented in terms of actual locking mechanisms, as shown below:

```
class ACE_MT_SYNCH {
public:
    typedef ACE_Thread_Mutex MUTEX;
    typedef ACE_Null_Mutex NULL_MUTEX;
    typedef ACE_Process_Mutex PROCESS_MUTEX;
    typedef ACE_Recursive_Thread_Mutex RECURSIVE_MUTEX;
    typedef ACE_RW_Thread_Mutex RW_MUTEX;
    typedef ACE_Condition_Thread_Mutex CONDITION;
    typedef ACE_Thread_Semaphore SEMAPHORE;
    typedef ACE_Null_Semaphore NULL_SEMAPHORE;
};
```

The `ACE_MT_SYNCH` traits class defines a strategy containing portable, efficient synchronizers suitable for multithreaded applications. The client logging daemon examples in Section 6.2 (page 180) and Section 7.4 (page 243) illustrate the use of the `ACE_MT_SYNCH` traits class.

Sidebar 40: The C++ Traits and Traits Class Idioms

A *trait* is a type that conveys information used by another class or algorithm to determine policies at compile time. A *traits class* [Jos99] is a useful way to collect a set of traits that should be applied in a given situation to alter another class's behavior appropriately. Traits and traits classes are C++ *policy-based class design* idioms [Ale01] that are widely used throughout the C++ standard library [Aus99].

For example, the `char_traits` class defines the traits of a character type, such as its data type and functions to compare, search for, and assign characters of that type. The C++ standard library provides specializations of `char_traits<>` for `char` and `wchar_t`. These character traits then modify the behavior of common classes, such as `basic_iostream<>` and `basic_string<>`. The `iostream` and `string` classes are defined by specializing the class templates with `char_traits<char>`. Similarly, the `wiostream` and `wstring` classes are defined by specializing the templates with `char_traits<wchar_t>`.

These C++ idioms are similar in spirit to the Strategy pattern [GoF], which allows substitution of class behavioral characteristics without requiring a change to the class itself. The Strategy pattern involves a defined interface that's commonly bound dynamically at run time using virtual methods. In contrast, the traits and traits class idioms involve substitution of a set of class members and/or methods that can be bound statically at compile time using C++ parameterized types.

Parameterizing the `ACE_Message_Queue` template with a traits class provides the following benefits.

- It allows `ACE_Message_Queue` to work in both single-threaded and multithreaded configurations without requiring changes to the class implementation.
- It allows the synchronization aspects of an instantiation of `ACE_Message_Queue` to be changed wholesale via the Strategized Locking pattern.

For example, the `ACE_Message_Queue`'s `MUTEX` and `CONDITION` traits resolve to `ACE_Null_Mutex` and `ACE_Null_Condition` if the `ACE_NULL_SYNCH` traits class is used. In this case, the resulting message queue class incurs no synchronization overhead. In contrast, if an `ACE_Message_Queue` is parameterized with the `ACE_MT_SYNCH` traits class, its `MUTEX` and `CONDITION` traits resolve to `ACE_Thread_Mutex` and `ACE_Condition_Thread_Mutex`. In this case, the resulting message queue class behaves in accordance with the Monitor Object design pattern [POSA2], which

- Synchronizes concurrent method execution to ensure that only one method at a time runs within an object
- Allows an object's methods to schedule their execution sequences cooperatively

Sidebar 49 (page 214) explains how ACE uses macros to implement `ACE_NULL_SYNCH` and `ACE_MT_SYNCH` for C++ compilers that lack support for traits classes in templates.

When ACE_Message_Queue is parameterized with ACE_NULL_SYNCH, calls to its enqueue and dequeue methods never block the calling thread when they reach the queue's boundary conditions. They instead return −1 with errno set to EWOULDBLOCK. Conversely, when an ACE_Message_Queue is instantiated with ACE_MT_SYNCH, its enqueue and dequeue methods support blocking, nonblocking, and timed operations. For example, when a synchronized queue is empty, calls to its dequeue methods will block by default until a message is enqueued and the queue is no longer empty. Likewise, when a synchronized queue is full, calls to its enqueue methods block by default until sufficient messages are dequeued to decrease the number of bytes in the queue below its low watermark and the queue is no longer full. This default blocking behavior can be modified by passing the following types of ACE_Time_Value values to these methods:

Value	Behavior
NULL ACE_Time_Value pointer	Indicates that the enqueue or dequeue method should wait indefinitely, that is, it will block until the method completes, the queue is closed, or a signal interrupts the call.
Non-NULL ACE_Time_Value pointer whose sec() and usec() methods return 0	Indicates that enqueue and dequeue methods should perform a nonblocking operation, that is, if the method doesn't succeed immediately return −1 and set errno to EWOULDBLOCK.
Non-NULL ACE_Time_Value pointer whose sec() or usec() method returns > 0	Indicates that enqueue or dequeue method should wait until the *absolute* time of day, returning −1 with errno set to EWOULDBLOCK if the method does not complete by this time. The call will also return earlier if the queue is closed or a signal interrupts the call.

Sidebar 6 (page 45) describes the different interpretations of timeout values used by various classes in ACE.

4. Shutdown and message release methods.   The following methods can be used to shut down, deactivate, and/or release the messages in an ACE_Message_Queue:

Method	Description
deactivate()	Changes the queue state to DEACTIVATED and wakes up all threads waiting on enqueue or dequeue operations. This method does not release any queued messages.
pulse()	Changes the queue state to PULSED and wakes up all threads waiting on enqueue or dequeue operations. This method does not release any queued messages.
state()	Returns the queue's state .
activate()	Changes the queue state to ACTIVATED.
~ACE_Message_Queue() close()	Deactivates the queue and releases any queued messages immediately.
flush()	Releases the messages in a queue, but doesn't change its state.

An ACE_Message_Queue is always in one of three states internally:

- ACTIVATED, in which all operations work normally (a queue always starts in the ACTIVATED state).
- DEACTIVATED, in which all enqueue and dequeue operations immediately return −1 and set errno to ESHUTDOWN until the queue is activated again.
- PULSED, the transition to which causes waiting enqueue and dequeue operations to return immediately as if the queue were deactivated; however, all operations initiated while in the PULSED state behave as in ACTIVATED state.

The DEACTIVATED and PULSED states are useful in situations in which it's necessary to notify all producer and consumer threads that some significant event has occurred. Transitioning to either state causes all waiting producer and consumer threads to wake up. The difference between them is the queue's enqueue/dequeue behavior after the transition. In the DEACTIVATED state, all enqueue and dequeue operations fail until the queue's state is changed to ACTIVATED. The PULSED state, however, is behaviorally equivalent to the ACTIVATED state, that is, all enqueue/dequeue operations proceed normally. The PULSED state is mainly informational—an awakened producer/consumer can decide whether to attempt further queue operations by examining the return value from the state() method. The *Example* portion of Section 7.4 (page 246) illustrates the use of the pulse() method to trigger connection reestablishment.

No messages are removed from the queue on any state transition. The messages in a queue can be released by the ACE_Message_Queue destructor, close(), or flush() methods. These methods release all the message blocks remaining in the message queue. The flush() method doesn't deactivate the queue, however, whereas the other two methods do. Sidebar 41 describes several protocols that shut ACE_Message_Queues down gracefully.

Sidebar 41: ACE_Message—uscoreQueue Graceful Shutdown Protocols

To avoid losing queued messages unexpectedly when an ACE_Message_Queue needs to be closed, producer and consumer threads can implement the following protocol:

1. A producer thread can enqueue a special message, such as a message block whose payload is size 0 and/or whose type is MB_STOP, to indicate that it wants the queue closed.
2. The consumer thread can close the queue when it receives this shutdown message, after processing any other messages ahead of it in the queue.

A variant of this protocol can use the ACE_Message_Queue::enqueue_prio() method to boost the priority of the shutdown message so it takes precedence over lower-priority messages that may already reside in the queue.

Example

This example shows how ACE_Message_Queue can be used to implement a client logging daemon. As shown in Figure 1.10 (page 21), a client logging daemon runs on every host participating in the networked logging service and performs the following tasks:

- It uses a local IPC mechanism, such as shared memory, pipes, or loopback sockets, to receive log records from client applications on the client logging daemon's host.
- It uses a remote IPC mechanism, such as TCP/IP, to forward log records to a server logging daemon running on a designated host.

Our example uses two threads to implement a *bounded buffer* concurrency model [BA90] based on a synchronized ACE_Message_Queue using the ACE_MT_SYNCH traits class (page 164).

In our client logging daemon, the main thread uses an event handler and the ACE Reactor framework to read log records from sockets connected to client applications via the network loopback device. The event handler queues each log record in the synchronized ACE_Message_Queue. A separate forwarder thread runs concurrently, performing the following steps continuously:

1. Dequeueing messages from the message queue
2. Buffering the messages into larger chunks
3. Forwarding the chunks to the server logging daemon over a TCP connection

By using a synchronized message queue, the main thread can continue to read log records from client applications as long as the message queue isn't full. Overall server concurrency can therefore be enhanced, even if the forwarder thread blocks occasionally when sending log records to the logging server over a flow controlled connection.

The client logging daemon plays multiple roles, including accepting connections from client applications, receiving log records, establishing connections to the logging server, and forwarding log records. We therefore can't implement it by reusing our Reactor_Logging_Server class from the *Example* portion of Section 3.5. Instead, we define a new group of classes shown in Figure 6.4. The role of each class is outlined below:

Class	Description
CLD_Handler	Target of callbacks from the ACE_Reactor. Receives log records from clients, converts them into ACE_Message_Blocks, and inserts them into the synchronized message queue that's processed by a separate thread and forwarded to the logging server.
CLD_Acceptor	A factory that passively accepts connections from clients and registers them with the ACE_Reactor to be processed by the CLD_Handler.
CLD_Connector	A factory that actively establishes (and when necessary reestablishes) connections with the logging server.
Client_Logging_Daemon	A facade class that integrates the other three classes together.

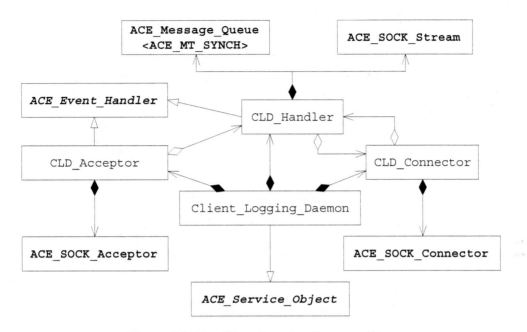

Figure 6.4: The Client Logging Daemon Classes

As shown in Figure 6.4, the classes in this client logging daemon implementation are designed in accordance with the Acceptor-Connector pattern. CLD_Acceptor plays the acceptor role, CLD_Connector plays the connector role, and CLD_Handler plays the service handler role. The relationships between the main thread, the forwarder thread, the classes in Figure 6.4, and the synchronized ACE_Message_Queue that joins them are shown in Figure 6.5 (page 170).

We start our implementation by including the necessary ACE header files.

```
#include "ace/OS.h"
#include "ace/Event_Handler.h"
#include "ace/INET_Addr.h"
#include "ace/Get_Opt.h"
#include "ace/Log_Record.h"
#include "ace/Message_Block.h"
#include "ace/Message_Queue.h"
#include "ace/Reactor.h"
#include "ace/Service_Object.h"
#include "ace/Signal.h"
#include "ace/Synch.h"
#include "ace/SOCK_Acceptor.h"
#include "ace/SOCK_Connector.h"
#include "ace/SOCK_Stream.h"
#include "ace/Thread_Manager.h"
#include "Logging_Acceptor.h"
#include "CLD_export.h"
```

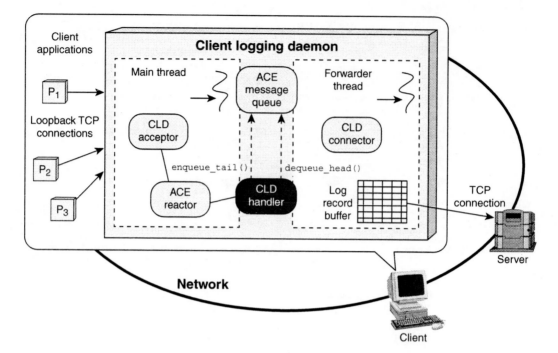

Figure 6.5: Interactions between Objects in the Client Logging Daemon

Each class in Figure 6.4 is defined in the `Client_Logging_Daemon.cpp` file and described below.

CLD_Handler.   This class provides the following capabilities:

- It receives log records from clients.
- It converts the log records into `ACE_Message_Blocks`.
- It enqueues the message blocks in a synchronized message queue.
- It runs a separate thread that dequeues the message blocks and forwards them to the logging server in large chunks.

The `CLD_Handler` class is shown below:

```
#if !defined (FLUSH_TIMEOUT)
#define FLUSH_TIMEOUT 120 /* 120 seconds == 2 minutes. */
#endif /* FLUSH_TIMEOUT */

class CLD_Handler : public ACE_Event_Handler {
public:
  enum { QUEUE_MAX = sizeof (ACE_Log_Record) * ACE_IOV_MAX };

  // Initialization hook method.
  virtual int open (CLD_Connector *);
```

```
// Shut down hook method.
virtual int close ();

// Accessor to the connection to the logging server.
virtual ACE_SOCK_Stream &peer () { return peer_; }

// Reactor hook methods.
virtual int handle_input (ACE_HANDLE handle);
virtual int handle_close (ACE_HANDLE = ACE_INVALID_HANDLE,
                          ACE_Reactor_Mask = 0);
protected:
// Forward log records to the server logging daemon.
virtual ACE_THR_FUNC_RETURN forward ();

// Send buffered log records using a gather-write operation.
virtual int send (ACE_Message_Block *chunk[], size_t &count);

// Entry point into forwarder thread of control.
static ACE_THR_FUNC_RETURN run_svc (void *arg);

// A synchronized <ACE_Message_Queue> that queues messages.
ACE_Message_Queue<ACE_MT_SYNCH> msg_queue_;

// Manage the forwarder thread.
ACE_Thread_Manager thr_mgr_;

// Pointer to our <CLD_Connector>.
CLD_Connector *connector_;

// Connection to the logging server.
ACE_SOCK_Stream peer_;
};
```

There's no need for a constructor or destructor in CLD_Handler since its open() and close() hooks perform initialization and destruction activities when called by the CLD_ Acceptor factory class (page 176). CLD_Handler performs two roles—*input* and *output*—which are explained below.

   • **Input role.**   Since CLD_Handler inherits from ACE_Event_Handler, it can use the ACE Reactor framework to wait for log records to arrive from client applications connected to the client logging daemon via loopback TCP sockets. When a log record arrives at the client logging daemon, the singleton ACE_Reactor dispatches the following CLD_Handler::handle_input() hook method:

```
1 int CLD_Handler::handle_input (ACE_HANDLE handle) {
2   ACE_Message_Block *mblk = 0;
3   Logging_Handler logging_handler (handle);
4
5   if (logging_handler.recv_log_record (mblk) != -1)
```

```
 6          if (msg_queue_.enqueue_tail (mblk->cont ()) != -1) {
 7            mblk->cont (0);
 8            mblk->release ();
 9            return 0; // Success return.
10          } else mblk->release ();
11       return -1; // Error return.
12     }
```

Lines 3–5 Use the `Logging_Handler` from Chapter 4 of C++NPv1 to read a log record out of the socket handle parameter and store the record in an `ACE_Message_Block`.

Lines 6–8 Insert the message into the synchronized queue serviced by the forwarder thread. The server logging daemon expects to receive a marshaled log record, but not a hostname string, so we enqueue only the log record data (which is referenced by `mblk->cont ()`) and *not* the hostname (which is referenced by `mblk`). When the server logging daemon receives the log record, it prepends the name of the client logging host, just as this client logging daemon recorded the name of the logging client. If the `enqueue_tail ()` call succeeds, the continuation field is set to `NULL` to ensure that `mblk->release ()` only reclaims the message block that stores the hostname.

Lines 10–11 If a client application disconnects the TCP connection or an error occurs, the `handle_input ()` hook method returns −1 (Sidebar 13 on page 61 discusses strategies for handling peers that simply stop communicating). This value triggers the reactor to call the following `handle_close ()` hook method that closes the socket:

```
int CLD_Handler::handle_close (ACE_HANDLE handle,
                               ACE_Reactor_Mask)
{ return ACE_OS::closesocket (handle); }
```

Note that we needn't delete `this` object in `handle_close ()` since the memory is managed by the `Client_Logging_Daemon` class (page 180).

  • **Output role.** The `CLD_Handler` object is initialized when `CLD_Connector`'s `connect ()` method (page 179) calls the following `open ()` hook method:

```
1 int CLD_Handler::open (CLD_Connector *connector) {
2   connector_ = connector;
3   int bufsiz = ACE_DEFAULT_MAX_SOCKET_BUFSIZ;
4   peer ().set_option (SOL_SOCKET, SO_SNDBUF,
5                       &bufsiz, sizeof bufsiz);
6   msg_queue_.high_water_mark (CLD_Handler::QUEUE_MAX);
7   return thr_mgr_.spawn (&CLD_Handler::run_svc,
8                          this, THR_SCOPE_SYSTEM);
9 }
```

Lines 2–5 Store a pointer to the `CLD_Connector` and increase the `peer ()` socket send buffer to its largest size to maximize throughput over long-delay and/or high-speed networks.

Line 6 Set the `msg_queue_`'s high watermark to `sizeof(ACE_Log_Record)` ×
ACE_IOV_MAX. Since log records are buffered in groups of up to ACE_IOV_MAX before being sent to the server logging daemon, the queue's high watermark is set to accomodate at
least ACE_IOV_MAX log records. Although the queued log records will be CDR-marshaled,
using the maximum sized demarshaled log record (`ACE_Log_Record`) is a fair approxi-
mation.

Lines 7–8 Use the `ACE_Thread_Manager` from Chapter 9 of C++NPv1 to spawn a
system-scoped thread that executes the `CLD_Handler::run_svc()` static method concurrently with respect to the main thread.[1] The `run_svc()` static method casts its `void`
pointer argument to a `CLD_Handler` pointer and then delegates its processing to the `for-`
`ward()` method, as shown below:

```
ACE_THR_FUNC_RETURN CLD_Handler::run_svc (void *arg) {
  CLD_Handler *handler = ACE_static_cast (CLD_Handler *, arg);
  return handler->forward ();
}
```

We now show the `CLD_Handler::forward()` method, which runs in its own
thread and forwards log records to the server logging daemon. As shown below, this method
optimizes network throughput by buffering log records until a maximum number have arrived or a maximum time elapses.

```
 1 ACE_THR_FUNC_RETURN CLD_Handler::forward () {
 2   ACE_Message_Block *chunk[ACE_IOV_MAX];
 3   size_t message_index = 0;
 4   ACE_Time_Value time_of_last_send (ACE_OS::gettimeofday ());
 5   ACE_Time_Value timeout;
 6   ACE_Sig_Action no_sigpipe ((ACE_SignalHandler) SIG_IGN);
 7   ACE_Sig_Action original_action;
 8   no_sigpipe.register_action (SIGPIPE, &original_action);
 9
10   for (;;) {
11     if (message_index == 0) {
12       timeout = ACE_OS::gettimeofday ();
13       timeout += FLUSH_TIMEOUT;
14     }
15     ACE_Message_Block *mblk = 0;
16     if (msg_queue_.dequeue_head (mblk, &timeout) == -1) {
17       if (errno != EWOULDBLOCK) break;
18       else if (message_index == 0) continue;
19     } else {
20       if (mblk->size () == 0
21           && mblk->msg_type () == ACE_Message_Block::MB_STOP)
22         { mblk->release (); break; }
```

---

[1]Since the `CLD_Handler::close()` method (page 176) waits for this thread to exit, we needn't pass
the THR_DETACHED flag to `spawn()`.

```
23              chunk[message_index] = mblk;
24              ++message_index;
25          }
26      if (message_index >= ACE_IOV_MAX
27          || (ACE_OS::gettimeofday () - time_of_last_send
28              >= FLUSH_TIMEOUT)) {
29          if (send (chunk, message_index) == -1) break;
30          time_of_last_send = ACE_OS::gettimeofday ();
31          }
32      }
33
34      if (message_index > 0) send (chunk, message_index);
35      msg_queue_.close ();
36      no_sigpipe.restore_action (SIGPIPE, original_action);
37      return 0;
38 }
```

Lines 2–5   We will buffer as many blocks as can be sent in a single gather-write operation. We therefore declare an array of ACE_Message_Block pointers to hold pointers to the blocks that will be dequeued. We also define an index to keep track of the number of buffered records and ACE_Time_Value objects to record the last time a log record was sent and the next flush timeout. These ACE_Time_Value objects are used to bound the amount of time log records are buffered before they're transmitted to the logging server.

Lines 6–8   UNIX systems will raise the SIGPIPE signal if send() fails due to the peer closing the connection. The default behavior for SIGPIPE is to abort the process. We use the ACE_Sig_Action class to ignore the SIGPIPE signal in this method, which will allow us to handle any send() failures in the normal (nonsignal) execution path.

Line 10   This loop will run until the message queue is deactivated.

Lines 11–14   Reset the flush timeout on the first iteration, after a timeout, and after message blocks are forwarded.

Lines 15–16   Wait up to the next flush timeout to dequeue a pointer to the next ACE_Message_Block from the msg_queue_.

Lines 17–18   If the dequeue operation failed, and it wasn't because of a timeout, break out of the loop. If it was a timeout, but there are no buffered log records, just continue the loop waiting to dequeue a message block.

Lines 19–22   After successfully dequeueing a message block, we first check to see if its size() is 0 and its type is MB_STOP. By convention, this application uses this type of message block to request the thread to shut down. When we receive the shutdown message, we release the message block and break out of the loop.

Lines 23–24   We store the log record block in the next available slot in the chunk array and increment the count of saved message blocks.

Lines 26–30 Whenever the buffer fills up or the FLUSH_TIMEOUT elapses, call the CLD_ Handler::send() method (see below) to flush the buffered log records in one gather-write operation. The send() method releases all the saved message blocks and resets message_index to reflect the fact that there are no valid blocks remaining. If the records were sent successfully, we record the time when the records were sent.

Line 34 If dequeue_head() fails or a shutdown message was received, any remaining buffered log records are flushed by a call to CLD_Handler::send().

Line 35 Close the message queue to release its resources.

Line 36 Restore the disposition of the SIGPIPE signal to its original action before the forward() method was called.

Line 37 Return from the CLD_Handler::forward() method, which exits the thread.

The CLD_Handler::send() method sends the buffered log records to the logging server. It's also responsible for reconnecting to the server if the connection is closed.

```
 1 int CLD_Handler::send (ACE_Message_Block *chunk[],
 2                        size_t &count) {
 3   iovec iov[ACE_IOV_MAX];
 4   size_t iov_size;
 5   int result = 0;
 6
 7   for (iov_size = 0; iov_size < count; ++iov_size) {
 8     iov[iov_size].iov_base = chunk[iov_size]->rd_ptr ();
 9     iov[iov_size].iov_len = chunk[iov_size]->length ();
10   }
11
12   while (peer ().sendv_n (iov, iov_size) == -1)
13     if (connector_->reconnect () == -1) {
14       result = -1;
15       break;
16     }
17
18   while (iov_size > 0) {
19     chunk[--iov_size]->release (); chunk[iov_size] = 0;
20   }
21   count = iov_size;
22   return result;
23 }
```

Lines 3–9 To set up the gather-write operation, we gather the data pointers and lengths from the supplied message blocks into an iovec array.

Lines 12–16 The ACE_SOCK_Stream::sendv_n() method flushes the buffered log records in one gather-write operation. If sendv_n() fails due to a broken connection, we attempt to reestablish the connection using the CLD_Connector::reconnect() method. If reconnect() succeeds, sendv_n() is reinvoked. As shown on page 179,

CLD_Connector::reconnect() tries upto MAX_RETRIES times to reestablish connections.

All the data is sent on each iteration of the while loop. Since there's no application-level transaction monitoring, there's no end-to-end acknowledgment that the transmitted log records were received and recorded. The sendv_n() can pass back the number of bytes successfully sent to the TCP layer for transmission, but offers no guarantee that any of the bytes were received at the peer host or read by the server logging daemon. Since there's no reliable way to tell how many log records were received and recorded, and logging a record multiple times does no harm, they are all re-sent if the connection must be reestablished.

Lines 18–21   The final loop in the method releases all the log record data and sets all the ACE_Message_Block pointers to 0. To reflect the fact that there are no valid log records remaining in chunk, we reset count to 0.

CLD_Handler::close() is a public method called by the CLD_Acceptor:: handle_close() method (page 178) or the Client_Logging_Daemon::fini() method (page 181) to shut the handler down. It inserts a 0-sized message of type MB_STOP into the message queue as follows:

```
int CLD_Handler::close () {
  ACE_Message_Block *shutdown_message = 0;
  ACE_NEW_RETURN
    (shutdown_message,
     ACE_Message_Block (0, ACE_Message_Block::MB_STOP), -1);
  msg_queue_.enqueue_tail (shutdown_message);
  return thr_mgr_.wait ();
}
```

When the forwarder thread receives the shutdown_message, it flushes its remaining log records to the logging server, closes the message queue, and exits the thread. We use the ACE_Thread_Manager::wait() method to block until the forwarder thread exits before returning. This method also reaps the exit status of the forwarder thread to prevent memory leaks.

CLD_Acceptor.   This class provides the following capabilities:

- It's a factory that passively accepts connections from clients.
- It then registers the connections with the ACE_Reactor. Log records sent from clients over the connections are then processed by an instance of the CLD_Handler shown above.

The CLD_Acceptor class definition is shown below:

```
class CLD_Acceptor : public ACE_Event_Handler {
public:
  // Initialization hook method.
  virtual int open (CLD_Handler *, const ACE_INET_Addr &,
                    ACE_Reactor * = ACE_Reactor::instance ());
```

```
  // Reactor hook methods.
  virtual int handle_input (ACE_HANDLE handle);
  virtual int handle_close (ACE_HANDLE = ACE_INVALID_HANDLE,
                            ACE_Reactor_Mask = 0);
  virtual ACE_HANDLE get_handle () const;

protected:
  // Factory that passively connects <ACE_SOCK_Stream>s.
  ACE_SOCK_Acceptor acceptor_;

  // Pointer to the handler of log records.
  CLD_Handler *handler_;
};
```

Since CLD_Acceptor inherits from ACE_Event_Handler, it can register itself
with the ACE Reactor framework to accept connections, as shown below:

```
int CLD_Acceptor::open (CLD_Handler *handler,
                        const ACE_INET_Addr &local_addr,
                        ACE_Reactor *r) {
  reactor (r); // Store the reactor pointer.
  handler_ = handler;
  if (acceptor_.open (local_addr) == -1
      || reactor ()->register_handler
           (this, ACE_Event_Handler::ACCEPT_MASK) == -1)
    return -1;
  return 0;
}
```

This method instructs the acceptor_ to start listening for connection requests and then
registers this object with the singleton reactor to accept new connections. The reactor
double-dispatches to the following CLD_Acceptor::get_handle() method to obtain
the acceptor_'s socket handle:

```
ACE_HANDLE CLD_Acceptor::get_handle () const
{ return acceptor_.get_handle (); }
```

When a connection request arrives at the client logging daemon, the singleton reactor
dispatches the following CLD_Acceptor::handle_input() hook method:

```
 1 int CLD_Acceptor::handle_input (ACE_HANDLE) {
 2   ACE_SOCK_Stream peer_stream;
 3   if (acceptor_.accept (peer_stream) == -1) return -1;
 4   else if (reactor ()->register_handler
 5                 (peer_stream.get_handle (),
 6                  handler_,
 7                  ACE_Event_Handler::READ_MASK) == -1)
 8      return -1;
 9   else return 0;
10 }
```

Lines 2–3   Accept the connection into `peer_stream`, which just accepts the connection and initializes the new socket handle registered with the reactor. It therefore needn't exist after `handle_input()` returns. The destructor of `ACE_SOCK_Stream` doesn't shut down the handle automatically for the reasons described in Chapter 3 of C++NPv1.

Lines 4–7   Use the three-parameter variant of `register_handler()` (page 73) to register a pointer to the `CLD_Handler` with the reactor for READ events. This `register_handler()` method enables the client logging daemon to reuse a single C++ object for all of its logging handlers. When log records arrive, the reactor will dispatch the `CLD_Handler::handle_input()` method (page 171).

The following `handle_close()` method is invoked automatically by the reactor if a failure occurs while accepting a connection or registering a handle and event handler:

```
int CLD_Acceptor::handle_close (ACE_HANDLE, ACE_Reactor_Mask) {
  acceptor_.close ();
  handler_->close ();
  return 0;
}
```

This method closes both the acceptor factory and the `CLD_Handler`. `CLD_Handler::close()` (page 176) triggers a shutdown of the message queue and forwarder thread.

CLD_Connector.   This class provides the following capabilities:

- It's a factory that actively establishes a connection from the client logging daemon to the server logging daemon.
- It activates the instance of `CLD_Handler` to forward log records concurrently to the logging server.

The `CLD_Connector` class definition is shown below:

```
class CLD_Connector {
public:
  // Establish a connection to the logging server
  // at the <remote_addr>.
  int connect (CLD_Handler *handler,
               const ACE_INET_Addr &remote_addr);

  // Re-establish a connection to the logging server.
  int reconnect ();

private:
  // Pointer to the <CLD_Handler> that we're connecting.
  CLD_Handler *handler_;

  // Address at which the logging server is listening
  // for connections.
  ACE_INET_Addr remote_addr_;
}
```

The `connect()` method is shown below:

```
 1 int CLD_Connector::connect
 2     (CLD_Handler *handler,
 3      const ACE_INET_Addr &remote_addr) {
 4   ACE_SOCK_Connector connector;
 5
 6   if (connector.connect (handler->peer (), remote_addr) == -1)
 7     return -1;
 8   else if (handler->open (this) == -1)
 9   { handler->handle_close (); return -1; }
10   handler_ = handler;
11   remote_addr_ = remote_addr;
12   return 0;
13 }
```

Lines 4–6   Use the ACE Socket wrapper facades from Chapter 4 of C++NPv1 to establish a TCP connection with the server logging daemon.

Lines 8–9   Activate the `CLD_Handler` by invoking its `open()` hook method (page 172). If successful, this method spawns a thread that runs the `CLD_Handler::forward()` method to forward log records to the logging server. If `open()` fails, however, we call the `handle_close()` method on the `handler` to close the socket.

Lines 10–11   Store the handler and the remote address to simplify the implementation of the `CLD_Connector::reconnect()` method, which is used to reconnect to the logging server when it closes client connections, either due to a crash or due to the Evictor pattern (page 66). As shown below, the `reconnect()` method uses an exponential backoff algorithm to avoid swamping a logging server with connection requests:

```
int CLD_Connector::reconnect () {
  // Maximum number of times to retry connect.
  const size_t MAX_RETRIES = 5;

  ACE_SOCK_Connector connector;
  ACE_Time_Value timeout (1); // Start with 1 second timeout.
  size_t i;
  for (i = 0; i < MAX_RETRIES; ++i) {
    if (i > 0) ACE_OS::sleep (timeout);
    if (connector.connect (handler_->peer (), remote_addr_,
                           &timeout) == -1)
      timeout *= 2; // Exponential backoff.
    else {
      int bufsiz = ACE_DEFAULT_MAX_SOCKET_BUFSIZ;
      handler_->peer ().set_option (SOL_SOCKET, SO_SNDBUF,
                                    &bufsiz, sizeof bufsiz);
      break;
    }
  }
  return i == MAX_RETRIES ? -1 : 0;
}
```

As earlier, we increase the `peer()` socket send buffer to its largest size to maximize throughput over long-delay and/or high-speed networks.

Client_Logging_Daemon.   This class is a facade that integrates the three classes described above to implement the client logging daemon. Its definition is shown below.

```
class Client_Logging_Daemon : public ACE_Service_Object {
public:
  // Service Configurator hook methods.
  virtual int init (int argc, ACE_TCHAR *argv[]);
  virtual int fini ();
  virtual int info (ACE_TCHAR **bufferp, size_t length = 0) const;
  virtual int suspend ();
  virtual int resume ();

protected:
  // Receives, processes, and forwards log records.
  CLD_Handler handler_;

  // Factory that passively connects the <CLD_Handler>.
  CLD_Acceptor acceptor_;

  // Factory that actively connects the <CLD_Handler>.
  CLD_Connector connector_;
};
```

`Client_Logging_Daemon` inherits from `ACE_Service_Object`. It can therefore be configured dynamically via a `svc.conf` file processed by the ACE Service Configurator framework described in Chapter 5. When an instance of `Client_Logging_Daemon` is linked dynamically, the ACE Service Configurator framework calls `Client_Logging_Daemon::init()`, which is shown below:

```
 1 int Client_Logging_Daemon::init (int argc, ACE_TCHAR *argv[]) {
 2   u_short cld_port = ACE_DEFAULT_SERVICE_PORT;
 3   u_short sld_port = ACE_DEFAULT_LOGGING_SERVER_PORT;
 4   ACE_TCHAR sld_host[MAXHOSTNAMELEN];
 5   ACE_OS_String::strcpy (sld_host, ACE_LOCALHOST);
 6
 7   ACE_Get_Opt get_opt (argc, argv, ACE_TEXT ("p:r:s:"), 0);
 8   get_opt.long_option (ACE_TEXT ("client_port"), 'p',
 9                        ACE_Get_Opt::ARG_REQUIRED);
10   get_opt.long_option (ACE_TEXT ("server_port"), 'r',
11                        ACE_Get_Opt::ARG_REQUIRED);
12   get_opt.long_option (ACE_TEXT ("server_name"), 's',
13                        ACE_Get_Opt::ARG_REQUIRED);
14
15   for (int c; (c = get_opt ()) != -1;)
16     switch (c) {
17     case 'p': // Client logging daemon acceptor port number.
```

```
18          cld_port = ACE_static_cast
19            (u_short, ACE_OS::atoi (get_opt.opt_arg ()));
20          break;
21        case 'r': // Server logging daemon acceptor port number.
22          sld_port = ACE_static_cast
23            (u_short, ACE_OS::atoi (get_opt.opt_arg ()));
24          break;
25        case 's': // Server logging daemon hostname.
26          ACE_OS_String::strsncpy
27            (sld_host, get_opt.opt_arg (), MAXHOSTNAMELEN);
28          break;
29        }
30
31    ACE_INET_Addr cld_addr (cld_port);
32    ACE_INET_Addr sld_addr (sld_port, sld_host);
33
34    if (acceptor_.open (&handler_, cld_addr) == -1)
35      return -1;
36    else if (connector_.connect (&handler_, sld_addr) == -1)
37    { acceptor_.handle_close (); return -1; }
38    return 0;
39 }
```

Lines 2–5   Assign the default client logging daemon listen port (cld_port) and the default server logging daemon port (sld_port) and hostname (sld_host). These network addresses can be changed by arguments passed into this method. In particular, the server logging daemon hostname will often need to be set using the -s option.

Lines 7–29   Use the ACE_Get_Opt iterator described in Sidebar 8 (page 47) to parse any options passed by the svc.conf file. The final parameter of 0 to ACE_Get_Opt ensures option parsing will begin at argv[0] rather than argv[1], which is the default. If any of the "-p", "-r", or "-s" options, or their long option equivalents, are passed in the argv parameter to init(), the appropriate port number or hostname is modified accordingly.

Lines 31–32   With the port numbers and server logging daemon's hostname now known, form the addresses needed to establish connections.

Lines 34–37   Initialize the acceptor_ (page 177) and connector_ (page 179).

When the client logging daemon is removed, the ACE Service Configurator framework calls the following Client_Logging_Daemon::fini() hook method:

```
int Client_Logging_Daemon::fini () {
  acceptor_.handle_close ();
  handler_.close ();
  return 0;
}
```

This `fini()` method closes the `ACE_SOCK_Acceptor` socket factory and the `CLD_Handler`, which triggers a shutdown of the message queue and forwarder thread. The ACE Service Configurator framework will delete the `Client_Logging_Daemon` instance after `fini()` returns.

Now that we've implemented all the client logging daemon's classes, we place the following ACE_FACTORY_DEFINE macro from Sidebar 32 (page 136) in the implementation file:[2]

```
ACE_FACTORY_DEFINE (CLD, Client_Logging_Daemon)
```

This macro defines the `_make_Client_Logging_Daemon()` factory function, which is used in the following `svc.conf` file:

```
dynamic Client_Logging_Daemon Service_Object *
CLD:_make_Client_Logging_Daemon() "-p $CLIENT_LOGGING_DAEMON_PORT"
```

This file directs the ACE Service Configurator framework to configure the client logging daemon via the following steps:

1. It dynamically links the CLD DLL into the address space of the process.

2. It uses the `ACE_DLL` class described in Sidebar 33 (page 143) to extract the `_make_Client_Logging_Daemon()` factory function address from the CLD DLL symbol table.

3. The factory function is called to obtain a pointer to a dynamically allocated `Client_Logging_Daemon` object.

4. The Service Configurator framework then calls `Client_Logging_Daemon::init()` on this new object, passing as its `argc`/`argv` argument the string `"-p"` followed by an expansion of the `CLIENT_LOGGING_DAEMON_PORT` environment variable designating the port number where the client logging daemon listens for client application connection requests. The `"-r"` and `"s"` options can also be passed in this manner.

5. If `init()` succeeds, the `Client_Logging_Daemon` pointer is stored in the `ACE_Service_Repository` under the name `"Client_Logging_Daemon"`.

Rather than write a new `main()` program, we reuse the one from `Configurable_Logging_Server` (page 147). The `svc.conf` file above simply configures in the Client Logging Daemon service when the program starts. The *Example* portion of Section 7.4 shows how the ACE Acceptor-Connector framework can be used to further simplify and enhance the multithreaded client logging daemon implementation shown above.

---

[2] We leave the `suspend()`, `resume()`, and `info()` hook methods as an exercise for the reader.

6.3   The ACE_Task Class

Motivation

The ACE_Message_Queue class described in Section 6.2 can be used to

- Decouple the flow of information from its processing
- Link threads that execute producer/consumer services concurrently

To use a producer/consumer concurrency model effectively in an object-oriented program, however, each thread should be associated with the message queue and any other service-related information. To preserve modularity and cohesion, and to reduce coupling, it's therefore best to encapsulate an ACE_Message_Queue with its associated data and methods into one class whose service threads can access it directly.

Thread-spawning capabilities provided by popular OS platforms are based on each spawned thread invoking a C-style function call. The ACE_Thread_Manager wrapper facade class described in Chapter 9 of C++NPv1 implements portable multithreading capabilities. However, programmers must still pass a C-style function to its spawn() and spawn_n() methods. Providing a spawned thread with access to a C++ object requires a bridge to the C++ object environment. The CLD_Handler::open() method (page 172) illustrated this technique. Since implementing this technique manually for each class is repetitive, it's a good candidate for reuse. The ACE Task framework therefore defines ACE_Task to encapsulate a class's messaging capability and provide a portable way for thread(s) to execute in the context of an object.

Class Capabilities

ACE_Task is the basis of ACE's object-oriented concurrency framework. It provides the following capabilities:

- It uses an instance of ACE_Message_Queue from Section 6.2 to separate data and requests from their processing.
- It uses the ACE_Thread_Manager class to activate the task so it runs as an active object [POSA2] that processes its queued messages in one or more threads of control. Since each thread runs a designated class method, they can access all of the task's data members directly.
- It inherits from ACE_Service_Object, so its instances can be configured dynamically via the ACE Service Configurator framework from Chapter 5.
- It's a descendant of ACE_Event_Handler, so its instances can also serve as event handlers in the ACE Reactor framework from Chapter 3.
- It provides virtual hook methods that application classes can reimplement for task-specific service execution and message handling.

Our focus in this section is on the ACE_Task capabilities for queueing and processing messages. It obtains its event-handling, configuration, and dynamic linking/unlinking capabilities as a consequence of inheriting from ACE classes described in previous chapters.

The interface for ACE_Task is shown in Figure 6.6. Since this class has a rich interface, we group the description of its methods into the three categories described below. Sidebar 60 (page 308) describes some additional ACE_Task methods that are related to the ACE Streams framework.

1. Task initialization methods. The methods used to initialize a task are shown in the following table:

Method	Description
ACE_Task()	Constructor that can assign pointers to the ACE_Message_Queue and ACE_Thread_Manager used by the task
open()	Hook method that performs application-defined initialization activities
thr_mgr()	Get and set a pointer to the task's ACE_Thread_Manager
msg_queue()	Get and set a pointer to the task's ACE_Message_Queue
activate()	Convert a task into an active object that runs in one or more threads

Applications can customize the startup behavior of an ACE_Task by overriding its open() hook method. This method allocates resources used by a task, such as connection handlers, I/O handles, and synchronization locks. Since open() is generally called after the init() method that's inherited via ACE_Service_Object, any options passed via the ACE Service Configurator framework have already been processed. Therefore, open() can act on those configured preferences. The open() method is also often used to convert a task into an active object by calling ACE_Task::activate() (page 187).

The thr_mgr() and msg_queue() methods make it possible to access and change the thread management and message queueing mechanisms used by a task. Alternative thread management and message queueing mechanisms can also be passed to the ACE_Task constructor when an instance of the class is created.

The activate() method uses the ACE_Thread_Manager pointer returned by the thr_mgr() accessor to spawn one or more threads that run within the task. This method converts the task into an active object whose thread(s) direct its own execution and response to events, rather than being driven entirely by passive method calls that borrow the thread of the caller. Sidebar 42 (page 186) describes how to avoid memory leaks when an activated task's thread(s) exit.

2. Task communication, processing, and synchronization methods. The following table describes the methods used to communicate between tasks and to process messages passively and actively within a task:

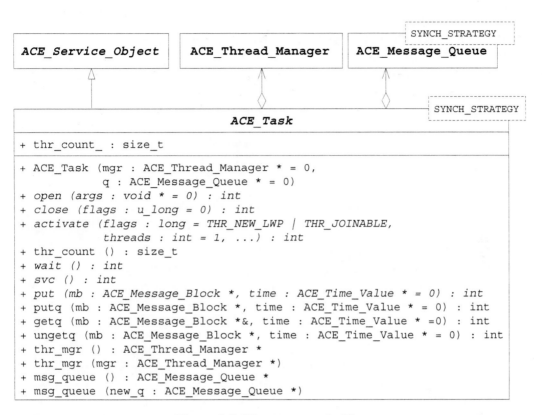

Figure 6.6: The ACE_Task Class

Method	Description
svc()	A hook method that can implement a task's service processing. It is executed by all threads spawned via the activate() method.
put()	A hook method that can be used to pass a message to a task, where it can be processed immediately or queued for subsequent processing by the svc() hook method.
putq() getq() ungetq()	Insert, remove, and replace messages from the task's message queue. The putq(), getq(), and ungetq() methods simplify access to the enqueue_tail(), dequeue_head(), and enqueue_head() methods of a task's message queue, respectively.

A subclass of ACE_Task can perform application-defined processing on messages passed to it by overriding its put() and svc() hook methods to implement the following two processing models:

1. Passive processing. The put() method is used to pass messages to an ACE_Task. Pointers to ACE_Message_Blocks are passed between tasks to avoid data copying overhead. Task processing can be performed entirely in the context of put(), where

---

Sidebar 42: Avoiding Memory Leaks When Threads Exit

Calls to the `ACE_Task::activate()` or the `ACE_Thread_Manager`'s `spawn()` and `spawn_n()` methods can include either of the following flags:

- THR_DETACHED, which designates the spawned thread(s) as *detached* so that when the thread exits, the `ACE_Thread_Manager` ensures the storage used for the thread's state and exit status is reclaimed.
- THR_JOINABLE, which designates the spawned thread(s) as *joinable* so that `ACE_Thread_Manager` ensures the identity and exit status of an exiting thread is retained until another thread reaps its exit status.

The terms *detached* and *joinable* stem from POSIX Pthreads [IEE96].

By default, `ACE_Thread_Manager` (and hence the `ACE_Task` class that uses it) spawns threads with the THR_JOINABLE flag. To avoid leaking resources that the OS holds for joinable threads, an application must call one of the following methods:

1. `ACE_Task::wait()`, which waits for all threads to exit an `ACE_Task` object
2. `ACE_Thread_Manager::wait_task()`, which waits for all threads to exit in a specified `ACE_Task` object
3. `ACE_Thread_Manager::join()`, which waits for a designated thread to exit.

If none of these methods are called, ACE and the OS won't reclaim the thread stack and exit status of a joinable thread, and the program will leak memory.

If it's inconvenient to wait for threads explicitly in your program, you can simply pass THR_DETACHED when spawning threads or activating tasks. Many networked application tasks and long-running daemon threads can be simplified by using detached threads. However, an application can't wait for a detached thread to finish with `ACE_Task::wait()` or obtain its exit status via `join()`. Applications can, however, use `ACE_Thread_Manager::wait()` to wait for both joinable and detached threads managed by an `ACE_Thread_Manager` to finish.

---

the caller's thread is borrowed for the duration of its processing. A task's `svc()` hook method need not be used if the task only processes requests *passively* in `put()`.

2. Active processing. A task's application-defined processing can also be performed *actively*. In this case, one or more threads execute the task's `svc()` hook method to process messages concurrently with respect to other activities in an application. If a task's `put()` method doesn't perform all the processing on a message, it can use `putq()` to enqueue the message and return to its caller immediately.

A task's `svc()` hook method can use `ACE_Task::getq()` to dequeue messages placed onto the message queue and process them concurrently. The `getq()` method blocks until either a message is available on the message queue or the specified absolute timeout elapses. The blocking nature of `getq()` allows the thread(s) of a task to block and only wake up when there's work available on the message queue.

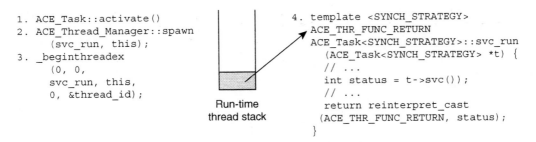

```
1. ACE_Task::activate()              4. template <SYNCH_STRATEGY>
2. ACE_Thread_Manager::spawn            ACE_THR_FUNC_RETURN
     (svc_run, this);                   ACE_Task<SYNCH_STRATEGY>::svc_run
3. _beginthreadex                          (ACE_Task<SYNCH_STRATEGY> *t) {
     (0, 0,                               // ...
      svc_run, this,                      int status = t->svc());
      0, &thread_id);                     // ...
                                          return reinterpret_cast
                                          (ACE_THR_FUNC_RETURN, status);
              Run-time                 }
              thread stack
```

Figure 6.7: Activating an ACE Task

Unlike `put()`, the `svc()` method is never invoked by a client of a task directly. It's instead invoked by one or more threads when a task becomes an active object after its `activate()` method is called. The `activate()` method uses the `ACE_Thread_Manager` associated with an `ACE_Task` to spawn one or more threads, as shown below:

```
template <class SYNCH_STRATEGY> int
ACE_Task<SYNCH_STRATEGY>::activate (long flags,
                                    int n_threads,
                                    /* Other params omitted */) {
  // ...
  thr_mgr ()->spawn_n (n_threads,
                       &ACE_Task<SYNCH_STRATEGY>::svc_run,
                       ACE_static_cast (void *, this),
                       flags, /* Other params omitted */);
  // ...
}
```

The THR_SCOPE_SYSTEM, THR_SCOPE_PROCESS, THR_NEW_LWP, THR_DETACHED, and THR_JOINABLE flags in the table on page 190 of C++NPv1 can be passed in the `flags` parameter to `activate()`. Sidebar 42 describes how THR_DETACHED and THR_JOINABLE can be used to avoid memory leaks when threads exit.

`ACE_Task::svc_run()` is a static method used by `activate()` as an adapter function. It runs in the newly spawned thread(s) of control, which provide an execution context for the `svc()` hook method. Figure 6.7 illustrates the steps associated with activating an `ACE_Task` using the Windows `_beginthreadex()` function to spawn the thread. Naturally, the `ACE_Task` class shields applications from OS-specific details.

When an `ACE_Task` subclass executes as an active object, its `svc()` method runs an event loop that uses its `getq()` method to wait for messages to arrive on the task's message queue. This queue can buffer a sequence of data messages and control messages for subsequent processing by a task's `svc()` method. As messages arrive and are enqueued by a task's `put()` method, its `svc()` method runs in separate thread(s), dequeueing the messages and performing application-defined processing concurrently, as shown in Figure 6.8.

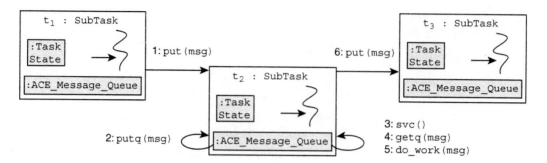

Figure 6.8: Passing Messages Between ACE_Task Objects

Sidebar 43 compares and contrasts the ACE_Task capabilities with Java's Runnable interface and Thread class.

3. Task destruction. The methods used in the destruction of all or parts of a task are shown in the following table:

Method	Description
~ACE_Task()	Deletes resources allocated in ACE_Task constructor, which includes the message queue, if it wasn't passed as a parameter to the constructor.
close()	Hook method that performs application-defined shutdown activities. This method should generally not be called directly by applications, particularly if the task is an active object.
flush()	Closes the message queue associated with the task, which frees all of its enqueued message blocks and releases any threads blocked on the queue.
thr_count()	Returns the number of threads currently active in the ACE_Task.
wait()	A barrier synchronizer that waits for all *joinable* threads running in this task to exit before returning.

The lifetime of an ACE_Task object is not tied to the lifetime of any threads activated in that object. Since deleting an ACE_Task object doesn't shut down any active threads, the threads must therefore exit before the task object can be deleted. ACE provides various ways to request a task's threads to exit, including the cooperative cancellation mechanism (pages 190–191 of C++NPv1). A task's message queue can also be used to pass a shutdown message to the task's threads, as described in Sidebar 41 (page 167).

Applications can customize an ACE_Task's destruction by overriding its close() hook method. This method can free application-defined resources allocated by a task, such as connection control blocks, I/O handles, and synchronization locks. Whereas the open() hook method should be called at most once per instance to initialize an object before it's activated, both the svc() and close() hook methods are called once in each thread. The svc() hook should therefore perform any needed per-thread initialization. The ACE Task framework will call the close() hook method in each thread after the svc() hook

---

Sidebar 43: ACE_Task vs. Java `Runnable` and `Thread`

If you've used Java's `Runnable` interface and `Thread` class [Lea00], the `ACE_Task` design should look familiar, as discussed below:

- `ACE_Task::activate()` is similar to the Java `Thread.start()` method since they both spawn internal threads. The Java `Thread.start()` method spawns only one thread, whereas `activate()` can spawn multiple threads within the same `ACE_Task`, making it easy to implement thread pools as shown in the *Example* part of this section.
- `ACE_Task::svc()` is similar to the Java `Runnable.run()` method since both methods are *hooks* that run in newly spawned thread(s) of control. The Java `run()` hook method executes in only a single thread per object, whereas the `ACE_Task::svc()` method can execute in multiple threads per task object.
- `ACE_Task` contains a message queue that allows applications to exchange and buffer messages. In contrast, this type of queueing capability must be added by Java developers explicitly.

---

method returns, so avoid calling a task's `close()` hook directly, particularly if a task is an active object. This asymmetry between the `open()` and `close()` hook methods is necessary because there's no reliable opportunity to clean up a task's resources except in the task's threads.

If a task activates multiple threads, the `close()` method must not free resources (or delete the task object itself) if other threads are still executing. The `thr_count()` method returns the number of threads still active in the task. `ACE_Task` decrements the thread count before calling `close()`, so if `thr_count()` returns a value greater than 0, the object is still active. The `wait()` method can be used to block until all threads running in this task exit, at which point `thr_count()` equals 0. Sidebar 44 (page 190) describes the steps to follow when destroying an `ACE_Task`.

Example

This example shows how to combine `ACE_Task` and `ACE_Message_Queue` with the `ACE_Reactor` from Chapter 3 and `ACE_Service_Config` from Chapter 5 to implement a concurrent logging server. This server design is based on the Half-Sync/Half-Async pattern [POSA2] and the eager spawning thread pool strategy described in Chapter 5 of C++NPv1. Figure 6.9 (page 191) shows how a pool of worker threads is prespawned when the logging server is launched. Log records can be processed concurrently until the number of simultaneous client requests exceeds the number of worker threads. At this point, the main thread buffers additional requests in a synchronized `ACE_Message_Queue` until a worker thread becomes available or until the queue becomes full.

Sidebar 44: Destroying an ACE_Task

Special care must be taken when destroying an `ACE_Task` that runs as an active object. Before destroying an active object, ensure that the thread(s) running its `svc()` hook method have exited. Sidebar 41 (page 167) describes several techniques to shut down `svc()` hook methods that are blocked on a task's message queue.

If a task's life cycle is managed externally, whether dynamically allocated or instantiated on the stack, one way to ensure a proper destruction sequence looks like this:

```
My_Task *task = new Task; // Allocate a new task dynamically.
task->open (); // Initialize the task.
task->activate (); // Run task as an active object.
// ... do work ...
// Deactive the message queue so the svc() method unblocks
// and the thread exits.
task->msg_queue ()->deactivate ();
task->wait (); // Wait for the thread to exit.
delete task; // Reclaim the task memory.
```

This technique relies on the task to exit all of its threads when the task's message queue is deactivated. This design introduces behavioral coupling, however, between the `Task` class and its users. Users depend on particular behavior when the message queue is deactivated, so any change to this behavior would cause undesired ripple effects throughout all systems that use the `Task` class.

If a task is allocated dynamically, it may therefore be better to have the task's `close()` hook delete itself when the last thread exits the task, rather than calling `delete` on a pointer to the task directly. You may still want to `wait()` on the threads to exit the task, however, particularly if you're preparing to shut down the process. On some OS platforms, when the main thread returns from `main()`, the entire process will be shut down immediately, whether there were other threads active or not.

The `ACE_Message_Queue` plays several roles in our thread pool logging server's half-sync/half-async concurrency design:

- **It decouples the main reactor thread from the thread pool.** This design allows multiple worker threads to be active simultaneously. It also offloads the responsibility for maintaining queues of log record data from kernel space to user space, which has more virtual memory to queue log records than the kernel.

- **It helps to enforce flow control between clients and the server.** When the number of bytes in the message queue reaches its high watermark, its flow control protocol blocks the main thread. As the underlying TCP socket buffers fill up, the flow control propagates back to the server's clients. This prevents clients from establishing new connections or sending log records until the worker threads have a chance to catch up and unblock the main thread.

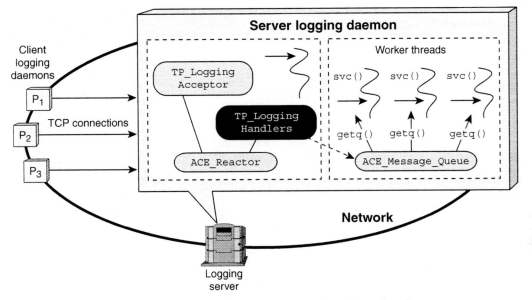

Figure 6.9: Architecture of the Thread Pool Logging Server

Prespawning and queueing help to amortize the cost of thread creation, as well as constrain the use of OS resources, which can significantly improve server scalability.

The following table outlines the classes that we'll cover in the thread pool logging server example below:

Class	Description
TP_Logging_Task	Runs as an active object, with a pool of threads that process and store log records inserted into its synchronized message queue
TP_Logging_Handler	Target of upcalls from the ACE_Reactor that receives log records from clients and inserts them into the TP_Logging_ Task's message queue
TP_Logging_Acceptor	A factory that accepts connections and creates TP_Logging_ Handler objects to process client requests
TP_Logging_Server	A facade class that integrates the other three classes together

The relationship between these classes is shown in Figure 6.10 (page 192). The TP_ Logging_Acceptor and TP_Logging_Handler classes play the reactive role in the Half-Sync/Half-Async pattern and the TP_Logging_Task::svc() method, which runs concurrently in the worker threads, plays the synchronous role in the pattern.

Each class in Figure 6.10 is described below. We start by including the necessary ACE header files into the TP_Logging_Server.h file:

```
#include "ace/OS.h"
#include "ace/Auto_Ptr.h"
```

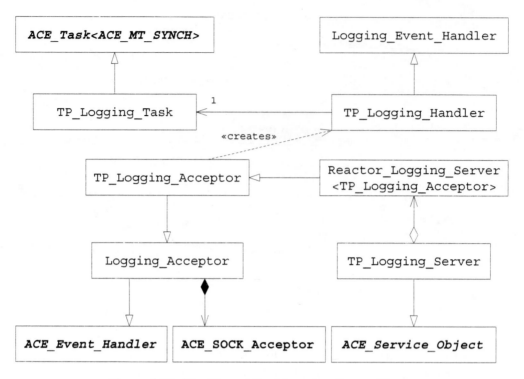

Figure 6.10: The Thread Pool Logging Server Classes

```
#include "ace/Singleton.h"
#include "ace/Synch.h"
#include "ace/Task.h"
#include "Logging_Acceptor.h"
#include "Logging_Event_Handler.h"
#include "Reactor_Logging_Server.h"
#include "TPLS_export.h"
```

TP_Logging_Task.   This class provides the following capabilities:

- It derives from ACE_Task, which it instantiates to provide a synchronized ACE_Message_Queue.
- It spawns a pool of worker threads that all run the same svc() method to process and store log records inserted into its synchronized message queue.

The TP_Logging_Task is shown below:

```
class TP_Logging_Task : public ACE_Task<ACE_MT_SYNCH> {
         // Instantiated with an MT synchronization trait.
public:
  enum { MAX_THREADS = 4 };
```

```
  // ...Methods defined below...
};
```

The `TP_Logging_Task::open()` hook method calls `ACE_Task::activate()` to convert this task into an active object, as follows:

```
virtual int open (void * = 0)
{ return activate (THR_NEW_LWP, MAX_THREADS); }
```

If `activate()` returns successfully, the `TP_Logging_Task::svc()` method will be running in MAX_THREADS separate threads. We show the `TP_Logging_Task::svc()` method (page 199) after we describe the `TP_Logging_Acceptor` and `TP_Logging_Handler` classes.

The `TP_Logging_Task::put()` method inserts a message block containing a log record into the queue.

```
virtual int put (ACE_Message_Block *mblk,
                 ACE_Time_Value *timeout = 0)
{ return putq (mblk, timeout); }
```

We need only one instance of `TP_Logging_Task`, so we convert it into a single-ton using the singleton adapter template described in Sidebar 45 (page 194). Since the `TP_Logging_Task` will be located in a DLL, however, we must use the `ACE_Unmanaged_Singleton` rather than `ACE_Singleton`. This design requires that we close the sin-gleton explicitly when the logging task shuts down in `TP_Logging_Server::fini()` (page 201).

```
typedef ACE_Unmanaged_Singleton<TP_Logging_Task, ACE_Null_Mutex>
        TP_LOGGING_TASK;
```

Since `TP_LOGGING_TASK::instance()` is only accessed from the main thread, we use `ACE_Null_Mutex` as the synchronization type parameter for `ACE_Unmanaged_Singleton`. If this singleton were accessed concurrently by other threads we'd need to parameterize it with `ACE_Recursive_Thread_Mutex` (Chapter 10 of C++NPv1) to serialize access.

TP_Logging_Acceptor.   This class is a factory that provides the following capabilities:

- It accepts connections from client logging daemons.
- It creates `TP_Logging_Handlers` that receive log records from connected clients.

The `TP_Logging_Acceptor` class is shown below:

Sidebar 45: The ACE_Singleton Template Adapters

Although it's possible to code the `TP_Logging_Task` explicitly to be a single-ton, this approach is tedious and error-prone. ACE therefore defines the following `ACE_Singleton` template adapter that applications can use to manage singleton life cycles:

```
template <class TYPE, class LOCK>
class ACE_Singleton : public ACE_Cleanup {
public:
  static TYPE *instance (void) {
    ACE_Singleton<TYPE, LOCK> *&s = singleton_;
    if (s == 0) {
      LOCK *lock = 0;
      ACE_GUARD_RETURN (LOCK, guard,
            ACE_Object_Manager::get_singleton_lock (lock), 0);
      if (s == 0) {
        ACE_NEW_RETURN (s, (ACE_Singleton<TYPE, LOCK>), 0);
        ACE_Object_Manager::at_exit (s);
      }
    }
    return &s->instance_;
  }
protected:
  ACE_Singleton (void); // Default constructor.
  TYPE instance_; // Contained instance.
  // Single instance of the <ACE_Singleton> adapter.
  static ACE_Singleton<TYPE, LOCK> *singleton_;
};
```

The `ACE_Singleton::instance()` static method uses the Double-Checked Locking Optimization pattern [POSA2] to construct and access an instance of the type-specific `ACE_Singleton`. It then registers the instance with the `ACE_Object_Manager` for cleanup at program termination. As described in Sidebar 23 of C++NPv1 (page 218), the `ACE_ObjectManager` assumes responsibility for destroying the `ACE_Singleton` instance, as well as the adapted `TYPE` instance.

A program can crash during singleton cleanup if the object code implementing `TYPE` is unlinked before the `ACE_Object_Manager` cleans up singletons, which is often the case for singletons located in dynamically linked services. We therefore rec-ommend using `ACE_Unmanaged_Singleton` when defining singletons in DLLs that will be linked and unlinked dynamically. This class offers the same double-checked locking optimization to create the singleton. To destroy the singleton, however, re-quires an explicit call to `ACE_Unmanaged_Singleton::close()`. A dynamic ser-vice's `fini()` method is a good place to call this `close()` method, as shown in the `TP_Logging_Server::fini()` method (page 201).

```
class TP_Logging_Acceptor : public Logging_Acceptor {
public:
  TP_Logging_Acceptor (ACE_Reactor *r = ACE_Reactor::instance ())
    : Logging_Acceptor (r) {}

  virtual int handle_input (ACE_HANDLE) {
    TP_Logging_Handler *peer_handler = 0;
    ACE_NEW_RETURN (peer_handler,
                    TP_Logging_Handler (reactor ()), -1);
    if (acceptor_.accept (peer_handler->peer ()) == -1) {
      delete peer_handler;
      return -1;
    } else if (peer_handler->open () == -1)
      peer_handler->handle_close (ACE_INVALID_HANDLE, 0);
    return 0;
  }
};
```

Since `TP_Logging_Acceptor` inherits from the `Logging_Acceptor` (page 54) it can override `handle_input()` to create instances of `TP_Logging_Handler`.

TP_Logging_Handler.   This class provides the following capabilities:

- It receives log records from a connected client.
- It enqueues the log records into the `TP_LOGGING_TASK` singleton's synchronized message queue.

The `TP_Logging_Handler` class is shown below:

```
class TP_Logging_Handler : public Logging_Event_Handler {
  friend class TP_Logging_Acceptor;
```

Since this class derives from `Logging_Event_Handler` (page 59 in Section 3.3), it can receive log records when dispatched by a reactor.

The destructor is defined as protected to ensure dynamic allocation. However, since the `TP_Logging_Acceptor::handle_input()` method deletes objects of this type, `TP_Logging_Acceptor` must be a friend of this class. Declaring a friend class is appropriate in this case because these classes exhibit a high degree of cohesion, and it's important to maintain the restriction on dynamic allocation of `TP_Logging_Handler`. The three data members are used to implement the protocol for closing `TP_Logging_Handler` objects concurrently, as described in Sidebar 46 (page 196).

```
protected:
  virtual ~TP_Logging_Handler () {} // No-op destructor.

  // Number of pointers to this class instance that currently
  // reside in the <TP_LOGGING_TASK> singleton's message queue.
  int queued_count_;
```

Sidebar 46: Closing TP_Logging_Handlers Concurrently

A challenge with thread pool servers is closing objects that can be accessed concurrently by multiple threads. In our thread pool logging server, TP_Logging_Handler pointers are used by TP_LOGGING_TASK threads. These service threads are separate from the thread running the reactor event loop that's driving callbacks to TP_Logging_Handler. We must therefore ensure that a TP_Logging_Handler object isn't destroyed while there are still pointers to it in use by TP_LOGGING_TASK.

When a logging client closes a connection, TP_Logging_Handler::handle_input() (page 197) returns −1. The reactor then calls the handler's handle_close() method, which ordinarily cleans up resources and deletes the handler. Unfortunately, that would wreak havoc if one or more pointers to that handler were still enqueued or being used by threads in the TP_LOGGING_TASK pool. We therefore use a reference counting protocol to ensure the handler isn't destroyed while a pointer to it is still in use. The UML activity diagram below illustrates the behavior this protocol enforces:

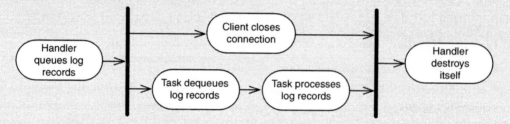

The protocol counts how many times a handler resides in the TP_LOGGING_TASK singleton's message queue. If the count is greater than 0 when the logging client socket is closed, TP_Logging_Handler::handle_close() can't yet destroy the handler. Later, as the TP_LOGGING_TASK processes each log record, the handler's reference count is decremented. When the count reaches 0, the handler can finish processing the close request that was deferred earlier.

```
// Indicates whether <Logging_Event_Handler::handle_close()>
// must be called to cleanup and delete this object.
int deferred_close_;

// Serialize access to <queued_count_> and <deferred_close_>.
ACE_Thread_Mutex lock_;
```

The public part of the class defines the constructor and a pair of methods dispatched by the reactor when certain events occur.

```
public:
  TP_Logging_Handler (ACE_Reactor *reactor)
```

```
      : Logging_Event_Handler (reactor),
        queued_count_  (0),
        deferred_close_  (0) {}

  // Called when input events occur, e.g., connection or data.
  virtual int handle_input (ACE_HANDLE);

  // Called when this object is destroyed, e.g., when it's
  // removed from a reactor.
  virtual int handle_close (ACE_HANDLE, ACE_Reactor_Mask);
};
```

ACE_FACTORY_DECLARE (TPLS, TP_Logging_Handler)

TP_Logging_Handler::handle_input() plays the reactive role in the Half-Sync/Half-Async pattern. It differs from the Logging_Event_Handler::handle_input() method (page 59) since it doesn't process a log record immediately after receiving it. Instead, it inserts each log record into the TP_LOGGING_TASK singleton's message queue, where it will be processed concurrently. However, while processing the log record, the TP_LOGGING_TASK needs to access this handler's log file (inherited from Logging_Event_Handler). To facilitate this, handle_input() combines the log record with a message block containing the handler's pointer and inserts the resulting composite message at the end of the TP_LOGGING_TASK singleton's message queue, as shown below:

```
 1 int TP_Logging_Handler::handle_input (ACE_HANDLE) {
 2   ACE_Message_Block *mblk = 0;
 3   if (logging_handler_.recv_log_record (mblk) != -1) {
 4     ACE_Message_Block *log_blk = 0;
 5     ACE_NEW_RETURN
 6       (log_blk, ACE_Message_Block
 7                   (ACE_reinterpret_cast (char *, this)), -1);
 8     log_blk->cont (mblk);
 9     ACE_GUARD_RETURN (ACE_Thread_Mutex, guard, lock_, -1);
10     if (TP_LOGGING_TASK::instance ()->put (log_blk) == -1)
11     { log_blk->release (); return -1; }
12     ++queued_count_;
13     return 0;
14   } else return -1;
15 }
```

Lines 2–3   Read a log record from a connected socket into a dynamically allocated ACE_Message_Block.

Lines 4–8   Create an ACE_Message_Block called log_blk that contains a pointer to this handler. The ACE_Message_Block constructor simply "borrows" the this pointer and sets the ACE_Message_Block::DONT_DELETE flag internally to ensure that the handler itself isn't destroyed when the message block is released in TP_Logging_

Task::svc() (page 199). The mblk is attached to log_blk's continuation chain to
form a composite message.

Lines 9–10   Use an ACE_Guard to acquire the lock_ that serializes access to queued_
count_. To avoid a race condition in which a service thread processes the record before
queued_count_ can be incremented, the lock is acquired *before* calling put() to insert
the composite message block into the TP_LOGGING_TASK singleton's message queue.

Lines 11–13   Release the log_blk resources and return −1 if put() fails. If it succeeds, increment the count of the number of times the handler's in the TP_LOGGING_
TASK's queue. In either case, the return statement causes the guard to release lock_.

Line 14   If the client closes the connection, or a serious error occurs, handle_input()
returns −1. This value causes the reactor to call TP_Logging_Handler::handle_
close(), which implements a key portion of the protocol for closing TP_Logging_
Handlers concurrently, as described in Sidebar 46 (page 196). The handle_close()
method is shown below:

```
 1 int TP_Logging_Handler::handle_close (ACE_HANDLE handle,
 2                                        ACE_Reactor_Mask) {
 3    int close_now = 0;
 4    if (handle != ACE_INVALID_HANDLE) {
 5      ACE_GUARD_RETURN (ACE_Thread_Mutex, guard, lock_, -1);
 6      if (queued_count_ == 0) close_now = 1;
 7      else deferred_close_ = 1;
 8    } else {
 9      ACE_GUARD_RETURN (ACE_Thread_Mutex, guard, lock_, -1);
10      queued_count_--;
11      if (queued_count_ == 0) close_now = deferred_close_;
12    }
13
14    if (close_now) return Logging_Event_Handler::handle_close ();
15    return 0;
16 }
```

Line 3   The close_now variable records whether the Logging_Event_Handler::
handle_close() method should be called on line 14. This decision depends on the
reference count decisions made in the rest of this method.

Lines 4–7   This code runs when handle_close() is called when handle_input()
returns −1. Lines 6–7 are performed within a critical section protected by an ACE_Guard
that acquires and releases the lock_ automatically within the scope of the if clause. If
queue_count_ equals 0, there are no references to this object remaining in the TP_
LOGGING_TASK, so we set the close_now local variable to 1. Otherwise, we set the
deferred_close_ data member to note that as soon as the reference count reaches 0
this handler should be destroyed since the client has already closed its socket endpoint. As
log records are processed, the TP_Logging_Task::svc() method (page 199) calls
handle_close() again, and will execute the lines described below.

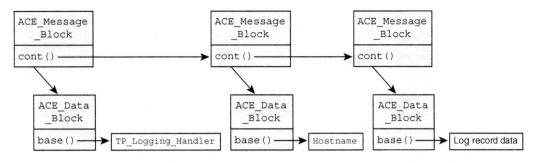

Figure 6.11: Message Block Chain of Log Record Information

Lines 8–12   The handle equals ACE_INVALID_HANDLE when handle_close() is called in TP_Logging_Task::svc() (page 199) *after* the handler has been removed from the task's message queue. We therefore decrement the queue_count_. If the count is now 0, we record whether we need to finish processing a close request that was deferred earlier. As in lines 5–7, we use an ACE_Guard to acquire and release the lock_ automatically within the scope of the else clause.

Line 14   Call Logging_Event_Handler::handle_close() (page 60) if the local variable close_now is true to close the socket and log file, and then delete itself.

Now that we've shown the TP_Logging_Handler class, we can show the TP_Logging_Task::svc() method, which runs concurrently in each of the worker threads and implements the synchronous role in the Half-Sync/Half-Asynch pattern. This method runs its own event loop that blocks on the synchronized message queue. After a message is enqueued by TP_Logging_Handler::handle_input() (page 197), it will be dequeued by an available worker thread and written to the appropriate log file corresponding to the client, as shown below.

```
 1 int TP_Logging_Task::svc () {
 2   for (ACE_Message_Block *log_blk; getq (log_blk) != -1; ) {
 3     TP_Logging_Handler *tp_handler = ACE_reinterpret_cast
 4       (TP_Logging_Handler *, log_blk->rd_ptr ());
 5     Logging_Handler logging_handler (tp_handler->log_file ());
 6     logging_handler.write_log_record (log_blk->cont ());
 7     log_blk->release ();
 8     tp_handler->handle_close (ACE_INVALID_HANDLE, 0);
 9   }
10   return 0;
11 }
```

Lines 2–4   Call the getq() method, which blocks until a message block is available. As shown in Figure 6.11, each message block is a composite message containing three message blocks chained together via their continuation pointers in the following order:

1. A pointer to the `TP_Logging_Handler` that contains the log file where the log record will be written
2. The hostname of the connected client
3. The marshaled log record contents

Lines 5–6   Initialize `logging_handler` with the `log_file` and then call `Logging_Handler::write_log_record()`, which writes the log record to the log file. The `write_log_record()` method is responsible for releasing its message block chain, as shown in Chapter 4 of C++NPv1.

Lines 7–8   Call `log_blk->release()` to reclaim allocated resources. Since the `TP_Logging_Handler` pointer is borrowed rather than allocated dynamically, however, we must explicitly call `TP_Logging_Handler::handle_close()` (page 198) on `tp_handler`. This method decreases the `TP_Logging_Handler` reference count and cleans up the object properly, using the protocol described in Sidebar 46 (page 196).

TP_Logging_Server.   This facade class inherits from `ACE_Service_Object`, contains a `Reactor_Logging_Server`, and uses the `TP_LOGGING_TASK` singleton, as shown below.

```
class TP_Logging_Server : public ACE_Service_Object {
protected:
  // Contains the reactor, acceptor, and handlers.
  typedef Reactor_Logging_Server<TP_Logging_Acceptor>
          LOGGING_DISPATCHER;
  LOGGING_DISPATCHER *logging_dispatcher_;

public:
  TP_Logging_Server (): logging_dispatcher_ (0) {}

  // Other methods defined below...
};
```

The `TP_Logging_Server::init()` hook method enhances the reactive logging server implementation from Chapter 3 as follows:

```
virtual int init (int argc, ACE_TCHAR *argv[]) {
  int i;
  char **array = 0;
  ACE_NEW_RETURN (array, char*[argc], -1);
  ACE_Auto_Array_Ptr<char *> char_argv (array);

  for (i = 0; i < argc; ++i)
    char_argv[i] = ACE::strnew (ACE_TEXT_ALWAYS_CHAR (argv[i]));
  ACE_NEW_NORETURN
    (logging_dispatcher_,
     TP_Logging_Server::LOGGING_DISPATCHER
       (i, char_argv.get (), ACE_Reactor::instance ()));
```

```
    for (i = 0; i < argc; ++i) ACE::strdelete (char_argv[i]);
    if (logging_dispatcher_ == 0) return -1;
    else return TP_LOGGING_TASK::instance ()->open ();
}
```

This init() method is similar to the one on page 122. It allocates an instance of TP_
Logging_Server::LOGGING_DISPATCHER and stores its pointer in the logging_
dispatcher_ member. It also calls TP_Logging_Task::open() to prespawn a
pool of worker threads that process log records concurrently.

The TP_Logging_Server::fini() method is shown next:

```
1 virtual int fini () {
2   TP_LOGGING_TASK::instance ()->flush ();
3   TP_LOGGING_TASK::instance ()->wait ();
4   TP_LOGGING_TASK::close ();
5   delete logging_dispatcher_;
6   return 0;
7 }
```

Line 2   Call the flush() method of the TP_LOGGING_TASK singleton, thereby closing the message queue associated with the task, which deletes all the queued messages and
signals the threads in the pool to exit.

Lines 3–4   Use the ACE_Thread_Manager's barrier synchronization feature to wait for
the pool of threads spawned by TP_Logging_Task::open() to exit and then explicitly
close the singleton because this DLL is about to be unlinked.

Lines 5–6   Delete the logging_dispatcher_ allocated in init() and return.

For brevity, we omit the suspend(), resume(), and info() hook methods, which are
similar to those shown in earlier examples.

Finally, we place ACE_FACTORY_DEFINE into TP_Logging_Server.cpp.

```
ACE_FACTORY_DEFINE (TPLS, TP_Logging_Server)
```

This macro automatically defines the _make_TP_Logging_Server() factory function
that's used in the following svc.conf file:

```
dynamic TP_Logging_Server Service_Object *
TPLS:_make_TP_Logging_Server() "$TP_LOGGING_SERVER_PORT"
```

This file directs the ACE Service Configurator framework to configure the thread pool logging server via the following steps:

1. Dynamically link the TPLS DLL into the address space of the process.

2. Use the ACE_DLL class to extract the _make_TP_Logging_Server() factory function from the TPLS DLL symbol table.

3. This function is called to obtain a pointer to a dynamically allocated TP_Logging_ Server.

4. The Service Configurator framework calls the TP_Logging_Server::init() hook method through this pointer, passing the value of the TP_LOGGING_SERVER_ PORT environment variable as its single argument. This string designates the port number where the logging server listens for client connection requests.

5. If init() succeeds, the TP_Logging_Server pointer is stored in the ACE_ Service_Repository under the name "TP_Logging_Server".

Once again, the ACE Service Configurator framework enables us to reuse the main() program from Configurable_Logging_Server.cpp (page 147).

6.4 Summary

The ACE Task framework allows developers to create and configure concurrent networked applications using powerful and extensible object-oriented designs. This framework provides the ACE_Task class that integrates multithreading with object-oriented programming and queueing. The queueing mechanism in ACE_Task uses the ACE_Message_ Queue class to transfer messages between tasks efficiently. Since ACE_Task derives from the ACE_Service_Object in Section 5.2, it's easy to design services that can be configured dynamically to run as active objects and be dispatched by the ACE Reactor framework.

This chapter illustrated how the ACE Reactor framework can be combined with the ACE Task framework to implement variants of the Half-Sync/Half-Async pattern [POSA2]. The ACE Task framework classes can also be combined with the ACE_Future, ACE_ Method_Request, and ACE_Activation_List classes to implement the Active Object pattern [POSA2]. A subset of the ACE_Message_Queue implementation is presented in Chapter 10 of C++NPv1.

CHAPTER 7

The ACE Acceptor-Connector Framework

This chapter describes the design and use of the ACE Acceptor-Connector framework. This framework implements the Acceptor-Connector pattern [POSA2], which decouples the connection and initialization of cooperating peer services in a networked application from the processing they perform after being connected and initialized. The Acceptor-Connector framework allows applications to configure key properties of their connection topologies independently from the services they provide. We illustrate how this framework can be combined with the ACE Reactor and Task frameworks and applied to enhance the reusability, extensibility, security, and scalability of our networked logging service.

7.1 Overview

Many networked applications, such as e-mail, remote file backups, and Web services, use connection-oriented services containing classes that play the following roles:

- The **connection role** determines how an application establishes connections.
- The **communication role** determines whether an application plays the role of a client, a server, or both client and server in a peer-to-peer configuration.

Networked applications that communicate via connection-oriented protocols (e.g., TCP/IP) are typified by the following asymmetric connection roles between clients and servers:

- Servers often wait passively to accept connections by listening on a designated TCP port.
- Clients often initiate connections actively by connecting to a server's listening port.

Even in peer-to-peer applications, where applications play both client and server roles, connections must be initiated actively by one peer and accepted passively by the other. To enhance reuse and extensibility, networked applications should be designed to easily change connection and communication roles to support different requirements and environments.

The ACE Acceptor-Connector framework implements the Acceptor-Connector design pattern [POSA2], which enhances software reuse and extensibility by decoupling the activities required to connect and initialize cooperating peer services in a networked application from the processing they perform once they're connected and initialized. This chapter describes the following ACE Acceptor-Connector framework classes that networked applications can use to establish connections and initialize peer services:

ACE Class	Description
ACE_Svc_Handler	Represents the local end of a connected service and contains an IPC endpoint used to communicate with a connected peer.
ACE_Acceptor	This factory waits passively to accept a connection and then initializes an ACE_Svc_Handler in response to an active connection request from a peer.
ACE_Connector	This factory actively connects to a peer acceptor and then initializes an ACE_Svc_Handler to communicate with its connected peer.

The most important relationships between the ACE Acceptor-Connector framework's classes are shown in Figure 7.1. These classes play the following roles in accordance with the Acceptor-Connector pattern [POSA2]:

- **Event infrastructure layer classes** perform generic, application-independent strategies for dispatching events. The ACE Reactor framework described in Chapter 3 is commonly used as the event infrastructure layer.

- **Connection management layer classes** perform application-independent connection and initialization services. These classes include the ACE_Svc_Handler, ACE_Acceptor, and ACE_Connector.

- **Application layer classes** customize the generic strategies performed by the other two layers via subclassing and/or template instantiation to create objects that establish connections, exchange data, and perform service-specific processing. In the ACE Acceptor-Connector framework, application layer classes are descendants and template instantiations of the connection management layer classes outlined above.

By being descendants of ACE_Event_Handler, these classes all offer integration with the ACE Reactor framework from Chapter 3. Chapter 8 describes a variant of the Acceptor-Connector framework based on the ACE Proactor framework for applications in which asynchronous I/O is more appropriate or beneficial.

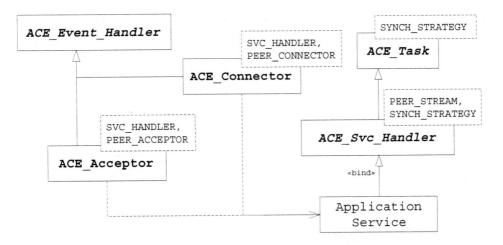

Figure 7.1: The ACE Acceptor-Connector Framework Classes

The ACE Acceptor-Connector framework provides the following benefits:

- **Reusability and extensibility.** Connection-oriented networked applications often contain a significant amount of low-level code that establishes connections and initializes services. This code is largely independent of the processing that connected service handlers perform on the data they exchange. The ACE Acceptor-Connector framework refactors this low-level code into reusable, application-independent acceptor and connector classes that know how to establish a connection and initialize its associated service handler after the connection is established. As a result, service handlers can focus solely on their application-defined processing. This separation of concerns makes it easier to add new types of application services, service implementations, authentication protocols, and communication protocols without affecting existing connection establishment and service initialization configuration code.

- **Portability.** The class templates in the framework are all parameterized by the type of IPC mechanism needed to establish connections and to transfer data. The flexibility offered by this template-based extensibility is useful when developing applications that must run portably and efficiently across multiple OS platforms. The IPC class parameters for the Acceptor-Connector templates can be any network programming classes that conform to the interface expected by the templates. For example, depending on certain properties of the underlying OS platform, such as whether it's a BSD or System V variant of UNIX, a server can instantiate the framework classes to use the ACE Socket wrapper facades or the ACE TLI wrapper facades. For non-TCP/IP applications, the templates can be instantiated with many of ACE's IPC wrapper facades, or any privately developed classes that export the necessary interface.

- **Robustness.** By strongly decoupling a service handler from its acceptor, the framework can ensure that passive-mode transport endpoints aren't accidentally used to read or write data. This added type safety eliminates a subtle and pernicious class of errors that can arise when programming with weakly typed network programming interfaces, such as the Socket or TLI APIs defined in C.

- **Efficiency.** The Acceptor-Connector pattern can actively establish connections with a large number of peers asynchronously and efficiently over long-latency wide area networks. Asynchrony is important in these situations because large-scale networked applications may have hundreds or thousands of peers to connect.

The remainder of this chapter motivates and describes the capabilities of the ACE Acceptor-Connector framework classes. It shows how service handlers are initialized and destroyed, and motivates key framework design choices. It also shows how this framework can be layered on top of the ACE Reactor and ACE Task frameworks to handle connection requests and data exchanged between client and server logging daemons. If you're not familiar with the Acceptor-Connector pattern from POSA2 we recommend you read about it first before delving into the detailed examples in this chapter. We also recommend you read about the ACE Reactor and Task frameworks in Chapters 3 and 6, respectively.

7.2   The ACE_Svc_Handler Class

Motivation

Chapter 2 defined a service as a set of functionality offered to a client by a server. A *service handler* is the portion of a networked application that either implements or accesses (or both, in the case of a peer-to-peer arrangement) a service. Connection-oriented networked applications require at least two communicating service handlers—one for each end of every connection. Incidentally, applications using multicast or broadcast communication may have multiple service handlers. Although these connectionless communication protocols don't cleanly fit the Acceptor-Connector model, the ACE_Svc_Handler class is often a good choice for implementing a service handler and should be considered.

When designing the service handlers involved in a service, developers should also take into account the communication design dimensions discussed in Chapter 1 of C++NPv1. In general, the application functionality defined by a service handler can be decoupled from the following design aspects:

- How the service handler was connected (actively or passively) and initialized
- The protocols used to connect, authenticate, and exchange messages between two service handlers
- The network programming API used to access the OS IPC mechanisms

In general, connection/authentication protocols and service initialization strategies change less frequently than the service handler functionality implemented by an application. To separate these concerns and allow developers to focus on the functionality of their service handlers, the ACE Acceptor-Connector framework defines the ACE_Svc_Handler class.

Class Capabilities

ACE_Svc_Handler is the basis of ACE's synchronous and reactive data transfer and service processing mechanisms. This class provides the following capabilities:

- It provides the basis for initializing and implementing a service in a synchronous and/or reactive networked application, acting as the target of the ACE_Connector and ACE_Acceptor connection factories.
- It provides an IPC endpoint used by a service handler to communicate with its peer service handler(s). The type of this IPC endpoint can be parameterized with many of ACE's IPC wrapper facade classes, thereby separating lower-level communication mechanisms from application-level service processing policies.
- Since ACE_Svc_Handler derives from ACE_Task (and ACE_Task from ACE_Event_Handler), it inherits the concurrency, synchronization, dynamic configuration, and event handling capabilities described in Chapters 3 through 6.
- It codifies the most common practices of reactive network services, such as registering with a reactor when a service is opened and closing the IPC endpoint when unregistering a service from a reactor.

The interface for ACE_Svc_Handler is shown in Figure 7.2 (page 208). As shown in the figure, this class template is parameterized by:

- A PEER_STREAM traits class, which is able to transfer data between connected peer service handlers. It also defines an associated PEER_STREAM::PEER_ADDR trait that represents the address class for identifying the peers to the service. The PEER_STREAM parameter is often instantiated by one of the ACE IPC wrapper facades, such as the ACE_SOCK_Stream described in Chapter 3 of C++NPv1.
- A SYNCH_STRATEGY traits class, which applies the Strategized Locking pattern [POSA2] to parameterize the synchronization traits of an ACE_Message_Queue in the parent ACE_Task class. This parameter is often instantiated by either the ACE_NULL_SYNCH or ACE_MT_SYNCH traits classes (page 163).

Sidebar 40 (page 165) describes the C++ traits and traits class idioms.

Since ACE_Svc_Handler is a descendant of ACE_Event_Handler, an instance of it can be registered with the ACE Reactor framework for various types of events. For example, it can be registered to handle READ and WRITE events. Its handle_input() and handle_output() hook methods will then be dispatched automatically by a reactor when its data-mode socket handle is ready to receive or send data, respectively.

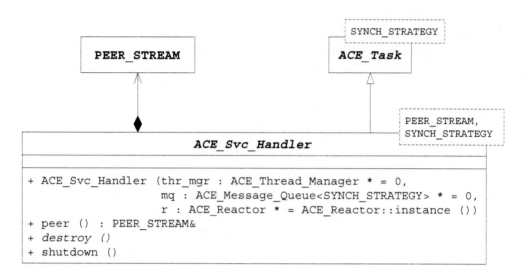

Figure 7.2: The ACE_Svc_Handler Class

The ACE_Svc_Handler class has a rich interface that exports both its capabilities and the capabilities of its parent classes. We therefore group the description of its methods into the three categories described below.

1. Service creation and activation methods. The ACE Acceptor-Connector framework can modify various service handler creation and initialization aspects at compile time and at run time. By default, an ACE_Svc_Handler subclass is allocated dynamically by an acceptor or connector factory, which use the following methods to create and activate it:

Method	Description
ACE_Svc_Handler()	Constructor called by an acceptor or connector when it creates a service handler
open()	Hook method called automatically by an acceptor or connector to initialize a service handler

Sidebar 47 explains why the ACE Acceptor-Connector framework decouples service handler creation from activation.

Pointers to ACE_Thread_Manager, ACE_Message_Queue, and ACE_Reactor objects can be passed to the ACE_Svc_Handler constructor to override its defaults. The open() hook method can perform activities that initialize a service handler, such as:

- Spawning a thread (or pool of threads) that will perform service processing via the svc() hook method
- Registering one or more event sources, such as input events or timeouts, with a reactor

> ### Sidebar 47: Decoupling Service Handler Creation from Activation
>
> The motivations for decoupling service activation from service creation in the ACE Acceptor-Connector framework include:
>
> - **To make service handler creation flexible.** ACE allows for wide flexibility in the way an application creates (or reuses) service handlers. Many applications create new handlers dynamically as needed, but some may recycle handlers or use a single handler for all connections, as discussed in Sidebar 53 (page 240).
> - **To simplify error handling.** ACE doesn't rely on native C++ exceptions for the reasons described in Appendix A.6 of C++NPv1. The constructor used to create a service handler therefore shouldn't perform any operations that can fail. Instead, any such operations should be placed in the open() hook method, which must return −1 if activation fails.
> - **To ensure thread safety.** If a thread is spawned in a constructor it's not possible to ensure that the object has been initialized completely before the thread begins to run. To avoid this potential race condition, the ACE Acceptor-Connector framework decouples service handler creation from activation.

- Opening log files and initializing usage statistics
- Initializing locks or other resources

If these initialization activities complete successfully, open() returns 0. If a failure occurs and the service cannot or should not continue, however, open() must report this event to its caller by returning −1. Since the service handler doesn't control how it was instantiated, a failure in open() must be reported back to the caller so that cleanup activities can be performed. By default, the service handler is deleted automatically if open() returns −1, as shown in the various activate_svc_handler() methods of the acceptor and connector factories (page 221).

The ACE_Svc_Handler defines a default implementation of open() that performs the common set of operations shown below:

```
template <class PEER_STREAM, class SYNCH_STRATEGY> int
ACE_Svc_Handler<PEER_STREAM, SYNCH_STRATEGY>::open
    (void *factory) {
  if (reactor () && reactor ()->register_handler
      (this, ACE_Event_Handler::READ_MASK) == -1) return -1;
  else return 0;
}
```

The void * parameter to open() is a pointer to the acceptor or connector factory that created the service handler. By default, a service handler registers itself with a reactor and processes incoming events reactively. The *Example* part of this section (page 214) illustrates a service handler that activates itself in its open() method to become an active object and process incoming events concurrently. Since a service handler is responsible for its life cycle management after being activated successfully, it rarely interacts with the acceptor that created and activated it. As shown in the *Example* part of Section 7.4, however, a service handler often uses a connector to reestablish connections if failures occur.

2. Service processing methods. As outlined above, a service handler can perform its processing in several ways. For example, it can process events reactively using a reactor or it can process them concurrently via one or more processes or threads. The following methods inherited from ACE_Svc_Handler's ancestors can be overridden by its subclasses and used to perform service handler processing:

Method	Description
svc()	ACE_Svc_Handler inherits the svc() hook method from the ACE_Task class described in Section 6.3. After a service handler's activate() method is invoked, much of its subsequent processing can be performed concurrently within its svc() hook method.
handle_*()	ACE_Svc_Handler inherits the handle_*() methods from the ACE_Event_Handler class described in Section 3.3. A service handler can therefore register itself with a reactor to receive callbacks, such as handle_input(), when various events of interest occur, as described in Chapter 3.
peer()	Returns a reference to the underlying PEER_STREAM. A service handler's PEER_STREAM is ready for use when its open() hook method is called. Any of the service processing methods can use this accessor to obtain a reference to the connected IPC mechanism.

Although the ACE_Svc_Handler SYNCH_STRATEGY template argument parameterizes the ACE_Message_Queue inherited from ACE_Task, it has no effect on the PEER_STREAM IPC endpoint. It's inappropriate for the ACE Acceptor-Connector framework to unilaterally serialize use of the IPC endpoint since it's often not accessed concurrently. For example, a service handler may run as an active object with a single thread or be driven entirely by callbacks from a reactor in a single-threaded configuration.

It is possible, however, for a service handler's open() hook method to spawn multiple threads that access its IPC endpoint concurrently. In such cases, the application code in the service handler must perform any necessary synchronization. Chapter 10 of C++NPv1 describes ACE synchronization mechanisms that applications can use. For example, if more than one thread writes to the same socket handle, it's a good idea to serialize it with an ACE_Thread_Mutex to avoid interleaving data from different send() calls into the same TCP bytestream.

3. Service shutdown methods. A service handler can be used in many ways. For example, it can be dispatched by a reactor, run in its own thread or process, or form part of a thread pool. The ACE_Svc_Handler class therefore provides the following methods to shut a service handler down:

Method	Description
`destroy()`	Can be called to shut a service handler down directly
`handle_close()`	Calls `destroy()` via a callback from a reactor
`close()`	Calls `handle_close()` on exit from a service thread

Service handlers are often closed in accordance with an application-defined protocol, such as when a peer service handler closes a connection or when a serious communication error occurs. Regardless of the particular circumstance, however, a service handler's shutdown processing usually undoes the actions performed by the service handler's `open()` hook method, and deletes the service handler when needed. The shutdown methods listed in the table above can be divided into the following three categories:

• **Direct shutdown.**   An application can invoke the `destroy()` method directly to shut a service handler down. This method performs the following steps:

1. Remove the handler from the reactor.
2. Cancel any timers associated with the handler.
3. Close the peer stream object to avoid handle leaks.
4. If the object was allocated dynamically, delete it to avoid memory leaks.

Chapter 3 of C++NPv1 explained why the destruction of an `ACE_SOCK`-derived object doesn't close the encapsulated socket. `ACE_Svc_Handler` is at a higher level of abstraction, however, and, because it's part of a framework, it codifies common usage patterns. Since closing the socket is such a common part of shutting down a service handler, the ACE Acceptor-Connector framework performs this task automatically.

`ACE_Svc_Handler` uses the Storage Class Tracker C++ idiom described in Sidebar 48 (page 212) to check if it was allocated dynamically or statically. Its `destroy()` method can therefore tell if a service handler was allocated dynamically and, if so, delete it. If the service handler was not allocated dynamically, `destroy()` doesn't delete it.

If a service handler is registered with a reactor, it's best to not call `destroy()` from a thread that's not running the reactor event loop. Doing so could delete the service handler object out from under a reactor that's dispatching events to it, causing undefined (and undesired) behavior (this is similar to the issue discussed in Sidebar 46 on page 196). Rather than calling `destroy()` directly, therefore, use the `ACE_Reactor::notify()` method (page 77) to transfer control to a thread dispatching reactor events, where `destroy()` is safer to use. An even better approach, however, is to alter the design to use the reactive shutdown technique described next.

• **Reactive shutdown.**   When an `ACE_Svc_Handler` is registered with the ACE Reactor framework, it often detects that the peer application has closed the connection and initiates shutdown locally. A reactor invokes a service handler's `handle_close()` method when instructed to remove the handler from its internal tables, usually when the

---

Sidebar 48: Determining a Service Handler's Storage Class

ACE_Svc_Handler objects are often allocated dynamically by the ACE_Acceptor and ACE_Connector factories in the ACE Acceptor-Connector framework. There are situations, however, when service handlers are allocated differently, such as statically or on the stack. To reclaim a handler's memory correctly, without tightly coupling it with the classes and factories that may instantiate it, the ACE_Svc_Handler class uses the C++ *Storage Class Tracker* idiom [vR96]. This idiom performs the following steps to determine automatically whether a service handler was allocated statically or dynamically and act accordingly:

1. ACE_Svc_Handler overloads operator new, which allocates memory dynamically and sets a flag in thread-specific storage that notes this fact.
2. The ACE_Svc_Handler constructor inspects thread-specific storage to see if the object was allocated dynamically, recording the result in a data member.
3. When the destroy() method is eventually called, it checks the "dynamically allocated" flag. If the object was allocated dynamically, destroy() deletes it; if not, it will simply let the ACE_Svc_Handler destructor clean up the object when it goes out of scope.

---

service handler's handle_input() method returns −1 after a peer closes a connection. Reactive handlers should consolidate shutdown activities in the handle_close() method, as discussed in Sidebar 9 (page 51). As shown in Figure 7.3, the default handle_close() method calls the destroy() method (page 211). The handle_close() method can be overridden in subclasses if its default behavior is undesirable.

• **Thread shutdown.** As described on page 188, a service handler's close() hook method is called in each of a task's threads when its svc() method returns. Whereas a reactive service uses the reactor shutdown mechanism to initiate shutdown activity, an active thread that's handling a peer connection can simply return when the peer closes the connection. Since a single thread executing the service is a common use case, the default ACE_Svc_Handler::close() hook method implementation calls the handle_close() method described above. This method can be overridden in subclasses to perform application-specific cleanup code if its default behavior is undesirable.

Example

This example illustrates how to use the ACE_Svc_Handler class to implement a logging server based on the thread-per-connection concurrency model described in Chapter 5 of C++NPv1. The example code is in the TPC_Logging_Server.cpp and TPC_Logging_Server.h files. The header file declares the example classes, and starts by including the necessary header files.

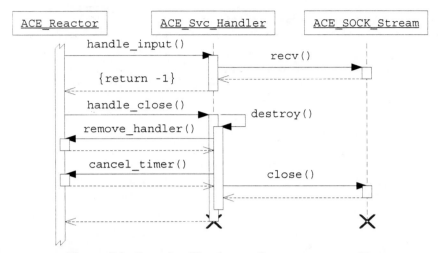

Figure 7.3: Reactive Shutdown of ACE_Svc_Handler

```
#include "ace/Acceptor.h"
#include "ace/INET_Addr.h"
#include "ace/Reactor.h"
#include "ace/Svc_Handler.h"
#include "ace/FILE_IO.h"
#include "Logging_Handler.h"
```

The TPC_Logging_Handler shown below inherits from ACE_Svc_Handler.

```
class TPC_Logging_Handler
  : public ACE_Svc_Handler<ACE_SOCK_Stream, ACE_NULL_SYNCH> {
```

We parameterize the ACE_Svc_Handler template with an ACE_SOCK_Stream data transfer class and the ACE_NULL_SYNCH traits class, which designates a no-op synchronization strategy. Sidebar 49 (page 214) explains how ACE handles C++ compilers that don't support traits classes in templates.

   TPC_Logging_Handler defines the following two data members that are initialized in its constructor.

```
protected:
  ACE_FILE_IO log_file_; // File of log records.

  // Connection to peer service handler.
  Logging_Handler logging_handler_;

public:
  TPC_Logging_Handler (): logging_handler_ (log_file_) {}
```

As usual, we reuse the Logging_Handler from Chapter 4 of C++NPv1 to read a log record out of the socket handle parameter and store it into an ACE_Message_Block.

Sidebar 49: Workarounds for Lack of Traits Class Support

If you examine the ACE Acceptor-Connector framework source code closely, you'll notice that the IPC class template argument to `ACE_Acceptor`, `ACE_Connector`, and `ACE_Svc_Handler` is a macro rather than a type parameter. Likewise, the synchronization strategy parameter to the `ACE_Svc_Handler` is a macro rather than a type parameter. ACE uses these macros to work around the lack of support for traits classes and templates in some C++ compilers. To work portably on those platforms, ACE class types, such as `ACE_INET_Addr` or `ACE_Thread_Mutex`, must be passed as explicit template parameters, rather than accessed as traits of traits classes, such as `ACE_SOCK_Addr::PEER_ADDR` or `ACE_MT_SYNCH::MUTEX`.

To simplify the efforts of application developers, ACE defines a set of macros that conditionally expand to the appropriate types. For example, the following table describes the `ACE_SOCK*` macros:

ACE Class	Description
`ACE_SOCK_ACCEPTOR`	Expands to either `ACE_SOCK_Acceptor` or `ACE_SOCK_Acceptor` and `ACE_INET_Addr`
`ACE_SOCK_CONNECTOR`	Expands to either `ACE_SOCK_Connector` or to `ACE_SOCK_Connector` and `ACE_INET_Addr`
`ACE_SOCK_STREAM`	Expands to either `ACE_SOCK_Stream` or to `ACE_SOCK_Stream` and `ACE_INET_Addr`

These macros supply addressing classes that work properly with all C++ compilers supported by ACE. For example, they expand to a single class if template traits are supported and two classes if not.

ACE uses the `ACE_SOCK_STREAM` macro internally as the IPC class parameter to the `ACE_Svc_Handler` template macro rather than the `ACE_SOCK_Stream` class to avoid problems when porting code to older C++ compilers. Most modern C++ compilers no longer have these problems, so you needn't use these macros in your application code unless portability to legacy compilers is essential. For simplicity, the code in this book assumes that your C++ compiler fully supports template traits and traits classes, and therefore doesn't use the ACE macros. The C++NPv2 example code included with ACE, however, does use the macros to ensure portability to all ACE platforms.

Each instance of `TPC_Logging_Handler` is allocated dynamically by the `TPC_Logging_Acceptor` (page 222) when a connection request arrives from a peer connector. `TPC_Logging_Handler` overrides the `ACE_Svc_Handler::open()` hook method to initialize the handler, as shown below:

```
1 virtual int open (void *) {
2    static const ACE_TCHAR LOGFILE_SUFFIX[] = ACE_TEXT (".log");
3    ACE_TCHAR filename[MAXHOSTNAMELEN + sizeof (LOGFILE_SUFFIX)];
```

```
 4     ACE_INET_Addr logging_peer_addr;
 5
 6     peer ().get_remote_addr (logging_peer_addr);
 7     logging_peer_addr.get_host_name (filename, MAXHOSTNAMELEN);
 8     ACE_OS_String::strcat (filename, LOGFILE_SUFFIX);
 9
10     ACE_FILE_Connector connector;
11     connector.connect (log_file_,
12                        ACE_FILE_Addr (filename),
13                        0, // No timeout.
14                        ACE_Addr::sap_any, // Ignored.
15                        0, // Don't try to reuse the addr.
16                        O_RDWR|O_CREAT|O_APPEND,
17                        ACE_DEFAULT_FILE_PERMS);
18
19     logging_handler_.peer ().set_handle (peer ().get_handle ());
20
21     return activate (THR_NEW_LWP | THR_DETACHED);
22   }
```

Lines 2–17   Initialize a log file using the same logic described in the Logging_Event_ Handler::open() method (page 59).

Line 19   Borrow the socket handle from the service handler and assign it to logging_ handler_, which is then used to receive and process client log records.

Line 21   Convert TPC_Logging_Handler into an active object. The newly spawned detached thread runs the following TPC_Logging_Handler::svc() hook method:

```
virtual int svc () {
  for (;;)
    switch (logging_handler_.log_record ()) {
    case -1: return -1; // Error.
    case 0: return 0; // Client closed connection.
    default: continue; // Default case.
    }
  /* NOTREACHED */
  return 0;
  }
};
```

This method focuses solely on reading and processing client log records. We break out of the for loop and return from the method when the log_record() method detects that its peer service handler has closed the connection or when an error occurs. Returning from the method causes the thread to exit, which in turn triggers ACE_Task::svc_run() to call the inherited ACE_Svc_Handler::close() method on the object. By default, this method closes the peer stream and deletes the service handler if it was allocated dynamically, as described in the table on page 210. Since the thread was spawned using the THR_DETACHED flag, there's no need to wait for it to exit.

You may notice that `TPC_Logging_Handler::svc()` provides no way to stop the thread's processing if the server is somehow asked to shut down before the peer closes the socket. Adding this capability is left as an exercise for the reader. Some common techniques for providing this feature are described in Sidebar 50.

Sidebar 50: Techniques for Shutting Down Blocked Service Threads

Service threads often perform blocking I/O operations, as shown by the thread-per-connection concurrency model in `TPC_Logging_Handler::svc()` (page 215). If the service thread must be stopped before its normal completion, however, the simplicity of this model can cause problems. Some techniques for forcing service threads to shut down, along with their potential drawbacks, include:

- Exit the server process, letting the OS abruptly terminate the peer connection, as well as any other open resources, such as files (a log file, in the case of this chapter's examples). This approach can result in lost data and leaked resources. For example, System V IPC objects are vulnerable in this approach.

- Enable asynchronous thread cancellation and cancel the service thread. This design isn't portable and can also abandon resources if not programmed correctly.

- Close the socket, hoping that the blocked I/O call will abort and end the service thread. This solution can be effective, but doesn't work on all platforms.

- Rather than blocking I/O, use timed I/O and check a shutdown flag, or use the `ACE_Thread_Manager` cooperative cancellation mechanism, to cleanly shut down between I/O attempts. This approach is also effective, but may delay the shutdown by up to the specified timeout.

7.3   The ACE_Acceptor Class

Motivation

Many connection-oriented server applications tightly couple their connection establishment and service initialization code in ways that make it hard to reuse existing code. For example, if you examine the `Logging_Acceptor` (page 58), `Logging_Acceptor_Ex` (page 67), `Logging_Acceptor_WFMO` (page 112), `CLD_Acceptor` (page 176), and `TP_Logging_Acceptor` (page 193) classes, you'll see that the `handle_input()` method was rewritten for each logging handler, even though the structure and behavior of the code was nearly identical. The ACE Acceptor-Connector framework defines the `ACE_Acceptor` class so that application developers needn't rewrite this code repeatedly.

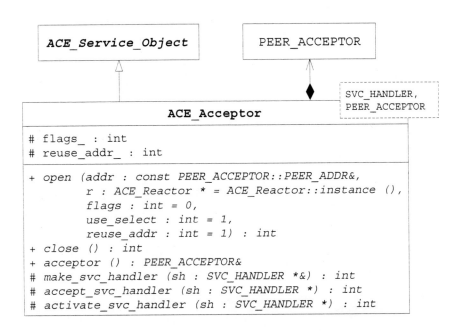

Figure 7.4: The ACE_Acceptor Class

Class Capabilities

ACE_Acceptor is a factory that implements the Acceptor role in the Acceptor-Connector pattern [POSA2]. This class provides the following capabilities:

- It decouples the passive connection establishment and service initialization logic from the processing performed by a service handler after it's connected and initialized.
- It provides a passive-mode IPC endpoint used to listen for and accept connections from peers. The type of this IPC endpoint can be parameterized with many of ACE's IPC wrapper facade classes, thereby separating lower-level connection mechanisms from application-level service initialization policies.
- It automates the steps necessary to connect the IPC endpoint passively and create/activate its associated service handler.
- Since ACE_Acceptor is derived from ACE_Service_Object, it inherits the event-handling and configuration capabilities described in Chapters 3 and 5.

The interface for ACE_Acceptor is shown in Figure 7.4. As shown in the figure, this class template is parameterized by:

- An SVC_HANDLER class, which provides an interface for processing services defined by clients, servers, or both client and server roles in peer-to-peer services. This parameter is instantiated by a subclass of the `ACE_Svc_Handler` class described in Section 7.2.

- A `PEER_ACCEPTOR` class, which is able to accept client connections passively. This parameter is often specified as one of the ACE IPC wrapper facades, such as the `ACE_SOCK_Acceptor` described in Chapter 3 of C++NPv1.

Since `ACE_Acceptor` is a descendant of `ACE_Event_Handler`, an instance of it can be registered with the ACE Reactor framework to process ACCEPT events. Its `handle_input()` method will be dispatched automatically by a reactor when a new connection request arrives from a client.

The `ACE_Acceptor` class has a flexible interface that can be customized extensively by application developers. We therefore group the description of its methods into the two categories described below.

1. Acceptor initialization, destruction, and accessor methods. The following methods are used to initialize and destroy an `ACE_Acceptor`:

Method	Description
`ACE_Acceptor()` `open()`	Bind an acceptor's passive-mode IPC endpoint to a particular address, such as a TCP port number and IP host address, then listen for the arrival of connection requests.
`~ACE_Acceptor()` `close()`	Close the acceptor's IPC endpoint and release its resources.
`acceptor()`	Returns a reference to the underlying `PEER_ACCEPTOR`.

A portion of `ACE_Acceptor::open()` is shown below:

```
1 template <class SVC_HANDLER, class PEER_ACCEPTOR>
2 int ACE_Acceptor<SVC_HANDLER, PEER_ACCEPTOR>::open
3     (const ACE_TYPENAME PEER_ACCEPTOR::PEER_ADDR &addr,
4      ACE_Reactor * = ACE_Reactor::instance (),
5      int flags = 0,
6      /* ... Other parameters omitted ... */)
7 { /* ... */ }
```

Line 3   To designate the proper type of IPC addressing class, a `PEER_ACCEPTOR` template parameter must define a `PEER_ADDR` trait. Sidebar 5 in Chapter 3 in C++NPv1 illustrates how the `ACE_SOCK_Acceptor` class meets this criteria.

Line 4   By default, the `open()` method uses the singleton `ACE_Reactor` to register the acceptor to handle ACCEPT events. This reactor can be changed on a per-instance basis, which is useful when a process uses multiple reactors, for example, one per thread.

Line 5   The `flags` parameter indicates whether a service handler's IPC endpoint initialized by the acceptor should start in blocking mode (the default) or in nonblocking mode (ACE_NONBLOCK).

2. Connection establishment and service handler initialization methods. The following `ACE_Acceptor` methods can be used to establish connections passively and initialize their associated service handlers:

Method	Description
`handle_input()`	This template method is called by a reactor when a connection request arrives from a peer connector. It can use the three methods outlined below to automate the steps necessary to connect an IPC endpoint passively, and to create and activate its associated service handler.
`make_svc_handler()`	This factory method creates a service handler to process data requests emanating from its peer service handler via its connected IPC endpoint.
`accept_svc_handler()`	This hook method uses the acceptor's passive-mode IPC endpoint to create a connected IPC endpoint and encapsulate the endpoint with an I/O handle that's associated with the service handler.
`activate_svc_handler()`	This hook method invokes the service handler's open() hook method, which allows the service handler to finish initializing itself.

Figure 7.5 (page 220) shows the default steps that an `ACE_Acceptor` performs in its `handle_input()` template method:

1. It calls the `make_svc_handler()` factory method to create a service handler dynamically.
2. It calls the `accept_svc_handler()` hook method to accept a connection and store it in the service handler.
3. It calls the `activate_svc_handler()` hook method to allow the service handler to finish initializing itself.

Sidebar 47 (page 209) explains why the `ACE_Acceptor::handle_input()` template method decouples service handler creation from activation.

`ACE_Acceptor::handle_input()` uses the Template Method pattern [GoF] to allow application designers to change the behavior of any of the three steps outlined above. The default behaviors of `make_svc_handler()`, `accept_svc_handler()`, and `activate_svc_handler()` can therefore be overridden by subclasses. This design allows a range of behavior modification and customization to support many use cases. The three primary variation points in `ACE_Acceptor::handle_input()` are described and illustrated in more detail below.

1. Service handler creation. The `ACE_Acceptor::handle_input()` template method calls the `make_svc_handler()` factory method to create a new service handler. The default implementation of `make_svc_handler()` is shown below:

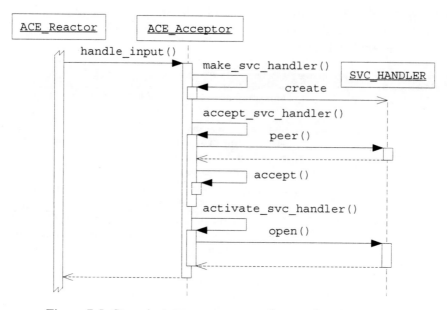

Figure 7.5: Steps in ACE_Acceptor Connection Acceptance

```
1 template <class SVC_HANDLER, class PEER_ACCEPTOR> int
2 ACE_Acceptor<SVC_HANDLER, PEER_ACCEPTOR>::make_svc_handler
3    (SVC_HANDLER *&sh) {
4  ACE_NEW_RETURN (sh, SVC_HANDLER, -1);
5  sh->reactor (reactor ());
6  return 0;
7 }
```

Line 4 Allocate an instance of SVC_HANDLER dynamically. The SVC_HANDLER constructor should initialize any pointer data members to NULL to avoid subtle run-time problems that can otherwise arise if failures are detected in ACE_Acceptor::handle_input() template method and the SVC_HANDLER must be closed.

Line 5 Set the reactor of the newly created service handler to the same reactor associated with the acceptor.

Subclasses can override make_svc_handler() to create service handlers in any way that they like, such as:

- Creating service handlers based on some criteria, such as the number of CPUs available, a stored configuration parameter, calculated historical load average, or the current host workload.
- Always returning a singleton service handler (page 247) or
- Dynamically linking the handler from a DLL by using the ACE_Service_Config or ACE_DLL classes described in Chapter 5.

2. Connection establishment. The `ACE_Acceptor::handle_input()` template method calls the `accept_svc_handler()` hook method to passively accept a new connection from a peer connector. The default implementation of this method delegates to the `PEER_ACCEPTOR::accept()` method, as shown below:

```
template <class SVC_HANDLER, class PEER_ACCEPTOR> int
ACE_Acceptor<SVC_HANDLER, PEER_ACCEPTOR>::accept_svc_handler
    (SVC_HANDLER *sh) {
  if (acceptor ().accept (sh->peer ()) == -1)
  { sh->close (0); return -1; }
  return 0;
}
```

For this `accept_svc_handler()` implementation to compile, the `PEER_ACCEPTOR` template parameter must have a public `accept()` method. `ACE_SOCK_Acceptor` (Chapter 3 of C++NPv1) meets this requirement, as do most ACE IPC wrapper facades.

Subclasses can override `accept_svc_handler()` to add extra processing required before or after the connection is accepted, but before it can be used. For example, this method can authenticate a new connection before activating the service. The authentication process could validate the peer's host and/or port number, perform a login sequence, or set up an SSL session on the new socket. The *Example* section on page 222 illustrates how to implement authentication by overriding the `accept_svc_handler()` hook method to perform SSL authentication before activating the service. Use caution, however, when performing exchanges with the peer in this situation. If `activate_svc_handler()` is called via a reactor callback, the application's entire event dispatching loop may block for an unacceptably long amount of time.

3. Service handler activation. The `ACE_Acceptor::handle_input()` template method calls the `activate_svc_handler()` hook method to activate a new service after it has been created and a new connection has been accepted on its behalf. The default behavior of this method is shown below:

```
 1 template <class SVC_HANDLER, class PEER_ACCEPTOR> int
 2 ACE_Acceptor<SVC_HANDLER, PEER_ACCEPTOR>::activate_svc_handler
 3     (SVC_HANDLER *sh) {
 4   int result = 0;
 5   if (ACE_BIT_ENABLED (flags_, ACE_NONBLOCK)) {
 6     if (sh->peer ().enable (ACE_NONBLOCK) == -1)
 7       result = -1;
 8   } else if (sh->peer ().disable (ACE_NONBLOCK) == -1)
 9     result = -1;
10
11   if (result == 0 && sh->open (this) == -1)
12     result = -1;
13   if (result == -1) sh->close (0);
14   return result;
15 }
```

Lines 5–9   The blocking/nonblocking status of a service handler is set to reflect the flags stored by the acceptor in its constructor. If the acceptor's `flag_` designates nonblocking mode, we enable nonblocking I/O on the service handler's peer stream. Otherwise, the peer stream is set to blocking mode.

Lines 11–14   The service handler's `open()` hook method is called to activate the handler (see page 209 for an example). If service activation fails, the service handler's `close()` hook method is called to release any resources associated with the service handler.

Subclasses can override `activate_svc_handler()` to activate the service in some other way, such as associating it with a thread pool or spawning a new process or thread to process data sent by clients. Since the `ACE_Acceptor::handle_input()` method is virtual it's possible (though rare) to change the sequence of steps performed to accept a connection and initialize a service handler. Regardless of whether the default `ACE_Acceptor` steps are used or not, the functionality of the service handler itself is decoupled completely from the steps used to passively connect and initialize it. This design maintains the modularity and separation of concerns that are so important to minimize the cost of the service's future maintenance and development.

Example

This example is another variant of our server logging daemon. It uses the `ACE_Acceptor` instantiated with an `ACE_SOCK_Acceptor` to listen on a passive-mode TCP socket handle defined by the "`ace_logger`" service entry in the system's services database, which is usually `/etc/services`. This revision of the server uses the thread-per-connection concurrency model to handle multiple clients simultaneously.

As shown in Figure 7.6, the main thread uses a reactor to wait for new connection requests from clients. When a connection arrives, the acceptor uses the OpenSSL [Ope01] authentication protocol outlined in Sidebar 51 (page 224) to ensure that the client logging daemon is permitted to connect with the server. If the client is legitimate, the acceptor dynamically creates a `TPC_Logging_Handler` from the *Example* part of Section 7.2 to handle the connection. The `TPC_Logging_Handler::open()` method (page 214) spawns a thread to process log records sent by the client over the connection.

Since much of the code is reused from the ACE Acceptor-Connector framework and OpenSSL library, this example mostly extends, instantiates, and uses existing capabilities. We subclass `ACE_Acceptor` and override its `open()` method and `accept_svc_handler()` hook method to define the server end of its authentication protocol. The `TPC_Logging_Acceptor` class and its protected data members are declared as follows:

```
#include "ace/SOCK_Acceptor.h"
#include <openssl/ssl.h>
```

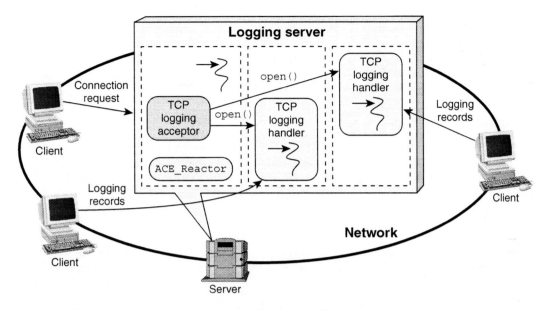

Figure 7.6: Architecture of the Thread-per-Connection Logging Server

```
class TPC_Logging_Acceptor
   : public ACE_Acceptor<TPC_Logging_Handler, ACE_SOCK_Acceptor> {
protected:
  // The SSL ''context'' data structure.
  SSL_CTX *ssl_ctx_;

  // The SSL data structure corresponding to authenticated
  // SSL connections.
  SSL *ssl_;
```

The `ssl_ctx_` and `ssl_` data members are passed to the OpenSSL API calls made by the following public methods in `TPC_Logging_Acceptor`.

```
public:
  typedef ACE_Acceptor<TPC_Logging_Handler, ACE_SOCK_Acceptor>
          PARENT;
  typedef ACE_SOCK_Acceptor::PEER_ADDR PEER_ADDR;

  TPC_Logging_Acceptor (ACE_Reactor *)
    : PARENT (r), ssl_ctx_ (0), ssl_ (0) {}

  // Destructor frees the SSL resources.
  virtual ~TPC_Logging_Acceptor (void) {
    SSL_free (ssl_);
    SSL_CTX_free (ssl_ctx_);
  }
```

```
   // Initialize the acceptor instance.
   virtual int open
     (const ACE_SOCK_Acceptor::PEER_ADDR &local_addr,
      ACE_Reactor *reactor = ACE_Reactor::instance (),
      int flags = 0, int use_select = 1, int reuse_addr = 1);

   // <ACE_Reactor> close hook method.
   virtual int handle_close
     (ACE_HANDLE = ACE_INVALID_HANDLE,
      ACE_Reactor_Mask = ACE_Event_Handler::ALL_EVENTS_MASK);

   // Connection establishment and authentication hook method.
   virtual int accept_svc_handler (TPC_Logging_Handler *sh);
};
```

Sidebar 51: An Overview of Authentication and Encryption Protocols

To protect against potential attacks or third-party discovery, many networked applications must authenticate the identities of their peers and encrypt sensitive data sent over a network. To provide these capabilities, various cryptography packages, such as OpenSSL [Ope01], and security protocols, such as Transport Layer Security (TLS) [DA99], have been developed. These packages and protocols provide library calls that ensure authentication, data integrity, and confidentiality between two communicating applications. For example, the TLS protocol can encrypt/decrypt data sent/received across a TCP/IP network. TLS is based on an earlier protocol named the Secure Sockets Layer (SSL), which was developed by Netscape.

The OpenSSL toolkit used by the examples in this chapter is based on the SSLeay library written by Eric Young and Tim Hudson. It is open source, under active development, and runs on multiple platforms, including most platforms ACE supports, such as Linux, FreeBSD, OpenBSD, NetBSD, Solaris, AIX, IRIX, HP-UX, OpenUNIX, DG/UX, ReliantUNIX, UnixWare, Cray T90 and T3E, SCO Unix, Microsoft Windows, and MacOS. OpenSSL is a highly successful open-source package, as evidenced by its extensive commercial and noncommerical user community.

`TPC_Logging_Acceptor::open()` (in `TPC_Logging_Server.cpp`) initializes itself using its base class implementation and establishes the server's identity as follows:

```
1 #include "ace/OS.h"
2 #include "Reactor_Logging_Server_Adapter.h"
3 #include "TPC_Logging_Server.h"
4 #include "TPCLS_export.h"
5
6 #if !defined (TPC_CERTIFICATE_FILENAME)
7 #  define TPC_CERTIFICATE_FILENAME "tpc-cert.pem"
8 #endif /* !TPC_CERTIFICATE_FILENAME */
9 #if !defined (TPC_KEY_FILENAME)
```

```
10 #  define TPC_KEY_FILENAME "tpc-key.pem"
11 #endif /* !TPC_KEY_FILENAME */
12
13 int TPC_Logging_Acceptor::open
14    (const ACE_SOCK_Acceptor::PEER_ADDR &local_addr,
15             ACE_Reactor *reactor,
16             int flags, int use_select, int reuse_addr) {
17   if (PARENT::open (local_addr, reactor, flags,
18                     use_select, reuse_addr) != 0)
19      return -1;
20   OpenSSL_add_ssl_algorithms ();
21   ssl_ctx_ = SSL_CTX_new (SSLv3_server_method ());
22   if (ssl_ctx_ == 0) return -1;
23
24   if (SSL_CTX_use_certificate_file (ssl_ctx_,
25                                     TPC_CERTIFICATE_FILENAME,
26                                     SSL_FILETYPE_PEM) <= 0
27        || SSL_CTX_use_PrivateKey_file (ssl_ctx_,
28                                     TPC_KEY_FILENAME,
29                                     SSL_FILETYPE_PEM) <= 0
30        || !SSL_CTX_check_private_key (ssl_ctx_))
31      return -1;
32   ssl_ = SSL_new (ssl_ctx_);
33   return ssl_ == 0 ? -1 : 0;
34 }
```

Lines 6–11   Since our logging server doesn't have a user interface, its server certificate and accompanying key are assumed to exist in a default set of files. However, the application may override the default filenames by defining the specified preprocessor macros.

Lines 17–18   Initialize the ACE_Acceptor using the default open() implementation.

Line 20   Initialize the OpenSSL library. For brevity, we place the OpenSSL_add_ssl_algorithms() call in TPC_Logging_Acceptor::open(). Although this function can be called safely multiple times per process, ideally this call should be made only once per process. Initialization must be synchronized if multiple threads can call the function, however, since this OpenSSL function isn't thread safe.

Lines 21–22   Set up for SSL version 3 connection and create the SSL structure corresponding connections to be authenticated.

Lines 24–31   Set up the certificate and accompanying private key used to identify the server when establishing connections and then verify that the private key matches the correct certificate. This code assumes that the certificate and key are encoded in *Privacy Enhanced Mail* (PEM) format within the specified files.

Lines 32–33   Initialize a new SSL data structure, which is used in the TPC_Logging_Acceptor::accept_svc_handler() hook method when establishing SSL connections via the OpenSSL API, as follows:

```
 1  int TPC_Logging_Acceptor::accept_svc_handler
 2        (TPC_Logging_Handler *sh) {
 3    if (PARENT::accept_svc_handler (sh) == -1) return -1;
 4    SSL_clear (ssl_);  // Reset for new SSL connection.
 5    SSL_set_fd
 6        (ssl_, ACE_reinterpret_cast (int, sh->get_handle ()));
 7
 8    SSL_set_verify
 9        (ssl_,
10        SSL_VERIFY_PEER | SSL_VERIFY_FAIL_IF_NO_PEER_CERT,
11        0);
12    if (SSL_accept (ssl_) == -1
13        || SSL_shutdown (ssl_) == -1) return -1;
14    return 0;
15  }
```

Line 3   Accept the TCP connection using the default `accept_svc_handler()` implementation.

Lines 4–6   Reset the SSL data structures for use with a new SSL connection.

Lines 8–11   Configure the SSL data structures so that client authentication is performed and enforced when accepting an SSL connection.

Line 12   Perform the actual SSL connection and negotiation. If authentication of the client fails, the `SSL_accept()` call will fail.

Line 13   Shut down the SSL connection if authentication succeeds. Since we don't actually encrypt the log record data we simply communicate via the TCP stream from here on. If data encryption were required, we could use the ACE wrapper facades for OpenSSL described in Sidebar 52.

By overriding the `open()` and `accept_svc_handler()` hook methods, we added authentication to our server logging daemon without affecting any other part of its implementation. This extensibility illustrates the power of the Template Method pattern used in the `ACE_Acceptor` class design.

When our example service is shut down via the ACE Service Configurator framework, `Reactor_Logging_Server_Adapter::fini()` (page 123) will end up calling the following `handle_close()` method:

```
int TPC_Logging_Acceptor::handle_close (ACE_HANDLE h,
                                        ACE_Reactor_Mask mask) {
  PARENT::handle_close (h, mask);
  delete this;
  return 0;
}
```

Sidebar 52: ACE Wrapper Facades for OpenSSL

Although the OpenSSL API provides a useful set of functions, it suffers from the usual problems incurred by native OS APIs written in C (see Chapter 2 in C++NPv1). To address these problems, ACE provides classes that encapsulate OpenSSL using an API similar to the ACE C++ Socket wrapper facades. For example, the `ACE_SOCK_Acceptor`, `ACE_SOCK_Connector`, and `ACE_SOCK_Stream` classes described in Chapter 3 of C++NPv1 have their SSL-enabled counterparts: `ACE_SSL_SOCK_Acceptor`, `ACE_SSL_SOCK_Connector`, and `ACE_SSL_SOCK_Stream`.

The ACE SSL wrapper facades allow networked applications to ensure the integrity and confidentiality of data exchanged across a network. They also follow the same structure and APIs as their Socket API counterparts, which makes it easy to replace them wholesale using C++ parameterized types and the `ACE_Svc_Handler` template class. For example, to apply the ACE wrapper facades for OpenSSL to our networked logging server we can simply remove all the OpenSSL API code and instantiate the `ACE_Acceptor`, `ACE_Connector`, and `ACE_Svc_Handler` with the `ACE_SSL_SOCK_Acceptor`, `ACE_SSL_SOCK_Connector`, and `ACE_SSL_SOCK_Stream`, respectively.

This method calls `ACE_Acceptor::handle_close()` to close the listening acceptor socket and unregister it from the reactor framework. To avoid memory leaks, the method then deletes `this` object, which was allocated dynamically when the service was initialized.

We finally create the `TPC_Logging_Server` type definition:

```
typedef Reactor_Logging_Server_Adapter<TPC_Logging_Acceptor>
        TPC_Logging_Server;

ACE_FACTORY_DEFINE (TPCLS, TPC_Logging_Server)
```

We also use the ACE_FACTORY_DEFINE macro described in Sidebar 32 (page 136) to automatically generate the `_make_TPC_Logging_Server()` factory function, which is used in the following `svc.conf` file:

```
dynamic TPC_Logging_Server Service_Object *
TPCLS:_make_TPC_Logging_Server() "$TPC_LOGGING_SERVER_PORT"
```

This file directs the ACE Service Configurator framework to configure the thread-per-connection logging server via the following steps:

1. It dynamically links the `TPCLS` DLL into the address space of the process.

2. It uses the `ACE_DLL` class to extract the `_make_TPC_Logging_Server()` factory function from the `TPCLS` DLL symbol table.

3. This function is called to allocate a `TPC_Logging_Server` dynamically and return a pointer to it.

4. The ACE Service Configurator framework then calls `TPC_Logging_Server::init()` through this pointer, passing as its `argc/argv` argument an expansion of the `TPC_LOGGING_SERVER_PORT` environment variable that designates the port number where the logging server listens for client connection requests. The port number is ultimately passed down to the `Reactor_Logging_Server` constructor (page 83).

5. If `init()` succeeds, the `TPC_Logging_Server` pointer is stored in the `ACE_Service_Repository` under the name `"TPC_Logging_Server"`.

The various `*Logging_Acceptor*` classes written by hand for our previous logging server examples are no longer needed. Their purpose has been subsumed by `TPC_Logging_Acceptor`, which inherits from `ACE_Acceptor`. The first template argument to the `ACE_Acceptor` base class is `TPC_Logging_Handler`, which derives from `ACE_Svc_Handler`.

In the `TPC_Logging_Server` service, the ACE Acceptor-Connector framework performs most of the basic work of authenticating a client connection, as well as initializing and operating a service handler. Since the `ACE_Acceptor` refactors the functionality of accepting connections, authenticating clients, and activating service handlers into well-defined steps in its `handle_input()` template method, the source code for our logging server daemon shrank considerably. In particular, `ACE_Acceptor` supplied all of the code we previously had to write manually to

- Listen for and accept connections
- Create and activate new service handlers

Our thread-per-connection logging server also reused classes from earlier solutions that provided the following capabilities:

- Initialize the network listener address using the `Reactor_Logging_Server_Adapter` template defined in Section 5.2 (page 122).
- Dynamically configure the logging server and run the ACE Reactor's event loop in the `main()` function.

Therefore, the only code of any consequence we had to write was the `TPC_Logging_Handler` class (page 213), which spawned a thread per connection to receive and process log records, and the `TPC_Logging_Acceptor::accept_svc_handler()` method (page 222), which implemented the server end of the protocol that authenticates the identity of the client and server logging daemons. Once again, due to the flexibility offered by the ACE Service Configurator framework, we simply reuse the `Configurable_Logging_Server` main program from Chapter 5.

7.4   The ACE_Connector Class

Motivation

Section 7.3 focused on how to decouple the functionality of service handlers from the steps required to passively connect and initialize them. It's equally useful to decouple the functionality of service handlers from the steps required to actively connect and initialize them. Moreover, networked applications that communicate with a large number of peers may need to actively establish many connections concurrently, handling completions as they occur. To consolidate these capabilities into a flexible, extensible, and reusable abstraction, the ACE Acceptor-Connector framework defines the `ACE_Connector` class.

Class Capabilities

`ACE_Connector` is a factory class that implements the Connector role in the Acceptor-Connector pattern [POSA2]. This class provides the following capabilities:

- It decouples the active connection establishment and service initialization logic from the processing performed by a service handler after it's connected and initialized.

- It provides an IPC factory that can actively establish connections with a peer acceptor either synchronously or reactively. The type of this IPC endpoint can be parameterized with many of ACE's IPC wrapper facade classes, thereby separating lower-level connection mechanisms from application-level service initialization policies.

- It automates the steps necessary to connect the IPC endpoint actively as well as to create and activate its associated service handler.

- Since `ACE_Connector` derives from `ACE_Service_Object` it inherits all the event handling and dynamic configuration capabilities described in Chapters 3 and 5, respectively.

The interface for `ACE_Connector` is shown in Figure 7.7 (page 230). This template class is parameterized by:

- An `SVC_HANDLER` class, which provides an interface for processing services defined by clients, servers, or both client and server roles in peer-to-peer services. This parameter should be an `ACE_Svc_Handler` subclass, as described in Section 7.2.

- A `PEER_CONNECTOR` class, which is able to establish client connections actively. This parameter is often specified as one of ACE's IPC wrapper facades, such as the `ACE_SOCK_Connector` described in Chapter 3 of C++NPv1.

The `ACE_Connector` class has a flexible interface that can be customized extensively by developers. We therefore group the description of its methods into the two categories described on the following page.

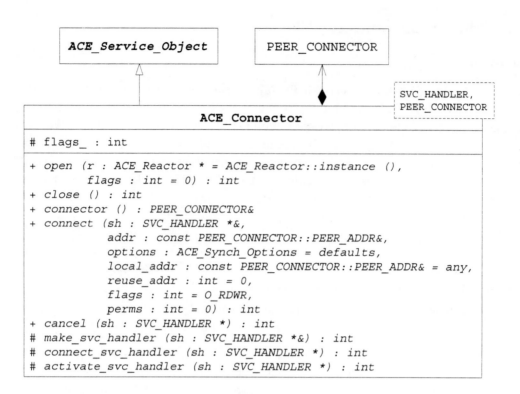

Figure 7.7: The ACE_Connector Class

1. Connector initialization, destruction methods, and accessor methods.   The following methods are used to initialize, destroy, and access an ACE_Connector:

Method	Description
ACE_Connector() open()	Methods that initialize a connector.
~ACE_Connector() close()	Methods that release the resources used by a connector.
connector()	Returns a reference to the underlying PEER_CONNECTOR.

The ACE_Connector's constructor and open() method can be passed a flag indicating whether a service handler's IPC endpoint initialized by the connector should start in blocking (the default) or nonblocking (ACE_NONBLOCK) mode. These methods can also be passed the reactor associated with the connector. They use the singleton ACE_Reactor by default, just like the ACE_Svc_Handler and ACE_Acceptor.

An ACE_Connector object is closed either when it's destroyed or when its close() method is called explicitly. An ACE_Connector allocates no resources for synchronous connections, so there's nothing to clean up if it's used only synchronously. For asynchronous connections, however, these methods release the resources a connector allocates to track pending connections that haven't completed by the time the connector is closed. Each remaining unconnected service handler is also closed by invoking its close() hook method.

2. Connection establishment and service handler initialization methods.   The following ACE_Connector methods can be used to establish connections actively and initialize their associated service handlers:

Method	Description
connect()	This template method is called by an application when it wants to connect a service handler to a listening peer. It can use the following three methods to automate the steps necessary to actively connect an IPC endpoint, as well as to create and activate its associated service handler.
make_svc_handler()	This factory method supplies a service handler that will use the connected IPC endpoint.
connect_svc_handler()	This hook method uses the service handler's IPC endpoint to actively connect the endpoint, either synchronously or asynchronously.
activate_svc_handler()	This hook method invokes the service handler's open() hook method, which allows the service handler to finish initializing itself after the connection is established.
handle_output()	This template method is called by a reactor after an asynchronously initiated connection request completes. It calls the activate_svc_handler() method to allow the service handler to initialize itself.
cancel()	Cancel a service handler whose connection was initiated asynchronously. The caller—not the connector—is responsible for closing the service handler.

Networked applications use the connect() template method to initiate a connection attempt actively, regardless of whether its completion is handled synchronously or asynchronously. This method uses the following steps to connect and initialize a new service handler:

1. It obtains a service handler, either by using the handler passed by the caller or by invoking the make_svc_handler() factory method.
2. It then calls the connect_svc_handler() method to initiate the connection. Whereas passive connection establishment is usually immediate, active connection establishment can take a longer amount of time, particularly over wide-area networks. The ACE_Connector can therefore be instructed to use the ACE Reactor framework to handle connection completions asynchronously as they occur, whether they succeed or fail.

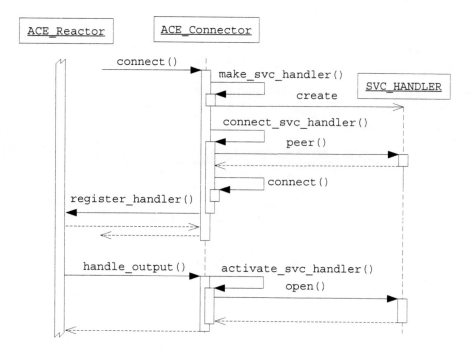

Figure 7.8: Steps in ACE_Connector Asynchronous Connection Establishment

3. For synchronous connections, connect() calls activate_svc_handler()
   to allow the service handler to finish initializing itself. For asynchronous connections, the reactor calls ACE_Connector::handle_output() to finish service
   handler initialization after the connection completes. Figure 7.8 illustrates the steps
   for the asynchronous case.

Since ACE_Connector::connect() uses the Template Method pattern [GoF], application designers can change the behavior of any or all of the three steps outlined above.

As shown in Figure 7.7 (page 230), the ACE_Connector::connect() method is
passed the following arguments:

- A reference to a pointer to a SVC_HANDLER. If the pointer is NULL, the make_
  svc_handler() factory method is called to obtain one. The default version of
  make_svc_handler() allocates one dynamically.
- An address argument whose signature matches the peer connector and stream types
  via C++ traits. The address specifies the endpoint to which the peer connects. For
  instance, it could be an ACE_INET_Addr containing a port number and IP address
  for service handlers using ACE_SOCK_Stream. For other IPC mechanisms, it could
  be the name used to locate a service via a naming service or it could be the hostname
  of a port mapping server—it's up to the application designer to decide.

- A reference to an `ACE_Synch_Options` object that consolidates the values of options used to determine the `ACE_Connector`'s behavior.

Each `connect()` call tries to establish a connection with the designated peer. If `connect()` gets an immediate indication of connection success or failure, it ignores the `ACE_Synch_Options` parameter. If it doesn't get an immediate indication of connection success or failure, however, `connect()` uses its `ACE_Synch_Options` parameter to vary the completion processing via two orthogonal factors:

1. Whether to use the ACE Reactor framework to detect the connection completion
2. How long to wait for the connection to complete

If the reactor is used, the `connect()` method can register both the `PEER_CONNECTOR` (for connect completion detection) and a timer (for the caller-specified time limit) with the reactor and returns −1 to its caller with `errno` set to `EWOULDBLOCK`. The ultimate success or failure of the connect will result in the `ACE_Connector::activate_svc_handler()` method's activating the handler for success or the service handler's `close()` method for failure. The application runs the reactor's event loop, and the appropriate call will be made during the course of the reactor's normal event loop processing.

If the reactor isn't used, the `connect()` method doesn't return until the connect attempt completes, fails, or times out. Its success or failure still results in a call to either the `activate_svc_handler()` method or the service handler's `close()` method, respectively. The table below summarizes the `ACE_Connector`'s behavior, based on the `ACE_Synch_Options` values, if the connect request doesn't complete immediately.

Reactor	Timeout	Behavior
Yes	0,0	Return −1 with `errno` EWOULDBLOCK; service handler is closed via reactor event loop.
Yes	Time	Return −1 with `errno` EWOULDBLOCK; wait up to specified amount of time for completion using the reactor.
Yes	NULL	Return −1 with `errno` EWOULDBLOCK; wait for completion indefinitely using the reactor.
No	0,0	Close service handler directly; return −1 with `errno` EWOULDBLOCK.
No	Time	Block in `connect_svc_handler()` up to specified amount of time for completion; if still not completed, return −1 with `errno` ETIME.
No	NULL	Block in `connect_svc_handler()` indefinitely for completion.

Regardless of how connections are established, any or all of the default `make_svc_handler()`, `connect_svc_handler()`, and `activate_svc_handler()` methods can be overridden by subclasses. This extensible Template Method pattern design allows a range of behavior modification and customization to support many use cases. We describe the three primary variation points in `ACE_Connector::connect()` on the following page.

1. Obtain a service handler. Since an acceptor is often driven by upcalls from a reactor, its `make_svc_handler()` factory method usually creates a new service handler. In contrast, a connector can choose to connect and initialize a service handler as either

- **Caller created,** wherein the caller passes a pointer to an existing service handler to the connector's `connect()` method
- **Connector created,** wherein the caller passes a NULL service handler pointer to the connector's `connect()` method, thereby instructing the `make_svc_handler()` factory method to obtain a pointer to the service handler (or even defer this activity altogether until the `connect_svc_handler()` method to enable connection caching).

The default implementation of `ACE_Connector::make_svc_handler()` handles these two cases, as follows:

```
template <class SVC_HANDLER, class PEER_CONNECTOR> int
ACE_Connector<SVC_HANDLER, PEER_CONNECTOR>::make_svc_handler
    (SVC_HANDLER *&sh) {
  if (sh == 0) ACE_NEW_RETURN (sh, SVC_HANDLER, -1);
  sh->reactor (reactor ());
  return 0;
}
```

This method looks similar to `ACE_Acceptor::make_svc_handler()` (page 219). However, `ACE_Connector::make_svc_handler()` allocates a new service handler only if the pointer passed to it by reference is NULL, which enables the client application to determine if the caller or the connector should create the service handler.

2. Connection establishment. The `ACE_Connector::connect()` template method calls its `connect_svc_handler()` hook method to initiate a new connection with a peer acceptor. The default implementation of this method simply forwards to the PEER_CONNECTOR::connect() method to initiate the connection, as shown below:

```
template <class SVC_HANDLER, class PEER_CONNECTOR> int
ACE_Connector<SVC_HANDLER, PEER_CONNECTOR>::connect_svc_handler
    (SVC_HANDLER *sh,
     const ACE_TYPENAME PEER_CONNECTOR::PEER_ADDR &remote_addr,
     ACE_Time_Value *timeout,
     const ACE_TYPENAME PEER_CONNECTOR::PEER_ADDR &local_addr,
     int reuse_addr, int flags, int perms) {
  return connector_.connect (svc_handler->peer (),
                             remote_addr,
                             timeout,
                             local_addr,
                             reuse_addr, flags, perms);
}
```

More powerful implementations of `connect_svc_handler()` can be defined by subclasses of `ACE_Connector`. Here are some examples:

- **Connection caching.** The `connect_svc_handler()` method can be overridden to search a cache of existing, connected service handlers. If there's no suitable cached handler, a new `SVC_HANDLER` can be created and connected. Since the decision to create a new `SVC_HANDLER` or not is made in `connect_svc_handler()` (which is called after `make_svc_handler()`), the subclass would probably define its `make_svc_handler()` method as a no-op.

- **Authentication.** The `connect_svc_handler()` method can be overridden to always connect synchronously and then implement an authentication protocol on the new connection. For example, it may send an encrypted login password and negotiate access rights with a secure server. If authentication fails, the overridden `connect_svc_handler()` method can close the connection and return -1 to indicate an error to `ACE_Connector::connect()` so the service handler isn't activated. The *Example* section below illustrates how to implement SSL authentication by overrriding `connect_svc_handler()`.

3. Service handler activation. The `ACE_Connector` can activate service handlers in the following two ways, depending on how the connection was initiated:

- If a connection is completed synchronously, the service handler is activated by `ACE_Connector::connect()` after `connect_svc_handler()` returns successfully. At this point, `connect()` calls `activate_svc_handler()` so the service handler can finish initializing itself.

- If a connection completion is handled asynchronously using the Reactor framework, the reactor calls `ACE_Connector::handle_output()` to inform the connector that the IPC endpoint is connected. At this point, `handle_output()` calls the `activate_svc_handler()` hook method so the service handler can finish initializing itself.

The default behavior of `ACE_Connector::activate_svc_handler()` is identical to the `ACE_Acceptor::activate_svc_handler()` (page 221). This commonality between the `ACE_Acceptor` and `ACE_Connector` underscores the power of the ACE Acceptor-Connector framework, which completely decouples passive and active connection establishment from the initialization and use of a service handler.

Example

This example applies the ACE Acceptor-Connector framework to implement another client logging daemon that extends the one shown in the *Example* portion of Section 6.2. Rather than using the *ad hoc* Acceptor-Connector pattern implementation shown in Figure 6.4 (page 169), we use the `ACE_Acceptor`, `ACE_Connector`, and `ACE_Svc_Handler` classes described in this chapter. The resulting implementation is more concise and portable since much of the code we had to write manually in the previous client logging daemon is available as reusable classes from the ACE Acceptor-Connector framework. Our new implementation is also more powerful since it provides an authentication protocol that's interposed transparently to ensure that the client logging daemon is permitted to connect to the server logging daemon.

Like the earlier client logging daemon, our new version uses two threads, which perform the following tasks using various ACE framework classes:

- **Input processing**—The main thread uses the singleton `ACE_Reactor`, an `ACE_Acceptor`, and an `ACE_Svc_Handler` passive object to read log records from sockets connected to client applications via the network loopback device. Each log record is queued in a second `ACE_Svc_Handler` that runs as an active object.

- **Output processing**—The active object `ACE_Svc_Handler` runs in its own thread. It dequeues messages from its message queue, buffers the messages into chunks, and forwards these chunks to the server logging daemon over a TCP connection. A subclass of `ACE_Connector` is used to establish (and when necessary reestablish) and authenticate connections with the logging server.

The classes comprising the new client logging daemon based on the ACE Acceptor-Connector framework are shown in Figure 7.9. The role of each class is outlined below:

Class	Description
AC_Input_Handler	A target of callbacks from the singleton `ACE_Reactor` that receives log records from clients, stores each in an `ACE_Message_Block`, and passes them to the `AC_Output_Handler` for processing.
AC_Output_Handler	An active object that runs in its own thread. Its `put()` method enqueues message blocks passed to it from the `AC_Input_Handler`. Its `svc()` method dequeues messages from its synchronized message queue and forwards them to the logging server.
AC_CLD_Acceptor	A factory that passively accepts connections from clients and registers them with the singleton `ACE_Reactor` to be processed by the `AC_Input_Handler`.
AC_CLD_Connector	A factory that actively (re)establishes and authenticates connections with the logging server.
AC_Client_Logging_Daemon	A facade class that integrates the other classes together.

The interactions between instances of these classes are shown in Figure 7.10 (page 238). When the service is operating, there are two threads. The first is the initial program thread and it runs the reactor event loop. This thread performs the following processing:

- It accepts new logging client connections via `AC_CLD_Acceptor`.
- It receives log records and identifies broken logging client connections via `AC_Input_Handler`; log records are enqueued on the `AC_Output_Handler` message queue.

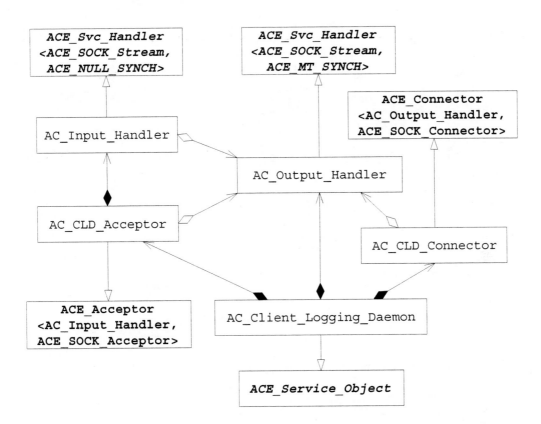

Figure 7.9: Classes in the Acceptor-Connector Client Logging Daemon

- It detects broken logging server connections in AC_Output_Handler and reconnects with the server via AC_CLD_Connector.

The forwarder thread is started when the initial connection to the logging server is made and continues to run until the service is terminated. This thread runs the AC_Output_Handler active object service thread.

We start our implementation by including the necessary ACE header files.

```
#include "ace/OS.h"
#include "ace/Acceptor.h"
#include "ace/Connector.h"
#include "ace/Get_Opt.h"
#include "ace/Handle_Set.h"
#include "ace/INET_Addr.h"
#include "ace/Log_Record.h"
#include "ace/Message_Block.h"
#include "ace/Reactor.h"
#include "ace/Service_Object.h"
```

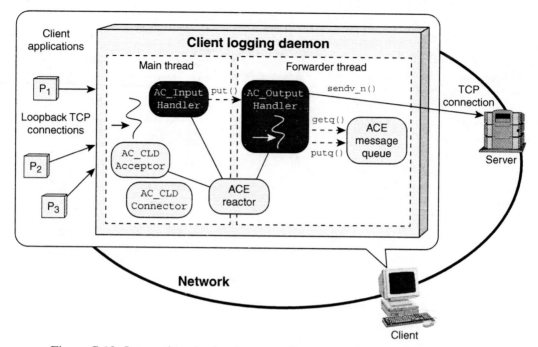

Figure 7.10: Interactions in the Acceptor-Connector Client Logging Daemon

```
#include "ace/Signal.h"
#include "ace/Svc_Handler.h"
#include "ace/Synch.h"
#include "ace/SOCK_Acceptor.h"
#include "ace/SOCK_Connector.h"
#include "ace/SOCK_Stream.h"
#include "ace/Thread_Manager.h"
#include "Logging_Handler.h"
#include "AC_CLD_export.h"
#include <openssl/ssl.h>
```

The classes in Figure 7.9 (page 237) are defined in the AC_Client_Logging_Daemon.
cpp file and described below.

AC_Input_Handler.   This class provides the following capabilities:

- It receives log records from clients.
- It stores each log record in an ACE_Message_Block.
- It passes the message blocks to the AC_Output_Handler for processing.

The AC_Input_Handler class is shown below:

```
class AC_Input_Handler
  : public ACE_Svc_Handler<ACE_SOCK_Stream, ACE_NULL_SYNCH> {
```

```
public:
  AC_Input_Handler (AC_Output_Handler *handler = 0)
    : output_handler_ (handler) {}
  virtual int open (void *); // Initialization hook method.
  virtual int close (u_long = 0); // Shutdown hook method.

protected:
  // Reactor hook methods.
  virtual int handle_input (ACE_HANDLE handle);
  virtual int handle_close (ACE_HANDLE = ACE_INVALID_HANDLE,
                            ACE_Reactor_Mask = 0);

  // Pointer to the output handler.
  AC_Output_Handler *output_handler_;

  // Keep track of connected client handles.
  ACE_Handle_Set connected_clients_;
};
```

Since `AC_Input_Handler` uses no per-client state, only a single instance is defined in `AC_CLD_Acceptor` (page 247) to handle input from all connected clients. We therefore define an `ACE_Handle_Set`, which is a wrapper facade for `fd_set` defined in Chapter 7 of C++NPv1. This `ACE_Handle_Set` keeps track of all connected client socket handles so we can remove them from the singleton reactor when the `AC_Input_Handler` is closed. Sidebar 53 (page 240) discusses the pros and cons of different strategies for using multiple versus single service handlers.

Since `AC_Input_Handler` inherits from `ACE_Svc_Handler` it can use the singleton `ACE_Reactor` to wait for log records to arrive from any client applications connected to the client logging daemon via loopback TCP sockets. It therefore doesn't use its message queue, so it instantiates the `ACE_Svc_Handler` with the `ACE_NULL_SYNCH` strategy to minimize its synchronizer usage. When a log record arrives at the client logging daemon, the singleton `ACE_Reactor` dispatches the following `AC_Input_Handler::handle_input()` hook method:

```
int AC_Input_Handler::handle_input (ACE_HANDLE handle) {
  ACE_Message_Block *mblk = 0;
  Logging_Handler logging_handler (handle);

  if (logging_handler.recv_log_record (mblk) != -1)
    if (output_handler_->put (mblk->cont ()) != -1) {
      mblk->cont (0);
      mblk->release ();
      return 0; // Success return.
    } else mblk->release ();
  return -1; // Error return.
}
```

Sidebar 53: Multiple versus Single Service Handlers

The server logging daemon implementation in the *Example* part of Section 7.3 dynamically allocates a new service handler for each connected client. In contrast, the client logging daemon implementation in this example uses a single service handler for all connected clients. The rationale and tradeoffs for these approaches are:

- If each service handler maintains separate state information for each client (in addition to the connection handle) then allocating a service handler per client is generally the most straightforward design.
- If each service handler does *not* maintain separate state for each client, then a server that allocates one service handler for all clients can potentially use less space and perform faster than if it allocates a handler dynamically for each client. The effect of these improvements increases as the number of concurrently connected clients grows.
- It's generally much easier to manage memory if a separate service handler is allocated dynamically for each client since the ACE Acceptor-Connector framework classes embody the most common behavior for this case—the service handler simply calls `destroy()` from its `handle_close()` hook method. In contrast, memory management is trickier if one service handler is shared by all the clients.
- If service handler initialization can be performed from multiple threads, such as when using multiple dispatching threads with `ACE_WFMO_Reactor`, the design must take possible race conditions into account and use appropriate synchronization to avoid mishandling connections.

For completeness, we show both approaches in this chapter. In general, however, the multiple service handler approach is much easier to program. We therefore recommend using this design in practice, unless there's a need to save space.

This method uses the `Logging_Handler` from Chapter 4 of C++NPv1 to read a log record out of the socket handle parameter, store the record into an `ACE_Message_Block`, and pass this message to the `AC_Output_Handler` (page 243), which will queue it and service it in a separate thread. We only enqueue the log record data (which is referenced by `mblk->cont()`) and *not* the hostname (which is referenced by `mblk`).

If a client application disconnects the socket or an error occurs, `handle_input()` returns −1. This value triggers the singleton reactor to call the following `handle_close()` hook method that closes the socket.

```
int AC_Input_Handler::handle_close (ACE_HANDLE handle,
                                    ACE_Reactor_Mask) {
  connected_clients_.clr_bit (handle);
  return ACE_OS::closesocket (handle);
}
```

Note that we needn't delete `this` object in `handle_close()` since the `AC_Input_Handler`'s memory is managed by the `AC_CLD_Acceptor` (page 247). The `handle_close()` method also removes the specified handle from the `connected_clients_` handle set, where it was added when the connection was opened.

When a connection request arrives at the client logging daemon from a client application, `AC_CLD_Acceptor::handle_input()` will dispatch the following `AC_Input_Handler::open()` hook method:

```
1  int AC_Input_Handler::open (void *) {
2    ACE_HANDLE handle = peer ().get_handle ();
3    if (reactor ()->register_handler
4          (handle, this, ACE_Event_Handler::READ_MASK) == -1)
5      return -1;
6    connected_clients_.set_bit (handle);
7    return 0;
8  }
```

Lines 2–5   The client logging daemon reuses a single `AC_Input_Handler` object for all of its logging handlers. When `AC_CLD_Acceptor::accept_svc_handler()` is called to accept the new connection, it therefore reuses the handle in the `AC_Input_Handler`'s `ACE_SOCK_Stream` for each connection. We use the three-parameter `ACE_Reactor::register_handler()` method (page 73) to register a pointer to this single object with the singleton reactor for READ events. When log records arrive, the singleton reactor will dispatch `AC_Input_Handler::handle_input()` (page 239).

Recall from Sidebar 53 that singleton service handlers and multithreaded event dispatching may introduce a race condition. We may lose track of some connections if the `AC_Input_Handler` class is used with a multithreaded reactor event loop since the `AC_Input_Handler` object's `ACE_SOCK_Stream` member can be changed by multiple threads. Each involved event dispatching thread does the following:

1. Calls the `AC_CLD_Acceptor::accept_svc_handler()` method, which accepts a new socket and stores its handle in `AC_Input_Handler`
2. Calls the `AC_CLD_Acceptor::activate_svc_handler()` method, which in turn calls `AC_Input_Handler::open()` shown above

If thread *B* accepts a new connection before thread *A* completes the two steps above, it's likely that the `AC_Input_Handler::open()` invocation in thread *A* will actually register the socket accepted from thread *B*. If so, the first socket accepted would still be open, but never registered with the reactor and, thus, abandoned.

To prevent this race condition, synchronization is needed around the code that accesses the shared `ACE_SOCK_Stream` object in the `AC_Input_Handler`. Unfortunately, the synchronization scope includes the two steps listed above and so must be done from their caller, `ACE_Acceptor::handle_input()`. The use of multiple reactor event dispatching threads would therefore end up requiring a new implementation of `handle_input` to properly synchronize concurrent connection acceptance. The example in this section therefore uses a single reactor event dispatching thread.

Line 6   Record the handle of the connected client in the `connected_clients_` `ACE_Handle_Set`. We keep track of connected client handles so we can remove them from the reactor when `AC_Input_Handler::close()` is called. This method is called by `AC_CLD_Acceptor::handle_close()` (page 247) or `AC_Client_Logging_Daemon::fini()` (page 253) to shut down the client logging daemon:

```
 1 int AC_Input_Handler::close (u_long) {
 2   ACE_Message_Block *shutdown_message = 0;
 3   ACE_NEW_RETURN
 4     (shutdown_message,
 5      ACE_Message_Block (0, ACE_Message_Block::MB_STOP), -1);
 6   output_handler_->put (shutdown_message);
 7
 8   reactor ()->remove_handler
 9     (connected_clients_, ACE_Event_Handler::READ_MASK);
10   return output_handler_->wait ();
11 }
```

Lines 2–6   Insert a 0-sized message block of type `MB_STOP` into the message queue. When the forwarder thread running `AC_Output_Handler::svc()` (page 244) dequeues this `shutdown_message` it will flush its remaining log records to the logging server, close the message queue, and exit the thread.

Lines 8–9   Remove all handles in the `connected_clients_` handle set in one operation. Each removed handle will generate a reactor callback to `AC_Input_Handler::handle_close()` on its behalf, where the socket handle is closed.

Line 10   Use the `output_handler_`'s `wait()` method to block until its `svc()` hook method exits before returning from `AC_Input_Handler::close()`. This method reaps the exit status of the forwarder thread to prevent memory leaks.

AC_Output_Handler.   This class provides the following capabilities:

- It inserts message blocks passed to it from the `AC_Input_Handler` into its synchronized message queue.
- It runs as an active object in its own thread, dequeueing message blocks from its synchronized message queue, buffering them into chunks, and forwarding the chunks to the logging server.
- It registers with the singleton `ACE_Reactor` to process disconnects from the logging server and reestablish connections.

The `AC_Output_Handler` class is shown below:

```
class AC_Output_Handler
    : public ACE_Svc_Handler<ACE_SOCK_Stream, ACE_MT_SYNCH> {
public:
  enum { QUEUE_MAX = sizeof (ACE_Log_Record) * ACE_IOV_MAX };

  virtual int open (void *); // Initialization hook.

  // Entry point into the <AC_Output_Handler>.
  virtual int put (ACE_Message_Block *, ACE_Time_Value * = 0);

protected:
  // Pointer to connection factory for <AC_Output_Handler>.
  AC_CLD_Connector *connector_;

  // Handle disconnects from the logging server.
  virtual int handle_input (ACE_HANDLE handle);

  // Hook method forwards log records to server logging daemon.
  virtual int svc ();

  // Send buffered log records using a gather-write operation.
  virtual int send (ACE_Message_Block *chunk[], size_t &count);
};

#if !defined (FLUSH_TIMEOUT)
#define FLUSH_TIMEOUT 120 /* 120 seconds == 2 minutes. */
#endif /* FLUSH_TIMEOUT */
```

Since `AC_Output_Handler` is derived from `ACE_Svc_Handler` and instantiates its synchronization traits with `ACE_MT_SYNCH`, it inherits the `ACE_SOCK_Stream`, `ACE_Thread_Manager`, and synchronized `ACE_Message_Queue`, as well as the ability to activate itself to become an active object.

   `AC_Input_Handler::handle_input()` (page 239) plays the reactive role in the variant of the Half-Sync/Half-Async pattern we use to structure the concurrency architecture of this client logging daemon. It passes log records to the `AC_Output_Handler` via the following `put()` method:

```
int AC_Output_Handler::put (ACE_Message_Block *mb,
                            ACE_Time_Value *timeout) {
  int result;
  while ((result = putq (mb, timeout)) == -1)
    if (msg_queue ()->state () != ACE_Message_Queue_Base::PULSED)
      break;
  return result;
}
```

This method simply enqueues the message block onto the `AC_Output_Handler`'s synchronized message queue. If the `putq()` call is blocked and the message queue is pulsed, it simply reexecutes the putq () call to try again. The following two methods explain how this class uses queue pulsing.

The AC_CLD_Connector factory (page 248) initializes the AC_Output_Handler by calling its open () hook method shown below:

```
 1  int AC_Output_Handler::open (void *connector) {
 2    connector_ =
 3      ACE_static_cast (AC_CLD_Connector *, connector);
 4    int bufsiz = ACE_DEFAULT_MAX_SOCKET_BUFSIZ;
 5    peer ().set_option (SOL_SOCKET, SO_SNDBUF,
 6                          &bufsiz, sizeof bufsiz);
 7    if (reactor ()->register_handler
 8        (this, ACE_Event_Handler::READ_MASK) == -1)
 9      return -1;
10    if (msg_queue ()->activate ()
11        == ACE_Message_Queue_Base::ACTIVATED) {
12      msg_queue ()->high_water_mark (QUEUE_MAX);
13      return activate (THR_SCOPE_SYSTEM);
14    } else return 0;
15  }
```

Lines 2–3 Save the pointer to the AC_CLD_Connector factory that called this method. If the connection to the server must be reconnected, the same factory will be used.

Lines 4–6 Increase the connected socket's send buffer to its largest size to maximize throughput over long-delay and/or high-speed networks.

Lines 7–8 Register this object with the singleton reactor so that its handle_input () method (page 246) will be notified immediately if the logging server disconnects.

Lines 10–13 This method is called each time a new connection to the logging server is established. On the initial connection, the message queue will be in the ACTIVATED state, so we set the message queue's high watermark to sizeof(ACE_Log_Record) × ACE_IOV_MAX, just like we do on line 6 of CLD_Handler::open() (page 172). We then spawn a system-scoped thread that runs the AC_Input_Handler::svc() hook method concurrently. Since AC_Input_Handler::close() (page 242) waits for this thread to exit we don't pass the THR_DETACHED flag to activate().

If the message queue was not in the ACTIVATED state, however, we know the logging server connection was reestablished. In this case, the message queue's high watermark was already set and the service thread is already executing.

We now show the AC_Output_Handler::svc() hook method, which runs in its own thread and forwards log records to the server logging daemon. As shown below, this method optimizes network throughput by buffering log records until a maximum number have arrived or a maximum time elapses.

```
 1 int AC_Output_Handler::svc () {
 2   ACE_Message_Block *chunk[ACE_IOV_MAX];
 3   size_t message_index = 0;
 4   ACE_Time_Value time_of_last_send (ACE_OS::gettimeofday ());
 5   ACE_Time_Value timeout;
 6   ACE_Sig_Action no_sigpipe ((ACE_SignalHandler) SIG_IGN);
 7   ACE_Sig_Action original_action;
 8   no_sigpipe.register_action (SIGPIPE, &original_action);
 9
10   for (;;) {
11     if (message_index == 0) {
12       timeout = ACE_OS::gettimeofday ();
13       timeout += FLUSH_TIMEOUT;
14     }
15     ACE_Message_Block *mblk = 0;
16     if (getq (mblk, &timeout) == -1) {
17       if (errno == ESHUTDOWN) {
18         if (connector_->reconnect () == -1) break;
19         continue;
20       } else if (errno != EWOULDBLOCK) break;
21       else if (message_index == 0) continue;
22     } else {
23       if (mblk->size () == 0
24           && mblk->msg_type () == ACE_Message_Block::MB_STOP)
25         { mblk->release (); break; }
26       chunk[message_index] = mblk;
27       ++message_index;
28     }
29     if (message_index >= ACE_IOV_MAX
30         || (ACE_OS::gettimeofday () - time_of_last_send
31             >= FLUSH_TIMEOUT)) {
32       if (send (chunk, message_index) == -1) break;
33       time_of_last_send = ACE_OS::gettimeofday ();
34     }
35   }
36
37   if (message_index > 0) send (chunk, message_index);
38   no_sigpipe.restore_action (SIGPIPE, original_action);
39   return 0;
40 }
```

We omit the AC_Output_Handler::send() implementation since it's identical to CLD_Handler::send() (page 175), which sends log records to the logging server and reconnects to the server if the connection is closed during the send. In fact, AC_Output_Handler::svc() is similar to CLD_Handler::forward() (page 173). The primary difference is that lines 17 through 20 above check to see if the queue was pulsed in response to the logging server disconnecting. The pulse is performed by the AC_Output_Handler::handle_input() method below, which is dispatched by the singleton reactor when the server closes a connection to the client logging daemon. When the connection is reestablished via AC_Connector::reconnect(), the ACE_Connector class calls `AC_Output_Handler::open()` (page 244), which changes the message queue's state back to ACTIVATED.

```
1  int AC_Output_Handler::handle_input (ACE_HANDLE h) {
2    peer ().close ();
3    reactor ()->remove_handler
4      (h, ACE_Event_Handler::READ_MASK
5         | ACE_Event_Handler::DONT_CALL);
6    msg_queue ()->pulse ();
7    return 0;
8  }
```

Line 2 Close the connection to release the socket handle.

Lines 3–5 Remove the socket handle from the reactor since it's no longer valid. Since we've now taken care of all required cleanup and this object is not being deleted, the DONT_CALL flag is passed to `remove_handler()`. When the connection to the server logging daemon is reestablished, `open()` will be called again, and a new socket will be registered for this object.

Line 6 To avoid trying to reconnect to the server logging daemon while the forwarder thread may be attempting the same thing, transfer the work to the forwarder thread using the `pulse()` method (page 166). If the forwarder thread is waiting on the synchronized message queue (page 244) (and therefore unaware that the connection is closed), it will wake up and immediately begin a reconnect. The `AC_Input_Handler::handle_input()` method can continue to queue message blocks, ensuring that flow control is properly back-propagated to client applications if the connection can't be reestablished for a long amount of time.

The `ACE_Svc_Handler::close()` method will be called automatically by the ACE Acceptor-Connector framework when the thread running the `svc()` hook method exits. This method cleans up all the dynamically allocated resources, such as the synchronized message queue and its contents, and removes the `AC_Output_Handler` from the singleton reactor.

AC_CLD_Acceptor. This class provides the following capabilities:[1]

- It's a factory that creates a single instance of the `AC_Input_Handler` (page 238).

- It passively accepts connections from clients.

- It activates the single instance of `AC_Input_Handler`, which registers all connections with the singleton `ACE_Reactor`.

---

[1] Although `AC_CLD_Acceptor` doesn't perform any authentication on the new logging client, this could be added to both `AC_CLD_Acceptor` and in the logging client code. These additions are left as an exercise for the reader.

The AC_CLD_Acceptor class definition is shown below:

```
class AC_CLD_Acceptor
  : public ACE_Acceptor<AC_Input_Handler, ACE_SOCK_Acceptor> {
public:
  AC_CLD_Acceptor (AC_Output_Handler *handler = 0)
    : output_handler_ (handler), input_handler_ (handler) {}

protected:
  typedef ACE_Acceptor<AC_Input_Handler, ACE_SOCK_Acceptor>
          PARENT;

  // <ACE_Acceptor> factory method.
  virtual int make_svc_handler (AC_Input_Handler *&sh);

  // <ACE_Reactor> close hook method.
  virtual int handle_close (ACE_HANDLE = ACE_INVALID_HANDLE,
                            ACE_Reactor_Mask = 0);

  // Pointer to the output handler.
  AC_Output_Handler *output_handler_;

  // Single input handler.
  AC_Input_Handler input_handler_;
};
```

AC_CLD_Acceptor is a subclass of ACE_Acceptor, so it inherits all the capabilities described in Section 7.3. Since we only need one instance of AC_Input_Handler we override the ACE_Acceptor::make_svc_handler() method as follows:

```
int AC_CLD_Acceptor::make_svc_handler (AC_Input_Handler *&sh)
{ sh = &input_handler_; return 0; }
```

This method sets the service handler to the address of the input_handler_ data member, which ensures there's only one instance of AC_Input_Handler, regardless of the number of clients that connect.

The following AC_CLD_Acceptor::handle_close() method is invoked by the reactor automatically if a failure occurs while accepting a connection or registering a handle and event handler with the reactor:

```
1 int AC_CLD_Acceptor::handle_close (ACE_HANDLE,
2                                    ACE_Reactor_Mask) {
3   PARENT::handle_close ();
4   input_handler_.close ();
5   return 0;
6 }
```

Line 3   Call up to its parent's handle_close() method to close the acceptor.

Line 4   Call the input_handler_'s close() method (page 242) to clean up the AC_Input_Handler's resources and shut down the AC_Output_Handler's message queue and svc() thread.

AC_CLD_Connector.   This class provides the following capabilities:

- It actively establishes (and when necessary reestablishes) and authenticates connections with the logging server.
- It activates a single instance of `AC_Output_Handler`, which forwards log records to the logging server concurrently with respect to the reception of log records by the `AC_Input_Handler`.

The `AC_CLD_Connector` class definition is shown below:

```
class AC_CLD_Connector
  : public ACE_Connector<AC_Output_Handler, ACE_SOCK_Connector> {
public:
  typedef ACE_Connector<AC_Output_Handler, ACE_SOCK_Connector>
          PARENT;

  AC_CLD_Connector (AC_Output_Handler *handler = 0)
    : handler_ (handler), ssl_ctx_ (0), ssl_ (0) {}

  virtual ~AC_CLD_Connector (void) { // Frees the SSL resources.
    SSL_free (ssl_);
    SSL_CTX_free (ssl_ctx_);
  }

  // Initialize the Connector.
  virtual int open (ACE_Reactor *r = ACE_Reactor::instance (),
                    int flags = 0);
  int reconnect (); // Re-establish connection to server.

protected:
  // Connection establishment and authentication hook method.
  virtual int connect_svc_handler
    (AC_Output_Handler *&svc_handler,
     const ACE_SOCK_Connector::PEER_ADDR &remote_addr,
     ACE_Time_Value *timeout,
     const ACE_SOCK_Connector::PEER_ADDR &local_addr,
     int reuse_addr, int flags, int perms);

  // Pointer to <AC_Output_Handler> we're connecting.
  AC_Output_Handler *handler_;

  // Address at which logging server listens for connections.
  ACE_INET_Addr remote_addr_;

  // The SSL "context" data structure.
  SSL_CTX *ssl_ctx_;

  // The SSL data structure corresponding to authenticated SSL
  // connections.
  SSL *ssl_;
};
```

The CLD_Connector::open() method implementation performs the canonical ACE_Connector initialization, in addition to using OpenSSL to establish the client's identity.

```
#if !defined (CLD_CERTIFICATE_FILENAME)
#  define CLD_CERTIFICATE_FILENAME "cld-cert.pem"
#endif /* !CLD_CERTIFICATE_FILENAME */
#if !defined (CLD_KEY_FILENAME)
#  define CLD_KEY_FILENAME "cld-key.pem"
#endif /* !CLD_KEY_FILENAME */

int AC_CLD_Connector::open (ACE_Reactor *r, int flags) {
  if (PARENT::open (r, flags) != 0) return -1;
  OpenSSL_add_ssl_algorithms ();
  ssl_ctx_ = SSL_CTX_new (SSLv3_client_method ());
  if (ssl_ctx_ == 0) return -1;

  if (SSL_CTX_use_certificate_file (ssl_ctx_,
                                    CLD_CERTIFICATE_FILENAME,
                                    SSL_FILETYPE_PEM) <= 0
      || SSL_CTX_use_PrivateKey_file (ssl_ctx_,
                                      CLD_KEY_FILENAME,
                                      SSL_FILETYPE_PEM) <= 0
      || !SSL_CTX_check_private_key (ssl_ctx_))
    return -1;

  ssl_ = SSL_new (ssl_ctx_);
  if (ssl_ == 0) return -1;
  return 0;
}
```

This code initializes and validates the OpenSSL data structures using essentially the same logic as the implementation of TPC_Logging_Acceptor::open() (page 224).

Unlike CLD_Connector, AC_CLD_Connector needn't implement a connect() method. Instead, it reuses the ACE_Connector::connect() template method. When a connection is completed via ACE_Connector, the framework calls the following AC_CLD_Connector::connect_svc_handler() hook method, which uses OpenSSL to implement an authentication protocol that ensures the client logging daemon is permitted to connect with the server logging daemon. The server's identity is also verified. The server logging daemon's end of this protocol appears in TPC_Logging_Acceptor::accept_svc_handler() (page 222) and the client logging daemon's end is shown below:

```
1 int AC_CLD_Connector::connect_svc_handler
2     (AC_Output_Handler *&svc_handler,
3      const ACE_SOCK_Connector::PEER_ADDR &remote_addr,
4      ACE_Time_Value *timeout,
5      const ACE_SOCK_Connector::PEER_ADDR &local_addr,
6      int reuse_addr, int flags, int perms) {
```

```
 7    if (PARENT::connect_svc_handler
 8         (svc_handler, remote_addr, timeout,
 9          local_addr, reuse_addr, flags, perms) == -1) return -1;
10    SSL_clear (ssl_);
11    SSL_set_fd (ssl_, ACE_reinterpret_cast
12                         (int, svc_handler->get_handle ()));
13
14    SSL_set_verify (ssl_, SSL_VERIFY_PEER, 0);
15
16    if (SSL_connect (ssl_) == -1
17         || SSL_shutdown (ssl_) == -1) return -1;
18    remote_addr_ = remote_addr;
19    return 0;
20 }
```

Lines 7–9   Establish the TCP connection using the default `connect_svc_handler()`.

Lines 10–12   Reset the SSL data structures for use with a new SSL connection.

Line 14   Configure the SSL data structures so that authentication of the server is performed and enforced when establishing the SSL connection.

Line 16   Perform the actual SSL connection/negotiation. If authentication of the server fails, the `SSL_connect()` call will fail.

Line 17   Shutdown the SSL connection if authentication succeeds. Since we don't actually encrypt the data we can communicate through the TCP stream from here on. If data encryption is also required, Sidebar 52 (page 227) describes how the ACE wrapper facades for OpenSSL can be applied.

Line 18   Save the address of the connected server logging daemon in case the connection needs to be reestablished using the `AC_CLD_Connector::reconnect()` method discussed below.

By overriding the `open()` and `connect_svc_handler()` hook methods, we can add authentication to our client logging daemon without affecting any other part of its implementation. This extensibility illustrates the power of the Template Method pattern used in the `ACE_Connector` class design.

The following `AC_CLD_Connector::reconnect()` method uses the same exponential backoff algorithm as `CLD_Connector::reconnect()` (page 179) to avoid swamping a logging server with connection requests:

```
int AC_CLD_Connector::reconnect () {
  // Maximum number of times to retry connect.
  const size_t MAX_RETRIES = 5;
  ACE_Time_Value timeout (1);
  size_t i;
  for (i = 0; i < MAX_RETRIES; ++i) {
```

```
      ACE_Synch_Options options (ACE_Synch_Options::USE_TIMEOUT,
                                 timeout);
      if (i > 0) ACE_OS::sleep (timeout);
      if (connect (handler_, remote_addr_, options) == 0)
        break;
      timeout *= 2; // Exponential backoff.
    }
    return i == MAX_RETRIES ? -1 : 0;
}
```

AC_Client_Logging_Daemon.   This class is a facade that integrates the other classes described above to implement the new client logging daemon. Its definition is shown below:

```
class AC_Client_Logging_Daemon : public ACE_Service_Object {
protected:
  // Factory that passively connects the <AC_Input_Handler>.
  AC_CLD_Acceptor acceptor_;

  // Factory that actively connects the <AC_Output_Handler>.
  AC_CLD_Connector connector_;

  // The <AC_Output_Handler> connected by <AC_CLD_Connector>.
  AC_Output_Handler output_handler_;

public:
  AC_Client_Logging_Daemon ()
    : acceptor_ (&output_handler_),
      connector_ (&output_handler_) {}

  // Service Configurator hook methods.
  virtual int init (int argc, ACE_TCHAR *argv[]);
  virtual int fini ();
  virtual int info (ACE_TCHAR **bufferp, size_t length = 0) const;
  virtual int suspend ();
  virtual int resume ();
};
```

AC_Client_Logging_Daemon inherits from ACE_Service_Object. It can therefore be configured dynamically via a svc.conf file that's processed by the ACE Service Configurator framework described in Chapter 5. When an instance of AC_Client_Logging_Daemon is linked dynamically, the ACE Service Configurator framework calls the AC_Client_Logging_Daemon::init() hook method shown below:

```
1 int AC_Client_Logging_Daemon::init
2       (int argc, ACE_TCHAR *argv[]) {
3   u_short cld_port = ACE_DEFAULT_SERVICE_PORT;
4   u_short sld_port = ACE_DEFAULT_LOGGING_SERVER_PORT;
5   ACE_TCHAR sld_host[MAXHOSTNAMELEN];
6   ACE_OS_String::strcpy (sld_host, ACE_LOCALHOST);
```

```
 7    ACE_Get_Opt get_opt (argc, argv, ACE_TEXT ("p:r:s:"), 0);
 8    get_opt.long_option (ACE_TEXT ("client_port"), 'p',
 9                         ACE_Get_Opt::ARG_REQUIRED);
10    get_opt.long_option (ACE_TEXT ("server_port"), 'r',
11                         ACE_Get_Opt::ARG_REQUIRED);
12    get_opt.long_option (ACE_TEXT ("server_name"), 's',
13                         ACE_Get_Opt::ARG_REQUIRED);
14
15    for (int c; (c = get_opt ()) != -1;)
16      switch (c) {
17      case 'p': // Client logging daemon acceptor port number.
18        cld_port = ACE_static_cast
19          (u_short, ACE_OS::atoi (get_opt.opt_arg ()));
20        break;
21      case 'r': // Server logging daemon acceptor port number.
22        sld_port = ACE_static_cast
23          (u_short, ACE_OS::atoi (get_opt.opt_arg ()));
24        break;
25      case 's': // Server logging daemon hostname.
26        ACE_OS_String::strsncpy
27          (sld_host, get_opt.opt_arg (), MAXHOSTNAMELEN);
28        break;
29      }
30
31    ACE_INET_Addr cld_addr (cld_port);
32    ACE_INET_Addr sld_addr (sld_port, sld_host);
33
34    if (acceptor_.open (cld_addr) == -1) return -1;
35    AC_Output_Handler *oh = &output_handler_;
36    if (connector_.connect (oh, sld_addr) == -1)
37    { acceptor_.close (); return -1; }
38    return 0;
39 }
```

Lines 3–6 Assign the default client logging daemon listen port (`cld_port`) and the default server logging daemon port (`sld_port`) and hostname (`sld_host`). These can be changed by arguments passed into this method. In particular, the server logging daemon hostname will often need to be set using the `-s` option.

Lines 7–29 The `ACE_Get_Opt` iterator describe in Sidebar 8 (page 47) parses options passed by the `svc.conf` file. The final parameter of 0 to `ACE_Get_Opt` ensures option parsing begins at `argv[0]` rather than `argv[1]`, which is the default. If any of the `"-p"`, `"-r"`, or `"-s"` options, or their long option equivalents, are passed in the `argv` parameter to `init()`, the appropriate port number or hostname is modified accordingly.

Lines 31–32 With the port numbers and server logging daemon's hostname now known, form the addresses needed to establish connections.

Lines 34–37 Initialize the `acceptor_` (page 247) and `connector_` (page 248).

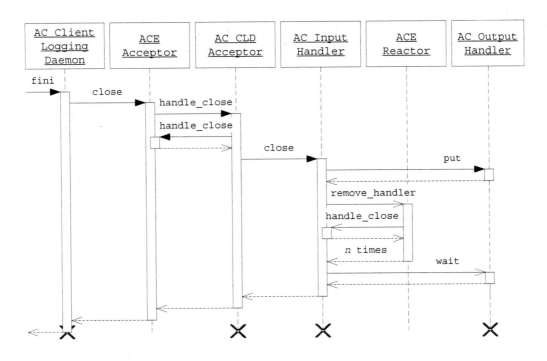

Figure 7.11: AC_Client_Logging_Daemon Shutdown Sequence

When the client logging daemon is removed, the ACE Service Configurator framework calls the following AC_Client_Logging_Daemon::fini() hook method:

```
int AC_Client_Logging_Daemon::fini ()
{ return acceptor_.close (); }
```

The fini() method calls the close() method inherited by AC_CLD_Acceptor. This method in turn calls AC_CLD_Acceptor::handle_close() to trigger a shutdown of the message queue and forwarder thread. The ACE Service Configurator framework deletes the AC_Client_Logging_Daemon instance after fini() returns. This shutdown sequence is depicted in Figure 7.11.

Now that we've implemented all the client logging daemon's classes, we can add the ACE_FACTORY_DEFINE macro.[2]

```
ACE_FACTORY_DEFINE (AC_CLD, AC_Client_Logging_Daemon)
```

This macro automatically defines the _make_AC_Client_Logging_Daemon() factory function, which is used in the following svc.conf file:

---

[2]We leave the suspend(), resume(), and info() hook methods as an exercise for the reader.

```
dynamic AC_Client_Logging_Daemon Service_Object *
AC_CLD:_make_AC_Client_Logging_Daemon()
  "-p $CLIENT_LOGGING_DAEMON_PORT"
```

This file directs the ACE Service Configurator framework to configure the client logging daemon via the following steps:

1. It dynamically links the AC_CLD DLL into the address space of the process.

2. It uses the ACE_DLL class described in Sidebar 33 (page 143) to extract the _make_ AC_Client_Logging_Daemon() factory function from the AC_CLD DLL symbol table.

3. This function is called to obtain a pointer to a dynamically allocated AC_Client_ Logging_Daemon.

4. The framework then calls AC_Client_Logging_Daemon::init() through this pointer, passing as its argc/argv argument the string -p followed by an expansion of the CLIENT_LOGGING_DAEMON_PORT environment variable that designates the port number where the client logging daemon listens for client application connection requests.

5. If init() succeeds, the AC_Client_Logging_Daemon pointer is stored in the ACE_Service_Repository as the "AC_Client_Logging_Daemon".

We're now ready to show the main() function, in SR_Configurable_Logging_ Server.cpp. It's similar to the Configurable_Logging_Server.cpp program used for other services, but requires slightly different tactics. Sidebar 11 (page 55) discusses some problems that can arise when event handlers don't control their own life cycle. The AC_Client_Logging_Daemon service in this chapter is allocated dynamically by the ACE Configurator framework when it's activated. However, its acceptor and service handlers are member objects in the service, and therefore don't control their own life cycle. Although our design carefully manages all the handlers's life cycle activities, problems can still occur on Windows because of the ACE_WFMO_Reactor deferred cleanup semantics (page 107). We therefore explicitly set the ACE_Reactor singleton to be an ACE_Select_Reactor.

```
 1 #include "ace/OS.h"
 2 #include "ace/Reactor.h"
 3 #include "ace/Select_Reactor.h"
 4 #include "ace/Service_Config.h"
 5
 6 int ACE_TMAIN (int argc, ACE_TCHAR *argv[]) {
 7   ACE_Select_Reactor *select_reactor;
 8   ACE_NEW_RETURN (select_reactor, ACE_Select_Reactor, 1);
 9   ACE_Reactor *reactor;
10   ACE_NEW_RETURN (reactor, ACE_Reactor (select_reactor, 1), 1);
```

```
11    ACE_Reactor::close_singleton ();
12    ACE_Reactor::instance (reactor, 1);
13
14    ACE_Service_Config::open (argc, argv);
15
16    ACE_Reactor::instance ()->run_reactor_event_loop ();
17    return 0;
18 }
```

Lines 7–8   The reactor implementation-specific examples in Chapter 4 used automatic instances of the desired reactor types. In this example, however, the reactor must persist until after the ACE_Object_Manager terminates services at shutdown time. To ensure this, we allocate the reactor dynamically. The third argument to the ACE_NEW_RETURN macro is the value to return from main() if allocation fails.

Lines 9–10   The ACE_Reactor is also allocated dynamically. The ACE_Select_ Reactor is passed as the implementation to use. The second argument to the ACE_ Reactor constructor tells the new ACE_Reactor instance to delete the implementation object when the reactor closes.

Lines 11–12   Close any existing ACE_Reactor singleton and replace it with the new ACE_Select_Reactor-based instance. The second argument to ACE_Reactor:: instance() explcitly turns control of the ACE_Reactor instance's memory to the ACE_Reactor singleton management mechanism. This design ensures that the reactor singleton shutdown activity generated by the ACE_Object_Manager will close the re-actor and free the dynamically allocated memory after the services are shut down.

Lines 14–16   As usual, configure services and run the reactor event loop.

The examples in this chapter have illustrated a number of powerful ACE Acceptor-Connector techniques and strategies:

- Using a single ACE_Svc_Handler to process many network connections
- Using nondynamic service handlers with a reactor
- Pulsing a service handler's message queue to communicate with the handler's service thread
- Reconnecting a TCP socket using an exponential backoff strategy
- Replacing the singleton ACE_Reactor with one that ACE deletes automatically

The capabilities in this chapter's client and server logging daemons could clearly be implemented using different mechanisms and protocols. Due to ACE's highly refined framework design, however, none of the different ways to redesign these daemons will require rewriting the networking code, buffer management, queueing mechanisms, concurrency strategies, or demultiplexing techniques. The only changes are in the networked service implementation itself.

7.5   Summary

The ACE Acceptor-Connector framework decouples a service's connection and initialization strategies from its service handling strategy. This separation of concerns allows each set of strategies to evolve independently and promotes a modular design of networked applications. The ACE Acceptor-Connector framework factors connection and initialization strategies into the `ACE_Acceptor` and `ACE_Connector` class templates, and the service handling strategy into the `ACE_Svc_Handler` class template.

The ACE Reactor, Service Configurator, and Task frameworks described in earlier chapters use class inheritance and virtual methods as their primary extensibility mechanisms. The ACE Acceptor-Connector framework uses these mechanisms as well, primarily as the means to configure different strategies for connection establishment, communication, concurrency, and service behavior. Unlike the frameworks in previous chapters, however, classes in the ACE Acceptor-Connector framework share an inherent relationship in networked application services, so the use of parameterized types plays a more significant role here. To allow and enforce the relationships between the strategies, both `ACE_Acceptor` and `ACE_Connector` include an `ACE_Svc_Handler`-derived class in their template arguments to act as the target of the connection factory.

This chapter defined and illustrated the communication and connection roles that networked application services play, as well as the passive and active connection modes that connection-oriented services use. Although the ACE Socket wrapper facades described in Chapter 3 of C++NPv1 assist with mastering the problems associated with C operating system APIs, this chapter illustrated how the design of the ACE Acceptor-Connector framework encourages modular separation of roles leading to highly extensible and maintainable designs. The examples showed how easy it is to define an application's service handlers by defining class(es) derived from `ACE_Svc_Handler` and adding the service-specific behavior in the hook and callback methods inherited from `ACE_Svc_Handler`, `ACE_Task`, and `ACE_Event_Handler`. Although the ACE Acceptor-Connector framework encapsulates the most common use-cases for service establishment, this chapter showed how the framework uses the Template Method pattern [GoF] to allow application developers to customize the behavior of each service establishment step to match the requirements, environment, and resources of specific networked applications.

CHAPTER 8

The ACE Proactor Framework

CHAPTER SYNOPSIS

This chapter outlines the asynchronous I/O mechanisms available on today's popular OS platforms and then describes the design and use of the ACE Proactor framework. This framework implements the Proactor pattern [POSA2], which allows event-driven applications to efficiently demultiplex and dispatch service requests triggered by the completion of asynchronous I/O operations. This chapter shows how to enhance our client logging daemon to use a proactive model that (1) initiates I/O operations, (2) demultiplexes I/O completion events, and (3) dispatches those completion events to application-defined completion handlers that process the results of asynchronous I/O operations.

8.1 Overview

Chapter 3 described the ACE Reactor framework, which is most often used with a *reactive I/O* model. An application based on this model registers event handler objects that are notified by a reactor when it's possible to perform one or more desired I/O operations, such as receiving data on a socket, with a high likelihood of immediate completion. I/O operations are often performed in a single thread, driven by the reactor's event dispatching loop. Although reactive I/O is a common programming model, each thread can execute only one I/O operation at a time. The sequential nature of the I/O operations can be a bottleneck since applications that transfer large amounts of data on multiple endpoints can't use the parallelism available from the OS and/or multiple CPUs or network interfaces.

One way to alleviate the bottlenecks of reactive I/O is to use *synchronous I/O* in conjunction with a multithreading model, such as the thread pool model in Chapter 6 or the thread-per-connection model in Chapter 7. Multithreading can help parallelize an application's I/O operations and may improve performance. However, adding multiple threads to a design requires appropriate synchronization mechanisms to avoid concurrency hazards, such as *race conditions* and *deadlocks* [Tan92]. These additional considerations require expertise in concurrency and synchronization techniques. They also add complexity to both design and code, increasing the risk of subtle defects. Moreover, multithreading can incur non-trivial time/space overhead due to the resources needed to allocate run-time stacks, perform context switches [SS95b], and move data between CPU caches [SKT96].

A *proactive I/O* model is often a more scalable way to alleviate reactive I/O bottlenecks without introducing the complexity and overhead of synchronous I/O and multithreading. This model allows an application to execute I/O operations via the following two phases:

1. The application can initiate one or more asynchronous I/O operations on multiple I/O handles in parallel without having to wait until they complete.

2. As each operation completes, the OS notifies an application-defined *completion handler* that then processes the results from the completed I/O operation.

The two phases of the proactive I/O model are essentially the inverse of those in the reactive I/O model, in which an application

1. Uses an event demultiplexer to determine when an I/O operation is possible, and likely to complete immediately, and then

2. Performs the operation synchronously

In addition to improving application scalability via asynchrony, the proactive I/O model can offer other benefits, depending on the platform's implementation of asynchronous I/O. For example, if multiple asynchronous I/O operations can be initiated simultaneously and each operation carries extended information, such as file positions for file I/O, the OS can optimize its internal buffering strategy to avoid unnecessary data copies. It can also optimize file I/O performance by reordering operations to minimize disk head movement and/or increase cache hit rates.

The ACE Proactor framework simplifies the development of programs that use the proactive I/O model. In this context, the ACE Proactor framework is responsible for

- Initiating asynchronous I/O operations

- Saving each operation's arguments and relaying them to the completion handler

- Waiting for completion events that indicate these operations have finished

- Demultiplexing the completion events to their associated completion handlers and

- Dispatching to hook methods on the handlers to process the events in an application-defined manner

In addition to its I/O-related capabilities, the ACE Proactor framework offers the same timer queue mechanisms offered by the ACE Reactor framework in Section 3.4.

This chapter describes the following ACE Proactor framework classes:

ACE Class	Description
`ACE_Handler`	Defines the interface for receiving the results of asynchronous I/O operations and handling timer expirations.

`ACE_Asynch_Read_Stream`
`ACE_Asynch_Write_Stream`
`ACE_Asynch_Result`
	Initiate asynchronous read and write operations on an I/O stream and associate each with an `ACE_Handler` object that will receive the results of those operations.

`ACE_Asynch_Acceptor` `ACE_Asynch_Connector`	An implementation of the Acceptor-Connector pattern that establishes new TCP/IP connections asynchronously.
`ACE_Service_Handler`	Defines the target of the `ACE_Asynch_Acceptor` and `ACE_Asynch_Connector` connection factories and provides the hook methods to initialize a TCP/IP-connected service.
`ACE_Proactor`	Manages timers and asynchronous I/O completion event demultiplexing. This class is analogous to the `ACE_Reactor` class in the ACE Reactor framework.

The most important relationships between the classes in the ACE Proactor framework are shown in Figure 8.1 (page 260). These classes play the following roles in accordance with the Proactor pattern [POSA2]:

- **Asynchronous I/O infrastructure layer classes** perform application-independent strategies that initiate asynchronous I/O operations, demultiplex completion events to their completion handlers, and then dispatch the associated completion handler hook methods. The infrastructure layer classes in the ACE Proactor framework include `ACE_Asynch_Acceptor`, `ACE_Asynch_Connector`, `ACE_Asynch_Result`, `ACE_Asynch_Read_Stream`, `ACE_Asynch_Write_Stream`, and various implementations of `ACE_Proactor`. The infrastructure layer also uses the `ACE_Time_Value` and ACE timer queue classes from Sections 3.2 and 3.4.

- **Application layer classes** include completion handlers that perform application-defined processing in their hook methods. In the ACE Proactor framework, these classes are descendants of `ACE_Handler` and/or `ACE_Service_Handler`.

The power of the ACE Proactor framework comes from the separation of concerns between its infrastructure classes and application classes. By decoupling completion demultiplexing and dispatching mechanisms from application-defined event processing policies, the ACE Proactor framework provides the following benefits:

- **Improve portability.** Applications can take advantage of the proactive I/O model on many platforms that have diverse asynchronous I/O mechanisms. It uses *overlapped I/O* on Windows (requires Windows NT version 4.0 and higher) and the Asynchronous I/O (AIO) option of the POSIX.4 Realtime Extension standard [POS95] on platforms that implement it, including HP-UX, IRIX, Linux, LynxOS, and Solaris.

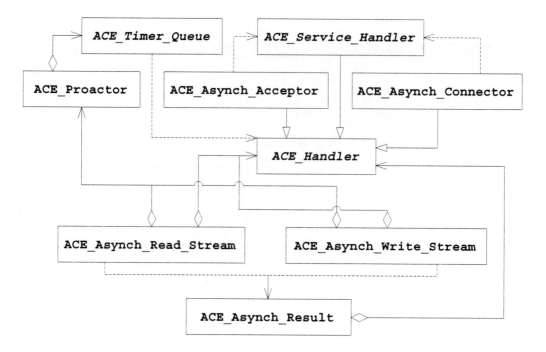

Figure 8.1: The ACE Proactor Framework Classes

- **Automates completion detection, demultiplexing, and dispatching.** The ACE Proactor framework isolates native OS I/O initiation and completion demultiplexing APIs, as well as timer support, in infrastructure layer framework classes. Applications can use these object-oriented mechanisms to initiate asynchronous operations, and only need to implement application-defined completion handlers.

- **Support transparent extensibility.** As shown in Section 8.5, the ACE Proactor framework uses the Bridge pattern [GoF] to export an interface with uniform, well-defined behavior. This design allows the framework internals to change and adapt to varying OS-provided asynchronous I/O implementations and shortcomings without requiring any application-layer changes.

- **Increase reuse and minimize error-prone programming details.** By separating asynchronous I/O mechanisms from application-defined policies and behavior, the ACE Proactor framework can be reused across many diverse application domains.

- **Thread safety.** Applications can use I/O parallelism offered by the OS platform without needing complicated application-level synchronization strategies. When application operation initiation and completion handling code is processed in a single thread, there are only simple data access rules to follow, such as "don't manipulate a buffer that's been given to the OS for I/O before that I/O is complete."

The ACE Proactor framework is a whitebox framework since networked application event handlers must descend from ACE_Handler, similar to the ACE Reactor framework.

The following sections motivate and describe the capabilities of each class in the ACE Proactor framework. They also illustrate how this framework can be used to apply asynchronous I/O to our client logging daemon. If you aren't familiar with the Proactor pattern from POSA2, we recommend that you read about it first before delving into the detailed examples in this chapter.

8.2   The Asynchronous I/O Factory Classes

Motivation

The proactive I/O model is generally harder to program than reactive and synchronous I/O models because

- I/O initiation and completion are distinct activities that must be handled separately.

- Multiple I/O operations can be initiated simultaneously, which requires more record-keeping.

- There's no guaranteed completion order when multiple I/O operations complete simultaneously.

- In a multithreaded service a completion handler may execute in a thread other than the one that initiated the I/O operation.

The proactive I/O model therefore requires a factory to initiate asynchronous I/O operations. Since multiple I/O operations can execute simultaneously and complete in any order, the proactive model also requires an explicit binding between each asynchronous operation, its parameters (such as the I/O handle, data buffer, and buffer size), and the completion handler that will process the results of the operation.

In theory, designing classes to generate asynchronous I/O operations and bind them to their completion handlers should be relatively straightforward. In practice, however, the design is complicated by the fact that asynchronous I/O is implemented in different ways across today's popular OS platforms. Two common examples include:

- **Windows.** The Windows ReadFile() and WriteFile() system functions can either perform synchronous I/O or initiate an overlapped I/O operation.

- **POSIX.** The POSIX aio_read() and aio_write() functions initiate asynchronous read and write operations, respectively. These functions are separate from the read() and write() (and Sockets recv() and send()) functions that are used in ACE's IPC wrapper facade classes (see Chapter 3 in C++NPv1).

Each platform's asynchronous I/O facility also includes its own mechanism for binding an I/O operation with its parameters, such as buffer pointer and transfer size. For example, POSIX AIO provides an AIO control block (`aiocb`), whereas Windows provides the `OVERLAPPED` structure and a completion key argument to the I/O completion port facility. Sidebar 54 discusses other challenges with OS asynchronous I/O mechanisms.

Sidebar 54: Asynchronous I/O Portability Issues

Unlike synchronous I/O and reactive I/O, which are available on most modern operating systems, asynchronous I/O is not ubiquitous. The following OS platforms supported by ACE provide asynchronous I/O mechanisms:

- **Windows platforms** that support both overlapped I/O and I/O completion ports [Ric97]. Overlapped I/O is an efficient and scalable I/O mechanism on Windows [Sol98]. Windows performs completion event demultiplexing via I/O completion ports and event handles. An I/O completion port is a queue managed by the Windows kernel to buffer I/O completion events.

- **POSIX platforms** that implement the POSIX.4 AIO specification [POS95]. This specification was originally designed for disk file I/O [Gal95], but can also be used for network I/O with varying degress of success. An application thread can wait for completion events via `aio_suspend()` or be notified by real-time signals, which are tricky to integrate into an event-driven application. In general, POSIX.4 AIO requires extra care to program the proactive model correctly and efficiently. Despite UNIX's usual interchangeability of I/O system functions across IPC mechanisms, integration of the POSIX AIO facility with other IPC mechanisms, such as the Socket API, leaves much to be desired on some platforms. For example, Socket API functions such as `connect()` and `accept()` are not integrated with the POSIX AIO model, and some AIO implementations can't handle multiple outstanding operations on a handle under all conditions.

Asynchronous I/O performance characteristics can also vary widely. For example, some operating systems implement the POSIX AIO functions by spawning a thread for each asynchronous I/O operation. Although this is a compliant implementation, it provides no performance gain relative to an application spawning the thread itself. In fact, this implementation can actually degrade the performance of I/O-intensive applications rather than improve it! Hopefully, OS asynchronous I/O implementations will soon improve, allowing wider use of this powerful mechanism.

All the asynchronous I/O mechanisms discussed above use an I/O handle to refer to the IPC channel or file on which to perform the I/O. The ACE Proactor framework defines a set of classes that initiate asynchronous I/O on various IPC mechanisms. These classes enhance portability, minimize complexity, and avoid reintroducing the I/O handle-related problems mastered in C++NPv1. This book examines the two most popular classes for networked applications, `ACE_Asynch_Read_Stream` and `ACE_Asynch_Write_Stream`.

Class Capabilities

`ACE_Asynch_Read_Stream` and `ACE_Asynch_Write_Stream` are factory classes that enable applications to initiate portable asynchronous `read()` and `write()` operations, respectively. These classes provide the following capabilities:

- They can initiate asynchronous I/O operations on a stream-oriented IPC mechanism, such as a TCP socket.
- They bind an I/O handle, an `ACE_Handler` object, and an `ACE_Proactor` to process I/O completion events correctly and efficiently.
- They create an object that carries an operation's parameters through the ACE Proactor framework to its completion handler.
- They derive from `ACE_Asynch_Operation`, which provides the interface to initialize the object and to request cancellation of outstanding I/O operations.

`ACE_Asynch_Read_Stream` and `ACE_Asynch_Write_Stream` define nested `Result` classes to represent the binding between an operation and its parameters. The ACE Proactor framework abstracts common results-oriented behavior into the `ACE_Asynch_Result` class from which the nested `Result` classes derive. Together, this set of classes provides a completion handler with the following capabilities:

- It can obtain the original parameters for an I/O operation, such as the requested transfer byte count and the memory address.
- It can determine the success or failure of the associated operation.
- It can be passed an *asynchronous completion token (ACT)* [POSA2] that provides a method to extend the amount and type of information communicated between the operation initiator and the completion handler.

The interfaces for `ACE_Asynch_Result`, `ACE_Asynch_Read_Stream`, `ACE_Asynch_Write_Stream` and their `Result` nested classes are shown in Figure 8.2 (page 264). The following table lists the key methods in `ACE_Asynch_Read_Stream`:

Method	Description
`open()`	Initialize object to prepare for initiating asynchronous `read()` operations.
`cancel()`	Attempt to cancel outstanding `read()` operations initiated via this object.
`read()`	Initiate an asynchronous operation to read from the associated IPC stream.

The key methods in the `ACE_Asynch_Write_Stream` class are shown in the following table:

Method	Description
`open()`	Initialize object to prepare for initiating asynchronous `write()` operations.
`cancel()`	Attempt to cancel outstanding `write()` operations initiated via this object.
`write()`	Initiate an asynchronous operation to write to the associated IPC stream.

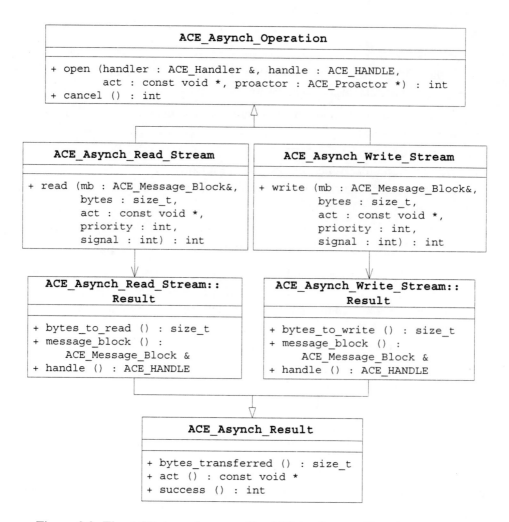

Figure 8.2: The ACE Asynchronous Read/Write Stream Class Relationships

The open() methods bind the asynchronous I/O factory object to

- The handle that's used to initiate I/O operations
- The ACE_Proactor object that will detect and demultiplex completion events for those I/O operations
- The ACE_Handler object that will handle proactor-dispatched I/O completions

The act parameter is an asynchronous completion token that will be associated with each I/O operation issued via the I/O factory object. When the operation completes, the act parameter can be retrieved using the act() method in ACE_Asynch_Result. This feature is specific to Windows, however, so we don't show its use in this book.

The `read()` and `write()` methods use an `ACE_Message_Block` to receive into and send from, respectively, thereby providing the following benefits:

- **Simplified buffer management.** Since asynchronous I/O initiation and completion are handled in separate classes, information concerning buffer addresses, available space, and used space must be associated with each I/O operation. Reusing `ACE_Message_Block` addresses these needs portably and efficiently.

- **Automatic transfer count udpate.** The `write()` method starts transferring bytes from the message block's read pointer, that is, it reads bytes out of the message. Conversely, the `read()` method starts reading into the message block beginning at its write pointer, that is, it writes new bytes into the message. After successful completion of an I/O operation, the message block's read and write pointers are updated to reflect the number of bytes transferred successfully. Applications therefore needn't adjust message buffer pointers or sizes since the ACE Proactor framework handles this automatically. Sidebar 55 (page 275) further describes how the ACE Proactor framework manages `ACE_Message_Block` pointers.

- **Easy integration with other ACE frameworks.** The `ACE_Message_Block` provides a convenient mechanism to obtain or forward data for further processing in the ACE Task framework (Chapter 6), ACE Acceptor-Connector framework (Chapter 7), and the ACE Streams framework (Chapter 9).

In contrast to the ACE IPC wrapper facades, such as `ACE_SOCK_Stream` described in C++NPv1, `ACE_Asynch_Read_Stream` and `ACE_Asynch_Write_Stream` don't encapsulate any underlying IPC mechanisms. Instead, they define the interface for initiating asynchronous I/O operations. This design yields the following benefits:

- It allows reuse of ACE's IPC wrapper facade classes, such as `ACE_SOCK_Stream` and `ACE_SPIPE_Stream`, in the ACE Proactor framework and avoids recreating a parallel set of IPC classes usable only in the Proactor framework.
- It imposes a structure to avoid misuse of I/O handles by exposing only the desired I/O operation initiators.
- It facilitates use of the same IPC classes for synchronous and asynchronous I/O by giving the I/O handle to the asynchronous operation factory.

Therefore, networked applications written with ACE can use any combination of synchronous, reactive, and proactive I/O. The decision concerning which I/O mechanism to use can be made at compile time or run time if desired. In fact, the decision can be deferred until after the IPC object is set up! For example, an application may decide which mechanism to use after establishing a socket connection [HPS97].

The ACE Proactor framework also contains factory classes for initiating datagram I/O operations (`ACE_Asynch_Read_Dgram` and `ACE_Asynch_Write_Dgram`) and file I/O operations (`ACE_Asynch_Read_File`, `ACE_Asynch_Write_File`, and `ACE_`

Asynch_Transmit_File). The designs and capabilities of these classes are similar to those described in this chapter. Please consult the online ACE documentation at http://ace.ece.uci.edu/Doxygen/ or http://www.riverace.com/docs/ for details.

Example

This chapter reimplements the client logging daemon service from Chapter 7 using the ACE Proactor framework. Although the classes used in the proactive client logging daemon service are similar to those in the Acceptor-Connector version, the proactive version uses a single application thread to initiate and handle completions for all its I/O operations.

The classes comprising the client logging daemon based on the ACE Proactor framework are shown in Figure 8.3. The role of each class is outlined below:

Class	Description
AIO_Output_Handler	A message forwarder that initiates asynchronous write operations to forward messages to the logging server
AIO_CLD_Connector	A factory that actively (re)establishes and authenticates connections with the logging server and activates an AIO_Output_Handler
AIO_Input_Handler	Processes log record data received from logging clients via asynchronous read() operations and passes completed log records to AIO_Output_Handler for output processing
AIO_CLD_Acceptor	A factory that accepts connections from logging clients and creates a new AIO_Input_Handler for each
AIO_Client_Logging_Daemon	A facade class that integrates the other classes together

The interactions between instances of these classes are shown in Figure 8.4 (page 268). We'll start describing the AIO_Output_Handler class in this example and present the other classes in subsequent sections in this chapter.

The source code for this example is in the AIO_Client_Logging_Daemon.cpp file. The AIO_Output_Handler class forwards log records to a server logging daemon. A portion of its class definition follows:

```
class AIO_Output_Handler
  : public ACE_Task<ACE_NULL_SYNCH>,
    public ACE_Service_Handler {
```

AIO_Output_Handler inherits from ACE_Task to reuse its ACE_Message_Queue. This queue is unsynchronized since all work in this service occurs in one application thread. Since AIO_Output_Handler derives from ACE_Service_Handler, it can process completion events (described in Section 8.3) and act as the target of the AIO_CLD_Connector asynchronous connection factory (described in Section 8.4).

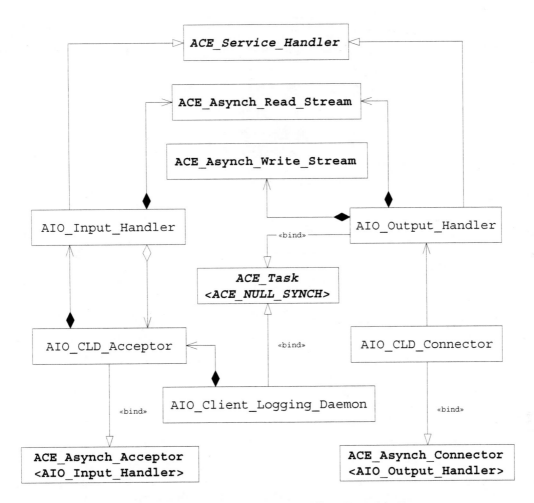

Figure 8.3: Classes in the Proactive Client Logging Daemon

```
public:
  AIO_Output_Handler (): can_write_ (0) {}

  virtual ~AIO_Output_Handler ();

  // Entry point into the <AIO_Output_Handler>.
  virtual int put (ACE_Message_Block *, ACE_Time_Value * = 0);

  // Hook method called when server connection is established.
  virtual void open (ACE_HANDLE new_handle,
                     ACE_Message_Block &message_block);

protected:
  ACE_Asynch_Read_Stream reader_; // Detects connection loss.
```

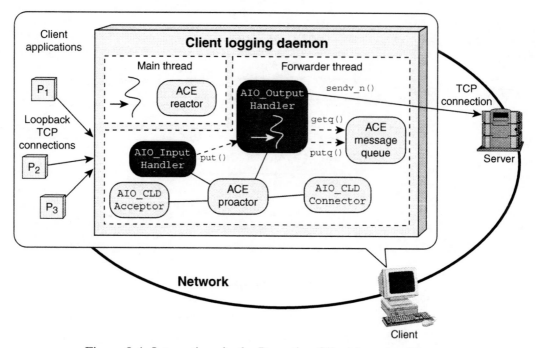

Figure 8.4: Interactions in the Proactive Client Logging Daemon

```
  ACE_Asynch_Write_Stream writer_; // Sends records to server.
  int can_write_; // Safe to begin sending a log record?

  // Initiate the send of a log record.
  void start_write (ACE_Message_Block *mblk = 0);
};

typedef ACE_Unmanaged_Singleton<AIO_Output_Handler,
                                ACE_Null_Mutex>
        OUTPUT_HANDLER;
```

AIO_Output_Handler contains an ACE_Asynch_Read_Stream to detect when the
server connection closes. It also contains an ACE_Asynch_Write_Stream to initiate
asynchronous write() operations that send log records to the server logging daemon.

Since there's one TCP connection to the server logging daemon, we use a single AIO_
Output_Handler to forward log records to the server logging daemon. We therefore define OUTPUT_HANDLER as an ACE_Unmanaged_Singleton (page 194). It's unmanaged to ensure that we control its life cycle since this service may be stopped and unlinked
before the end of the program. The synchronization traits class is ACE_Null_Mutex
because all access to the singleton occurs in one thread.

When the server logging daemon connection is established, the following open()
hook method is dispatched by the ACE Proactor framework:

```
1  void AIO_Output_Handler::open
2      (ACE_HANDLE new_handle, ACE_Message_Block &) {
3    ACE_SOCK_Stream temp_peer (new_handle);
4    int bufsiz = ACE_DEFAULT_MAX_SOCKET_BUFSIZ;
5    temp_peer.set_option (SOL_SOCKET, SO_SNDBUF,
6                              &bufsiz, sizeof bufsiz);
7
8    reader_.open (*this, new_handle, 0, proactor ());
9    writer_.open (*this, new_handle, 0, proactor ());
10
11   ACE_Message_Block *mb;
12   ACE_NEW (mb, ACE_Message_Block (1));
13   reader_.read (*mb, 1);
14   ACE_Sig_Action no_sigpipe ((ACE_SignalHandler) SIG_IGN);
15   no_sigpipe.register_action (SIGPIPE, 0);
16   can_write_ = 1;
17   start_write (0);
18 }
```

Lines 3–6   Increase the new socket's send buffer to its largest size to maximize throughput over long-delay and/or high-speed networks. We use a temporary `ACE_SOCK_Stream` object to set the buffer in a type-safe manner.

Lines 8–9   Initialize the `reader_` and `writer_` objects. Each specifies `this` object as the completion handler, the new socket handle to issue operations on, and the same `ACE_Proactor` used to open the connection. The completion key (ACT) facility isn't used, so the third argument is 0. After initialization, the `reader_` and `writer_` are used to initiate asynchronous I/O operations.

Lines 11–13   The client logging daemon in the *Example* part of Section 7.4 registered the server socket for input events in a reactor. In the proactive model, we initiate an asynchronous `read()` for one byte. If this operation ever completes, either the server sent data (which violates the protocol) or the server closed its socket endpoint.

Lines 14–15   As in other examples that rely on a READ event to detect a closed socket, ignore the SIGPIPE signal so that asynchronous `write()` operations won't abort the program if the connection is closed.

Lines 16–17   To avoid interleaving log records in the presence of partial writes, we only transmit one log record at a time. The `can_write_` flag indicates whether it's safe to start writing a new log record or not. Since this connection is newly opened, it's now safe to write, so we set the flag and then call the following `start_write()` method to initiate an asynchronous `write()` operation:

```
1  void AIO_Output_Handler::start_write
2      (ACE_Message_Block *mblk) {
3    if (mblk == 0) {
4      ACE_Time_Value nonblock (0);
```

```
5       getq (mblk, &nonblock);
6     }
7     if (mblk != 0) {
8       can_write_ = 0;
9       if (writer_.write (*mblk, mblk->length ()) == -1)
10        ungetq (mblk);
11    }
12 }
```

Lines 1–6 The start_write () method can be called with one of two arguments

- A NULL pointer, which indicates that the first message in the queue should be dequeued and sent
- A non-NULL ACE_Message_Block, which indicates to start writing immediately

Lines 7–11 If there's no log record available for sending, we return without doing anything. Otherwise, we reset can_write_ to 0 to prevent further message blocks from being sent until the current one is finished. The writer_ object initiates an asynchronous write () operation to send the message block. If the write () initiation fails, the message block is put back on the queue with the assumption that the socket is closed. The reconnection strategy (page 293) will trigger an asynchronous write () as soon as the connection is reestablished.

When log records are received from logging clients, they are passed to the AIO_Output_Handler using the following put () method reimplemented from ACE_Task:

```
int AIO_Output_Handler::put (ACE_Message_Block *mb,
                             ACE_Time_Value *timeout) {
  if (can_write_) { start_write (mb); return 0; }
  return putq (mb, timeout);
}
```

If there's no write () operation in progress, call start_write () to immediately initiate sending of the specified ACE_Message_Block. If a write () can't be started now, we queue the message for later.

8.3 The ACE_Handler Class

Motivation

A chief differentiator between the proactive and reactive I/O models is that proactive I/O initiation and completion are distinct steps that occur separately. Moreover, these two steps may occur in different threads of control. Using separate classes for the initiation and completion processing avoids unnecessarily coupling the two. Section 8.2 described the ACE_Asynch_Read_Stream and ACE_Asynch_Write_Stream classes used to initiate asynchronous I/O operations; this section focuses on I/O completion handling.

Completion events signify that a previously initiated I/O operation has finished. To process the result of the I/O operation correctly and efficiently, a completion handler must know all of the arguments specified for the I/O operation, in addition to the result. Together, this information includes

- What type of operation was initiated
- Whether or not the operation completed successfully
- The error code, if the operation failed
- The I/O handle that identifies the communication endpoint
- The memory address for the transfer
- The requested and actual number of bytes transferred

Asynchronous I/O completion processing requires more information than is available to callback methods in the ACE Reactor framework. The ACE_Event_Handler class presented in Section 3.3 is therefore not suitable for use in the ACE Proactor framework. Since completion handling also depends on the asynchronous I/O mechanism offered by the underlying OS platform, it has the same portability issues discussed in Section 8.2. Addressing these issues in each application is unnecessarily tedious and costly, which is why the ACE Proactor framework provides the ACE_Handler class.

Class Capabilities

ACE_Handler is the base class of all asynchronous completion handlers in the ACE Proactor framework. This class provides the following capabilities:

- It provides hook methods to handle completion of all asynchronous I/O operations defined in ACE, including connection establishment and I/O operations on an IPC stream.
- It provides a hook method to handle timer expiration.

The interface for ACE_Handler is shown in Figure 8.5 (page 272) and its key methods are shown in the following table:

Method	Description
handle()	Obtains the handle used by this object
handle_read_stream()	Hook method called on completion of a read() operation initiated by ACE_Asynch_Read_Stream
handle_write_stream()	Hook method called on completion of a write() operation initiated by ACE_Asynch_Write_Stream
handle_time_out()	Hook method called when a timer scheduled via ACE_Proactor expires

```
                        ACE_Handler
─────────────────────────────────────────────────────
# proactor_  : ACE_Proactor *
─────────────────────────────────────────────────────
+ handle ()  : ACE_HANDLE
+ handle_read_stream (result :
          const ACE_Asynch_Read_Stream::Result &)
+ handle_write_stream (result :
          const ACE_Asynch_Write_Stream::Result &)
+ handle_time_out (tv : const ACE_Time_Value &,
                    act : const void *)
+ handle_accept (result :
          const ACE_Asynch_Accept::Result &)
+ handle_connect (result :
          const ACE_Asynch_Connect::Result &)
```

Figure 8.5: The ACE_Handler Class

The handle_time_out() method is called when a timer scheduled with an ACE_
Proactor expires. Its tv argument is the absolute time of day that the timer was scheduled to expire. The actual time may be different depending on activity level and dispatched
handler delays. Note that this behavior is slightly different than the ACE_Time_Value
passed to ACE_Event_Handler::handle_timeout() (page 49), which is the actual time of day the timer event hook method was dispatched by the ACE proactor framework.

The handle_read_stream() and handle_write_stream() hook methods
are called with a reference to the Result object associated with an asynchronous operation
that has completed. The most useful Result object methods that are accessible from
handle_read_stream() and handle_write_stream() are shown in context in
Figure 8.2 (page 264) and listed in the following table:

Method	Description
success()	Indicates whether or not the asynchronous operation succeeded
handle()	Obtains the I/O handle used by the asynchronous I/O operation
message_block()	Obtains a reference to the ACE_Message_Block used in the operation
bytes_transferred()	Indicates how many bytes were actually transferred in the asynchronous operation
bytes_to_read()	Indicates how many bytes were requested for an asynchronous read() operation
bytes_to_write()	Indicates how many bytes were requested for an asynchronous write() operation

Example

All previous logging daemons, both client and server, have used the Logging_Handler class developed in Chapter 4 of C++NPv1 to receive log records from logging clients. The Logging_Handler::recv_log_record() method uses synchronous input operations to receive a log record. Synchronous input operations are relatively straightforward to program since the activation record of the receiving thread's run-time stack can be used to store bookkeeping information and data fragments.

In contrast, asynchronous input handling is harder to program since the bookkeeping details and data fragments must be managed explicitly, rather than implicitly on the run-time stack. In this example, the new AIO_Input_Handler class receives log records from logging clients by initiating asynchronous read() operations and assembling the data fragments into log records that are then forwarded to the server logging daemon. This class uses the proactive I/O model and asynchronous input operations to achieve maximum concurrency across all logging clients using a single thread of control.

As shown in Figure 8.3 (page 267), the AIO_Input_Handler class is a descendant of ACE_Handler (Section 8.4 discusses ACE_Service_Handler, which derives from ACE_Handler) and is defined as follows:

```
class AIO_Input_Handler : public ACE_Service_Handler {
public:
  AIO_Input_Handler (AIO_CLD_Acceptor *acc = 0)
    : acceptor_ (acc), mblk_ (0) {}

  virtual ~AIO_Input_Handler ();

  // Called by <ACE_Asynch_Acceptor> when a client connects.
  virtual void open (ACE_HANDLE new_handle,
                     ACE_Message_Block &message_block);

protected:
  enum { LOG_HEADER_SIZE = 8 };       // Length of CDR header.
  AIO_CLD_Acceptor *acceptor_;        // Our creator.
  ACE_Message_Block *mblk_;           // Block to receive log record.
  ACE_Asynch_Read_Stream reader_;     // Asynchronous read() factory.

  // Handle input from logging clients.
  virtual void handle_read_stream
    (const ACE_Asynch_Read_Stream::Result &result);
};
```

The logging client sends each log record in CDR format, starting with a fixed-length header (Section 4.4.2 in C++NPv1 presents complete details on the CDR marshaling and log record format). The header has an ACE_CDR::Boolean to indicate the byte order and an ACE_CDR::ULong holding the length of the payload following the header. From CDR encoding and alignment rules, we know this to be 8 bytes, so we define the LOG_HEADER_SIZE enumerator as 8.

When a logging client connects to the client logging daemon, the following `open()` hook method is dispatched by the ACE Proactor framework:

```
void AIO_Input_Handler::open
    (ACE_HANDLE new_handle, ACE_Message_Block &) {
  reader_.open (*this, new_handle, 0, proactor ());
  ACE_NEW_NORETURN
    (mblk_, ACE_Message_Block (ACE_DEFAULT_CDR_BUFSIZE));
  ACE_CDR::mb_align (mblk_);
  reader_.read (*mblk_, LOG_HEADER_SIZE);
}
```

This method allocates an `ACE_Message_Block` to receive the log record header from the client. Rather than simply allocating just enough for the header, the message will be large enough for the entire record in many cases. Moreover, it can be resized when needed. The block's write pointer is aligned correctly for CDR demarshaling, and then passed to an asynchronous `read()` operation that's initiated to receive the header.

When the `read()` operation completes, the following completion handler method is invoked by the ACE Proactor framework:

```
 1 void AIO_Input_Handler::handle_read_stream
 2     (const ACE_Asynch_Read_Stream::Result &result) {
 3   if (!result.success () || result.bytes_transferred () == 0)
 4     delete this;
 5   else if (result.bytes_transferred() < result.bytes_to_read())
 6     reader_.read (*mblk_, result.bytes_to_read () -
 7                           result.bytes_transferred ());
 8   else if (mblk_->length () == LOG_HEADER_SIZE) {
 9     ACE_InputCDR cdr (mblk_);
10
11     ACE_CDR::Boolean byte_order;
12     cdr >> ACE_InputCDR::to_boolean (byte_order);
13     cdr.reset_byte_order (byte_order);
14
15     ACE_CDR::ULong length;
16     cdr >> length;
17
18     mblk_->size (length + LOG_HEADER_SIZE);
19     reader_.read (*mblk_, length);
20   }
21   else {
22     if (OUTPUT_HANDLER::instance ()->put (mblk_) == -1)
23       mblk_->release ();
24
25     ACE_NEW_NORETURN
26       (mblk_, ACE_Message_Block (ACE_DEFAULT_CDR_BUFSIZE));
27     ACE_CDR::mb_align (mblk_);
28     reader_.read (*mblk_, LOG_HEADER_SIZE);
29   }
30 }
```

Lines 3–4   Delete `this` object if `read()` failed or if the peer logging client closed the connection. `AIO_Input_Handler`'s destructor releases resources to prevent leaks.

Lines 5–7   If fewer bytes were received than requested, initiate another asynchronous `read()` operation to receive the remaining bytes. We needn't adjust any pointers when requesting that more data be added to the message block. Sidebar 55 describes how the ACE Proactor framework manages `ACE_Message_Block` pointers automatically.

Lines 8–19   If all requested data was received, and it's the size of a log record header, we received the header, not payload. This test is safe since the data portion of a log record is always larger than the header. We then use the `ACE_InputCDR` class to demarshal the header, yielding the number of payload bytes in the record. `mblk_` is resized to accomodate the remaining data and an asynchronous `read()` is initiated to receive the payload. This method will be called again upon completion and, if necessary, will continue initiating asynchronous `read()` operations until the complete record is received or an error occurs.

Lines 22–23   When the complete log record is received, it's forwarded via the `AIO_Output_Handler::put()` method (page 270). After forwarding the log record, `AIO_Output_Handler` will release the message block. If the record can't be forwarded, however, the message is released immediately, discarding the log record.

Lines 25–28   Allocate a new `ACE_Message_Block` object for the next log record and initiate an asynchronous `read()` operation to receive its header.

Sidebar 55: How ACE_Message_Block Pointers are Managed

When initiating an asynchronous `read()` or `write()` operation, the request must specify an `ACE_Message_Block` to either receive or supply the data. The ACE Proactor framework's completion handling mechanism updates the `ACE_Message_Block` pointers to reflect the amount of data read or written as follows:

Operation	Pointer Usage
Read	The initial read buffer pointer is the message's `wr_ptr()`. At completion, the `wr_ptr` is advanced by the number of bytes read.
Write	The initial write buffer pointer is the message's `rd_ptr()`. At completion, the `rd_ptr` is advanced by the number of bytes written.

It may seem counterintuitive to use the write pointer for reads and the read pointer for writes. It may therefore help to consider that when reading data, it's being *written* into the message block. Similarly, when writing data, it's being *read* from the message block. Upon completion, the updated length of data in the `ACE_Message_Block` is larger for reads (because the write pointer has advanced) and smaller for writes (because the read pointer has advanced).

The AIO_Output_Handler::start_write() method (page 269) initiates an asynchronous write() operation to send a log record to the server logging daemon. When a write() completes, the following method is called by the ACE Proactor framework.

```
 1 void AIO_Output_Handler::handle_write_stream
 2         (const ACE_Asynch_Write_Stream::Result &result) {
 3   ACE_Message_Block &mblk = result.message_block ();
 4   if (!result.success ()) {
 5     mblk.rd_ptr (mblk.base ());
 6     ungetq (&mblk);
 7   }
 8   else {
 9     can_write_ = handle () == result.handle ();
10     if (mblk.length () == 0) {
11       mblk.release ();
12       if (can_write_) start_write ();
13     }
14     else if (can_write_) start_write (&mblk);
15     else { mblk.rd_ptr (mblk.base ()); ungetq (&mblk); }
16   }
17 }
```

Lines 4–7 If the write() operation failed, reset the message block's rd_ptr() to the beginning of the block. We assume that if a write() fails, the socket is closed and will be reconnected later, at which point the message block will be resent from the beginning.

Line 9 Re-enable can_write_ only if the socket hasn't been closed. If the socket closes while asynchronous write() operations are queued or in progress, there is no guarantee that the OS will deliver the completions in a given order. Thus, we check the handle, which is set to ACE_INVALID_HANDLE when the socket close is handled.

Lines 10–13 If the entire block has been written, release it. If another write() is possible, initiate it.

Line 14 The write() succeeded, but only part of the message was sent. If the socket is still connected, initiate an asynchronous write() to send the rest of the message.

Line 15 The message block was partially written, but the socket has been disconnected, so rewind the message's rd_ptr() to the beginning of the block and put it back on the message queue to be resent later.

If a write() operation fails, we don't try to clean up the socket since it has an outstanding read() operation to detect this problem. When the server logging daemon closes the socket, the asynchronous read() operation started in AIO_Output_Handler::open() (page 268) completes. Upon completion, the following method is called by the ACE Proactor framework:

```
 1 void AIO_Output_Handler::handle_read_stream
 2         (const ACE_Asynch_Read_Stream::Result &result) {
 3   result.message_block ().release ();
```

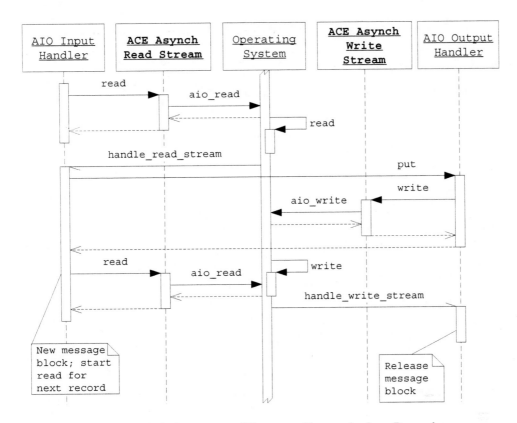

Figure 8.6: Sequence of Events to Forward a Log Record

```
4    writer_.cancel ();
5    ACE_OS::closesocket (result.handle ());
6    handle (ACE_INVALID_HANDLE);
7    can_write_ = 0;
8    CLD_CONNECTOR::instance ()->reconnect ();
9  }
```

Lines 3–5   Release the ACE_Message_Block that was allocated for the read() operation, cancel any outstanding write() operations, and close the socket.

Lines 6–8   Since the connection is now closed, set the handle to ACE_INVALID_HANDLE and reset the can_write_ flag to prevent any log record transmissions from being initiated until after we reestablish the server connection (the reconnection mechanism is explained on page 293). Section 8.4 discusses how to passively and actively establish connections in the ACE Proactor framework.

Figure 8.6 shows the sequence of events that occur when receiving a log record from a logging client and forwarding it to the server logging daemon.

8.4   The Proactive Acceptor-Connector Classes

Motivation

TCP/IP connection establishment is a two-step process:

1. The application either binds a listening socket to a port and listens, or learns of a listening application and initiates an active connection request.
2. The connect operation completes after OS-mediated TCP protocol exchanges open the new connection.

This two-step process is often performed using either a reactive or synchronous I/O model, as shown in Chapter 3 of C++NPv1 and in Chapter 7 of this book. However, the initiate/complete protocol of TCP connection establishment lends itself well to the proactive model. Networked applications that benefit from asynchronous I/O can therefore also benefit from asynchronous connection establishment capabilities.

OS support for asynchronous connection establishment varies. For example, Windows supports asynchronous connection establishment, whereas POSIX.4 AIO does not. It's possible, however, to emulate asynchronous connection establishment where it doesn't exist by using other OS mechanisms, such as multithreading (Sidebar 57 on page 283 discusses the ACE Proactor framework's emulation for POSIX). Since redesigning and rewriting code to encapsulate or emulate asynchronous connection establishment for each project or platform is tedious and error prone, the ACE Proactor framework provides the ACE_Asynch_Acceptor, ACE_Asynch_Connector, and ACE_Service_Handler classes.

Class Capabilities

ACE_Asynch_Acceptor is another implementation of the acceptor role in the Acceptor-Connector pattern [POSA2]. This class provides the following capabilities:

- It initiates asynchronous passive connection establishment.
- It acts as a factory, creating a new service handler for each accepted connection.
- It can cancel a previously initiated asynchronous accept() operation.
- It provides a hook method to obtain the peer's address when the new connection is established.
- It provides a hook method to validate the peer before initializing the new service handler.

ACE_Asynch_Connector plays the connector role in the ACE Proactor framework's implementation of the Acceptor-Connector pattern. This class provides the following capabilities:

- It initiates asynchronous active connection establishment.
- It acts as a factory, creating a new service handler for each completed connection.

- It can cancel a previously initiated asynchronous `connect()` operation.
- It provides a hook method to obtain the peer's address when the new connection is established.
- It provides a hook method to validate the peer before initializing the new service handler.

Unlike the ACE Acceptor-Connector framework described in Chapter 7, these two classes only establish TCP/IP connections. As discussed in Section 8.2, the ACE Proactor framework focuses on encapsulating operations, not I/O handles, and these classes encapsulate operations to establish TCP/IP connections. Connectionless IPC mechanisms (for example, UDP and file I/O) don't require a connection setup, so they can be used directly with the ACE Proactor framework's I/O factory classes.

Similar to `ACE_Acceptor` and `ACE_Connector`, `ACE_Asynch_Acceptor` and `ACE_Asynch_Connector` are template class factories that can create a service handler to execute a service on the new connection. The template parameter for both `ACE_Asynch_Acceptor` and `ACE_Asynch_Connector` is the service class the factory generates, known as `ACE_Service_Handler`. This class acts as the target of connection completions from `ACE_Asynch_Acceptor` and `ACE_Asynch_Connector`.

`ACE_Service_Handler` provides the following capabilities:

- It provides the basis for initializing and implementing a networked application service, acting as the target of the `ACE_Asynch_Connector` and `ACE_Asynch_Acceptor` connection factories.
- It receives the connected peer's address, which is important on Windows since this address isn't available after an asynchronous connection completes.
- It inherits the ability to handle asynchronous completion events since it derives from `ACE_Handler`.

Sidebar 56 (page 280) discusses the rationale behind the decision to not reuse `ACE_Svc_Handler` for the ACE Proactor framework.

The interfaces for all three of the classes in the Proactive Acceptor-Connector mechanism are shown in Figure 8.7 (page 281). The following table outlines the key methods in the `ACE_Asynch_Acceptor` class:

Method	Description
`open()`	Initialize and issue one or more asynchronous `accept()` operations.
`cancel()`	Cancels all asynchronous `accept()` operations initiated by the acceptor.
`validate_connection()`	Hook method to validate the peer address before opening a service for the new connection.
`make_handler()`	Hook method to obtain a service handler object for the new connection.

Sidebar 56: ACE_Service—uscoreHandler versus ACE_Svc_Handler

The `ACE_Service_Handler` class plays a role analogous to that of the ACE Acceptor-Connector framework's `ACE_Svc_Handler` class covered in Section 7.2. Although the ACE Proactor framework could have reused `ACE_Svc_Handler` as the target of `ACE_Asynch_Acceptor` and `ACE_Asynch_Connector`, a separate class was chosen for the following reasons:

- Networked applications that use proactive connection establishment also often use proactive I/O. The target of asynchronous connection completions should therefore be a class that can participate seamlessly with the rest of the ACE Proactor framework.
- `ACE_Svc_Handler` encapsulates an IPC object. The ACE Proactor framework uses I/O handles internally, so the additional IPC object could be confusing.
- `ACE_Svc_Handler` is designed for use with the ACE Reactor framework since it descends from `ACE_Event_Handler`. ACE maintains separation in its frameworks to avoid unnecessary coupling and faciliate ACE toolkit subsets.

For use cases in which an `ACE_Service_Handler` benefits by using the ACE Task framework, a common design is to add `ACE_Task` as a base class to the service class derived from `ACE_Service_Handler`. `ACE_Svc_Handler` can also be used since it's derived from `ACE_Task`, but use of `ACE_Task` is more common. In fact, this use case is illustrated in the `AIO_Output_Handler` class (page 266).

The `open()` method initializes the listening TCP socket and initiates one or more asynchronous `accept()` operations. If the argument for `reissue_accept` is 1 (the default), a new `accept()` operation will automatically be started as needed.

`ACE_Asynch_Acceptor` implements the `ACE_Handler::handle_accept()` method (Figure 8.5 on page 272) to process each `accept()` completion as follows

- Collect the `ACE_INET_Addr` representing each endpoint of the new connection.
- If the `validate_new_connection` parameter to `open()` was 1, invoke the `validate_connection()` method, passing the connected peer's address. If `validate_connection()` returns -1, the connection is aborted.
- Call the `make_handler()` hook method to obtain the service handler for the new connection. The default implementation uses `operator new` to allocate a new handler dynamically.
- Set the new handler's `ACE_Proactor` pointer.
- If the `pass_address` parameter to `open()` was 1, call the `ACE_Service_Handler::addresses()` method with both the local and peer addresses.
- Set the new connection's I/O handle and call the new service handler's `open()` method.

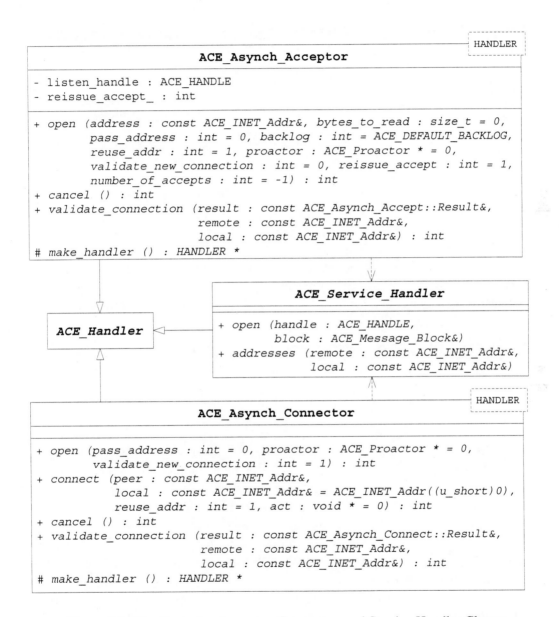

Figure 8.7: The Proactive Acceptor, Connector, and Service Handler Classes

The ACE_Asynch_Connector class provides methods that are similar to those in ACE_Asynch_Acceptor and are outlined in the following table:

Method	Description
open()	Initializes information for the active connection factory
connect()	Initiates an asynchronous connect() operation
cancel()	Cancels all asynchronous connect() operations
validate_connection()	Hook method to learn the connect disposition and validate the peer address before opening a service for the new connection
make_handler()	Hook method to obtain a service handler object for the new connection.

The open() method accepts fewer arguments than ACE_Asynch_Acceptor::open(). In particular, since addressing information can be different on each connect() operation, it's specified in parameters to the connect() method.

ACE_Asynch_Connector implements ACE_Handler::handle_connect() (Figure 8.5 on page 272) to process each connection completion. The processing steps are the same as for ACE_Asynch_Acceptor, above.

Each networked application service class in the ACE Proactor framework derives from ACE_Service_Handler. Its key methods are shown in the following table:

Method	Description
open()	Hook method called to initialize the service after establishing a new connection
addresses()	Hook method to capture the local and remote addresses for the service connection

As mentioned above, ACE_Asynch_Acceptor and ACE_Asynch_Connector both call the ACE_Service_Handler::open() hook method for each new connection established. The handle argument is the handle for the connected socket. The ACE_Message_Block argument may contain data from the peer if the bytes_to_read parameter to ACE_Asynch_Acceptor::open() was greater than 0. Since this Windows-specific facility is often used with non-IP protocols (e.g., X.25), we don't discuss its use here. The ACE Proactor framework manages the ACE_Message_Block, so the service need not be concerned with it.

If the service handler requires either the local or peer addresses on the new connection, it must implement the addresses() hook method to capture them when the connection is established. The ACE Proactor framework calls this method if the pass_address argument to the asynchronous connection factory was 1. This method is more significant on Windows because the connection addresses cannot be obtained any other way when asynchronous connection establishment is used.

Sidebar 57: Emulating Asynchronous Connections on POSIX

Windows has native capability for asynchronously connecting sockets. In contrast, the POSIX.4 AIO facility was designed primarily for use with disk I/O, so it doesn't include any capability for asynchronous TCP/IP connection establishment. To provide uniform capability across all asynchronous I/O-enabled platforms, ACE emulates asynchronous connection establishment where needed.

To emulate asynchronous connection establishment, active and passive connection requests are begun in nonblocking mode by the ACE_Asynch_Acceptor and ACE_Asynch_Connector. If the connection doesn't complete immediately (which is always the case for passive connections), the socket handle is registered with an instance of ACE_Select_Reactor managed privately by the framework. An ACE Proactor framework-spawned thread (unseen by the application) runs the private reactor's event loop. When the connection request completes, the framework regains control via a reactor callback and posts the completion event. The original application thread receives the completion event back in the ACE_Asynch_Acceptor or ACE_Asynch_Connector class, as appropriate.

Example

As with the client logging daemons in Chapters 6 and 7, the classes in the proactive implementation are separated into separate input and output roles that are explained below.

Input role. The input role of the proactive client logging daemon is performed by the AIO_CLD_Acceptor and AIO_Input_Handler classes. AIO_Input_Handler was described on page 273, so here we focus on AIO_CLD_Acceptor, which derives from ACE_Asynch_Acceptor as shown in Figure 8.3 (page 267). The class definition for AIO_CLD_Acceptor is shown below:

```
class AIO_CLD_Acceptor
    : public ACE_Asynch_Acceptor<AIO_Input_Handler> {
public:
  // Cancel accept and close all clients.
  void close (void);

  // Remove handler from client set.
  void remove (AIO_Input_Handler *ih)
  { clients_.remove (ih); }

protected:
  // Service handler factory method.
  virtual AIO_Input_Handler *make_handler (void);

  // Set of all connected clients.
  ACE_Unbounded_Set<AIO_Input_Handler *> clients_;
};
```

Since the ACE Proactor framework only keeps track of active I/O operations, it doesn't maintain a set of registered handlers like the ACE Reactor framework does. Applications must therefore locate and clean up handlers when necessary. In this chapter's example, the `AIO_Input_Handler` objects are allocated dynamically, and they must be readily accessible when the service shuts down. To satisfy this requirement, the `AIO_CLD_Acceptor::clients_` member is an `ACE_Unbounded_Set` that holds pointers to all active `AIO_Input_Handler` objects. When a logging client connects to this server, `ACE_Asynch_Acceptor::handle_accept()` calls the following factory method:

```
AIO_Input_Handler * AIO_CLD_Acceptor::make_handler (void) {
  AIO_Input_Handler *ih;
  ACE_NEW_RETURN (ih, AIO_Input_Handler (this), 0);
  if (clients_.insert (ih) == -1) { delete ih; return 0; }
  return ih;
}
```

`AIO_CLD_Acceptor` reimplements the `make_handler()` factory method that keeps track of each allocated service handler's pointer in `clients_`. If the new handler's pointer can't be inserted for some reason, it's deleted; returning 0 will force the ACE Proactor framework to close the newly accepted connection.

The `make_handler()` hook method passes its object pointer to each dynamically allocated `AIO_Input_Handler` (page 273). When `AIO_Input_Handler` detects a failed `read()` (most likely because the logging client closed the connection), its `handle_read_stream()` method (page 274) simply deletes itself. The `AIO_Input_Handler` destructor cleans up all held resources, and calls the `AIO_CLD_Acceptor::remove()` method (page 283) to remove itself from the `clients_` set, as shown below:

```
AIO_Input_Handler::~AIO_Input_Handler () {
  reader_.cancel ();
  ACE_OS::closesocket (handle ());
  if (mblk_ != 0) mblk_->release ();
  mblk_ = 0;
  acceptor_->remove (this);
}
```

When this service shuts down in the `AIO_Client_Logging_Daemon::svc()` method (page 295), all the remaining `AIO_Input_Handler` connections and objects are cleaned up by calling the `close()` method below:

```
void AIO_CLD_Acceptor::close (void) {
  ACE_Unbounded_Set_Iterator<AIO_Input_Handler *>
    iter (clients_.begin ());
  AIO_Input_Handler **ih;
  while (iter.next (ih)) delete *ih;
}
```

This method simply iterates through all of the active `AIO_Input_Handler` objects, deleting each one.

Output role.   The output role of the proactive client logging daemon is performed by the AIO_CLD_Connector and AIO_Output_Handler classes. The client logging daemon uses the AIO_CLD_Connector to

- Establish (and, when necessary, reestablish) a TCP connection to a server logging daemon
- Implement the connector half of the SSL authentication with the server logging daemon (the server logging daemon's SSL authentication is shown on page 224)

It then uses the AIO_Output_Handler to asynchronously forward log records from connected logging clients to the server logging daemon.

Part of the AIO_CLD_Connector class definition is below:

```
class AIO_CLD_Connector
  : public ACE_Asynch_Connector<AIO_Output_Handler> {
public:
  enum { INITIAL_RETRY_DELAY = 3, MAX_RETRY_DELAY = 60 };

  // Constructor.
  AIO_CLD_Connector ()
    : retry_delay_ (INITIAL_RETRY_DELAY), ssl_ctx_ (0), ssl_ (0)
  { open (); }

  // Hook method to detect failure and validate peer before
  // opening handler.
  virtual int validate_connection
    (const ACE_Asynch_Connect::Result &result,
     const ACE_INET_Addr &remote, const ACE_INET_Addr &local);

protected:
  // Template method to create a new handler
  virtual AIO_Output_Handler *make_handler (void)
  { return OUTPUT_HANDLER::instance (); }

  // Address at which logging server listens for connections.
  ACE_INET_Addr remote_addr_;

  // Seconds to wait before trying the next connect
  int retry_delay_;

  // The SSL "context" data structure.
  SSL_CTX *ssl_ctx_;

  // The SSL data structure corresponding to authenticated
  // SSL connections.
  SSL *ssl_;
};

typedef ACE_Unmanaged_Singleton<AIO_CLD_Connector, ACE_Null_Mutex>
        CLD_CONNECTOR;
```

The `AIO_CLD_Connector` class is accessed as an unmanaged singleton (see Sidebar 45 on page 194) via the `CLD_CONNECTOR typedef`. When `AIO_CLD_Connector` is instantiated, its constructor calls the `ACE_Asynch_Connector::open()` method. By default, the `validate_connection()` method (page 293) will be called on completion of each `connect()` attempt.

8.5   The ACE_Proactor Class

Motivation

Asynchronous I/O operations are handled in two steps: *initiation* and *completion*. Since multiple steps and classes are involved, there must be a way to demultiplex the completion events and efficiently associate each completion event with the operation that completed and the completion handler that will process the result. The diversity of OS asynchronous I/O facilities plays a deeper role here than in the reactive I/O model because

- Platforms have different ways to receive completion notifications. For example, Windows uses I/O completion ports or events, whereas POSIX.4 AIO uses real-time signals or the `aio_suspend()` system function to wait for a completion.
- Platforms use different data structures to maintain state information for asynchronous I/O operations. For example, Windows uses the `OVERLAPPED` structure, whereas POSIX.4 AIO uses `struct aiocb`.

Thus, the chain of knowledge concerning platform-specific mechanisms and data structures runs from initiation operations through dispatching and into completion handling. In addition to being complicated and hard to reimplement continually, it's easy to tightly couple proactive I/O designs. To resolve these issues and provide a portable and flexible completion event demultiplexing and dispatching facility, the ACE Proactor framework defines the `ACE_Proactor` class.

Class Capabilities

`ACE_Proactor` implements the Facade pattern [GoF] to define an interface that applications can use to access the various ACE Proactor framework features portably and flexibly. This class provides the following capabilities:

- It centralizes event loop processing in a proactive application.
- It dispatches timer expirations to their associated `ACE_Handler` objects.
- It demultiplexes completion events to completion handlers and dispatches the appropriate hook methods on completion handlers that then perform application-defined processing in response to the completion events.

- It can decouple the thread(s) performing completion event detection, demultiplexing, and dispatching from thread(s) initiating asynchronous operations.
- It mediates between classes that initiate I/O operations and platform-specific asynchronous I/O implementation details.

The interface for ACE_Proactor is shown in Figure 8.8 (page 288). This class has a rich interface that exports all the features in the ACE Proactor framework. We therefore group its method descriptions into the four categories described below.

1. Life cycle management methods.   The following methods initialize, destroy, and access an ACE_Proactor:

Method	Description
ACE_Proactor() open()	These methods initialize proactor instance.
~ACE_Proactor() close()	These methods clean up the resources allocated when a proactor was initialized.
instance()	A static method that returns a pointer to a singleton ACE_Proactor, which is created and managed by the Singleton pattern [GoF] combined with the Double-Checked Locking Optimization [POSA2].

The ACE_Proactor can be used in two ways:

- **As a singleton** [GoF] via the instance() method shown in the table above.
- **By instantiating one or more instances.** This capability can be used to support multiple proactors within a process. Each proactor is often associated with a thread running at a particular priority [Sch98].

2. Event loop management methods.   Inversion of control is supported by the ACE Proactor framework. Similar to the ACE Reactor framework, ACE_Proactor implements the following event loop methods that control application completion handler dispatching:

Method	Description
handle_events()	Waits for completion events to occur and then dispatches the associated completion handler(s). A timeout parameter can limit the time spent waiting for an event.
proactor_run_event_loop()	Calls the handle_events() method repeatedly until it fails, proactor_event_loop_done() returns true, or an optional timeout occurs.
proactor_end_event_loop()	Instructs a proactor to shut down its event loop.
proactor_event_loop_done()	Returns 1 when the proactor's event loop has been ended, for example, via a call to proactor_end_event_loop().

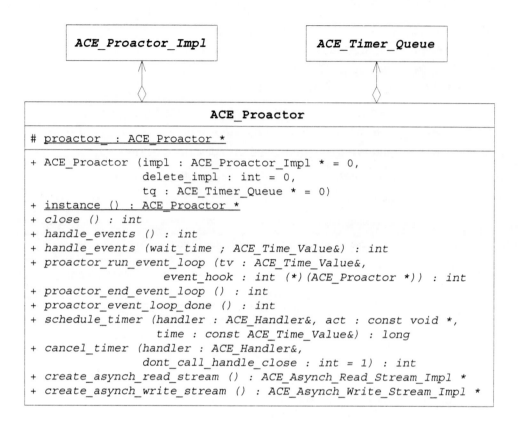

Figure 8.8: The ACE_Proactor Class

The ACE Proactor event loop is separate from that provided by the ACE Reactor framework. To use both ACE Reactor and ACE Proactor event loops in the same application and remain portable across all asynchronous I/O platforms, the two event loops must be executed in separate threads. However, the Windows implementation of ACE_Proactor can register its I/O completion port handle with an ACE_WFMO_Reactor instance to tie the two event loop mechanisms together, allowing them to both be used in one thread. Sidebar 58 (page 290) describes how to do this.

3. Timer management methods. By default, ACE_Proactor uses the ACE_Timer_ Heap timer queue mechanism described in Section 3.4 to schedule and dispatch event handlers in accordance to their timeout deadlines. The timer management methods exposed by the ACE_Proactor include:

Method	Description
schedule_timer()	Registers an ACE_Handler that will be dispatched after a user-specified amount of time
cancel_timer()	Cancels one or more timers that were previously registered

When a timer expires, `ACE_Handler::handle_time_out()` (page 271) is dispatched on the registered handler.

4. I/O operation facilitator methods. The `ACE_Proactor` class has visibility into the platform's asynchronous I/O implementation details that are useful for operation initiation and completion event processing. Making `ACE_Proactor` the central mediator of platform-specific knowledge prevents coupling between the classes in the ACE Proactor framework. In particular, the ACE Proactor framework uses the Bridge pattern [GoF].

`ACE_Asynch_Read_Stream` and `ACE_Asynch_Write_Stream` use the Bridge pattern to access flexible implementations of their I/O operation factories that are specific to the OS platform. Since `ACE_Proactor` is the mediator of this platform-specific knowledge, it defines the following methods used by the `ACE_Asynch_Read_Stream` and `ACE_Asynch_Write_Stream` classes:

Method	Description
`create_asynch_read_stream()`	Create an instance of a platform-specific subclass of `ACE_Asynch_Read_Stream_Impl` appropriate for initiating asynchronous `read()` operations.
`create_asynch_write_stream()`	Create an instance of a platform-specific subclass of `ACE_Asynch_Write_Stream_Impl` appropriate for initiating asynchronous `write()` operations.

As seen in Figure 8.8, the `ACE_Proactor` class refers to an object of type `ACE_Proactor_Impl`, similar to the design of ACE Reactor framework shown in Figure 4.1 (page 89). All work dependent on platform-specific mechanisms is forwarded to the Proactor implementation class for handling. We briefly describe the platform-specific ACE Proactor framework implementations below.

The ACE_WIN32_Proactor Class

`ACE_WIN32_Proactor` is the `ACE_Proactor` implementation on Windows. This class works on Windows NT 4.0 and newer Windows platforms, such as Windows 2000 and Windows XP. It doesn't work on Windows 95, 98, Me, or CE, however, since these platforms don't support asynchronous I/O.

Implementation overview. `ACE_WIN32_Proactor` uses an I/O completion port for completion event detection. When initializing an asynchronous operation factory, such as `ACE_Asynch_Read_Stream` or `ACE_Asynch_Write_Stream`, the I/O handle is associated with the Proactor's I/O completion port. In this implementation, the Windows `GetQueuedCompletionStatus()` function paces the event loop.

Sidebar 58: Integrating Proactor and Reactor Events on Windows

The ACE Reactor and ACE Proactor event loops require different event detection and demultiplexing mechanisms. As a result, they are often executed in separate threads. On Windows, however, ACE provides a way to integrate the two event loop mechanisms so they can both be driven by a single thread. The advantage of using a single event-loop thread is that it can simplify application-defined event handlers and completion handlers, since they may no longer require synchronizers to prevent race conditions.

The `ACE_Proactor` Windows implementation uses an I/O completion port to detect completion events. When one or more asynchronous operations complete, Windows signals the corresponding I/O completion port handle. This handle can therefore be registered with an instance of `ACE_WFMO_Reactor` (Chapter 4). Using this scheme, the `ACE_WFMO_Reactor` dispatches the I/O completion port's "signaled" event to the `ACE_Proactor`, which in turn dispatches completion events and returns to the reactor's event loop.

To use the scheme outlined above, an application must instantiate an `ACE_Proactor` with a particular set of nondefault options. The following code fragment shows how to accomplish this, and should be executed immediately at program startup:

```
1 ACE_Proactor::close_singleton ();
2 ACE_WIN32_Proactor *impl = new ACE_WIN32_Proactor (0, 1);
3 ACE_Proactor::instance (new ACE_Proactor (impl, 1), 1);
4 ACE_Reactor::instance ()->register_handler
5   (impl, impl->get_handle ());
// ... Other registration and initiation code omitted.
6 ACE_Reactor::instance ()->run_reactor_event_loop ();
7 ACE_Reactor::instance ()->remove_handler
8   (impl->get_handle (), ACE_Event_Handler::DONT_CALL);
```

Line 1 Close the existing proactor singleton.

Line 2 Creates a Windows-specific proactor implementation. The second argument specifies that this proactor will be used with a reactor.

Line 3 Create a new `ACE_Proactor` for the reactor-enabled implementation and make it the singleton. The second argument to `ACE_Proactor` says to delete the implementation when the `ACE_Proactor` is closed. The second argument to `instance()` says to delete the `ACE_Proactor` object when it's closed.

Lines 4–6 Register the I/O completion port handle with the reactor and run the reactor event loop.

Lines 7–8 After the event loop ends, remove the proactor's I/O completion port from the reactor.

All the `Result` classes defined for use with the `ACE_WIN32_Proactor` are derived from the Windows `OVERLAPPED` structure. Additional information is added to each depending on the operation being performed. When `GetQueuedCompletionStatus()` returns a pointer to the completed operation's `OVERLAPPED` structure, the `ACE_WIN32_Proactor` converts it to a pointer to a `Result` object. This design allows completions to be dispatched efficiently to the correct `ACE_Handler`-derived completion handler when I/O operations complete. The *Implementation* section of the Proactor pattern in POSA2 illustrates how to implement a proactor using the Windows asynchrony mechanisms and the Asynchronous Completion Token pattern.

Concurrency considerations.   Multiple threads can execute the event loop of an `ACE_WIN32_Proactor` simultaneously. Since all event registration and dispatching is handled by the I/O completion port mechanism, and not by the `ACE_WIN32_Proactor` itself, there's no need to synchronize access to registration-related data structures, as in the `ACE_WFMO_Reactor` implementation (page 106).

The timer queue expiry management is handled in a separate thread that's managed by the `ACE_WIN32_Proactor`. When a timer expires, the timeout mechanism uses the `PostQueuedCompletionStatus()` function to post a completion to the proactor's I/O completion port. This design cleanly integrates the timer mechanism with the normal completion dispatching mechanism. It also ensures that only one thread is awakened to dispatch the timer since all completion-detection threads wait only for completion events and needn't worry about waking up for a scheduled timer expiration.

The ACE_POSIX_Proactor Class

The ACE Proactor implementations on POSIX systems present multiple mechanisms for initiating I/O operations and detecting their completions. Moreover, Sun's Solaris Operating Environment offers its own proprietary version of asynchronous I/O. On Solaris 2.6 and above, the performance of the Sun-specific asynchronous I/O functions is significantly higher than that of Solaris's POSIX.4 AIO implementation. To take advantage of this performance improvement, ACE also encapsulates this mechanism in a separate set of classes.

Implementation overview.   The POSIX implementations of asynchronous I/O use a control block (`struct aiocb`) to identify each asynchronous I/O request and its controlling information. Each `aiocb` can be associated with only one I/O request at a time. The Sun-specific asynchronous I/O uses an additional structure named `aio_result_t`.

Although the encapsulated POSIX asynchronous I/O mechanisms support `read()` and `write()` operations, they don't support any TCP/IP connection-related operations. To support the functions of `ACE_Asynch_Acceptor`, and `ACE_Asynch_Connector`, a separate thread is used to perform connection-related operations. This asynchronous connection emulation is described in Sidebar 57 (page 283).

The three variants of the `ACE_POSIX_Proactor` implementation are described in the following table:

ACE Proactor Variant	Description
`ACE_POSIX_AIOCB_Proactor`	This implementation maintains a parallel list of `aiocb` structures and `Result` objects. Each outstanding operation is represented by an entry in each list. The `aio_suspend()` function suspends the event loop until one or more asynchronous I/O operations complete.
`ACE_POSIX_SIG_Proactor`	This implementation is derived from `ACE_POSIX_AIOCB_Proactor`, but uses POSIX real-time signals to detect asynchronous I/O completion. The event loop uses the `sigtimedwait()` and `sigwaitinfo()` functions to pace the loop and retrieve information about completed operations. Each asynchyronous I/O operation started using this proactor has a unique value associated with its `aiocb` that's communicated with the signal noting its completion. This design makes it easy to locate the `aiocb` and its parallel `Result` object, and dispatch the correct completion handler.
`ACE_SUN_Proactor`	This implementation is also based on `ACE_POSIX_AIOCB_Proactor`, but it uses the Sun-specific asynchronous I/O facility instead of the POSIX.4 AIO facility. This implementation works much like `ACE_POSIX_AIOCB_Proactor`, but uses the Sun-specific `aiowait()` function to detect I/O completions.

Concurrency considerations. The `ACE_POSIX_SIG_Proactor` is the default proactor implementation on POSIX.4 AIO-enabled platforms. Its completion event demultiplexing mechanism uses the `sigtimedwait()` function. Each `ACE_POSIX_SIG_Proactor` instance can specify the set of signals to use with `sigtimedwait()`. To use multiple threads at different priorities with different `ACE_POSIX_SIG_Proactor` instances, therefore, each instance should use a different signal, or set of signals.

Limitations and characteristics of some platforms directly affect which `ACE_POSIX_Proactor` implementation can be used. On Linux, for instance, threads are actually cloned processes. Since signals can't be sent across processes, and asynchronous I/O operations and Proactor timer expirations are both implemented using threads, the `ACE_POSIX_SIG_Proactor` doesn't work well on Linux. Thus, `ACE_POSIX_AIOCB_Proactor` is the default proactor implementation on Linux. The `aio_suspend()` demultiplexing mechanism used in `ACE_POSIX_AIOCB_Proactor` is thread safe, so multiple threads can run its event loop simultaneously.

Example

The `AIO_CLD_Connector` reconnection mechanism was mentioned in the discussion of the `AIO_Output_Handler::handle_read_stream()` method (page 276). The reconnection mechanism is initiated using the `AIO_CLD_Connector::reconnect()` method below:

```
int reconnect (void) { return connect (remote_addr_); }
```

This method simply initiates a new asynchronous connection request to the server logging daemon. An exponential backoff strategy is used to avoid continually initiating connection attempts when, for example, there's no server logging daemon listening. We use the following `validate_connection()` hook method to insert application-defined behavior into `ACE_Asynch_Connector`'s connection completion handling. This method learns the disposition of each asynchronous connection request and schedules a timer to retry the connect if it failed. If the connect succeeded, this method executes the SSL authentication with the server logging daemon.

```
 1  int AIO_CLD_Connector::validate_connection
 2          (const ACE_Asynch_Connect::Result &result,
 3           const ACE_INET_Addr &remote, const ACE_INET_Addr &) {
 4    remote_addr_ = remote;
 5    if (!result.success ()) {
 6      ACE_Time_Value delay (retry_delay_);
 7      retry_delay_ *= 2;
 8      if (retry_delay_ > MAX_RETRY_DELAY)
 9        retry_delay_ = MAX_RETRY_DELAY;
10      proactor ()->schedule_timer (*this, 0, delay);
11      return -1;
12    }
13    retry_delay_ = INITIAL_RETRY_DELAY;
14
15    if (ssl_ctx_ == 0) {
16      OpenSSL_add_ssl_algorithms ();
17      ssl_ctx_ = SSL_CTX_new (SSLv3_client_method ());
18      if (ssl_ctx_ == 0) return -1;
19
20      if (SSL_CTX_use_certificate_file (ssl_ctx_,
21                                        CLD_CERTIFICATE_FILENAME,
22                                        SSL_FILETYPE_PEM) <= 0
23          || SSL_CTX_use_PrivateKey_file (ssl_ctx_,
24                                          CLD_KEY_FILENAME,
25                                          SSL_FILETYPE_PEM) <= 0
26          || !SSL_CTX_check_private_key (ssl_ctx_)) {
27        SSL_CTX_free (ssl_ctx_);
28        ssl_ctx_ = 0;
29        return -1;
30      }
31      ssl_ = SSL_new (ssl_ctx_);
```

```
32      if (ssl_ == 0) {
33         SSL_CTX_free (ssl_ctx_); ssl_ctx_ = 0;
34         return -1;
35      }
36    }
37
38    SSL_clear (ssl_);
39    SSL_set_fd
40      (ssl_, ACE_reinterpret_cast (int, result.connect_handle()));
41
42    SSL_set_verify (ssl_, SSL_VERIFY_PEER, 0);
43
44    if (SSL_connect (ssl_) == -1
45        || SSL_shutdown (ssl_) == -1) return -1;
46    return 0;
47 }
```

Line 4   Save the peer address we tried to connect to so it can be reused for future connection attempts, if needed.

Lines 5–12   If the connect operation failed, set a timer to retry the connection later, then double the retry timer, up to the number of seconds specified by MAX_RETRY_DELAY.

Line 13   If the connection succeeded, we reset the retry_delay_ back to its initial value for the next reconnection sequence.

Lines 15–46   The rest of validate_connection() is similar to TPC_Logging_Acceptor::open() (page 224), so we don't explain it here. If the SSL authentication fails, validate_connection() returns −1, causing ACE_Asynch_Connector to close the new connection before opening a service handler for it. Note that the SSL function calls on lines 43 and 44 are synchronous, and therefore the proactor event loop is not processing completion events while these calls are being made. As with the Reactor framework, developers must be aware of this type of delay in a callback method.

When a timer set by the handle_connection() method expires, the following handle_time_out() hook method is called by the ACE Proactor framework:

```
void AIO_CLD_Connector::handle_time_out (const ACE_Time_Value &,
                                         const void *)
{ connect (remote_addr_); }
```

This method simply initiates another asynchronous connect() attempt which will trigger another call to validate_connection(), regardless of whether it succeeds or fails.

The AIO client logging daemon service is represented by the following AIO_Client_Logging_Daemon class:

```
class AIO_Client_Logging_Daemon: public ACE_Task<ACE_NULL_SYNCH> {
protected:
  ACE_INET_Addr cld_addr_; // Our listener address.
```

```
ACE_INET_Addr sld_addr_; // The logging server's address.

// Factory that passively connects the <AIO_Input_Handler>.
AIO_CLD_Acceptor acceptor_;
public:
// Service Configurator hook methods.
virtual int init (int argc, ACE_TCHAR *argv[]);
virtual int fini ();
virtual int svc (void);
};
```

This class is similar to the AC_Client_Logging_Daemon class (page 251). The primary difference is that AIO_Client_Logging_Daemon spawns a new thread to run the proactor event loop that the service depends on, whereas AC_Client_Logging_Daemon relies on the main program thread to run the singleton reactor's event loop. To activate this thread easily, AIO_Client_Logging_Daemon derives from ACE_Task rather than ACE_Service_Config.

We start a new thread for the proactor event loop because we do still rely on the reactor event loop for service reconfiguration activity as described in Chapter 5. If our service was designed solely for Windows, we could integrate the proactor and reactor event loops, as described in Sidebar 58 (page 290). However, this client logging daemon implementation is portable to all AIO-enabled ACE platforms. After our AIO_Client_Logging_Daemon::init() method processes the argument list and forms addresses, it then calls ACE_Task::activate() to spawn a thread running the following svc() method:

```
1 int AIO_Client_Logging_Daemon::svc (void) {
2   if (acceptor_.open (cld_addr_) == -1) return -1;
3   if (CLD_CONNECTOR::instance ()->connect (sld_addr_) == 0)
4     ACE_Proactor::instance ()->proactor_run_event_loop ();
5   acceptor_.close ();
6   CLD_CONNECTOR::close ();
7   OUTPUT_HANDLER::close ();
8   return 0;
9 }
```

Lines 2–3   Initialize the acceptor_ object to begin listening for logging client connections and initiate the first connection attempt to the server logging daemon.

Line 4   Call ACE_Proactor::proactor_run_event_loop() to handle asynchronous operation completions. The proactor event loop is terminated when the service is shut down via the following fini() method:

```
int AIO_Client_Logging_Daemon::fini () {
  ACE_Proactor::instance ()->proactor_end_event_loop ();
  wait ();
  return 0;
}
```

This method calls `ACE_Proactor::proactor_end_event_loop()` which ends the event loop in the `svc()` method. It then calls `ACE_Task::wait()` to wait for the `svc()` method to complete and exit its thread.

Lines 5–7 Close all open connections and singleton objects and exit the `svc()` thread.

Lastly, we add the necessary ACE_FACTORY_DEFINE macro to generate the service's factory function:

```
ACE_FACTORY_DEFINE (AIO_CLD, AIO_Client_Logging_Daemon)
```

Our new proactive client logging daemon service uses the ACE Service Configurator framework to configure itself into any main program, such as the `Configurable_Logging_Server` (page 147) by including the following entry in a `svc.conf` file:

```
dynamic AIO_Client_Logging_Daemon Service_Object *
AIO_CLD:_make_AIO_Client_Logging_Daemon()
  "-p $CLIENT_LOGGING_DAEMON_PORT"
```

8.6 Summary

This chapter explored the concept of proactive I/O and outlined how the proactive model differs from the reactive model. It also showed how the proactive I/O model can be used to overcome the performance limitations of the reactive I/O model without incurring certain liabilities associated with the use of multithreaded synchronous I/O. However, the proactive I/O model presents several challenges:

- **Design challenges.** The multistep nature of this model increases the likelihood of overly coupling the I/O mechanisms that initiate asynchronous operations with the processing of the completions of operations.

- **Portability challenges.** There are highly divergent standards and implementations for asynchronous I/O offered by today's computing platforms.

The Proactor pattern [POSA2] defines a set of roles and relationships to help simplify applications that use proactive I/O. The ACE Proactor framework implements the Proactor pattern across a range of operating systems that support asynchronous I/O. The ACE Proactor framework provides a set of classes that simplify networked application use of asynchronous I/O capabilities across all platforms that offer it. This chapter discussed each class in the framework, covering their motivations and capabilities. It showed an implementation of the client logging daemon that uses the proactive I/O model for all of its network operations. This version of the client logging daemon works portably on all ACE platforms that offer asynchronous I/O mechanisms.

CHAPTER 9

The ACE Streams Framework

CHAPTER SYNOPSIS

This chapter describes the design and use of the ACE Streams framework. This framework implements the Pipes and Filters pattern [POSA1], which is an architectural pattern that provides a structure for systems that process streams of data. We illustrate how the ACE Streams framework can be used to develop a utility program that formats and prints files of log records stored by our logging servers.

9.1 Overview

The Pipes and Filters architectural pattern is a common way of organizing layered/modular applications [SG96]. This pattern defines an architecture for processing a stream of data in which each processing step is encapsulated in some type of filter component. Data is passed between adjacent filters via a communication mechanism, which can range from IPC channels connecting local or remote processes to simple pointers that reference objects within the same process. Each filter can add, modify, or remove data before passing it along to the next filter. Filters are often stateless, in which case data passing through the filter are transformed and passed along to the next filter without being stored.

Common examples of the Pipes and Filters pattern include

- The UNIX pipe IPC mechanism [Ste92] used by UNIX shells to create unidirectional pipelines
- System V STREAMS [Rit84], which provides a framework for integrating bidirectional protocols into the UNIX kernel

The ACE Streams framework is based on the Pipes and Filters pattern. This framework simplifies the development of layered/modular applications that can communicate via bidirectional processing modules. This chapter describes the following classes in the ACE Streams framework:

ACE Class	Description
ACE_Task	A cohesive unit of application-defined functionality that uses messages to communicate requests, responses, data, and control information and can queue and process messages sequentially or concurrently.
ACE_Module	A distinct bidirectional processing layer in an application that contains two ACE_Task objects—one for "reading" and one for "writing"
ACE_Stream	Contains an ordered list of interconnected ACE_Module objects that can be used to configure and execute layered application-defined services

The most important relationships between classes in the ACE Streams framework are shown in Figure 9.1. These classes play the following roles in accordance with the Pipes and Filters pattern [POSA1]:

- **Filter classes** are the processing units in a stream that enrich, refine, or transform input data. The filter classes in the ACE Streams framework are implemented by subclasses of ACE_Task.

- **Pipe classes** denote the interconnections between the filters. The pipe classes in the ACE Streams framework are provided by ACE_Module objects that contain interconnected ACE_Task objects linked together to create a complete bidirectional ACE_Stream. Application-defined methods in adjacent interconnected tasks collaborate by exchanging data and control message blocks.

The ACE Streams framework provides the following benefits:

- **Enhanced reuse and flexibility.** Any ACE_Task can be plugged into any ACE_Module and any ACE_Module can be plugged into any ACE_Stream. This flexibility enables multiple applications to systematically reuse existing modules and tasks, all of which can be configured dynamically.

- **Transparent, incremental evolution.** Application functionality can be implemented in a controlled manner by adding, removing, and changing modules and tasks. This ability to evolve an application's design and functionality is particularly useful in agile development processes, such as Extreme Programming (XP) [Bec00].

- **Macro-level performance tuning.** Applications can adapt to varying deployment scenarios and run-time environments by selectively omitting unnecessary service functionality or reconfiguring a mixture of ACE_Task and ACE_Module objects to provide contextually optimal service functionality.

- **Inherent modularity.** The structure enforced by the ACE Streams framework promotes well-accepted design practices of strong cohesion and minimal coupling. Modular designs help to reduce the complexity of each layer and improve the overall implementation of networked applications and services. Testing and documentation are also more easily accomplished when based on a highly modular design, making application maintenance and systematic reuse easier, as well.

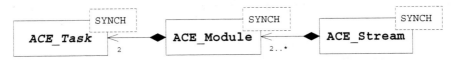

Figure 9.1: The ACE Streams Framework Classes

- **Easy to learn.** The ACE Streams framework contains an intuitive class structure based on the patterns and design of the System V STREAMS framework, as discussed in Sidebar 59. However, even developers who haven't been exposed to System V STREAMS can quickly grasp the structure of the Pipes and Filters pattern and then use that pattern as a basis for learning the rest of the ACE Streams framework classes.

The ACE_Task class was described in Chapter 6. This chapter therefore focuses largely on describing the capabilities provided by the ACE_Module and ACE_Stream classes. However, we illustrate how all the classes in the ACE Streams framework can be used to develop a utility program that formats and prints log records stored by our logging servers. If you aren't familiar with the Pipes and Filters pattern from POSA1, we recommend that you read about it first before delving into the detailed examples in this chapter.

Sidebar 59: ACE Streams Relationship to System V STREAMS

The class names and design of the ACE Streams framework correspond to similar componentry in System V STREAMS [Rit84, Rag93]. The techniques used to support extensibility and concurrency in these two frameworks differ significantly, however. For example, application-defined functionality is added in System V STREAMS via tables of pointers to C functions, whereas in the ACE Streams framework it's added by subclassing from ACE_Task, which provides greater type safety and extensibility. The ACE Streams framework also uses the ACE Task framework to enhance the coroutine-based concurrency mechanisms used in System V STREAMS. These ACE enhancements enable more effective use of multiple CPUs on shared memory multiprocessing platforms [SS95b] by reducing the likelihood of deadlock and simplifying flow control between ACE_Task active objects in an ACE_Stream.

9.2   The ACE_Module Class

Motivation

Many networked applications can be modeled as an ordered series of processing layers that are related hierarchically and that exchange messages between adjacent layers. For example, kernel-level [Rit84, Rag93] and user-level [SS95b, HJE95] protocol stacks, call center managers [SS94], and other families of networked applications can benefit from a message-passing design based on a layered/modular service architecture. As discussed in Section 2.1.4, each layer can handle a self-contained portion (such as input or output, event analysis, event filtering, or service processing) of a service or networked application.

The ACE_Task class provides a reuseable component that can easily be used to separate processing into stages and pass data between them. Since ACE_Task objects are independent, however, additional structure is required to order ACE_Task objects into bidirectional "reader-writer" pairs that can be assembled and managed as a unit. Redeveloping this structure in multiple projects is tedious and unnecessary because the structure is fundamentally application independent. To avoid this redundant development effort, therefore, the ACE Streams framework defines the ACE_Module class.

Class Capabilities

ACE_Module defines a distinct layer of application-defined functionality. This class provides the following capabilities:

- Each ACE_Module is a bidirectional application-defined processing layer containing a pair of reader and writer tasks that derive from ACE_Task. Layered designs can be expressed easily using ACE_Module, which simplifies development, training, and evolution.
- The ACE Service Configurator framework supports dynamic construction of ACE_Module objects that can be configured into an ACE_Stream at run time. Layered designs based on ACE_Module are therefore highly extensible.
- The reader and writer ACE_Task objects contained in an ACE_Module collaborate with adjacent ACE_Task objects by passing messages via a public hook method, which promotes loose coupling and simplifies reconfiguration.
- The objects composed into an ACE_Module can be varied and replaced independently, which lowers maintenance and enhancement costs.

The interface for ACE_Module is shown in Figure 9.2 and its key methods are shown in the following table:

Method	Description
ACE_Module() open()	Initialize a module and allocate its resources.
~ACE_Module() close()	Destroy a module and release its resources.
reader() writer()	Set/get the reader- and writer-side tasks.
name()	Set/get the name of the module.

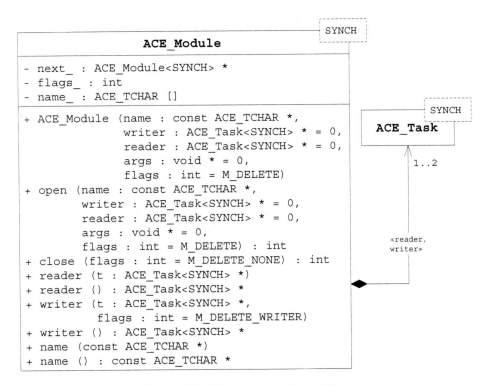

Figure 9.2: The ACE_Module Class

The ACE_Task class described in Section 6.3 provides an object-oriented process-ing abstraction that can be specialized to target any particular application domain, such as network protocol stacks [SW95] or customer care call center management [SS94]. The ACE_Task message passing and queueing mechanism provides a straightforward way to divide a domain's work into distinct steps and move work and data between them efficiently and bidirectionally. Many domains have symmetric processing steps for data being read and written. For example, protocol processing often involves symmetric tasks for verifying and applying security transforms, such as encryption. An ACE_Module provides a uni-form and flexible composition mechanism that relates instances of these application-defined ACE_Task objects into

- A "reader" side to process messages sent upstream to the ACE_Module layer
- A "writer" side to process messages sent downstream to the ACE_Module layer

The two tasks that comprise a bidirectional module are referred to as *siblings*. In the en-cryption example, for instance, the reader task would verify and decrypt received data while its sibling writer task would encrypt data before it's written. An ACE_Module would be composed from one of each of these tasks, and configured into the stream appropriately.

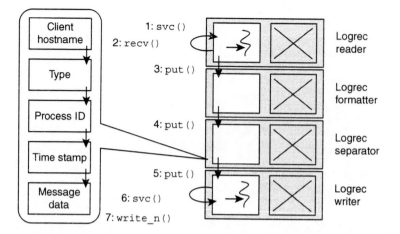

Figure 9.3: The ACE_Stream Structure for the display_logfile Program

In cases where a layer actively processes data in only one direction, the inactive sibling task can be specified as a NULL pointer, which triggers the ACE_Module to install an ACE_Thru_Task that simply forwards all messages to the next module's task without modifying them. This design maintains the layering even when layers are rearranged, added, or removed.

Example

This example develops a utility program called display_logfile, which reads log records stored by our logging servers, formats the information, and prints it in a human-readable format. As shown on page 90 in C++NPv1, most fields in a log record are stored in a CDR-encoded binary format, which is concise but not easily understood by humans. To implement the display_logfile program, we implement the following classes derived from ACE_Module:

- **Logrec Reader** is a module that converts the log records in a logfile into a canonical format that's then passed to, and processed by, other modules in an ACE_Stream.
- **Logrec Formatter** is a module that determines how the fields in the log record will be formatted, for example by converting them from binary to ASCII.
- **Logrec Separator** is a module that inserts message blocks containing a separator string between the existing message blocks in a composite log record message.
- **Logrec Writer** is a module that prints formatted log record messages to the standard output, where they can be redirected to a file, printer, or console.

Figure 9.3 illustrates the structure of the modules in the ACE_Stream that comprise the display_logfile program. This program uses a producer/consumer concurrency model, where the `Logrec_Reader` and the `Logrec_Writer` run as active objects that produce and consume messages, respectively. Figure 9.3 also illustrates the structure of the composite `ACE_Message_Block` created by the **Logrec Reader** module and manipulated by the other filter modules in the `ACE_Stream`.

In the example below, we inherit from `ACE_Task` and `ACE_Module` to create the **Logrec Reader**, **Logrec Formatter**, **Logrec Separator**, and **Logrec Writer** modules. The following `Logrec_Module` template and `LOGREC_MODULE` macro are used to simplify many of the examples below:

```
template <class TASK>
class Logrec_Module : public ACE_Module<ACE_MT_SYNCH> {
public:
  Logrec_Module (const ACE_TCHAR *name) {
    this->open (name,
                &task_, // Initialize writer-side task.
                0,      // Ignore reader-side task.
                0,
                ACE_Module<ACE_SYNCH>::M_DELETE_READER);
  }
private:
  TASK task_;
};
#define LOGREC_MODULE(NAME) \
  typedef Logrec_Module<NAME> NAME##_Module
```

Since the flow of messages is unidirectional (from **Logrec Reader** to **Logrec Writer**) we initialize only the writer-side task in the `ACE_Module` constructor. By passing a NULL pointer to the reader-side task parameter, the `ACE_Module` constructor will create an instance of `ACE_Thru_Task` that forwards all messages along without modifying them. The `M_DELETE_READER` flag instructs the `ACE_Module` destructor to only delete the reader-side task and not the writer-side task.

Logrec_Reader_Module.   This module contains an instance of the `Logrec_Reader` task class that performs the following activities:

1. It opens the designated logfile.
2. It activates the `Logrec_Reader` instance to be an active object.
3. It converts the log records in the logfile into a set of chained message blocks, each containing a field from the demarshaled log record, which is then processed by subsequent modules in an `ACE_Stream`.

The `Logrec_Reader` class is shown below:

```
class Logrec_Reader : public ACE_Task<ACE_MT_SYNCH> {
private:
  ACE_TString filename_; // Name of logfile.
  ACE_FILE_IO logfile_;  // File containing log records.
```

```
public:
  enum {MB_CLIENT = ACE_Message_Block::MB_USER,
        MB_TYPE, MB_PID, MB_TIME, MB_TEXT};

  Logrec_Reader (const ACE_TString &file): filename_ (file) {}
  // ... Other methods shown below ...
};
```

We define five enumerators to identify the fields in a log record. Rather than store the field indicator in the data itself, we use the ACE_Message_Block type member to indicate the field type. ACE_Message_Block defines two ranges of type values—*normal* and *priority*—with a number of values in each range. It also defines a third range for user-defined message types. We initialize MB_CLIENT to the value of ACE_Message_Block::MB_USER, which is the first user-defined message type value guaranteed not to conflict with other values defined within ACE itself.

The Logrec_Reader::open() hook method opens the designated logfile and converts the task into an active object, as shown below.

```
virtual int open (void *) {
  ACE_FILE_Addr name (filename_.c_str ());
  ACE_FILE_Connector con;
  if (con.connect (logfile_, name) == -1) return -1;
  return activate ();
}
```

Logrec_Reader::svc() runs in the active object thread. It reads log records from the logfile, demarshals and stores each one in a composite message block, and passes each composite message block up the stream for further processing by other modules. The logfile is written as a series of log records, each consisting of:

- A string containing the name of the client that sent the log record
- A CDR-encoded ACE_Log_Record (see page 79 of C++NPv1 for the marshaling code of the record)

Each log record follows the previous one with no inter-record marker. As shown below, Logrec_Reader::svc() reads the file contents in large chunks and demarshals them as a stream of data. A for loop reads the file contents until EOF is reached. An inner for loop demarshals log records from the data chunks.

```
1   virtual int svc () {
2     const size_t FILE_READ_SIZE = 8 * 1024;
3     ACE_Message_Block mblk (FILE_READ_SIZE);
4
5     for (;; mblk.crunch ()) {
6       ssize_t bytes_read = logfile_.recv (mblk.wr_ptr (),
7                                           mblk.space ());
8       if (bytes_read <= 0) break;
9       mblk.wr_ptr (ACE_static_cast (size_t, bytes_read));
10      for (;;) {
```

```
11          size_t name_len = ACE_OS_String::strnlen
12                              (mblk.rd_ptr (), mblk.length ());
13          if (name_len == mblk.length ()) break;
14
15          char *name_p = mblk.rd_ptr ();
16          ACE_Message_Block *rec = 0, *head = 0, *temp = 0;
17          ACE_NEW_RETURN
18            (head, ACE_Message_Block (name_len, MB_CLIENT), 0);
19          head->copy (name_p, name_len);
20          mblk.rd_ptr (name_len + 1);    // Skip nul also
21
22          size_t need = mblk.length () + ACE_CDR::MAX_ALIGNMENT;
23          ACE_NEW_RETURN (rec, ACE_Message_Block (need), 0);
24          ACE_CDR::mb_align (rec);
25          rec->copy (mblk.rd_ptr (), mblk.length ());
26
27          ACE_InputCDR cdr (rec); rec->release ();
28          ACE_CDR::Boolean byte_order;
29          if (!cdr.read_boolean (byte_order)) {
30            head->release (); mblk.rd_ptr (name_p); break;
31          }
32          cdr.reset_byte_order (byte_order);
33
34          ACE_CDR::ULong length;
35          if (!cdr.read_ulong (length)) {
36            head->release (); mblk.rd_ptr (name_p); break;
37          }
38          if (length > cdr.length ()) {
39            head->release (); mblk.rd_ptr (name_p); break;
40          }
41          ACE_NEW_RETURN
42            (temp, ACE_Message_Block (length, MB_TEXT), 0);
43          ACE_NEW_RETURN
44            (temp,
45             ACE_Message_Block (2 * sizeof (ACE_CDR::Long),
46                                MB_TIME, temp), 0);
47          ACE_NEW_RETURN
48            (temp,
49             ACE_Message_Block (sizeof (ACE_CDR::Long),
50                                MB_PID, temp), 0);
51          ACE_NEW_RETURN
52            (temp,
53             ACE_Message_Block (sizeof (ACE_CDR::Long),
54                                MB_TYPE, temp), 0);
55          head->cont (temp);
56          // Extract the type...
57          ACE_CDR::Long *lp = ACE_reinterpret_cast
58                              (ACE_CDR::Long *, temp->wr_ptr ());
59          cdr >> *lp;
60          temp->wr_ptr (sizeof (ACE_CDR::Long));
61          temp = temp->cont ();
62          // Extract the PID...
```

```
63          lp = ACE_reinterpret_cast
64              (ACE_CDR::Long *, temp->wr_ptr ());
65          cdr >> *lp;
66          temp->wr_ptr (sizeof (ACE_CDR::Long));
67          temp = temp->cont ();
68          // Extract the timestamp...
69          lp = ACE_reinterpret_cast
70              (ACE_CDR::Long *, temp->wr_ptr ());
71          cdr >> *lp; ++lp; cdr >> *lp;
72          temp->wr_ptr (2 * sizeof (ACE_CDR::Long));
73          temp = temp->cont ();
74          // Extract the text length, then the text message
75          ACE_CDR::ULong text_len;
76          cdr >> text_len;
77          cdr.read_char_array (temp->wr_ptr (), text_len);
78          temp->wr_ptr (text_len);
79
80          if (put_next (head) == -1) break;
81          mblk.rd_ptr (mblk.length () - cdr.length ());
82        }
83      }
84
85    ACE_Message_Block *stop = 0;
86    ACE_NEW_RETURN
87      (stop,
88       ACE_Message_Block (0, ACE_Message_Block::MB_STOP), 0);
89    put_next (stop);
90    return 0;
91  }
```

Lines 5–9   Begin the loop that reads the file's contents into an ACE_Message_Block, using the space() method to find out how much free space is available in the block. The block's write pointer is updated to reflect the added data. The final clause in the for loop uses the ACE_Message_Block::crunch() method to shift any data in mblk to the beginning of the block's data buffer so there's room to append more data.

Lines 10–20   Begin the log record demarshaling loop. We use the ACE_OS_String:: strnlen() method to find the length of the hostname string, but will only look through the characters remaining in mblk. If mblk doesn't contain the whole name, we break out of the loop to read more data from the file. If the name is there, we remember the pointer where the name starts (name_p) in case we need to get more data and restart the demarshaling. The head ACE_Message_Block is allocated to hold the name; it will become the first block in the message block chain that's passed up the stream.

Lines 22–25   The mblk read pointer is now at the start of the CDR-encoded ACE_Log_ Record. Recall from Chapter 4 of C++NPv1 that a buffer from which ACE's CDR classes will demarshal data must be properly aligned. The current alignment of the mblk read pointer is unknown, and not likely to be properly aligned. We therefore allocate a new ACE_

Message_Block large enough to hold the remaining data in mblk, plus any needed bytes for CDR alignment. After calling ACE_CDR::mb_align() to align the new block's write pointer, we copy the remainder of the file data.

Lines 27–32   Create an ACE_InputCDR object to demarshal the log record contents from rec. Since the ACE_InputCDR constructor increments the reference count on rec, we call rec->release() to release our reference to it, preventing a memory leak. The first item demarshaled is the byte order indicator. It's used to reset the byte order of cdr so the remaining data can be demarshaled properly.

Lines 34–39   The header written for the marshaled ACE_Log_Record contains a length field designating the number of bytes in the marshaled log record. That value is demarshaled and compared to the number of bytes remaining in the cdr object. If not all of the needed bytes are present, release the client name block (head), reset the mblk read pointer to restart at the host name on the next demarshaling pass, and break out of the record-demarshaling loop to read more data from the file.

Lines 41–55   Allocate message blocks for all of the remaining log record fields. Each has the correct block type for proper identification in modules further down the stream. They're allocated in reverse order to make it easier to supply the cont pointer. When the last one is allocated, therefore, it's the first block in the chain after head and is connected via its continuation pointer.

Lines 57–61   Demarshal the type field into the first message block by casting the message block's write pointer to ACE_CDR::Long * and use the CDR extraction operator to demarshal the type field. Adjust the block's write pointer to reflect the data just read and move to the next message block in the chain.

Lines 63–73   The same technique is used to demarshal the process ID and timestamp.

Lines 75–78   The log record's data portion was marshaled as a counted sequence of bytes. The length of the sequence is demarshaled, and the bytes themselves are then demarshaled into the final message block in the chain.

Line 80   Use put_next() to pass the message block to the next module in the stream for further processing. Sidebar 60 (page 308) explains how put_next() works.

Line 81   Move the file-content block's read pointer up past all of the data that was just extracted. The cdr object has been adjusting its internal pointers as a result of the CDR operations, so the length() method indicates how much data is left. Since the beginning length was the same as mblk.length() (which has not been adjusted during all the demarshaling), we can determine how much of the original message block was consumed.

Lines 85–89   The entire file is processed, so send a 0-sized ACE_Message_Block with type MB_STOP down the stream. By convention, this message block instructs other modules in the stream to stop their processing.

Sidebar 60: ACE_Task Methods Related to ACE Streams Framework

The ACE_Task described in Section 6.3 also contains the following methods that can be used in conjunction with the ACE Streams framework:

Method	Description
module()	Returns a pointer to the task's module if there is one, else 0
next()	Returns a pointer to the next task in a stream if there is one, else 0
sibling()	Returns a pointer to a task's sibling in a module
put_next()	Passes a message block to the adjacent task in a stream
can_put()	Returns 1 if a message block can be enqueued via put_next() without blocking due to intrastream flow control, else 0
reply()	Passes a message block to the sibling task's adjacent task of a stream, which enables a task to reverse the direction of a message in a stream

An ACE_Task that's part of an ACE_Module can use put_next() to forward a message block to an adjacent module. This method follows the module's next() pointer to the right task, then calls its put() hook method, passing it the message block. The put() method borrows the thread from the task that invoked put_next(). If a task runs as an active object, its put() method can enqueue the message on the task's message queue and allow its svc() hook method to handle the message concurrently with respect to other processing in a stream. Sidebar 62 (page 317) outlines the concurrency models supported by the ACE Streams framework.

Since the name of the logfile is passed to the Logrec_Reader_Module constructor, we can't use the LOGREC_MODULE macro (page 303). Instead, we define the class explicitly, as shown below:

```
class Logrec_Reader_Module : public ACE_Module<ACE_MT_SYNCH> {
public:
  Logrec_Reader_Module (const ACE_TString &filename)
    : task_ (filename)
  {
    this->open (ACE_TEXT ("Logrec Reader"),
                &task_, // Initialize writer-side.
                0,      // Ignore reader-side.
                0,
                ACE_Module<ACE_SYNCH>::M_DELETE_READER);
  }
private:
  // Converts the logfile into chains of message blocks.
  Logrec_Reader task_;
};
```

Logrec_Formatter_Module. This module contains a `Logrec_Formatter` task that determines how the log record fields will be formatted, as shown below:

```
class Logrec_Formatter : public ACE_Task<ACE_MT_SYNCH> {
private:
  typedef void (*FORMATTER[5])(ACE_Message_Block *);
  static FORMATTER format_; // Array of format static methods.

public:
```

The synchronization trait for a stream's modules and tasks is set by the ACE_Stream that contains them. Since the modules and tasks defined above use ACE_MT_SYNCH, `Logrec_Formatter` also derives from ACE_Task<ACE_MT_SYNCH>. It runs as a *passive object*, however, since `Logrec_Formatter` never calls `activate()` and its `put()` method borrows the thread of its caller to format messages, as shown below:

```
  virtual int put (ACE_Message_Block *mblk, ACE_Time_Value *) {
    if (mblk->msg_type () == Logrec_Reader::MB_CLIENT)
      for (ACE_Message_Block *temp = mblk;
           temp != 0;
           temp = temp->cont ()) {
        int mb_type =
          temp->msg_type () - ACE_Message_Block::MB_USER;
        (*format_[mb_type])(temp);
      }
    return put_next (mblk);
  }
```

The `put()` method determines the message type of the ACE_Message_Block forwarded to this module. If the message type is `Logrec_Reader::MB_CLIENT`, then it's the first in a set of chained blocks containing log record fields. In this case, the method iterates through the record fields invoking the appropriate static methods to convert the fields into a human-readable format. After all the fields are formatted, the message block is passed along to the next module in the stream. If the forwarded block is *not* of type `Logrec_Reader::MB_CLIENT`, it's assumed to be the MB_STOP block and is simply forwarded to the next module in the stream.

The following static methods format their corresponding type of field. We start with `format_client()`:

```
  static void format_client (ACE_Message_Block *) { return; }
```

The MB_CLIENT block has a known-length text string in it. Since this needs no further formatting, `format_client()` simply returns. Note that the text is in ASCII. Any processing required to translate to a wide-character format or verify the name by looking up its IP address could be added here without disturbing the rest of the stream.

We use the following `format_long()` method to convert the log record's type and process id into an ASCII representation:

```
static void format_long (ACE_Message_Block *mblk) {
  ACE_CDR::Long type = * (ACE_CDR::Long *)mblk->rd_ptr ();
  mblk->size (11); // Max size in ASCII of 32-bit word.
  mblk->reset ();
  mblk->wr_ptr ((size_t) sprintf (mblk->wr_ptr (), "%d", type));
}
```

The `size()` method call ensures that there's enough space in the message block to hold the textual representation of the value, reallocating space if necessary. The `reset()` method call resets the message block's read and write pointers to the start of its memory buffer in preparation for the call to the standard C `sprintf()` function that does the actual formatting. The `sprintf()` function returns the number of characters used to format the value, not including the string-terminating NUL character. Since message blocks contain a specific count, we don't include the NUL character in the new length when updating the message block's write pointer.

The `format_time()` method is more complicated since it converts the seconds and microseconds of the time value into an ASCII string, as follows:

```
static void format_time (ACE_Message_Block *mblk) {
  ACE_CDR::Long secs = * (ACE_CDR::Long *)mblk->rd_ptr ();
  mblk->rd_ptr (sizeof (ACE_CDR::Long));
  ACE_CDR::Long usecs = * (ACE_CDR::Long *)mblk->rd_ptr ();
  char timestamp[26]; // Max size of ctime_r() string.
  time_t time_secs (secs);
  ACE_OS::ctime_r (&time_secs, timestamp, sizeof timestamp);
  mblk->size (26); // Max size of ctime_r() string.
  mblk->reset ();
  timestamp[19] = '\0'; // NUL-terminate after the time.
  timestamp[24] = '\0'; // NUL-terminate after the date.
  size_t fmt_len (sprintf (mblk->wr_ptr (),
                           "%s.%03d %s",
                           timestamp + 4,
                           usecs / 1000,
                           timestamp + 20));
  mblk->wr_ptr (fmt_len);
}
```

The final `format_string()` method is identical to `format_client()` since it also receives a known-length string. Again, if the string required some manipulation, this processing could easily be added here.

```
  static void format_string (ACE_Message_Block *) { return; }
};
```

We initialize the array of pointers to formatting methods as follows:

```
Logrec_Formatter::FORMATTER Logrec_Formatter::format_ = {
  format_client, format_long,
  format_long, format_time, format_string
};
```

We use pointers to static methods rather than pointers to nonstatic methods since there's no need to access `Logrec_Formatter` state.

We next instantiate the LOGREC_MODULE macro with the `Logrec_Formatter` class to create the `Logrec_Formatter_Module`:

```
LOGREC_MODULE (Logrec_Formatter);
```

Logrec_Separator_Module.   This module contains a `Logrec_Separator` object that inserts message blocks between the existing message blocks in a composite log record message, each new message block contains the separator string.

```
class Logrec_Separator : public ACE_Task<ACE_MT_SYNCH> {
private:
  ACE_Lock_Adapter<ACE_Thread_Mutex> lock_strategy_;
public:
```

This class is a passive object, so `Logrec_Separator::put()` borrows the thread of its caller to insert the separators:

```
 1  virtual int put (ACE_Message_Block *mblk,
 2                   ACE_Time_Value *) {
 3    if (mblk->msg_type () == Logrec_Reader::MB_CLIENT) {
 4      ACE_Message_Block *separator = 0;
 5      ACE_NEW_RETURN
 6         (separator,
 7          ACE_Message_Block (ACE_OS_String::strlen ("|") + 1,
 8                             ACE_Message_Block::MB_DATA,
 9                             0, 0, 0, &lock_strategy_), -1);
10      separator->copy ("|");
11
12      ACE_Message_Block *dup = 0;
13      for (ACE_Message_Block *temp = mblk; temp != 0; ) {
14         dup = separator->duplicate ();
15         dup->cont (temp->cont ());
16         temp->cont (dup);
17         temp = dup->cont ();
18      }
19      ACE_Message_Block *nl = 0;
20      ACE_NEW_RETURN (nl, ACE_Message_Block (2), 0);
21      nl->copy ("\n");
22      dup->cont (nl);
23      separator->release ();
24    }
25
26    return put_next (mblk);
27  }
```

Line 3   If the block's type is MB_STOP, it's forwarded to the next stream module. Since `Logrec_Separator` is a passive object, it needn't take any action when it's done.

Lines 4–10 Create a message block to hold the separator string, which is set to " | " (a more flexible implementation could make the separator string a parameter to the class constructor). Later in this method, we'll use the `ACE_Message_Block::duplicate()` method, which returns a "shallow" copy of the message that simply increments its reference count by one, but doesn't actually make a copy of the data itself. Sidebar 61 explains how and why we configured the `separator ACE_Message_Block` with an `ACE_Lock_Adapter<ACE_Thread_Mutex>` locking strategy.

Lines 12–18 Loop through the list of message blocks to insert a duplicate of `separator` that contains the separator string between each of the original message blocks.

Lines 19–22 After the separators are inserted, a final block containing a newline is appended to format the output cleanly when it's eventually written to the standard output.

Lines 23–26 The block from which all the separator blocks were duplicated is released, and the revised composite message is passed along to the next module in the stream.

Sidebar 61: Serializing ACE_Message_Block Reference Counts

If shallow copies of a message block are created and/or released in different threads there's a potential race condition on access to the reference count and shared data. Access to these data must therefore be serialized. Since there are multiple message blocks involved, an external locking strategy is applied. Hence, a message block can be associated with an instance of `ACE_Lock_Adapter`. `Logrec_Separator::put()` (page 311) accesses message blocks from multiple threads, so the `ACE_Lock_Adapter` is parameterized with an `ACE_Thread_Mutex`. This locking strategy serializes calls to the message block's `duplicate()` and `release()` methods to avoid race conditions when a message block is created and released concurrently by different threads. Although `Logrec_Separator::put()` calls `separator->release()` before forwarding the message block to the next module, we take this precaution because a subsequent module inserted in the stream may process the blocks using multiple threads.

We now instantiate the LOGREC_MODULE macro with the `Logrec_Separator` class to create the `Logrec_Separator_Module`:

```
LOGREC_MODULE (Logrec_Separator);
```

Logrec_Writer_Module. This module contains a `Logrec_Writer` task that performs the following activities:

- It activates the `Logrec_Writer` instance to be an active object.
- It receives formatted log record messages passed by an adjacent module and prints them to its standard output.

The `Logrec_Writer` class is shown below:

```
class Logrec_Writer : public ACE_Task<ACE_MT_SYNCH> {
public:
  // Initialization hook method.
  virtual int open (void *) { return activate (); }
```

The `open()` hook method converts `Logrec_Writer` into an active object. The other two methods in this class leverage the fact that its `ACE_Task` subclass is instantiated with the `ACE_MT_SYNCH` traits class. For example, `Logrec_Writer::put()` enqueues messages in its synchronized message queue:

```
  virtual int put (ACE_Message_Block *mblk, ACE_Time_Value *to)
  { return putq (mblk, to); }
```

Likewise, `Logrec_Writer::svc()` runs in its active object thread, dequeueing messages from its message queue and writing them to standard output:

```
  virtual int svc () {
    int stop = 0;
    for (ACE_Message_Block *mb; !stop && getq (mb) != -1; ) {
      if (mb->msg_type () == ACE_Message_Block::MB_STOP)
        stop = 1;
      else ACE::write_n (ACE_STDOUT, mb);

      put_next (mb);
    }
    return 0;
  }
};
```

When a `MB_STOP` block is received, the method will break out of the processing loop and return, ending the thread. The `ACE::write_n()` method prints out all other message blocks chained through their `cont()` pointers using an efficient gather-write operation. All the message blocks are forwarded to the next module in the stream. By default, the ACE Streams framework releases all message blocks that are forwarded "off the end" of the stream, as discussed in the coverage of `ACE_Stream_Tail` (page 314).

Finally, we instantiate the LOGREC_MODULE macro with the `Logrec_Writer` class to create the `Logrec_Writer_Module`:

```
LOGREC_MODULE (Logrec_Writer);
```

The *Example* portion of Section 9.3 illustrates how all the modules shown above can be configured in an `ACE_Stream` to create the complete `display_logfile` program.

9.3   The ACE_Stream Class

Motivation

The ACE_Module class described in Section 9.2 can be used to decompose a networked application into a series of interconnected, functionally distinct layers. Each module implements a different layer of application-defined functionality, such as a reader, formatter, separator, and writer of log records. ACE_Module provides methods to transfer messages between sibling tasks within a module, as well as between modules. It does not, however, provide a facility to connect or rearrange modules in a particular order. To enable developers to build and manage a series of hierarchically related module layers as a single object, the ACE Streams framework defines the ACE_Stream class.

Class Capabilities

ACE_Stream implements the Pipes and Filters pattern [POSA1] to enable developers to configure and execute hierarchically related services by customizing reusable application-independent framework classes. This class provides the following capabilities:

- It provides methods to dynamically add, replace, and remove ACE_Module objects to form various stream configurations.
- It provides methods to send/receive messages to/from an ACE_Stream.
- It provides a mechanism to connect two ACE_Stream streams together.
- It provides a way to shut down all modules in a stream and wait for them all to stop.

The interface for ACE_Stream is shown in Figure 9.4. Since this class exports many features of the ACE Streams framework, we group its method descriptions into the three categories described below.

1. Stream initialization and destruction methods.   The following methods initialize and destroy an ACE_Stream:

Method	Description
ACE_Stream() open()	Initialize a stream.
~ACE_Stream() close()	Destroy a stream by releasing its resources and popping (destroying) each module.
wait()	Synchronize with the final close of a stream.

By default, two ACE-created ACE_Module objects are installed in an ACE_Stream when it's initialized, one at the head of the stream and the other at the tail. The head module contains ACE_Stream_Head objects in both its reader and writer sides. Likewise, the tail module contains ACE_Stream_Tail objects in both sides. These two classes interpret

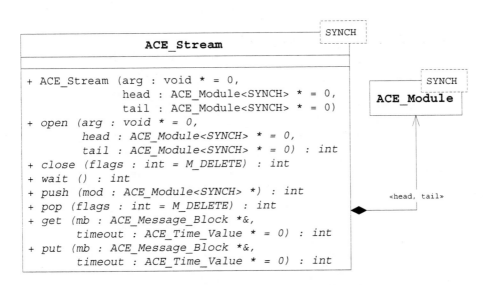

Figure 9.4: The ACE_Stream Class

predefined control messages and data message blocks that can be circulated through an
ACE_Stream at run time. The ACE_Message_Block class defines the types of these
message blocks as enumerators whose values are all less than MB_USER.

ACE_Stream_Head can queue messages between an application and an instance of
ACE_Stream. When a message is passed to the top module's writer-side ACE_Stream_
Head, it's forwarded to the next module in the stream. When a message is passed to the
top module's reader-side ACE_Stream_Head, it's queued on the task's message queue
(unless its type is MB_FLUSH, in which case the message queue is shut down).

To prevent resource leaks when messages reach the end of a stream without being processed, ACE_Stream_Tail::put() releases messages that it receives when acting as
writer. This behavior allows the Logrec_Writer module (page 313) to pass its message
blocks through to the next task. Most likely, the next task is an ACE_Stream_Tail. If
the program is extended to add another module at that point in the stream, however, the
module will continue to work as expected.

2. Stream configuration methods.   The following methods push and pop ACE_Module
objects onto and off of an ACE_Stream:

Method	Description
push()	Add a new module to the stream right below the stream head.
pop()	Remove the module right below the stream head and close it down.
top()	Return a pointer to the module right below the stream head.
insert()	Insert a new module below the designated module.
replace()	Replace the designated module with a new module.
remove()	Remove the designated module from a stream and close it down.

The push() and pop() methods allow applications to configure a stream at run time by inserting or removing an instance of ACE_Module at the top of a stream. When a module is pushed onto a stream, the open() hook methods of the module's writer- and reader-side tasks are called automatically. Likewise, when a module is popped from a stream the close() hook methods of its writer- and reader-side tasks are invoked.

Since a complete stream is represented as an interconnected series of independent modules, it's often useful to insert, remove, and replace modules at any point in a stream. To support these operations, therefore, ACE_Module objects are named in the stream, and the insert(), replace() and remove() methods can manipulate a stream's modules. ACE_Module objects can be composed in essentially arbitrary configurations that satisfy application requirements and enhance module reuse.

3. Stream communication methods.   The following methods are used to send and receive messages on an ACE_Stream:

Method	Description
get()	Receive the next message that's stored at the stream head.
put()	Send a message down a stream, starting at the module that's below the stream head.

The get() and put() methods allow applications to send and receive messages on an ACE_Stream object. Similar to inserting message blocks in an ACE_Message_Queue, the blocking behavior of these methods can be modified by passing the following types of ACE_Time_Value values:

Value	Behavior
NULL ACE_Time_Value pointer	Indicates that get() or put() should wait indefinitely, that is, it will block until the method completes.
Non-NULL ACE_Time_Value pointer whose sec() and usec() methods return 0	Indicates that get() or put() should perform a nonblocking operation, that is, if the method doesn't succeed immediately, return −1 and set errno to EWOULDBLOCK.
A non-NULL ACE_Time_Value pointer whose sec() or usec() method returns > 0	Indicates that get() or put() should wait until the *absolute* time of day, returning −1 with errno set to EWOULDBLOCK if the method does not complete by this time.

When message blocks arrive at an ACE_Stream they can pass through a series of interconnected ACE_Task objects by calling their put_next() methods, as discussed in Sidebar 60 (page 308). Message blocks can originate from various sources, such as an application thread, a reactor or proactor, or an ACE timer queue dispatcher. Sidebar 62 outlines the concurrency models supported by the ACE Streams framework.

Sidebar 62: ACE Streams Framework Concurrency Models

Section 5.6 of C++NPv1 describes the two canonical types of concurrency architectures, *task-based* and *message-based* [SS93], which are supported by the ACE
Streams framework. For example, a put() method may enqueue a message and
defer handling to its task's svc() method that executes concurrently in a separate
thread. This approach is illustrated by the task-based architecture shown below:

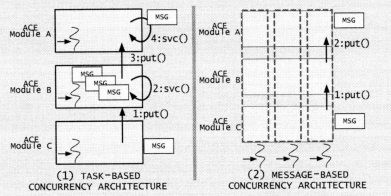

(1) TASK-BASED
CONCURRENCY ARCHITECTURE

(2) MESSAGE-BASED
CONCURRENCY ARCHITECTURE

Conversely, a put() method can borrow the thread of control from its caller to
handle a message immediately. This approach is illustrated by the message-based
architecture shown in the figure above. A stream's concurrency architecture has a
significant impact on performance and ease of programming, as described in [SS95b].

Example

We conclude by showing how to configure the display_logfile program with an
ACE_Stream object that contains the modules presented in Section 9.2. The program
below creates an ACE_Stream and then pushes all of the modules onto the stream.

```
int ACE_TMAIN (int argc, ACE_TCHAR *argv[]) {
  if (argc != 2) ACE_ERROR_RETURN
                ((LM_ERROR, "usage: %s logfile\n", argv[0]), 1);
  ACE_TString logfile (argv[1]);
  ACE_Stream<ACE_MT_SYNCH> stream;
  if (stream.push
      (new Logrec_Writer_Module (ACE_TEXT ("Writer"))) != -1
      && stream.push
      (new Logrec_Separator_Module (ACE_TEXT ("Separator"))) != -1
      && stream.push
      (new Logrec_Formatter_Module (ACE_TEXT ("Formatter"))) != -1
      && stream.push
      (new Logrec_Reader_Module (logfile)) != -1)
    return ACE_Thread_Manager::instance ()->wait () == 0 ? 0 : 1;
  return 1;
}
```

As each module is pushed onto the stream, the ACE Streams framework calls the `open()` hook method on its writer-side task, which initializes the task. The `Logrec_Writer_Module` and `Logrec_Reader_Module`'s `open()` hook methods convert their writer tasks into active objects. The main thread doesn't actually take part in the processing. After pushing all the modules onto the stream successfully, it simply waits for the other threads to exit from their active objects when they're done processing the logfile.

The `main()` function on the previous page allocates a number of modules dynamically at program startup and while processing the logfile. We omit most of the error handling logic from the `main()` function to save space. Although it's unlikely that this program would exhaust the heap at startup time, a well-designed production application should check for errors and handle them appropriately.

Implementing the `display_logfile` program with the ACE Streams framework enables the transparent, incremental evolution of application functionality. For example, it's straightforward to implement and configure a **Logrec Sorter** module that changes the order in which the fields in the log record are displayed. Likewise, the ACE Streams framework reduces the complexity of each module layer in the `display_logfile` program, thereby simplifying its implementation, testing, and maintenance.

9.4   Summary

The ACE Streams framework is an implementation of the Pipes and Filters pattern that employs object-oriented design techniques, the ACE Task framework, and C++ language features. The ACE Streams framework makes it easy to incorporate new or modified functionality into an `ACE_Stream` without modifying the application-independent framework classes. For example, incorporating a new layer of service functionality into an `ACE_Stream` involves the following steps:

1. Inheriting from the `ACE_Task` interface and overriding the `open()`, `close()`, `put()`, and `svc()` methods in the `ACE_Task` subclass to implement application-defined functionality.
2. Allocating a new `ACE_Module` that contains one or two instances of the application-defined `ACE_Tasks`, one for the reader-side and one for the writer-side.
3. Inserting the `ACE_Module` into an `ACE_Stream` object. Multiple `ACE_Modules` can be inserted into an `ACE_Stream` to form an ordered series of hierarchically related processing capabilities.

The ACE Streams framework enables developers to create layered, modular networked applications that are easily extended, tuned, maintained and configured. Moreover, the synergy between the ACE Task, Service Configurator, and Streams frameworks allows a wide range of designs and configurations that can be extended and modified to suit countless design situations, run-time environments, and OS platforms.

Glossary

Acceptor-Connector Pattern A design pattern that decouples the connection and initialization of cooperating peer services in a networked system from the processing they perform once connected and initialized.

Active Connection Establishment The connection role played by a peer application that initiates a connection to a remote peer (compare with *Passive Connection Establishment*).

Active Object An object that implements the Active Object pattern. Such objects generally execute service requests in a thread separate from the caller's (compare with *Passive Object*).

Active Object Pattern A design pattern that decouples method execution from method invocation in order to enhance concurrency and simplify synchronized access to objects that reside in their own threads of control.

Architectural Pattern A pattern that expresses a fundamental structural organization schema for software systems. It provides a set of predefined subsystems, specifies their responsibilities, and includes rules and guidelines for organizing the relationships between them.

Aspects A property of a program, such as memory management, synchronization, or fault tolerance, that cross-cuts module boundaries.

Asynchronous Completion Token (ACT) A developer-supplied value associated with an asynchronous operation. It is used to communicate information related to the operation to the operation's completion handler.

Asynchronous I/O A mechanism for sending or receiving data in which an I/O operation is initiated but the caller does not block waiting for the operation to complete.

Barrier Synchronization A thread synchronization mechanism that allows a designated group of threads to synchronize their progress when each attains a certain state, such as completion of some collective operation or task. A barrier represents a specific point in the execution path. Each thread that reaches the barrier point waits for the other threads to also reach that point. When all threads in the set reach the barrier, the barrier is "dropped" and all threads simultaneously continue execution.

Bounded Buffer A finite-sized buffer that allows two (or more) threads to share the buffer concurrently, with at least one thread inserting items into the buffer and at least one thread removing items from the buffer.

Bridge Pattern A design pattern that decouples an abstraction from its implementation so that the two can vary independently.

Busy Wait A technique used by a thread to wait for a lock by executing a tight loop and polling to see if the lock is available on each iteration, in contrast to waiting for the lock to be released by sleeping and allowing other threads to run.

Cache Affinity A thread scheduling optimization that gives preference to dispatching a thread on the CPU on which it most recently ran to maximize the probability of its state being present in the CPU's instruction and data caches.

Callback An object registered with a dispatcher, which calls back to a method on the object when a particular event occurs.

Collocation The locating of objects into a single process or host, often done to improve simplicity or performance (compare with *Distribution*).

Common Data Representation (CDR) The standard format defined by CORBA to marshal and demarshal data. It uses a bicanonical "receiver makes right" representation that only incurs overhead if the byte order of the sender differs from the byte order of the receiver.

Common Middleware Services This layer of middleware defines domain-independent services, such as event notifications, logging, multimedia streaming, persistence, security, global time synchronization, real-time scheduling and distributed resource management, fault tolerance, concurrency control, and recoverable transactions, that allocate, schedule, and coordinate various resources throughout a distributed system.

Completion Handler An object whose interface contains one or more hook methods designed to process completion events.

Component An encapsulated part of a software system that implements a specific service or set of services. A component has one or more interfaces that provide access to its services. Components serve as building blocks for the structure of a system. On a programming language level, components may be represented as modules, classes, objects, or a set of related functions. A component that does not implement all the elements of its interface is called an abstract component.

Component Configurator Pattern A design pattern that allows an application to link and unlink its component implementations at run time without having to modify, recompile, or relink the application statically.

Concurrency The ability of an object, component, or system to execute operations that are "logically simultaneous" (compare with *Parallelism*).

Condition Variable A synchronization mechanism used by collaborating threads to suspend themselves temporarily until condition expressions involving data shared between the threads attain desired states. A condition variable is always used in conjunction with a mutex, which the thread must acquire before evaluating the condition expression. If the condition expression is false the thread atomically suspends itself on the condition variable and releases the mutex, so that other threads can change the shared data. When a cooperating thread changes this data, it can notify the condition variable, which atomically resumes a thread that had previously suspended on the condition variable and acquires its mutex again.

Container A common name for data structures that hold a collection of elements. Examples of containers are lists, sets, and associative arrays. In addition, component models, such as EJB and ActiveX Controls, define containers that provide a run-time environment that shields components from the details of their underlying infrastructure, such as an operating system.

Critical Section Code that should not execute concurrently in an object or subsystem can be synchronized by a critical section. A critical section is a sequence of instructions that obeys the following invariant: while one thread or process is executing in the critical section, no other thread or process can execute in the critical section.

Daemon A server process that runs continuously in the background performing various services on behalf of clients.

Deadlock A concurrency hazard that occurs when multiple threads attempt to acquire multiple locks and become blocked indefinitely in a circular wait state.

Demarshaling The conversion of a *marshaled* message to a host-specific format from a host-independent format.

Demultiplexing A mechanism that routes incoming data from an input port to its intended receivers. There's a 1:N relationship between input port and receivers. Demultiplexing is commonly applied to incoming events and data streams. The reverse operation is known as multiplexing.

Design Pattern A design pattern provides a scheme for refining components of a software system or the relationships between them. It describes a commonly recurring structure of communicating components that solves a general design problem within a particular context.

Distribution The activities associated with placing an object into a different process or host than the clients that access it. Distribution is often applied to improve fault tolerance or to access remote resources (compare with *Collocation*).

Distribution Middleware This layer of middleware automates common network programming tasks, such as connection and memory management, marshaling and demarshaling, endpoint and request demultiplexing, synchronization, and multithreading, so that developers can program distributed applications much like stand-alone applications, that is, by invoking operations on target objects without concern for their location, language, OS, or hardware.

Domain Denotes concepts, knowledge and other items that are related to a particular problem area. Often used in "application domain" to denote the problem area addressed by an application. On the Internet, a domain is a logical addressing entity, such as uci.edu or riverace.com.

Domain Analysis An inductive, feedback-driven process that examines an application domain systematically to identify its core challenges and design dimensions in order to map them onto effective solution techniques.

Double-Checked Locking Optimization Pattern A design pattern that reduces contention and synchronization overhead whenever critical sections of code must acquire locks in a thread-safe manner just once during program execution.

Double-Dispatching This technique allows the execution of methods that depend on the type of request and the types of two receivers. The object that calls the method passes itself as a parameter to the receiver, so the receiver can act differently depending upon the type of the caller.

Dynamically Linked Library (DLL) A library that can be shared by multiple processes and linked into and out of a process address space dynamically to improve application flexibility and extensibility at run time.

Event A message that conveys the occurrence of a significant activity, together with any data associated with the activity.

Event Handler An object whose interface consists of one or more hook methods that can process application-specific events.

Event Loop A program structure that continuously waits for and processes events.

Factory A method or function that creates and assembles the resources needed to instantiate and initialize an object or component instance.

Flow Control A networking protocol mechanism that prevents a fast sender from overrunning the buffering and computing resources of a slow receiver.

Framework See *Object-Oriented Framework*.

Function Object An object that can be called as if it is a function. Also known as a Functor.

Gather-Write An output operation that transmits the contents of multiple noncontiguous data buffers in a single operation.

Generative Programming A programming technique focusing on designing and implementing software components that can be combined to generate specialized and highly optimized systems that fulfill specific requirements.

Generic Programming A programming technique that unites design patterns and C++ parameterized types to enable developers to achieve expressive, flexible, efficient, and highly reusable code.

Half-Sync/Half-Async Pattern An architectural pattern that decouples asynchronous and synchronous processing in concurrent systems, to simplify programming without reducing performance unduly. This pattern introduces two intercommunicating layers, one for asynchronous and one for synchronous service processing. A queueing layer mediates communication between services in the asynchronous and synchronous layers.

Handle A handle identifies resources that are managed by an operating system kernel. These resources commonly include, among others, network connections, open files, timers, and synchronization objects.

Hook Method A framework-prescribed virtual method that acts as the target of framework-initiated callbacks. Use of hook methods is a technique for integrating application code with framework code.

Host Infrastructure Middleware This layer of middleware encapsulates concurrency and IPC mechanisms available on hosts to create OO network programming capabilities that eliminate many tedious, error-prone, and nonportable aspects associated with developing networked applications via native OS APIs, such as Sockets or Pthreads.

Idiom A low-level pattern specific to a programming language. An idiom describes how to implement particular aspects of components or the relationships between them using the features of the given language.

Inheritance A feature of object-oriented languages that allows new classes to be derived from existing ones. Inheritance defines implementation reuse, a subtype relationship, or both. Depending on the programming language, single or multiple inheritance is possible.

Inlining A compile-time optimization technique that replaces a call to a function or method with the actual code body of that function or method. Inlining long function/method bodies can lead to code "bloat," with negative effects on storage consumption and paging.

Internet A worldwide "network of networks" that is based on the Internet Protocol (IP). Widely considered to be the most important human invention since fire and MTV.

Jitter The standard deviation of the latency for a series of operations.

Latency The delay experienced by operations.

Leader/Followers Pattern An architectural pattern that provides an efficient concurrency model where multiple threads take turns sharing a set of event sources in order to detect, demultiplex, dispatch, and process service requests that occur on the event sources.

Lock A mechanism used to implement some type of a *critical section*. A lock that can be acquired and released serially, such as a static mutex, may be added to a class. If multiple threads attempt to acquire the lock simultaneously, only one thread will succeed and the others will block until the lock is available. Other locking mechanisms, such as semaphores or readers/writer locks, define different synchronization semantics.

Manager Pattern   This design pattern controls the life cycle of, or the access to, objects of a class.

Marshaling   The conversion of a set of data from a host-specific format into a host-independent format.

Message   Messages are used to communicate between objects, threads, or processes. In an object-oriented system the term *message* is used to describe the selection and activation of an operation or the method of an object. This type of message is synchronous, which means that the sender waits until the receiver finishes the activated operation. Threads and processes often communicate asynchronously, in which the sender continues its execution without waiting for the receiver to reply.

Message Passing   An IPC mechanism used to exchange messages between threads or processes (compare with *Shared Memory*).

Middleware   A set of layers and components that provides reusable common services and network programming mechanisms. Middleware resides on top of an operating system and its protocol stacks but below the structure and functionality of any particular application.

Monitor Object Pattern   A design pattern that synchronizes the execution of concurrent methods to ensure that only one method at a time runs within an object. It also allows an object's methods to schedule their execution sequences cooperatively.

Mutex   A "mutual exclusion" locking mechanism that ensures only one thread at a time is active concurrently within a critical section in order to prevent *race conditions*.

Nonrecursive Mutex   A mutex that must be released before it can be reacquired by any thread, including the thread originally holding it. Compare with *Recursive Mutex*.

Object-Oriented Framework   An integrated set of classes that collaborate to provide a reusable software architecture for a family of related applications. In an object-oriented environment a framework consists of abstract and concrete classes. Instantiation of such a framework consists of composing and subclassing from existing classes.

Overlapped I/O   See *asynchronous I/O*.

Parallelism   The ability of an object, component, or system to execute operations that are "physically simultaneous" (compare with *Concurrency*).

Parameterized Type   A programming language feature that allows classes to be parameterized by various other types (compare with *Template*).

Passive Connection Establishment   The connection role played by a peer application that accepts a connection from a remote peer (compare with *Active Connection Establishment*).

Passive Object   An object that borrows the thread of its caller to execute its methods (compare with *Active Object*).

Pattern A pattern describes a particular recurring design problem that arises in specific design contexts and presents a well-proven solution for the problem. The solution is specified by describing its constituent participants, their responsibilities and relationships, and the ways in which they collaborate.

Pattern Language A family of interrelated patterns that define a process for resolving software development problems systematically.

Peer-to-Peer In a distributed system peers are processes that communicate with each other. In contrast to components in client-server architectures, peers may act as clients, as servers, or as both, and may change these roles dynamically.

Pipes and Filters Pattern An architectural pattern that provides a structure for systems that process a stream of data.

Platform The combination of hardware and/or software that a system uses for its implementation. Software platforms include operating systems, libraries, and frameworks. A platform implements a virtual machine with applications running on top of it.

Priority Inversion A scheduling hazard that occurs when a lower-priority thread or request blocks the execution of a higher-priority thread or request.

Proactive I/O An I/O method in which control returns to the caller initiating the operation immediately, often before the operation completes. The calling thread can perform other work while the OS carries out the I/O in parallel. The I/O operation's completion is noted at a later time. Compare with *Reactive I/O*.

Proactor Pattern An architectural pattern that allows event-driven applications to efficiently demultiplex and dispatch service requests triggered by the completion of asynchronous operations, to achieve the performance benefits of concurrency without incurring certain of its liabilities.

Process-Scope Contention A concurrency policy whereby the scope of threading or synchronization contention occurs within a process on a host (compare with *System-Scope Contention*).

Quality of Service (QoS) A collection of policies and mechanisms designed to control and enhance communication properties, such as availability, bandwidth, latency, and jitter.

Race Condition A race condition is a concurrency hazard that can occur when multiple threads simultaneously execute within a critical section that is not properly serialized.

Reactive I/O An I/O model in which an application is notified when desired I/O operation(s) on a particular source are likely to succeed. The application then performs the desired operation(s) one at a time. Compare with *Proactive I/O*.

Reactor Pattern An architectural pattern that allows event-driven applications to demultiplex and dispatch service requests that are delivered to an application from one or more clients.

Recursive Mutex A lock that can be reacquired by the thread that owns the mutex without incurring self-deadlock on the thread. Compare with *Nonrecursive Mutex*.

Refactoring An incremental activity that abstracts general-purpose behavior from existing software to enhance the structure and reusability of components and frameworks.

Reify The act of creating a concrete instance of an abstraction. For example, a concrete reactor implementation reifies the Reactor pattern and an object reifies a class.

Robust Iterator An iterator that ensures insertions and removals won't interfere with traversal.

Scatter-Read An input operation that stores data into multiple caller-supplied buffers instead of a single contiguous buffer.

Scoped Locking Idiom A C++ idiom that ensures a lock is acquired when control enters a scope and released automatically when control leaves the scope, regardless of the return path from the scope.

Semaphore A locking mechanism that maintains a count. As long as the count is greater than zero a thread can acquire the semaphore without blocking. After the count becomes zero, however, threads block on the semaphore until its count becomes greater than zero as a result of another thread releasing the semaphore, which increments the count.

Serialization A mechanism for ensuring that only one thread at a time executes within a critical section in order to prevent race conditions.

Service In the context of network programming, a service can either be (1) a well-defined capability offered by a server, such as the ECHO service provided by the INETD super-server, (2) a collection of capabilities offered by a server daemon, such as the INETD super-server itself, or (3) a collection of server processes that cooperate to achieve a common task, such as a collection of RWHO daemons in a local area network (LAN) subnet that periodically broadcast and receive status information reporting user activities to other hosts.

Shared Library See *Dynamically Linked Library* (DLL).

Smart Pointer A smart pointer is a C++ object that looks and acts like a built-in pointer but can achieve effects, such as caching, persistence, or thread-specific storage access, that built-in pointers don't support.

Socket A family of terms related to network programming. A socket is an endpoint of communication that identifies a particular network address and port number. The Socket API is a set of function calls supported by most operating systems and used by network applications to establish connections and communicate via socket endpoints. A data-mode socket can be used to exchange data between connected peers. A passive-mode socket is a factory that returns a handle to a connected data-mode socket.

Starvation A scheduling hazard that occurs when one or more threads are continually preempted by higher-priority threads and never execute.

Strategized Locking Pattern A design pattern that parameterizes synchronization mechanisms that protect a component's critical sections from concurrent access.

Strategy Pattern   A design pattern that defines a family of algorithms, encapsulates each one, and makes them interchangeable. Strategy lets the algorithms vary independently from clients that use it.

Synchronization Mechanism   A locking mechanism that coordinates the order in which threads execute.

Synchronized Message Queue   A *bounded buffer* where producer threads can block if the queue is full and consumer threads can block if the queue is empty.

Synchronous Event Demultiplexer   A mechanism, usually a system function, that demultiplexes events from disparate sources, allowing them to be processed as part of an application's normal execution flow.

Synchronous I/O   A mechanism for sending or receiving data in which an I/O operation is initiated and the caller blocks waiting for the operation to complete.

System-Scope Contention   A concurrency policy whereby the scope of threading or synchronization contention occurs between processes on a host (compare with *Process-Scope Contention*).

Task   An autonomous or semi-autonomous portion of an application that performs some specific portion of the application's work, such as receive and demarshal network input, or process requests. A task is executed using one or more *threads*.

Template   A C++ programming language feature that enables classes and functions to be parameterized by various types, constants, or pointers to functions. A template is often called a generic or parameterized type.

Thread   An independent sequence of instructions that executes within an address space that can be shared with other threads. Each thread has its own run-time stack and registers, which enables it to perform synchronous I/O without blocking other threads that are executing concurrently. Compared to processes, threads maintain minimal state information, require relatively little overhead to spawn, synchronize and schedule, and usually communicate with other threads via objects in their process's memory space, rather than shared memory.

Thread-per-Connection   A concurrency model that associates a separate thread with each network connection. This model handles each client that connects with a server in a separate thread for the duration of the connection. It is useful for servers that must support long-duration sessions with multiple clients. It is not useful for clients, such as HTTP 1.0 Web browsers, that associate a single request with each connection, which is effectively a *thread-per-request* model.

Thread-per-Request   A concurrency model that spawns a new thread for each request. This model is useful for servers that must handle long-duration request events from multiple clients, such as database queries. It is less useful for short-duration requests, due to the overhead of creating a new thread for each request. It can also consume a large number of operating system resources if many clients send requests simultaneously.

Thread Pool   A concurrency model that allocates a set of threads that can perform requests simultaneously. This model is a variant of *thread-per-request* that amortizes thread creation costs by prespawning a pool of threads. It is useful for servers that want to limit the number of operating system resources they consume. Client requests can be executed concurrently until the number of simultaneous requests exceeds the number of threads in the pool. At this point, additional requests must be queued until a thread becomes available.

Thread Safe   Safe from any undesired side effects (*race conditions*, data collisions, etc.) caused by multiple threads executing the same section of code concurrently.

Thread-Safe Interface Pattern   A design pattern that minimizes locking overhead and ensures that intracomponent method calls do not incur "self-deadlock" by trying to reacquire a lock that is held by the component already.

Thread-Specific Storage (TSS) Pattern   A design pattern that allows multiple threads to use one "logically global" access point to retrieve an object that is local to a thread, without incurring locking overhead on each object access.

Traits   A type that conveys information used by another class or algorithm to determine policies or implementation details at compile time.

Trojan Horse   A harmful piece of software that is hidden in a seemingly harmless software module such as a trusted run-time library.

Type Safe   A property enforced by a programming language's type system to ensure that only valid operations can be invoked upon instances of types.

Unicode   A standard for character representation that includes characters for most written languages as well as representations for punctuation, mathematical notations, and other symbols.

Weakly Typed   A datum whose declared data type does not fully reflect its intended or purported use.

Wrapper Facade   One or more classes that encapsulate functions and data within a type safe object-oriented interface.

Bibliography

[Ale01]   Andrei Alexandrescu. *Modern C++ Design: Generic Programming and Design Patterns Applied*. Addison-Wesley, Boston, 2001.

[All02]   Paul Allen. Model Driven Architecture. *Component Development Strategies*, 12(1), January 2002.

[Aus99]   Matthew H. Austern. *Generic Programming and the STL: Using and Extending the C++ Standard*. Addison-Wesley, Reading, MA, 1999.

[BA90]   M. Ben-Ari. *Principles of Concurrent and Distributed Programming*. Prentice Hall International Series in Computer Science, 1990.

[Bay02]   John Bay. Recent Advances in the Design of Distributed Embedded Systems. In *Proceedings of Proceedings of SPIE, Volume 47: Battlespace Digitization and Network Centric Warfare*, April 2002.

[Bec00]   Kent Beck. *Extreme Programming Explained: Embrace Change*. Addison-Wesley, Boston, 2000.

[Ber95]   Steve Berczuk. A Pattern for Separating Assembly and Processing. In James O. Coplien and Douglas C. Schmidt, editors, *Pattern Languages of Program Design*. Addison-Wesley, Reading, MA, 1995.

[BHLM94]   J. T. Buck, S. Ha, E. A. Lee, and D. G. Messerschmitt. Ptolemy: A Framework for Simulating and Prototyping Heterogeneous Systems. *International Journal of Computer Simulation, Special Issue on Simulation Software Development Component Development Strategies*, 4, April 1994.

[Bja00]   Bjarne Stroustrup. *The C++ Programming Language, Special Edition*. Addison-Wesley, Boston, 2000.

[BL88]   Ronald E. Barkley and T. Paul Lee. A Heap-based Callout Implementation to Meet Real-time Needs. In *Proceedings of the USENIX Summer Conference*, pages 213–222. USENIX Association, June 1988.

[Bla91]   U. Black. *OSI: A Model for Computer Communications Standards*. Prentice-Hall, Englewood Cliffs, NJ, 1991.

[BM98]   Gaurav Banga and Jeffrey C. Mogul. Scalable Kernel Performance for Internet
             Servers under Realistic Loads. In *Proceedings of the USENIX 1998 Annual Technical
             Conference*, New Orleans, LA, June 1998. USENIX.

[Boo94]   Grady Booch. *Object Oriented Analysis and Design with Applications, 2nd Edition.*
             Benjamin/Cummings, Redwood City, CA, 1994.

[Box98]   Don Box. *Essential COM.* Addison-Wesley, Reading, MA, 1998.

[BvR94]   Kenneth Birman and Robbert van Renesse. *Reliable Distributed Computing with the
             Isis Toolkit.* IEEE Computer Society Press, Los Alamitos, 1994.

[CB97]   John Crawford and Steve Ball. Monostate Classes: The Power of One. *C++ Report*,
             9(5), May 1997.

[CHW98]   James Coplien, Daniel Hoffman, and David Weiss. Commonality and Variability in
             Software Engineering. *IEEE Software*, 15(6), November/December 1998.

[CN02]   Paul Clements and Linda Northrop. *Software Product Lines: Practices and Patterns.*
             Addison-Wesley, Boston, 2002.

[C++NPv1]   Douglas C. Schmidt and Stephen D. Huston. *C++ Network Programming, Volume 1:
             Mastering Complexity with ACE and Patterns.* Addison-Wesley, Boston, 2002.

[Cul99]   Timothy R. Culp. Industrial Strength Pluggable Factories. *C++ Report*, 11(9),
             October 1999.

[DA99]   Tim Dierks and Christopher Allen. The TLS Protocol Version 1.0. *Network
             Information Center RFC 2246*, January 1999.

[Dim01]   Dimitri van Heesch. Doxygen. `http://www.doxygen.org`, 2001.

[Egr98]   Carlton Egremont, III. *Mr. Bunny's Guide to ActiveX.* Addison-Wesley, Reading,
             MA, 1998.

[FJS99a]   Mohamed Fayad, Ralph Johnson, and Douglas C. Schmidt, editors. *Building
             Application Frameworks: Object-Oriented Foundations of Framework Design.* Wiley
             & Sons, New York, 1999.

[FJS99b]   Mohamed Fayad, Ralph Johnson, and Douglas C. Schmidt, editors. *Implementing
             Application Frameworks: Object-Oriented Frameworks at Work.* Wiley & Sons, New
             York, 1999.

[FY00]   Brian Foote and Joe Yoder. Big Ball of Mud. In Brian Foote, Neil Harrison, and Hans
             Rohnert, editors, *Pattern Languages of Program Design 4*. Addison-Wesley, Boston,
             2000.

[Gal95]   Bill Gallmeister. *POSIX.4 Programming for the Real World.* O'Reilly, Sebastopol,
             CA, 1995.

[GLDW87]   R. Gingell, M. Lee, X. Dang, and M. Weeks. Shared Libraries in SunOS. In
             Proceedings of the Summer 1987 USENIX Technical Conference, Phoenix, Arizona,
             1987.

[GoF]   Erich Gamma, Richard Helm, Ralph Johnson, and John Vlissides. *Design Patterns: Elements of Reusable Object-Oriented Software*. Addison-Wesley, Reading, MA, 1995.

[GR93]   Jim Gray and Andreas Reuter. *Transaction Processing: Concepts and Techniques*. Morgan Kaufman, Boston, 1993.

[GSC02]   Chris Gill, Douglas C. Schmidt, and Ron Cytron. Multi-Paradigm Scheduling for Distributed Real-Time Embedded Computing. *IEEE Proceedings Special Issue on Modeling and Design of Embedded Software*, October 2002.

[GSNW02]   Aniruddha Gokhale, Douglas C. Schmidt, Balachandra Natarajan, and Nanbor Wang. Applying Model-Integrated Computing to Component Middleware and Enterprise Applications. *The Communications of the ACM Special Issue on Enterprise Components, Service and Business Rules*, 45(10), October 2002.

[HJE95]   Herman Hueni, Ralph Johnson, and Robert Engel. A Framework for Network Protocol Software. In *Proceedings of OOPSLA '95*, Austin, TX, October 1995. ACM.

[HJS]   Stephen D. Huston, James C. E. Johnson, and Umar Syyid. *The ACE Programmer's Guide*. Addison-Wesley, Boston (forthcoming).

[HLS97]   Timothy H. Harrison, David L. Levine, and Douglas C. Schmidt. The Design and Performance of a Real-time CORBA Event Service. In *Proceedings of OOPSLA '97*, pages 184–199, Atlanta, GA, October 1997. ACM.

[HMS98]   James Hu, Sumedh Mungee, and Douglas C. Schmidt. Principles for Developing and Measuring High-performance Web Servers over ATM. In *Proceedings of INFOCOM '98*, March/April 1998.

[Hol97]   Luke Holmann. *Journey of the Software Professional: The Sociology of Computer Programming*. Prentice Hall, Englewood Cliffs, NJ, 1997.

[HP91]   Norman C. Hutchinson and Larry L. Peterson. The *x*-kernel: An Architecture for Implementing Network Protocols. *IEEE Transactions on Software Engineering*, 17(1):64–76, January 1991.

[HPS97]   James Hu, Irfan Pyarali, and Douglas C. Schmidt. Measuring the Impact of Event Dispatching and Concurrency Models on Web Server Performance Over High-speed Networks. In *Proceedings of the 2nd Global Internet Conference*. IEEE, November 1997.

[HS99]   James Hu and Douglas C. Schmidt. JAWS: A Framework for High Performance Web Servers. In Mohamed Fayad and Ralph Johnson, editors, *Domain-Specific Application Frameworks: Frameworks Experience by Industry*. Wiley & Sons, New York, 1999.

[HV99]   Michi Henning and Steve Vinoski. *Advanced CORBA Programming with C++*. Addison-Wesley, Reading, MA, 1999.

[IEE96]   IEEE. *Threads Extension for Portable Operating Systems (Draft 10)*, February 1996.

[JF88]   Ralph Johnson and Brian Foote. Designing Reusable Classes. *Journal of Object-Oriented Programming*, 1(5):22–35, June/July 1988.

[JKN⁺01]   Philippe Joubert, Robert King, Richard Neves, Mark Russinovich, and John Tracey.
           High-Performance Memory-Based Web Servers: Kernel and User-Space
           Performance. In *Proceedings of the USENIX Technical Conference*, Boston, MA,
           June 2001.

[Joh97]   Ralph Johnson. Frameworks = Patterns + Components. *Communications of the ACM*,
           40(10), October 1997.

[Jos99]   Nicolai Josuttis. *The C++ Standard Library: A Tutorial and Reference*.
           Addison-Wesley, Reading, MA, 1999.

[KMC⁺00]   Eddie Kohler, Robert Morris, Benjie Chen, John Jannotti, and M. Frans Kaashoek.
           The Click Modular Router. *ACM Transactions on Computer Systems*, 18(3):263–297,
           August 2000.

[Koe92]   Andrew Koenig. When Not to Use Virtual Functions. *C++ Journal*, 2(2), 1992.

[Kof93]   Thomas Kofler. Robust Iterators for ET++. *Structured Programming*, 14(2):62–85,
           1993.

[KSS96]   Steve Kleiman, Devang Shah, and Bart Smaalders. *Programming with Threads*.
           Prentice Hall, Upper Saddle River, NJ, 1996.

[Kuh97]   Thomas Kuhne. The Function Object Pattern. *C++ Report*, 9(9), October 1997.

[LBM⁺01]   Akos Ledeczi, Arpad Bakay, Miklos Maroti, Peter Volgysei, Greg Nordstrom,
           Jonathan Sprinkle, and Gabor Karsai. Composing Domain-Specific Design
           Environments. *IEEE Computer*, November 2001.

[Lea00]   Doug Lea. *Concurrent Programming in Java: Design Principles and Patterns,
           Second Edition*. Addison-Wesley, Boston, 2000.

[Lew95]   Bil Lewis. *Threads Primer: A Guide to Multithreaded Programming*. Prentice-Hall,
           Englewood Cliffs, NJ, 1995.

[Lip96]   Stan Lippman. *Inside the C++ Object Model*. Addison-Wesley, 1996.

[MBKQ96]   Marshall Kirk McKusick, Keith Bostic, Michael J. Karels, and John S. Quarterman.
           The Design and Implementation of the 4.4BSD Operating System. Addison-Wesley,
           Reading, MA, 1996.

[McI68]   M. Doug McIlroy. Mass Produced Software Components. In *Proceedings of the
           NATO Software Engineering Conference*, October 1968.

[Mey96]   Scott Meyers. *More Effective C++*. Addison-Wesley, Reading, MA, 1996.

[Mey97]   Bertrand Meyer. *Object-Oriented Software Construction, 2nd Edition*. Prentice Hall,
           Englewood Cliffs, NJ, 1997.

[MH01]   Richard Monson-Haefel. *Enterprise JavaBeans, 3rd Edition*. O'Reilly and
           Associates, Inc., Sebastopol, CA, 2001.

[Obj98]   Object Management Group. *CORBAServices: Common Object Services Specification,
           Updated Edition*. Object Management Group, December 1998.

[Obj01a]   Object Management Group. *CORBA 3.0 New Components Chapters*, OMG TC Document ptc/2001-11-03 edition, November 2001.

[Obj01b]   Object Management Group. *Model Driven Architecture (MDA)*, OMG Document ormsc/2001-07-01 edition, July 2001.

[Obj02]   Object Management Group. *The Common Object Request Broker: Architecture and Specification*, 3.0 edition, June 2002.

[OOS01]   Ossama Othman, Carlos O'Ryan, and Douglas C. Schmidt. An Efficient Adaptive Load Balancing Service for CORBA. *IEEE Distributed Systems Online*, 2(3), March 2001.

[Ope01]   OpenSSL Project. Openssl. www.openssl.org/, 2001.

[OSI92a]   OSI Special Interest Group. *Data Link Provider Interface Specification*, December 1992.

[OSI92b]   OSI Special Interest Group. *Transport Provider Interface Specification*, December 1992.

[POS95]   Information Technology—Portable Operating System Interface (POSIX)—Part 1: System Application: Program Interface (API) [C Language], 1995.

[POS00]   Irfan Pyarali, Carlos O'Ryan, and Douglas C. Schmidt. A Pattern Language for Efficient, Predictable, Scalable, and Flexible Dispatching Mechanisms for Distributed Object Computing Middleware. In *Proceedings of the International Symposium on Object-Oriented Real-time Distributed Computing (ISORC)*, Newport Beach, CA, March 2000. IEEE/IFIP.

[POSA1]   Frank Buschmann, Regine Meunier, Hans Rohnert, Peter Sommerlad, and Michael Stal. *Pattern-Oriented Software Architecture—A System of Patterns*. Wiley & Sons, New York, 1996.

[POSA2]   Douglas C. Schmidt, Michael Stal, Hans Rohnert, and Frank Buschmann. *Pattern-Oriented Software Architecture: Patterns for Concurrent and Networked Objects, Volume 2*. Wiley & Sons, New York, 2000.

[Pre95]   Wolfgang Pree. *Design Patterns for Object-oriented Software Development*. Addison-Wesley, Reading, MA, 1995.

[Rag93]   Steve Rago. *UNIX System V Network Programming*. Addison-Wesley, Reading, MA, 1993.

[Ric97]   Jeffrey Richter. *Advanced Windows, 3rd Edition*. Microsoft Press, Redmond, WA, 1997.

[Rit84]   Dennis Ritchie. A Stream Input–Output System. *AT&T Bell Labs Technical Journal*, 63(8):311–324, October 1984.

[Rob99]   Robert Sedgwick. *Algorithms in C++, Parts 1–4: Fundamentals, Data Structure, Sorting, Searching, 3rd Edition*. Addison-Wesley, Reading, MA, 1999.

[Sch98]   Douglas C. Schmidt. Evaluating Architectures for Multi-threaded CORBA Object Request Brokers. *Communications of the ACM Special Issue on CORBA*, 41(10), October 1998.

[Sch00]   Douglas C. Schmidt. Why Software Reuse Has Failed and How to Make It Work for You. *C++ Report*, 12(1), January 2000.

[SG96]   Mary Shaw and Dave Garlan. *Software Architecture: Perspectives on an Emerging Discipline*. Prentice Hall, Englewood Cliffs, NJ, 1996.

[SK97]   Janos Sztipanovits and Gabor Karsai. Model-Integrated Computing. *IEEE Computer*, 30(4):110–112, April 1997.

[SKLN01]   Jonathan M. Sprinkle, Gabor Karsai, Akos Ledeczi, and Greg G. Nordstrom. The New Metamodeling Generation. In *IEEE Engineering of Computer Based Systems*, Washington, DC, April 2001. IEEE.

[SKT96]   James D. Salehi, James F. Kurose, and Don Towsley. The Effectiveness of Affinity-Based Scheduling in Multiprocessor Networking. In *IEEE INFOCOM*, San Francisco, USA, March 1996. IEEE Computer Society Press.

[SLM98]   Douglas C. Schmidt, David L. Levine, and Sumedh Mungee. The Design and Performance of Real-Time Object Request Brokers. *Computer Communications*, 21(4):294–324, April 1998.

[Sol98]   David A. Solomon. *Inside Windows NT, 2nd Edition*. Microsoft Press, Redmond, WA, 1998.

[Som98]   Peter Sommerland. The Manager Design Pattern. In Robert Martin, Frank Buschmann, and Dirk Riehle, editors, *Pattern Languages of Program Design 3*. Addison-Wesley, Reading, MA, 1998.

[SOP+00]   Douglas C. Schmidt, Carlos O'Ryan, Irfan Pyarali, Michael Kircher, and Frank Buschmann. Leader/Followers: A Design Pattern for Efficient Multi-threaded Event Demultiplexing and Dispatching. In *Proceedings of the 6th Pattern Languages of Programming Conference*, Monticello, IL, August 2000.

[SR00]   David A. Solomon and Mark E. Russinovich. *Inside Windows 2000, 3rd Edition*. Microsoft Press, Redmond, WA, 2000.

[SRL98]   H. Schulzrinne, A. Rao, and R. Lanphier. Real Time Streaming Protocol (RTSP). *Network Information Center RFC 2326*, April 1998.

[SS93]   Douglas C. Schmidt and Tatsuya Suda. Transport System Architecture Services for High-Performance Communications Systems. *IEEE Journal on Selected Areas in Communication*, 11(4):489–506, May 1993.

[SS94]   Douglas C. Schmidt and Tatsuya Suda. An Object-Oriented Framework for Dynamically Configuring Extensible Distributed Communication Systems. *IEE/BCS Distributed Systems Engineering Journal (Special Issue on Configurable Distributed Systems)*, 2:280–293, December 1994.

[SS95a]   Douglas C. Schmidt and Paul Stephenson. Experiences Using Design Patterns to
          Evolve System Software Across Diverse OS Platforms. In *Proceedings of the 9th
          European Conference on Object-Oriented Programming*, Aarhus, Denmark, August
          1995. ACM.

[SS95b]   Douglas C. Schmidt and Tatsuya Suda. Measuring the Performance of Parallel
          Message-based Process Architectures. In *Proceedings of the Conference on Computer
          Communications (INFOCOM)*, pages 624–633, Boston, April 1995. IEEE.

[SS02]   Richard E. Schantz and Douglas C. Schmidt. Middleware for Distributed Systems:
          Evolving the Common Structure for Network-centric Applications. In John Marciniak
          and George Telecki, editors, *Encyclopedia of Software Engineering*. Wiley & Sons,
          New York, 2002.

[Ste92]   W. Richard Stevens. *Advanced Programming in the UNIX Environment*.
          Addison-Wesley, Reading, MA, 1992.

[Ste94]   W. Richard Stevens. *TCP/IP Illustrated, Volume 1: The Protocols*. Addison-Wesley,
          Reading, MA, 1994.

[Ste98]   W. Richard Stevens. *UNIX Network Programming, Volume 1: Networking APIs:
          Sockets and XTI, 2nd Edition*. Prentice Hall, Englewood Cliffs, NJ, 1998.

[Ste99]   W. Richard Stevens. *UNIX Network Programming, Volume 2: Interprocess
          Communications, Second Edition*. Prentice Hall, Englewood Cliffs, NJ, 1999.

[SW95]   W. Richard Stevens and Gary R. Wright. *TCP/IP Illustrated, Volume 2: The
          Implementation*. Addison-Wesley, Reading, MA, 1995.

[SX01]   Randall Stewart and Qiaobing Xie. *Stream Control Transmission Protocol (SCTP) A
          Reference Guide*. Addison-Wesley, Boston, 2001.

[Szy98]   Clemens Szyperski. *Component Software—Beyond Object-Oriented Programming*.
          Addison-Wesley, Santa Fe, NM, 1998.

[Tan92]   Andrew S. Tanenbaum. *Modern Operating Systems*. Prentice Hall, Englewood Cliffs,
          NJ, 1992.

[TL01]   Thuan Thai and Hoang Lam. *.NET Framework Essentials*. O'Reilly, Sebastopol, CA,
          2001.

[VL97]   George Varghese and Tony Lauck. Hashed and Hierarchical Timing Wheels: Data
          Structures for the Efficient Implementation of a Timer Facility. *IEEE Transactions on
          Networking*, December 1997.

[Vli98a] John Vlissides. *Pattern Hatching: Design Patterns Applied*. Addison-Wesley,
          Reading, MA, 1998.

[Vli98b] John Vlissides. Pluggable Factory, Part 1. *C++ Report*, 10(10), November–December
          1998.

[Vli99]   John Vlissides. Pluggable Factory, Part 2. *C++ Report*, 11(2), February 1999.

[vR96]   Michael van Rooyen. Alternative C++: A New Look at Reference Counting and
            Virtual Destruction in C++. *C++ Report*, 8(4), April 1996.

[wKS00]   Martin Fowler with Kendall Scott. *UML Distilled—A Brief Guide to the Standard
            Object Modeling Language, 2nd Edition*. Addison-Wesley, Boston, 2000.

[WLS+85]   D. Walsh, B. Lyon, G. Sager, J. M. Chang, D. Goldberg, S. Kleiman, T. Lyon,
            R. Sandberg, and P. Weiss. Overview of the SUN Network File System. In
            Proceedings of the Winter USENIX Conference, Dallas, TX, January 1985.

[Woo97]   Bobby Woolf. The Null Object Pattern. In Robert Martin, Frank Buschmann, , and
            Dirk Riehle, editors, *Pattern Languages of Program Design 3*. Addison-Wesley,
            Reading, Massachusetts, 1997.

Index

The C++ In-Depth Series

Bjarne Stroustrup, Series Editor

Modern C++ Design
**Generic Programming and Design
Patterns Applied**
By Andrei Alexandrescu
0201704315
Paperback
352 pages
© 2001

Accelerated C++
Practical Programming by Example
By Andrew Koenig and
Barbara E. Moo
020170353X
Paperback
352 pages
© 2000

Essential C++
By Stanley B. Lippman
0201485184
Paperback
304 pages
© 2000

C++ Network Programming, Volume 1
**Mastering Complexity with ACE and
Patterns**
By Douglas C. Schmidt and
Stephen D. Huston
0201604647
Paperback
336 pages
© 2002

The Boost Graph Library
User Guide and Reference Manual
By Jeremy G. Siek, Lie-Quan Lee, and
Andrew Lumsdaine
0201729148
Paperback
352 pages
© 2002

Exceptional C++
**47 Engineering Puzzles, Programming
Problems, and Solutions**
By Herb Sutter
0201615622
Paperback
240 pages
© 2000

More Exceptional C++
**40 New Engineering Puzzles,
Programming Problems, and Solutions**
By Herb Sutter
020170434X
Paperback
304 pages
© 2002

C++ Network Programming, Volume 2
**Systematic Reuse with ACE and
Frameworks**
By Douglas C. Schmidt and
Stephen D. Huston
0201795256
Paperback
384 pages
© 2003

Applied C++
**Practical Techniques for
Building Better Software**
By Philip Romanik and Amy Muntz
0321108949
Paperback
352 pages
© 2003

Exceptional C++ Style
**40 New Engineering Puzzles, Programming
Problems, and Solutions**
By Herb Sutter
0201760428
Paperback
352 pages
© 2005

Also Available

The C++ Programming Language, Special Edition
By Bjarne Stroustrup
0201700735
Hardcover | 1,040 pages | © 2000

Written by the creator of C++, this is the most widely read and most trusted book on C++.

informIT

YOUR GUIDE TO IT REFERENCE

Articles

Keep your edge with thousands of free articles, in-depth features, interviews, and IT reference recommendations – all written by experts you know and trust.

Online Books

Answers in an instant from **InformIT Online Book's** 600+ fully searchable on line books. For a limited time, you can get your first 14 days **free**.

Catalog

Review online sample chapters, author biographies and customer rankings and choose exactly the right book from a selection of over 5,000 titles.

Register
Your Book

at www.awprofessional.com/register

You may be eligible to receive:
- Advance notice of forthcoming editions of the book
- Related book recommendations
- Chapter excerpts and supplements of forthcoming titles
- Information about special contests and promotions throughout the year
- Notices and reminders about author appearances, tradeshows, and online chats with special guests

Contact us

If you are interested in writing a book or reviewing manuscripts prior to publication, please write to us at:

Editorial Department
Addison-Wesley Professional
75 Arlington Street, Suite 300
Boston, MA 02116 USA
Email: AWPro@aw.com

Visit us on the Web: http://www.awprofessional.com